E-Commerce

Fundamentals and Applications

HENRY CHAN, RAYMOND LEE, THARAM DILLON
The Hong Kong Polytechnic University

ELIZABETH CHANG
The University of Newcastle, Australia

JOHN WILEY & SONS, LTD

Chichester • New York • Weinheim • Brisbane • Singapore • Toronto

Copyright © 2001 by John Wiley & Sons Ltd
Baffins Lane, Chichester,
West Sussex, PO19 1UD, England

National 01243 779777
International (+44) 1243 779777

e-mail (for orders and customer service enquiries): cs-books@wiley.co.uk

Visit our Home Page on http://www.wiley.co.uk
or
http://www.wiley.com

Other Wiley Editorial Offices

John Wiley & Sons, Inc., 605 Third Avenue,
New York, NY 10158-0012, USA

Wiley-VCH Verlag GmbH
Pappelallee 3, D-69469 Weinheim, Germany

John Wiley & Sons (Australia) Ltd, 33 Park Road, Milton,
Queensland 4064, Australia

John Wiley & Sons (Canada) Ltd, 22 Worcester Road
Rexdale, Ontario, M9W 1L1, Canada

John Wiley & Sons (Asia) Pte Ltd, 2 Clementi Loop #02-01,
Jin Xing Distripark, Singapore 129809

British Library Cataloguing in Publication Data

A catalogue record for this book is available from the British Library

ISBN 0 471 49303 1

Typeset in 10/12.5pt Sabon by TechBooks Ltd., New Delhi, India
Printed and bound in Great Britain by Biddles Ltd, Guildford and King's Lynn.
This book is printed on acid-free paper responsibly manufactured from sustainable forestry, for which at least two trees are planted for each one used for paper production.

E-Commerce

To
Cindy, Eric, and Brian – Henry
Iris – Raymond

Contents

Preface   xix

1 Introduction   1

1.1   Electronic commerce and physical commerce   2
1.2   The DIGITAL phenomenon   3
1.3   Looking at e-commerce from different perspectives   4
1.4   Different types of e-commerce   6
1.5   Examples of the types of e-commerce   8
    1.5.1   Amazon®: B2C e-commerce   8
    1.5.2   eBay: C2C e-commerce   9
    1.5.3   Trading process network: B2B e-commerce   10
    1.5.4   Priceline : C2B e-commerce   10
1.6   Some e-commerce scenarios   11
    1.6.1   Retailing   11
    1.6.2   Servicing   12
    1.6.3   Publishing   12
    1.6.4   Supply chain management   13
1.7   Changes brought by e-commerce   13
1.8   Advantages of e-commerce   14
1.9   Myths about e-commerce development and implementation   14
    1.9.1   Myth 1: e-commerce is about building a web page 16
    1.9.2   Myth 2: the successful implementation of an e-commerce system relies on web programmers   16
    1.9.3   Myth 3: e-commerce project is about translating the traditional business model into an electronic business model   17

1.10   System model and road map of this book   18
1.11   Summary   21
       References   23
       Recommended Reading   23

PART 1   Technologies (fundamentals)   25

2   Internet and world wide web   27

2.1   An Overview of the internet   28
       2.1.1   Basic network architecture   28
       2.1.2   Layered model   29
       2.1.3   Link layer   29
       2.1.4   Network layer   32
       2.1.5   Transport layer   35
       2.1.6   Application layer   36
       2.1.7   Next generation internet   38
2.2   Brief history of the web   38
2.3   Web system architecture   39
2.4   Uniform resource locator   40
2.5   Overview of the hypertext transfer
       protocol   41
2.6   Hypertext Transfer Protocol (HTTP)   42
       2.6.1   HTTP request   42
       2.6.2   Server response   44
2.7   Generation of dynamic web pages   46
2.8   Cookies   48
2.9   HTTP/1.1   49
2.10   Example   51
2.11   Summary   52
       References   52
       Recommended Reading   53

3   Client-side programming   55

3.1   Important factors in client-side or web programming   56
3.2   Web page design and production   61
       3.2.1   Define the audiences and the information
               requirements   61
       3.2.2   Develop the logical design of the web site   61

	3.2.3	Develop the perceptual design	62
	3.2.4	Content creation	63
	3.2.5	Programming	63
	3.2.6	Posting and hosting the site	63
3.3	Overview of HTML		63
3.4	Basic structure of an HTML document		64
3.5	Basic text formatting		66
	3.5.1	Heading	67
	3.5.2	Paragraph	67
	3.5.3	Font	68
	3.5.4	Other special tags for formatting text	68
	3.5.5	Horizontal rule	68
	3.5.6	Lists	68
3.6	Links		69
3.7	Images		71
3.8	ImageMap		72
3.9	Tables		73
3.10	Frames		75
3.11	Form		79
	3.11.1	Textbox	80
	3.11.2	Password textbox	80
	3.11.3	Checkbox	80
	3.11.4	Radio button	81
	3.11.5	Submit button	81
	3.11.6	File input field	81
	3.11.7	Hidden form field	81
	3.11.8	Textarea	82
	3.11.9	Select menu	82
3.12	Cascading style sheets		82
	3.12.1	External style sheets	83
	3.12.2	Embedded style sheets	84
	3.12.3	Inline style	85
3.13	JavaScript		86
	3.13.1	What is JavaScript?	86
	3.13.2	Basic structure of JavaScript	87
	3.13.3	A simple JavaScript example	88
	3.13.4	Form validation using JavaScript	89
3.14	Summary		92
	References		93
	Recommended Reading		93

4 Server-side programming I: servlet fundamentals   **95**

4.1   Revisiting the three-tier model   96
4.2   Common gateway interface (CGI)   98
     4.2.1   CGI fundamentals   98
     4.2.2   CGI languages   100
4.3   Active server page (ASP)   100
4.4   Overview of Java servlet   101
4.5   Java servlet architecture   103
4.6   Overview of the servlet API   103
4.7   Building the virtual bookstore – step by step   105
4.8   Your first servlet – welcome to VBS   107
4.9   Compilation and execution of servlets   109
4.10   An interactive servlet program example: topics of interest   110
4.11   Topics of interest: Cookie approach   115
4.12   Summary   122
     References   123
     Recommended Reading   123

5 Server-side programming II: database connectivity   **125**

5.1   Introduction   125
5.2   Relational database systems   126
     5.2.1   What is a relational database?   126
     5.2.2   A brief overview of relational databases: an example
          of book ordering   127
     5.2.3   Basic SQL statements   128
5.3   JDBC perspectives   134
     5.3.1   What is JDBC?   134
     5.3.2   Layered infrastructure of JDBC   134
     5.3.3   The JDBC drivers   134
     5.3.4   JDBC API   136
5.4   A JDBC program example: simple servlet book query   137
     5.4.1   Preparing for your first JDBC program   137
     5.4.2   Simple Book Query – ServletBookquery   138
     5.4.3   ServletBookquery – program summary   143
5.5   An advanced book query: ServletBookquerymulti   144
5.6   Advanced JDBC servlet: VBS advance book search engine   151
     5.6.1   VBS advance book search engine   151
     5.6.2   How does the SearchEngine.java work?   152

5.7   Summary   155
      References   156
      Recommended Reading   156

6   Server-side programming III: session tracking   159

6.1   Introduction   160
      6.1.1   A realistic case in session tracking: Shopping in VBS   160
      6.1.2   Issues involved in implementing the Shopping Cart
              object in the internet environment   161
6.2   Traditional session tracking techniques   161
      6.2.1   Hidden form field   162
      6.2.2   URL rewriting   170
      6.2.3   HTTP user authentication   175
      6.2.4   Cookies   175
      6.2.5   Comparison of the above session tracking methods 176
6.3   The servlet session tracking API   177
      6.3.1   Introduction   177
      6.3.2   How the servlet session tracking API works   178
      6.3.3   Some common methods for servlet session tracking 179
      6.3.4   A simple session tracking example   180
      6.3.5   A simple shopping cart example   185
6.4   A practical case: VBS shopping cart   195
      6.4.1   What is a shopping cart?   195
      6.4.2   Basic functions of the shopping cart object   196
6.5   Summary   201
      References   202
      Recommended Reading   202

7   Basic cryptography for enabling e-commerce   203

7.1   Security concerns   204
7.2   Security requirements   204
7.3   Encryption   205
7.4   Two basic principles for private key encryption   207
      7.4.1   Data encryption standard   208
      7.4.2   Other symmetric key encryption algorithm   208
7.5   The key distribution problem   209
7.6   Diffie–Hellman key exchange Protocol   209
7.7   Public key encryption   210

7.8	RSA encryption algorithm	210
7.9	Hybrid encryption	213
7.10	Other public key encryption methods	213
7.11	Stream cipher and block cipher	214
7.12	Message digest	214
	7.12.1 MD5 message digest algorithm	215
	7.12.2 Other message digest algorithms	216
7.13	Message authentication code	216
7.14	Digital signature	217
7.15	Digital signature standard	219
7.16	Authentication	219
	7.16.1 Public key infrastructure	220
	7.16.2 Digital certificate	220
	7.16.3 X.509: A digital certificate framework	221
	7.16.4 Certificate chain/verification path	222
	7.16.5 An hierarchical trust system	223
	7.16.6 Challenge and response authentication protocol	224
	7.16.7 Certificate revocation	225
7.17	Summary	225
	References	226
	Recommended Reading	226
8	**Internet security**	**229**
8.1	IPSec protocol	230
8.2	Setting up security associations	231
8.3	The authentication header (AH) service	232
8.4	The encapsulating security payload (ESP) service	233
8.5	Preventing replay attack	234
8.6	Application of IPSec: virtual private network	235
8.7	Firewalls	236
8.8	Different types of firewalls	237
	8.8.1 Packet filtering router	237
	8.8.2 Application gateway/proxy server	238
	8.8.3 Circuit level gateway	239
8.9	Examples of firewall systems	240
8.10	Secure socket layer (SSL)	242
	8.10.1 SSL handshake protocol	244
	8.10.2 SSL record protocol	247
	8.10.3 The SSL change cipher spec protocol and the alert protocol	247

8.11   Putting everything together   248
8.12   Summary   248
        References   249
        Recommended Reading   249

9   Advanced technologies for e-commerce   251

9.1   Introduction to mobile agents   252
       9.1.1   Overview of mobile agents   253
       9.1.2   Typical life cycle of an Aglet   254
       9.1.3   A simple programming example   256
       9.1.4   Overview of MAGICS   262
9.2   WAP: the enabling technology for mobile commerce   263
       9.2.1   The WAP model   264
       9.2.2   WAP architecture   265
       9.2.3   Benefits of WAP to e-commerce   267
9.3   XML (eXtensible Markup Language)   267
       9.3.1   HTML and XML   267
       9.3.2   Syntax of XML documents   267
       9.3.3   Displaying XML Documents – style sheets   271
       9.3.4   Processing XML documents and programming
                interfaces   271
       9.3.5   Applications of XML   273
       9.3.6   Architecture for XML and some features   275
9.4   Data mining   277
       9.4.1   Association rules   278
       9.4.2   Decision trees   279
       9.4.3   Web mining   280
       References   281
       Recommended XML Web sites   282

PART 2   Applications   283

10   Internet payment systems   285

10.1   Characteristics of payment systems   286
10.2   4C payment methods   286
10.3   SET Protocol for credit card payment   287
        10.3.1   SET network architecture   288
        10.3.2   SET digital certificate system   289

		10.3.3	Dual signature generation and verification	289
		10.3.4	Digital envelope	292
		10.3.5	SET protocol	293
		10.3.6	Purchase initiation	293
		10.3.7	Purchase request	294
		10.3.8	Payment authorization	295
		10.3.9	Payment capture	297
	10.4	E-cash		298
		10.4.1	Blind signature	298
		10.4.2	Payment by e-cash over the internet	299
	10.5	E-check		301
		10.5.1	Deposit-and-clear	301
		10.5.2	Cash-and-transfer	301
		10.5.3	Lockbox	303
		10.5.4	Direct fund transfer	303
	10.6	Micropayment system		303
		10.6.1	Millicent	303
		10.6.2	Payword	305
	10.7	Overview of smart card		306
	10.8	Overview of Mondex		309
	10.9	Putting it all together for payments in the VBS		310
	10.10	Summary		311
		References		311
		Recommended Reading		312

11   Consumer-oriented e-commerce   315

	11.1	Introduction		316
	11.2	Traditional retailing and e-retailing		317
		11.2.1	Traditional retailing	317
		11.2.2	E-retailing	318
	11.3	Benefits of e-retailing		319
		11.3.1	To the customer	319
		11.3.2	To the business	320
	11.4	Key success factors		321
		11.4.1	For traditional retailing	321
		11.4.2	For e-retailing	322
	11.5	Models of e-retailing		324
		11.5.1	Specialized e-stores	324

	11.5.2	Basic features of an e-retailing system	331
	11.5.3	Specialization by function	331
	11.5.4	Generalized e-stores	333
	11.5.5	E-malls	334
	11.5.6	Direct selling by the manufacturer	335
	11.5.7	Supplementary distribution channel	336
	11.5.8	Brokers or intermediaries	338
11.6	Features of e-retailing		341
	11.6.1	The future of e-retailing	341
11.7	Developing a consumer-oriented e-commerce system		341
	11.7.1	The emergent business model as the basis of e-commerce system development	342
	11.7.2	Process-oriented e-commerce development approach	344
	11.7.3	Steps in the development methodology	345
11.8	The PASS model		346
11.9	Summary		346
	References		347
	Recommended Reading		347

12 Business-oriented e-commerce — 349

12.1	Features of B2B e-commerce		351
12.2	Business models		352
	12.2.1	E-procurement and buyer-oriented e-commerce systems	353
	12.2.2	Buy-side e-commerce – intercompany activities of procurement	353
	12.2.3	Sell-side e-commerce	357
	12.2.4	Virtual markets	360
	12.2.5	Collaborative supply chain management	365
12.3	Integration		367
	12.3.1	Intercompany integration	367
	12.3.2	B2B e-commerce communication using XML	368
	12.3.3	Intracompany integration	370
12.4	Summary		371
	References		371
	Recommended Reading		371

13 E-services — 373

13.1	Categories of e-services		374
13.2	Web-enabled services		375

	13.2.1	E-banking	375
	13.2.2	E-stocktrading and e-investing	377
	13.2.3	E-education	378
13.3	Matchmaking services		379
	13.3.1	Travel services	379
	13.3.2	E-employment and e-jobs	381
	13.3.3	Others	381
13.4	Information-selling on the web		383
13.5	E-entertainment		384
13.6	Auctions and other specialized services		384
	13.6.1	C2C auction sites	386
	13.6.2	B2B auctions	386
13.7	Summary		387
	References		388

14 Web advertising and web publishing   389

14.1	Traditional versus internet advertising		390
14.2	Internet advertising techniques and strategies		392
	14.2.1	E-mail	392
	14.2.2	Banners	392
	14.2.3	Targeted advertising techniques	396
14.3	Business models for advertising and their revenue streams		398
14.4	Pricing models and measurement of the effectiveness of advertisements		399
14.5	Web publishing – goals and criteria		400
14.6	Web site development methodologies		401
	14.6.1	Definition of an audience	402
	14.6.2	Categories of systems	402
	14.6.3	Overview of design methodology	403
14.7	Logical design of the user interface I – abstract user interface object		407
14.8	Logical design of the user interface II – flow of interaction		411
	14.8.1	Illustrative example	414
14.9	Usability testing and quality assurance		414
	14.9.1	Usability testing	414
	14.9.2	Functional and system testing	419
	14.9.3	Web feature testing	421
14.10	Web Presence and visibility		423

14.11	Summary	424
	References	424
	Recommended Reading	425

15 Step-by-Step Exercises for Building the VBS   427

15.1	Introduction	427
	15.1.1 Typical e-shopping scenario	428
	15.1.2 VBS – system overview	429
15.2	Exercise 1 – VBS homepage design (weeks 1 and 2)	430
	15.2.1 Objectives	430
	15.2.2 Program instructions	430
	15.2.3 Program hints	432
15.3	Exercise 2 – Form validation using Javascript (weeks 3 and 4)	432
	15.3.1 Objectives	432
	15.3.2 Program instructions	432
	15.3.3 Program hints	434
15.4	Exercise 3 – search engines (weeks 5–7)	434
	15.4.1 VBS – system flow	434
	15.4.2 Objectives	436
	15.4.3 Search engine: program flow	437
15.5	Exercise 3A – quick search	438
	15.5.1 Program instructions	438
	15.5.2 Program hints	439
15.6	Exercise 3B – category search	441
	15.6.1 Objective	441
	15.6.2 Program instructions	441
	15.6.3 Program hints	441
15.7	Exercise 3C – advanced search	442
	15.7.1 Objective	442
	15.7.2 Program instructions	443
	15.7.3 Program hints	444
15.8	Exercise 4 – access control (weeks 8 and 9)	445
	15.8.1 Objective	445
	15.8.2 Program structure	446
15.9	Exercise 4A – CartLogin	447
	15.9.1 Objective	447
	15.9.2 Program instructions	449
	15.9.3 Program hints	449

15.10   Exercise 4B – create a new customer account   449
    15.10.1   Objective   449
    15.10.2   Program instructions   451
    15.10.3   Program hints   451
15.11   Exercise 4C – change password   452
    15.11.1   Objectives   452
    15.11.2   Program instructions   453
    15.11.3   Program hints   454
15.12   Exercise 4D – CartLogout   454
    15.12.1   Objective   454
    15.12.2   Program instructions   454
    15.12.3   Program hint   454
15.13   Exercise 5 – virtual Shopping (CartServices) (weeks 10 and 11)   455
    15.13.1   Objective   455
    15.13.2   Program structure   455
    15.13.3   CartServices: system flow   457
    15.13.4   Program instruction   457
15.14   Exercise 6 – e-payment (week 12)   459
    15.14.1   Objective   459
    15.14.2   Program structure   460
    15.14.3   Program instruction   460
    15.14.4   Program hints   462

Index   463

Preface

INTRODUCTION

Over the last few centuries, human beings have experienced two major revolutions: the industrial revolution and the electronic revolution. The former transformed our society from being agriculturally based to industrially based, whereas the latter transformed our society from being mechanically based to electronically based. As we enter the 21st century, we are seeing the beginning of a new revolution, namely the network revolution. It interconnects different parts of the world, enabling the seamless flow of information. The Internet is the engine of this revolution and electronic commerce (e-commerce) is its fuel.

In understanding the evolution of the Internet and the World Wide Web, one can distinguish four phases, namely

1. *The evolution of interconnections between different computing nodes*: This allowed the provision of specialized functions such as e-mail and file transfer services.
2. *The introduction of the World Wide Web*: This allowed the creation of hyperlinked web pages that could be accessed through browsers. This has facilitated the process of information retrieval and dissemination on the internet, and accelerated the growth of it explosively.
3. *The integration of the client-side web pages with backend applications, databases, and payment gateways*: This allowed the development of integrated e-commerce systems for order processing, payments, and dynamically updated information on web pages.

4. *The integration of mobile computing technologies and web-based applications*:
   This looks set to enable ubiquitous access to the Internet and mobile
   e-commerce.

In this book we concentrate essentially on the third phase and give a brief introduction to some technologies that underlie the fourth phase.

This book, therefore, is about the technical aspects of Internet Commerce, or
more specifically Web-based Electronic Business. Generally speaking, e-commerce
has a very wide scope, although most people like to refer to it as business transactions over the internet. To be consistent with this common terminology, we use
the term e-commerce to refer to web-based electronic business. E-commerce can be
taught both from the business/managerial or social aspects or alternatively from the
technical aspect. Here, we concentrate on the technical perspective but explain how
this underpins different categories of business applications. Teaching e-commerce
from the technical perspective is challenging and exciting because it involves nearly
all the different computing technologies, including networking, security, programming, human computer interface design, database design, etc. Therefore e-commerce
is a suitable final year elective subject. It allows students to reinforce their knowledge about these important computing technologies and discusses how to integrate
these technologies to build a useful application. This book can be used as a textbook
for a final year elective subject on e-commerce, or as an introductory subject on e-
commerce at the postgraduate level. It can also be used as a textbook for teaching
Internet Computing in general. This book can also serve as a useful reference for
programmers, e-commerce developers, information technology professionals, and
managers. While this book does not assume knowledge of any specific programming
languages, a general acquaintance with programming and an introductory knowledge
of Java programming would be useful.

FEATURES AND ONLINE MATERIALS

While a number of good e-commerce books have been published, most of them focus
on the business aspects, i.e., they frequently discuss some of the things e-commerce
systems do. This book focuses on the technical aspects, i.e., it discusses how to build
different parts of an e-commerce system and integrate them into a full system. The
contents of this book have been used for teaching technical/nontechnical courses in
e-commerce at both the undergraduate and graduate levels. The special features of
the book are summarized below.

- *Integrated book*: It is an integrated book on e-commerce covering both the
  technologies and the applications. In other words, you can find most of the

important information on e-commerce here, and it also points you to other references and more advanced texts.

- *Key underlying technologies*: It covers the key underlying technologies of e-commerce including the web system and web protocol, web publishing by using the hypertext markup language (HTML), web programming by using Java Servlets as an example, major cryptographic techniques, internet security, and internet payment systems. In discussing these, it focuses on those techniques most suitable for e-commerce application building. It also discusses these techniques from the point of view of integrating them into a complete end-to-end e-commerce system.

- *Advanced technologies*: It gives an overview of the advanced technologies for e-commerce, namely, mobile agents, wireless application protocol (WAP), eXtensible Markup Language (XML), and data mining techniques.

- *Running case study*: A special feature of the book is that it uses an ongoing case-study [Virtual Bookstore (VBS)] throughout the book to illustrate the basic concepts of building an e-commerce system.

- *Step-by-step programming exercise for building a virtual bookstore*: It provides a step-by-step exercise that guides you in the building of a VBS by using Java Servlets. The VBS incorporates many useful features such as a book search engine and shopping cart. This VBS system has many of the features currently available in business-to-consumer e-commerce systems and hence is a useful starting point for e-commerce application builders. *The sample programs (i.e., suggested answers to the exercises) are available from the web site of this book.*

- *Real-life e-commerce examples or case studies*: It provides many real-life examples or case studies to illustrate the applications of e-commerce, including consumer-oriented e-commerce and business-oriented e-commerce.

For instructors who adopt this book, you may download some teaching materials from the web site of this book. These include

- lecture slides (in Powerpoint format)
- source codes used in this book
- sample laboratory exercises for building the VBS (you may use them to develop your own laboratory exercises)
- links to other internet resources
- other supplementary teaching materials

As we are also using this book for teaching, we will update the web sites with new and updated materials regularly.

ORGANIZATION AND OUTLINE

There are two parts in this book. The first part (consisting of Chapters 2–10) is concerned with the underlying technologies for e-commerce, and the second part (consisting of Chapters 11–14) deals with e-commerce applications. In order to explain the key concepts, we will use an ongoing case-study (the VBS) through-out the book. We will also show you how to build this VBS by using Java Servlets through a step-by-step exercise. The organization of the book is as follows.

- Chapter 1 (Introduction) [HC,* TD] introduces the concept of e-commerce, describes its different categories, discusses its advantages, and outlines the basic system architecture.
- Chapter 2 (Internet and World Wide Web) [HC] presents the infrastructure of e-commerce by giving an overview of the internet, the web system, the hypertext transfer protocol, and cookies.
- Chapter 3 (Client-side programming) [EC, HC, RL] deals with client-side programming by using HTML and JavaScript. Essentially, it is about building the user-interface for an e-commerce system that the client uses to interact with the e-commerce system.
- Chapter 4 (Server-side programming I: Java servlet basics) [RL] introduces the fundamentals of Java Servlets for building dynamic web pages. Java Servlets will be used for building the VBS.
- Chapter 5 (Server-side programming II: Java servlet database connectivity) [RL] discusses the database programming techniques using Java Servlets. This is essential for generating dynamic web pages in general, and building the search engine for the VBS in particular.
- Chapter 6 (Server-side programming III: Java servlet session tracking) [RL] deals with the important issue of session tracking. As the hypertext transfer protocol is stateless, it is necessary to keep track of user's information. For example, session tracking is needed for building the shopping cart for the VBS.
- Chapter 7 (Basic cryptography for enabling e-commerce) [HC] presents the basic cryptographic techniques for addressing the confidentiality, integrity, and authentication requirements of e-commerce.
- Chapter 8 (Internet security) [HC] covers the security issues including firewalls, secure socket layer, and IPSec. These security technologies are essential for building a secure e-commerce system.

---

* The author(s) of each chapter is/are as indicated where HC: Henry Chan, RL: Raymond Lee, TD: Tharam Dillon and EC: Elizabeth Chang.

- Chapter 9 (Advanced technologies for e-commerce) [HC, RL, EC, TD] gives an overview of the advanced technologies for e-commerce, including mobile agents, WAP, XML, and data mining.

- Chapter 10 (Internet payment systems) [HC] presents the Secure Electronic Transaction protocol for credit card payment; the FSTC e-check system for check payment and fund transfer; and the e-cash system for supporting anonymous payment. It also gives an overview of the smart card payment methods and the emerging micropayment methods.

- Chapters 11–14 [TD, EC], present four key e-commerce applications, namely consumer-oriented e-commerce in Chapter 11, business-oriented e-commerce in Chapter 12, e-services in Chapter 13, and web advertising and publishing in Chapter 14.

- Chapter 15 (Building a virtual bookstore) [RL, HC] includes a step-by-step exercise to build the VBS by using Java Servlets. It involves the integration of various programming modules from previous chapters.

Current e-commerce applications are just "the tip of the iceberg." There may be many more innovative e-commerce applications "inside our heads." Once you have mastered the key technologies (in particular the web programming techniques) for e-commerce, you will be able to explore these applications and build them with your own "fingertips" (i.e., through programming).

We hope that you will find this book both instructive and enjoyable.

Henry Chan
Raymond Lee
Tharam Dillon
Elizabeth Chang

Acknowledgments

We express our sincere thanks to those who have contributed to the publication of this book. Many students at the Hong Kong Polytechnic University have helped us in various aspects. In particular, we thank Michael Siu, Gary Li, Ray Lam, Brian Sze, Irene Ho, and Sunny Ng for helping us in developing, testing and checking the programs, and Benjamin Lam, Stephen Ho, Catherine Chan, Portia Cheung, Violet

Chan, and Duncan Cheung for providing us with many useful ideas and valuable comments for the book. In fact, there are a lot more to name. Our thanks should go to all of them. We would also like to give special thanks to Ivy Sit who helped us to draw many nice diagrams used in the book.

Last but not least, we thank our colleagues at John Wiley & Sons and TechBooks for editing and publishing this book for us.

Henry Chan
Raymond Lee
Tharam Dillon
Elizabeth Chang

Contribution of individual author

Although I am the first author, I should only take part of the credits. I thank the other authors for writing part of the book. Without their contributions, the book could not have been completed.

The server-side programming chapters (Chapters 4–6) were written by Dr. Raymond Lee. He was also involved in writing Chapter 3 (the sections on Style Sheet, Image Map, Frames and Javascript particularly) and Chapter 15 (The VBS exercises). The e-commerce applications (Chapters 11–13) were written by Prof. Tharam Dillon. He also helped me to refine Chapter 1 and gave us many good suggestions and comments on improving the whole book. The first part of Chapter 3 (The introduction, Sections 3.1 and 3.2) and Chapter 14 (web advertising and web publishing) were written by Dr. Elizabeth Chang and Prof. Tharam Dillon. All of us involved in writing Chapter 9 (Advanced technologies for e-commerce) based on our research interests. While I wrote the mobile agent section, Dr. Raymond Lee wrote the WAP section, Dr. Elizabeth Chang wrote the XML section, and Prof. Tharam Dillon wrote the data mining section.

Thanks a lot Raymond, Tharam, and Elizabeth!

Henry Chan

1

Introduction

1.1   Electronic Commerce and Physical Commerce

1.2   The DIGITAL Phenomenon

1.3   Looking at E-commerce from Different Perspectives

1.4   Different Types of E-commerce

1.5   Examples of the Types of E-commerce

1.6   Some E-commerce Scenarios

1.7   Changes Brought by E-commerce

1.8   Advantages of E-commerce

1.9   Myths About E-commerce Development and Implementation

1.10   System Model and Road Map of this Book

1.11   Summary

        References

        Recommended Readings

Commerce is a basic economic activity involving trading or the buying and selling of goods (according to standard dictionaries). For example, a customer enters a bookshop, examines the books, selects a book, and pays for it. To fulfill the customer requirement, the bookshop needs to carry out other commercial transactions and business functions such as managing the supply chain, providing logistic support, handling payments, etc. As we enter the electronic age, an obvious question is whether these commercial transactions and business functions can be carried out electronically. In general, this means that no paperwork is involved, nor is any physical contact necessary. This is often referred to as electronic commerce (e-commerce). The earliest example of e-commerce is electronic funds transfer [Kalakota and Whinston, 1997]. This allows financial institutions to transfer funds between one another in a secure and efficient manner. Later, electronic data interchange (EDI) was introduced to facilitate interbusiness transactions. However, early EDI systems were typically operated over special networks that are complex to set up and costly to administer. For these reasons, EDI has not been as widely deployed as expected. With the advent of internet technologies and advanced cryptographic techniques, it is now feasible to implement e-commerce over a public network – the Internet. The development of the World Wide Web (www) greatly accelerates the development of e-commerce and expands its scope to cover different types of applications. In this chapter, we will give an introduction to e-commerce by discussing some primary concepts, advantages, and frameworks.

1.1 *ELECTRONIC COMMERCE AND PHYSICAL COMMERCE*

Generally speaking, e-commerce is about the sale and purchase of goods or services by electronic means, particularly over the internet. Figure 1.1 shows that in broad terms one can distinguish two types of commerce: physical commerce and e-commerce. In a physical or traditional commerce system, transactions take place via contact between humans usually in a physical outlet such as a store. For example, if you want to buy a book, you will go to a physical bookstore and buy the physical book from a salesman. In a pure e-commerce system, transactions take place via electronic means.

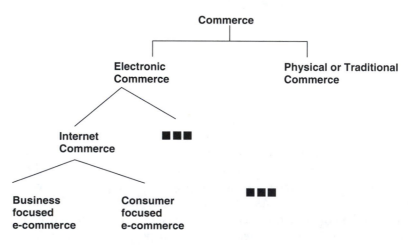

Figure 1.1 Types of commerce

In this case, you will access a cyber bookstore and download a digital book from a server computer. These two cases represent the extremes: the traditional commerce system on one side and the pure e-commerce system on the other. There are many variants and in many cases, e-commerce and physical commerce can complement each other. For example, a physical book is ordered by electronic means and it is sent to you via physical means [Turban *et al.*, 2000]. According to Schneider and Perry [2000], e-commerce is more suitable for standard goods, low-value goods, digital goods, and simple services (i.e. intangible goods), whereas traditional commerce is more suitable for nonstandard goods, perishable goods, expensive goods, and extremely low-value goods. Complex products such as cars and nonstandard services are better served by integrating e-commerce and physical commerce.

Strictly speaking, e-commerce has a very wide scope and can be further divided into different categories. The most popular type is, of course, Internet Commerce. It refers to business transactions over the internet and, in most cases, the transactions are carried out over a web system, so we may call it Web-based Electronic Business. Another broad categorization of e-commerce is to separate it into business-focused or customer-focused e-commerce. We discuss these in greater detail in Section 1.4.

In recent years, another term called e-business has emerged. In general, e-business has a wider perspective than e-commerce. It involves using information technologies in all aspects of the business. Hence, e-commerce can be viewed as a subset of e-business. However, like many other e-commerce books, we will use the following terms e-commerce, internet commerce, Web-based electronic business and e-business in an interchangeable manner.

1.2 *THE* **DIGITAL** *PHENOMENON*

Various statistics and forecasts have all indicated that e-commerce has an extremely promising future. A few years ago, Forrester Research forecasted that e-commerce sales would account for 1% of the global economy by 2002 [Korper and Ellis, 2001]. However, recent forecasts have all suggested that this may be too conservative. It is predicted that the number of e-commerce customers worldwide will reach 500 million by 2003, and the associated revenue will increase to $1.3 trillion as compared with $120 billion in 1999 [Dutta and Srivastava, 2001]. According to the Gartner Group, business-to-consumer e-commerce will account for 5–7% of the retail sales in the United States by 2004 [Derfler, 2001]. This represents at least a 500% growth from the year 2000. Based on research by Jupiter Communications, the revenue for business-to-business e-commerce in the United States will reach $6.3 trillion by 2005, representing a 2000% increase as compared with the same figure in 2000 [Derfler, 2001].

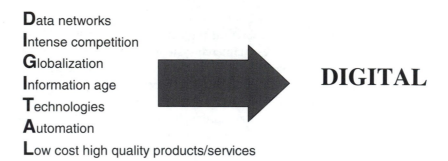

Data networks
Intense competition
Globalization
Information age
Technologies
Automation
Low cost high quality products/services

DIGITAL

Figure 1.2 The DIGITAL phenomenon

These figures indicate that there must be some "drivers" behind e-commerce. As e-commerce is about going "DIGITAL," we call this the DIGITAL phenomenon. Here we attempt to examine the possible drivers behind e-commerce (or the DIGITAL phenomenon) by the following "DIGITAL" acronym (see Figure 1.2). Hopefully, this can provide the basis for further discussion.

Let us explain the key words given in the figure in more detail in the following table (Table 1.1).

While each of the topics in this table can be explored in greater depth, they are introduced here to give one a feeling for the drivers behind e-commerce. For those who wish to follow up any of these in greater detail we include many references at the end of this chapter.

1.3 LOOKING AT E-COMMERCE FROM DIFFERENT PERSPECTIVES

E-commerce is changing our economy and affecting all aspects of business. Today, no company can afford to ignore e-commerce. It is even predicted that e-commerce will become part of core business functions just like accounting, marketing, etc. In recent years, many models, frameworks, and thoughts towards building a comprehensive picture of e-commerce are evolving. In this section, we go through some of them in order to look at e-commerce from different perspectives.

A three-layer model is commonly used to describe e-commerce such as the one proposed by Zwass [2000]. Zwass's model consists of an infrastructure layer, a services layer, and a products/structures layer. The three layers can be further divided into seven functional layers for carrying out different functions. The major functions are to provide the:

- technical infrastructure (e.g. the Internet and www)
- secure messaging services (e.g. EDI)
- supporting services (e.g. electronic payment)

Table 1.1 Summary of key drivers of e-commerce

Key drivers	Explanations
Data networks	With the advent of data networks such as the local area networks and the internet, dispersed computing systems can now be connected together. This not only allows seamless flow of information but also opens many new opportunities including e-commerce.
Intense competition	In nearly all businesses, competition is becoming increasingly intense. In order to survive, companies are constantly looking for more effective ways to provide better customer services. E-commerce is one of the effective ways.
Globalization	To maintain growth of profit, many companies are moving to the international market. However, one of the major obstacles is the geographical barrier. E-commerce provides an effective "vehicle" for companies to move to the international market because there is almost no geographical barrier in cyberspace. In other words, it is easier for a foreign company to compete with a local company under the cyber environment. Globalization is a complex issue and the reader is referred to the references for a more detailed discussion.
Information age	As we enter the information age, information becomes a valuable asset. Therefore, companies are looking for more effective ways to collect, update, and manipulate various types of information particularly for marketing purposes. E-commerce facilitates this.
Technologies	With the advent of technologies, many business ideas can now be realized. Technologies are the enabler for e-commerce.
Automation	As the cost of labor increases, there is a strong need for companies to look for alternative ways to do routine work. This is particularly true in handling the myriad paper transactions once an order is taken. With electronic messages one can reduce this considerably. E-commerce thus provides an attractive solution.
Low cost high quality products/services	"Low cost high quality products/services" has become one of the major business philosophies in the 21st century because of competitions and high customer expectations. Companies are looking for ways to satisfy these requirements.

- commercial products, services, and systems (e.g. e-retailing)
- electronic marketplace (e.g. on-line auctions)

For details, please refer to the insightful article by Zwass [2000].

Greenstein and Feinman [2000] discusses another three-layer model consisting of the existing market space, the three pillars of e-commerce (electronic information, electronic relationships, and electronic transactions), and the open market processes. Kalakota and Robinson [1999] view e-commerce from a wider perspective, using the term e-business. It is about integrating the frontend and backend applications with the business process. With the aim of maximizing customer value, it involves redefining the business model in conjunction with various information technologies. Eight business rules are proposed for achieving this goal. Schneider and Perry [2000] view e-commerce as an effective means to improve a value chain, which is used to link various functional activities (i.e. production, marketing, finance, etc.) of a company. This value chain concept can also be extended to link different companies to form an industry value chain. In general, e-commerce helps to facilitate information flow across the value chains and to reduce the associated transaction costs. It is also of interest to look at e-commerce from the point of view of relationship. At its root, every business needs to maintain three types of relationship: the relationship with its customer, the relationship with its business partners (e.g. suppliers), and the relationship with its employees [Derfler, 2001]. E-commerce provides an effective tool for building, managing, and enhancing these relationships. In the context of e-commerce, the first type of relationship is not just selling through the web but managing customer relationships in general. Special electronic customer relationship management software is available for this purpose. The second type of relationship is about procurement and supply chain management by electronic means. Virtual Private Networks and XML are the main facilitators in these areas. They will be described later in this book. While the first two types of relationship are external, the last one is internal. It involves building an effective Intranet for integrating different information systems and sharing information through which communication and productivity can be enhanced (see Derfler [2001] for details).

Furthermore, in both the popular press and in the general community, a number of ideas and commentaries are also gaining credence. It is worth looking at some of the more interesting of these in order to gain an appreciation of some aspects of e-commerce (see Figure 1.3).

1.4 DIFFERENT TYPES OF E-COMMERCE

The matrix in Figure 1.4 shows the different types of e-commerce from the perspective of the buyer and seller relationship. This is often used to categorize e-commerce applications. According to this relationship, e-commerce applications can be divided into the following four categories [Turban *et al.*, 2000; Korper and Ellis, 2001]:

a. *Business-to-consumer (B2C)* In this case, the seller is a business organization whereas the buyer is a consumer. This emulates the situation of physical retailing and so it is commonly called electronic retailing. Typically, electronic stores are set up on the internet to sell goods to the consumers. For example, our VBS sells books to the consumers through the internet. Note here that the business drives

Some interesting comments on e-commerce: what do you think?

- *E-commerce is the smartest way of doing business. You ask your customers to do the work for you such as filling in the order forms, checking the order status and downloading the product themselves so that you can save huge costs and manpower. Furthermore, they do not make any complaints and even think that you have done excellent work for them. Can you think of anything smarter than this?*

- *E-commerce is changing the traditional way of measuring business performance. People no longer look at the profit and loss account any more. Instead, the future value of a company becomes the major concern. As long as an e-commerce business "makes sense" (it does not need to "make cents"), it may still be backed by numerous investors.*

- *Many e-commerce companies are "burning money". There has even been the invention of a new term called "burn rate" to measure how "well" a company manages its e-commerce business. In order to survive, the business focus is not "how to make money quickly" but "how to burn money slowly".*

- *In both traditional commerce and e-commerce, companies and investors care about earning per share (EPS), but in a totally different way. In traditional commerce, investors care whether the EPS of a company is positive. In e-commerce, they care whether the EPS is negative. If the EPS is too positive, it may indicate that the company is too conservative (i.e., not aggressive enough).*

- *E-commerce is about focus. Many dotcoms (e-commerce companies are usually called dotcoms) sell only one product and in fact the company name may also be the product name.*

- *E-commerce relies heavily on IP: Innovation and People or Investment and Partnership.*

Figure 1.3   Some interesting comments on e-commerce

	Business (organization)	Consumer (individual)
Business (organization)	B2B (e.g. TPN)	B2C (e.g. Amazon)
Consumer (individual)	C2B (e.g. Priceline)	C2C (e.g. eBay)

Figure 1.4   Different types of e-commerce

the specification of the product and the customer chooses whether or not to buy a prefabricated product. An example of this in traditional commerce is purchasing suits "off the rack."

b. *Business-to-business (B2B)* In this case, both the buyer and the seller are business organizations. As described in Chapter 12, there are three types of systems, namely, buyer-oriented system, seller-oriented system, and virtual marketplace. In many situations, it is related to supply chain management. For example, the Virtual Bookstore (VBS) needs to order books from various publishers. The ordering process can be accomplished by using electronic data interchange.

c. *Consumer-to-consumer (C2C)* This refers to situations where both the seller and the buyer are consumers. With the advent of e-commerce, on-line auctions provide an effective means for supporting C2C e-commerce. For example, our VBS can provide on-line auction services for customers to sell used books to other customers through the VBS web site. In addition, a virtual community can be formed.

d. *Consumer-to-business (C2B)* As explained later, this is a new form of commerce in which a consumer specifies the requirements to a business, which provides a product that meets these requirements. These requirements could be as simple as an acceptable price, or could involve considerable customization of an existing standard product, or creation of a new product. An example of this in the traditional commerce setting is a "made to measure" tailor. The key distinction is related to who is driving the specification of the product being purchased. Unlike B2C, there is a strong element of customization.

1.5 EXAMPLES OF THE TYPES OF E-COMMERCE

The aforementioned categories of e-commerce can best be explained by four real life examples.

1.5.1 Amazon.com: B2C e-commerce

Established in 1995 by Jeff Bezos, Amazon.com (www.amazon.com) is one of the most well-known e-commerce site in general and internet bookseller in particular (see Figure 1.5). It is a typical example of B2C e-commerce in which a business sells already manufactured products to the consumers directly on the internet. Books are listed under different sections for ease of searching. This resembles organizing books in different bookshelves in a physical bookstore. Furthermore, a search facility is available for searching books according to user input. Our VBS also provides a similar function. Having selected a book, a consumer can put it into his shopping

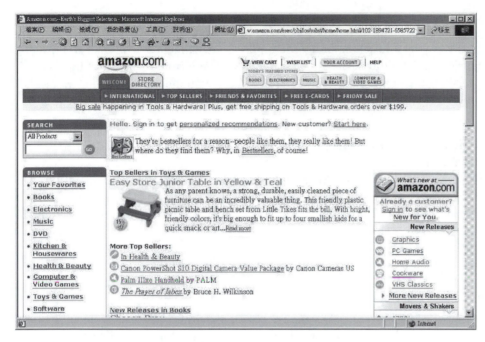

Figure 1.5 Homepage of Amazon.com (©2001 Amazon.com, Inc. All Rights Reserved Reproduced with permission of Amazon.com)

cart. Amazon.com makes use of data mining techniques to promote the selling of books. This is done by suggesting books to the customer based on the books in the shopping cart and the buying pattern of other customers with a similar profile. After shopping, consumers check out the books and pay by credit cards in most cases. Books are sent by mail or courier, whichever the customer prefers. Besides books, Amazon.com has now become a superstore (or a horizontal portal) by selling a variety of other things such as toys, wireless phones, cameras, and video games.

1.5.2 eBay*: C2C e-commerce

Established in 1995, eBay (www.eBay.com) provides the world's largest online trading service by means of online auctions. Basically, a user places an item on the eBay Web site for bidding. Other interested members then bid for it before the deadline. Where the English auction system is used, the highest bid wins. This is a typical C2C

---

* This subsection is based on information at eBay web site.

e-commerce example in which a consumer can sell to other consumers. Currently, eBay has more than 29 million members. By means of online auctions, they participate in the buying and selling of a wide range of items, including books, stamps, coins, music, etc. In addition to auctions, eBay creates a virtual community for its users to "talk" at the eBay Café (a chat room) and to communicate with other users via the bulletin boards.

1.5.3 Trading Process Network: B2B e-commerce

General Electric's Trading Process Network (TPN) (www.tpn.geis.com) is an internet-based trading network for buyers and sellers to carry out B2B e-commerce on the Internet. Unlike B2C e-commerce, it is buyer-driven rather than seller-driven. That means, a buyer submits a request to the system and then respective sellers respond to the request. In TPN, a typical purchase cycle (from the buyer's perspective) is described as follows based on the information at www.tpn.geis.com:

- *Step 1*: A buyer determines the requirements, prepares the Request For Quotation (RFQ), and searches for potential suppliers (sellers).
- *Step 2*: The buyer submits the RFQ and invites potential suppliers to respond.
- *Step 3*: Suppliers obtain the RFQ for processing.
- *Step 4*: Interested suppliers bid for the request accordingly.
- *Step 5*: The buyer and suppliers can negotiate the bids online.
- *Step 6*: Finally, the buyer selects the best bid and completes the purchase.

1.5.4 Priceline*: C2B e-commerce

Priceline (www.priceline.com) introduces a novel e-commerce application called the "demand collection system" (see Figure 1.6). It allows consumers to "name the price" and hence it is consumer driven not seller driven. According to the above definition, this is a C2B e-commerce application. Suppose that you want to buy an air-ticket. You can provide Priceline with your travel requirements (e.g. how many tickets you want to buy, departure/return date, departure/arrival city etc), the desirable price, and your credit card number. Then Priceline will try to find an airline that can meet your requirements. After finding a match, Priceline will buy the ticket(s) for you with your credit card. As you can "name the price", the deal is final

---

* This subsection is based on information at Priceline web site.

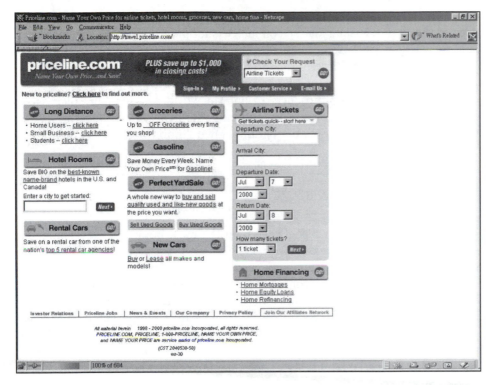

Figure 1.6 Homepage of Priceline (Reproduced with permission of Priceline.com)

(i.e. no alteration is allowed). Besides air-tickets, Priceline also handles the purchase of many other products/services such as cars, hotel rooms, long-distance calls and even mortgage.

1.6 *SOME E-COMMERCE SCENARIOS*

Let us examine some scenarios to see how e-commerce is changing our daily lives.

1.6.1 Retailing

In the main form of traditional retailing, when we want to buy something, we need to visit physical shops. Very often, we may not be able to buy the best product in the market because we can visit only a few shops near our home or our office. This is to some small extent modified in other forms of traditional retailing such as mail order or phone purchasing. With e-commerce, shopping can be done at any time by using our "fingertips" instead of our "feet". Furthermore, the geographical barrier becomes a blur. A shop located in another country and a shop next to your home are both "one finger-click" away. By using search engines, we can quickly select and compare different brands of products around the world. For some products such as software and music, we can even download the goods instantly. In the future, we may even send out intelligent software programs called "mobile agents" to shop around the internet for us.

1.6.2   Servicing

The classified advertisement has always been the most popular channel for selling used items (e.g. used car). If you have ever sold secondhand items through classified advertisements, you may have experienced the following headache. Tens or even hundreds of interested buyers contact you by telephone. As you can communicate with them only one at a time, it is difficult for you to negotiate the best price. Even after all the items have been sold, you may still receive calls from potential buyers. With e-commerce, a more effective channel is emerging: the on-line auction for facilitating this kind of C2C commerce transaction. By means of an on-line auction, not only can the seller reach a large number of potential buyers, but he can also find the best price in the market.

1.6.3   Publishing

The traditional publishing industry is based on a mass production model. Thus, there are only a few newspapers available and the format, layout, and news selection of these are done by the editorial staff. The degree of detail and slant on a particular news item is also fixed by the reporter or editorial staff. This is necessary for a mass production newspaper. By and large, the only choice the reader has is to select a particular newspaper. Once that is done he has to put up with the editorial layout and reporters' choices, even though these might not coincide with his own interests. E-commerce makes personalization possible at very little extra cost. Let us imagine that we have a web-based newspaper system available. Each reader can specify his/her favorite newspaper template. Information can then be filled into the personalized template accordingly from the databases. With personalization, electronic newspapers will be published according to customers' preferences (e.g. someone may want to see the headline news on the first page, while others may prefer to see the sports news or entertainment news on the first page). Obviously, this does not make economical sense in the traditional newspaper business. However, in the electronic newspaper scenario, the extra cost of printing a personalized newspaper is very small.

1.6.4 Supply chain management

In its most common forms, traditional supply chain management is supply driven. In other words, goods are "pushed" through the supply chain. One disadvantage of this model is that distributors may keep an unnecessary inventory. In order to overcome this, many manufacturers have introduced *Just-in-Time* (JIT) supply systems. These systems have some element of "pull" in them in the sense that the manufacturer's estimates of his needs for supplies in a short time horizon are used to determine purchases from suppliers, and suppliers must meet these orders within a specified time frame. Even here the manufacturer could easily see a buildup of the inventory of his manufactured products. What is necessary from the manufacturer's point of view is not simply JIT supply but also JIT production. Moreover, there may be a lot of paper-based information involved. With e-commerce, this whole process becomes demand-driven as controlled by the end consumer. That means, goods are now "pulled" down the chain by the customers. Thus, "supply chain management" becomes more "demand chain management." This makes JIT production management and mass customization possible.

1.7 CHANGES BROUGHT BY E-COMMERCE

No doubt, e-commerce is changing our daily lives. These changes occur along four different directions as illustrated by the aforementioned scenarios. In the first scenario, e-commerce provides an alternative solution. Even if we do not have cybershops, we can still make the purchase from physical shops. That means, cybershops are alternatives to physical shops. While cybershopping can be more convenient, some people may still want to shop at physical stores because of the physical shopping experience. In the second scenario, e-commerce provides a better solution. For instance, as explained in Section 1.6.2, the benefits brought by on-line auctions cannot be realized by the traditional classified advertisement and the on-line auction is therefore a better way to solve the same problem. In the third scenario, e-commerce is bringing in a new form of an already-existing service. In the traditional newspaper business, obviously it is not cost effective to print a different newspaper for everyone, so mass production is inevitable. However, with e-commerce, mass customization becomes possible at almost no extra cost. The final scenario illustrates that e-commerce is changing our business logic from a supply-driven model to a demand-driven model.

Turban *et al.* [2000] and Hartman, Sifonis, and Kador [2000] have summarized in a useful tabular form some of the changes e-commerce has made. Utilizing some of the information in these tables and drawing on other detailed sources and our own experience, we have developed an extended summary of the key changes brought about by e-commerce as shown in Table 1.2.

1.8 ADVANTAGES OF E-COMMERCE

E-commerce is bringing about advantages to both consumers and business organizations [Turban *et al.*, 2000; Schneider *et al.*, 2000]. For consumers, it is of interest to study the advantages in terms of the buying process, namely search, evaluate, and execute. With e-commerce, consumers can search the global market anytime and anywhere. By using search engines or search agents, consumers can easily compare products in the global market. This allows consumers to evaluate the best possible product efficiently. With certain digital goods such as software, consumers can execute the order conveniently and receive the goods instantly.

For business organizations, the prime objective is to manage this fundamental formula [Kalakota and Whinston, 1997]:

$$\text{Profit} = \text{Revenue} - \text{Cost}$$

According to Kalakota *et al.* [1997], e-commerce is attractive because it can be used to raise profit by increasing revenue while decreasing cost. With e-commerce, a company can increase revenue by exploring new opportunities and expanding into the global market. In fact, a local shop and a foreign shop are both "one click" away in the cyberspace. In other words, the geographical limitation is totally gone and international companies can now compete with local companies more easily. In terms of cost reduction, e-commerce can reduce manpower and operating expenses. The use of electronic documents not only speeds up processing time, but also greatly facilitates data updating (e.g. for updating an inventory). Consequently, business organizations can make use of e-commerce to enhance productivity.

1.9 MYTHS ABOUT E-COMMERCE DEVELOPMENT AND IMPLEMENTATION

While many companies realize the importance of e-commerce to their future growth, the true meaning of e-commerce may sometimes be overlooked. Here are three common myths about the development of an e-commerce system.

Table 1.2 Summary of changes brought about by e-commerce (extension of the work of Turban *et al.* [2000] and Hartman *et al.* [2000])

Traditional commerce	E-commerce	Remarks
Marketplace	Marketspace	Marketplace has many physical constraints whereas marketspace enables almost unlimited movement.
Mostly fixed pricing	Dynamic, customized, and group pricing	Many different pricing models such as dynamic pricing (e.g. by means of on-line auction), buyer-oriented pricing (e.g. Priceline), and group-oriented pricing (e.g. Mercata) become possible in e-commerce.
Standard product	Customized product	In traditional commerce, standard products are manufactured through mass production to achieve economies of scale. In e-commerce, mass customization is possible (or even becoming a norm) such that products can be tailor-made according to customers' requirements.
Physical catalogue (fixed and inflexible)	Digital catalogue (dynamic and flexible)	With digital catalogues, updating can be done easily and they can be linked directly to the ordering process.
Primarily mass marketing (one-to-many selling)	Multifunctional marketing, in particular one-to-one selling (direct selling) and many-to-many selling (community)	In traditional commerce, mass media is often used to convey a generic marketing message. With e-commerce, customers can receive a personalized message according to their profiles and buying behavior.
Supply (seller) driven	Demand (buyer) driven	In many e-commerce applications, buyers pull the goods down the demand chain. Companies now manage a "demand chain" instead of a "supply chain."
Physical goods	Digital goods	In e-commerce, some goods can be made completely digital. They can be bought and downloaded instantly.
Hierarchical organization	Networked organization	The internet together with other information technologies create "networked organizations" (e.g. Cisco), which are more effective and productive.
Tend to expand horizontally	Tend to expand vertically	In general, many dot.coms tend to be extremely specialized (go vertical) rather than generalized (go horizontal). This is because many business rules have changed. For example, no matter how big a company is, it is still limited by say the 15-in. computer screen. Also, no matter how far the competitors are, they are still "one-click" away in cyberspace.

1.9.1   Myth 1: E-commerce is about developing web pages

E-commerce is actually about building an integrated system not developing web pages. Very often, the web pages are just the tip of the iceberg in terms of cost and functions. The invisible parts or the backend systems are the real "heart" of the system. They are often many times more expensive than the web pages. In many e-commerce projects the most difficult task is not how to build an attractive web page, but how to integrate existing and new systems together in a cost-effective manner.

1.9.2   Myth 2: The successful implementation of an e-commerce system relies on web programmers

While web programmers play an important role in the implementation of an e-commerce system, everyone in the company should participate because e-commerce involves the integration of hardware, software, "peopleware," and business process. The following examples illustrate how different parties should typically participate in an e-commerce project [Turban *et al.*, 2000; Hartman, Sifonis, and Kador, 2000].

- Senior management should take the lead to define the strategic vision of an e-commerce project. Without top management support and a clear strategic direction, an e-commerce project is unlikely to be successful.

- Procurement department should use new procurement channels such as virtual marketplace to save cost and to improve efficiency.

- Production department should redefine the existing production process to support a buyer-driven supply chain. In particular, it should take into account the need for customization and JIT production.

- Marketing department should make use of new marketing channels and techniques such as banner exchanges, affiliation program, personalization software, and data mining for more effective promotion purposes. Another important opportunity is that the marketing process can now be linked directly to the ordering process.

- Finance/accounting department should investigate new alternatives for funding e-commerce projects. It should also participate in building a secure electronic payment system to complement the conventional payment methods.

- Personnel department should design more effective forms of compensation schemes such as options and to provide up-to-date training to the employees. This is an extremely important issue because of the worldwide shortage of people with technical expertise in specifying, architecting, designing, and implementing e-commerce systems.

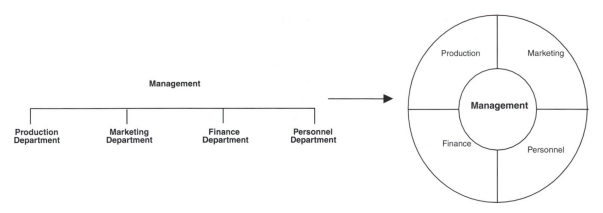

Figure 1.7 Transformation of a compartmentalized organization into an integrated organization

- Customer support department should make use of electronic customer relationship management software to provide better customer support.

To cope with the e-commerce environment, Figure 1.7 illustrates how a company may change its organization structure. In a traditional business organization, a compartmentalized organization structure is often used. In the new e-commerce environment, an integrated organization structure should be used. It looks like a "dynamic wheel" for driving a company to success.

1.9.3 Myth 3: E-commerce project is about translating the traditional business model into an electronic business model

The above statement often oversimplifies the whole picture. To implement e-commerce effectively, many business organizations need to reengineer themselves. The process is a "transformation" rather than a "translation." This may involve adopting a different business strategy. For example, with e-commerce, a manufacturer may sell goods directly to consumers. However, this may create conflicts with existing retailers. This example illustrates that e-commerce may introduce new opportunities as well as new threats. Another real life example is egghead.com, which moved its software retail outlet completely to the internet in 1997 [Zwass, 2000]. In general, an existing business can implement e-commerce using four different strategies*:

---

* This is based on the notes of Prof. Bennet P. Lientz's (UCLA) seminar on successful e-business implementation.

- *Separate* – implement by setting up a separate company
- *Overlay* – implement by adding a new department/branch to the existing company
- *Integrate* – implement by combining the traditional business and new business
- *Replace* – implement by replacing the traditional business with the new business

The first two approaches are less risky and so they are likely to be used by most companies. The third approach requires more work in general and the last approach, which has been adopted by egghead.com, is the most aggressive.

It is worth mentioning that many successful e-commerce applications go through the following development process:

1. *Tradition:* Study how the traditional model functions (e.g., customers visit a physical bookstore, choose some books from the bookshelves, and pay for them at the cash counter).
2. *Translation:* Translate the traditional model into the e-commerce model (e.g., customers visit the VBS, choose some books by browsing through the web pages, and pay for them at the check out page).
3. *Transformation*: Transform to a new and perhaps an even more effective model (e.g., in the case of the VBS, various new functions that are not available in the traditional model can be incorporated, such as search engine, shopping cart, promotion through data mining, etc.).

1.10 SYSTEM MODEL AND ROAD MAP OF THIS BOOK

The focus of this book is about building an e-commerce system. As a starting point, it is useful to define a generic system model. In general, nearly all e-commerce systems can be represented by the three-tier model as shown in Figure 1.8. This three-tier model has three main components, namely the client side, the service system, and the backend system. The service system and the backend system are often called the server side. This three-tier model is a client/server-based computing system. The client side connects users to the system, the service system serves the users' requests, and the backend system supports the service system in fulfilling the users' requests (e.g., by providing the required data). From the business perspective, the client side provides the customer interface, the service system handles the business logic, and the backend system provides the necessary information to complete a transaction.

To explain the basic concept of e-commerce, we will use an ongoing case-study [a Virtual Bookstore (VBS)] throughout the book. Figure 1.9 shows the typical

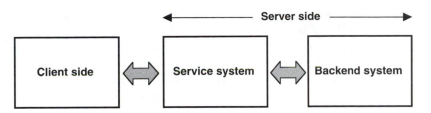

Figure 1.8   The three-tier technical model for an e-commerce system

architecture of a web-based e-commerce system in general and the VBS in particular. Referring to the three-tier model, the web server and the application server forms the service system, the web client or the web browser is the client side, and the database is the backend system.

The web server is responsible for interacting with the web client as well as the application server and the backend system. The internet provides the communication platform for transferring information between the web client and the web server. The information transfer is governed by an application protocol called the Hypertext Transfer Protocol (HTTP). This is a simple request/response protocol for the web client and the web server to "talk" to each other. Generally speaking, the web client issues a request to the web server and the web server returns a response to the web client. In Chapter 2, we will give an overview of the internet and the web system. It is important to learn them because they form the infrastructure of nearly all e-commerce systems.

To build the client side, we need a standard way to present text, images, graphics, and other multimedia information to users. For example, through the user interface, users can view product information and submit information to the web server.

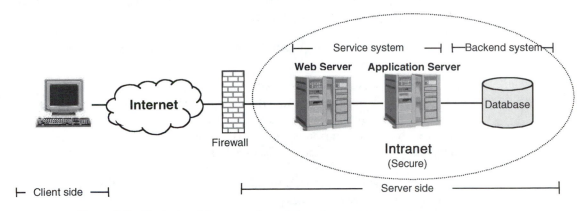

Figure 1.9   Typical architecture of a web-based e-commerce system

Currently, the most popular web publishing technique is to use the Hypertext Markup Language (HTML). In Chapter 3, we will give an overview of HTML and other techniques for building the client side.

In many cases, the web server's response is dynamic or is dependent on the user's input. For example, if a customer wants to search for some books, the web server's response will depend on the search criteria. To create a dynamic web page, the client's request invokes a program in the web server. In conjunction with the application server, the web server processes the client's request according to the program logic. In some cases, this may involve data retrieval from the database(s). After processing the client's request, the output will be returned to the client in the HTTP response message. The programs on the server side can be written in many languages. In this book, we will use Java Servlet as an example. As explained later, Java Servlet has many advantages over many other server-side programming techniques. In Chapter 4, we will discuss the fundamentals of Java Servlet programming and in Chapter 5, we will deal with the important issue of database connectivity.

HTTP is a simple request/response protocol, so it is stateless. In other words, a web server will not keep track of user state or user information. For example, a web server cannot know whether the current request is from a previous client or from a new client. In many e-commerce systems, knowing the user state is an important requirement. In technical terms, this is called session tracking. For example, in a shopping cart application, the web server needs to know the contents of each client's shopping cart so as to display the contents in the web page. Java servlets have an application programming interface (API) for performing session tracking. In Chapter 6, we will discuss the Java Servlet session tracking API. In particular, we will present ways to use the session tracking API for supporting user authentication and for building a shopping cart application.

In consumer-oriented systems, the client side is typically a user on a personal computer with a web browser to interact with the e-commerce system. In business-oriented systems, the client side could be:

1. a user on a personal computer with a web browser to interact with the e-commerce system.
2. an organizational system that is capable of carrying out purchasing and updating its own electronic documents and databases. Here there may be a direct connection between the client's organizational system and the seller's server-side system. Such communication is facilitated by electronic data interchange using business connectors. This issue is discussed in more detail in Chapter 12.

The internet, itself, is a nonsecure public network. Therefore, we need to protect the user against possible attacks from other users of the internet. Security is an important requirement in e-commerce. To build a secure e-commerce system, we need to employ various cryptographic techniques. These basically encode and decode the user information, putting it in a secure coded form during transmission over the insecure internet. In Chapter 7, we will present the basic cryptographic techniques for addressing these security requirements. As shown in Figure 1.9, the web server, the application server, and the database(s) of an organization are installed in a secure private network called an Intranet. This secure private intranet is protected from possible attacks from the insecure public internet by means of various security techniques such as firewalls. These are discussed in Chapter 8.

Besides these underlying technologies for e-commerce, we will also discuss some of the advanced technologies in Chapter 9. These include Mobile Agents, Wireless Application Protocol, eXtensible Markup Language, and Web Mining. They can be used to complement and enhance the existing e-commerce system.

Besides the above technologies, another important component of an e-commerce system is the payment system. In the traditional commerce system, we have four main types of payment methods, namely cash, check, credit card, and direct funds transfer. To build a complete e-commerce system, it is of great interest to implement these four types of payment methods in the cyberspace. In Chapter 10, we will give an overview of the internet payment systems.

By using the above technologies, many e-commerce applications can be built. In Chapters 11–14, we will give an overview of some of these e-commerce applications.

The road map of the book is shown in Figure 1.10.

Finally, it is important to mention that besides the technical issues, we also need to resolve many nontechnical ones before we can deploy e-commerce widely. Although these issues are beyond the scope of this book, we would like to mention them briefly here. Two important ones are related to law and taxation. As we break the geographical barrier, these two issues are becoming more critical. Imagine that someone starts a cyber shop in country A and sells goods to consumers in country B. Should the cyber shop be bound by the law in country B? If so, how can it be enforced? In terms of taxation, different countries have different taxation requirements. For example, some countries impose sales taxes while others do not. How can we fulfill different taxation requirements in such a complex environment? To explore these nontechnical issues further, please refer to the references and recommended readings at the end of this chapter.

1.11 *SUMMARY*

In this chapter, we have given an introduction to e-commerce. In general, e-commerce refers to business transactions by electronic means, especially by the internet. Various forecasts indicate that e-commerce has a very bright future. As a basis for further discussion, we attempt to capture the drivers behind e-commerce (or the DIGITAL

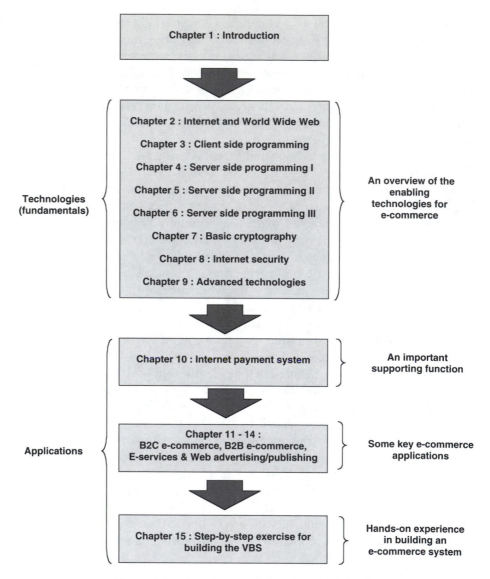

Figure 1.10 Roadmap and chapters of this book

phenomenon) by the acronym DIGITAL. We also look at e-commerce from many different perspectives. E-commerce applications are commonly classified in four categories, namely B2C, B2B, C2C, and C2B. Examples for each category are Amazon.com, TPN, eBay, and Priceline, respectively. E-commerce can bring about a number of advantages to both business organizations and consumers. At the same time, it is also bringing about many changes in our traditional commerce system.

In this book, our focus is on the technologies for building an e-commerce system. It is usually based on a three-tier system model involving the user interface, service system, and backend system. In a web-based e-commerce system, the user interface is the web client and the web server is the main part of the service system. We will discuss how to build this web-based e-commerce system in later chapters.

REFERENCES

Derfler, F. J. and the editors of PC Magazine, *E-business essentials*, Que, 2001.

Dutta, S. and Srivastava, S., *Embracing the Net*, Pearson Education Ltd., 2001.

Greenstein, M. and Feinman, T. M., *Electronic Commerce: Security, Risk Management and Control*, Irwin McGraw-Hill, 2000.

Hartman, A., Sifonis, J. G., and Kador, J., *Net Ready: Strategies for Success in the E-conomy*, McGraw-Hill, New York, 2000.

Kalakota, R. and Robinson, M., *E-business: Roadmap of Success*, Addison-Wesley, Reading, MA, 1999.

Kalakota, R. and Whinston, A. B., *Electronic Commerce – A Manager's Guide*, Addison-Wesley, Reading, MA, 1997.

Korper, S. and Ellis, J., *The E-commerce Book*, Academic Press, New York, 2001.

Kosiur, D. R., *Understanding Electronic Commerce*, Microsoft Press, 1997.

Schneider, G. P. and Perry, J. T., *Electronic Commerce*, Course Technology, 2000.

Turban, E., Lee, J., King, D., and Chung, H. M., *Electronic Commerce – A Managerial Perspective*, Prentice-Hall, Upper Saddle River, NJ, 2000.

Whiteley, D., *E-commerce: Strategy, Technologies and Applications*, McGraw-Hill, 2000.

Zwass, V., "Structure and macro-level impacts of electronic commerce: From technological infrastructure to electronic marketplaces," at http://www.gvsu.edu/ssb/ijec/. (An early version of the paper "Electronic commerce: Structures and issues" can be found in *International Journal of Electronic Commerce* **1** (1), 1996.)

RECOMMENDED READING

There are many good books on e-commerce, most of which focus on the business aspect. This book is devoted to the technical aspects.

Kosiur, D. R., *Understanding Electronic Commerce*, Microsoft Press, 1997.
  This is an introductory book that gives a good overview of e-commerce.

Kalakota, R. and Whinston, A. B., *Electronic Commerce – A Manager's Guide*, Addison-Wesley, Reading, MA, 1997.
  This is a book on e-commerce specially written for managers.

Kalakota, R. and Whinston, A. B., *Frontiers of Electronic Commerce*, Addison- Wesley, Reading, MA, 1996.
  This book describes the technical aspects of e-commerce in greater details.

Kalakota, R. and Robinson, M., *E-business: Roadmap of Success*, Addison-Wesley, Reading MA, 1999.

This is a recent book focusing on e-business.

Turban, E., Lee, J., King, D., and Chung, H. M., *Electronic Commerce – A Managerial Perspective*, Prentice-Hall, Upper Saddle River, NJ, 2000.

This is a textbook on e-commerce written from a managerial perspective. It gives a very good introduction to e-commerce and contains a lot of interesting case studies.

Schneider, G. P. and Perry, J. T., *Electronic Commerce*, Course Technology, 2000.

This is another textbook on e-commerce covering its major aspects, particularly the business aspects.

Greenstein, M. and Feinman, T. M., *Electronic Commerce: Security, Risk Management and Control*, Irwin McGraw-Hill, 2000.

This is an e-commerce textbook written from an accounting perspective.

IEEE Communication Magazine, **37**, Sept. 1999 (Articles on E-commerce)

Zwass, V. "Structure and macro-level impacts of electronic commerce: From technological infrastructure to electronic marketplaces," at http://www.gvsu.edu/ssb/ijec/. (An early version of the paper "Electronic commerce: Structures and issues" can be found in *International Journal of Electronic Commerce* **1** (1), 1996.)

These provide many insightful articles on e-commerce.

Hartman, A. Sifonis, J. G., and Kador, J., *Net Ready: Strategies for Success in the E-conomy*, McGraw-Hill, New York, 2000.

Carpenter, P., *eBRANDS*, Harvard Business School Press, 2000.

Dutta, S. and Srivastava, S., *Embracing the Net*, Pearson Education Ltd., 2001.

Derfler, F. J. and the editors of PC Magazine, *E-business essentials*, Que, 2001.

Smith, E. R., *E-loyalty*, HarperBusiness, New York, 2000.

Norris, G., Hurley, J. R., Hartley, K. M., Dunleavy, J. R., and Balls, J. D., *E-business and ERP*, John Wiley & Sons, New York, 2000.

These provide many interesting and valuable insights concerning e-commerce strategies and business issues.

To find the general information and latest news on e-commerce, please visit

www.ecommercetimes.com

www.zdnet.com

In particular, www.zdnet.com/pccomp/webmap/ gives some of the best web sites in different categories.

For research purposes, the following are two journals on e-commerce

International Journal of E-commerce (http://www.gvsu.edu/ssb/ijec/)

Journal of Electronic Commerce Research (http://www.baltzer.nl/ecr/ecr.asp)

Also, the Harvard Business School web site (http://www.hbsp.harvard.edu/products/cases/) contains many case studies on e-commerce.

Last but not least, governments should also play an important role in developing e-commerce. For example, some useful information can be found from the following web sites:

http://www.ecommerce.gov/framewrk.htm

http://www.info.gov.hk/digital21

Part 1

Technologies (Fundamentals)

2

Internet and World Wide Web

2.1   An Overview of the Internet

2.2   Brief History of the Web

2.3   Web System Architecture

2.4   Uniform Resource Locator

2.5   Overview of the Hypertext Transfer Protocol

2.6   HyperText Transfer Protocol (HTTP)

2.7   Generation of Dynamic Web Pages

2.8   Cookies

2.9   HTTP/1.1

2.10 Example

2.11 Summary

       References

       Recommended Reading

In Chapter 1, we introduced the three-tiered e-commerce system model. It consists of three main components: the client side, the internet, and the server side, which is composed of the service system and the backend system. In a web-based e-commerce system, the web browser (or web client) is the client interface and the web server and application server are the main parts of the service system. For example, in the VBS scenario, customers access the VBS's web server and e-commerce application over the internet through their web browsers. As the web clients and the web server are connected to the internet, we need a protocol enabling them to "talk" to each other over the internet. This protocol is called the Hypertext Transfer Protocol (HTTP).

The internet and the web system form the basic infrastructure of many e-commerce systems. In this chapter, we first give an overview of the internet and then describe the web system and the web protocol.

2.1 *AN OVERVIEW OF THE INTERNET*

2.1.1 Basic network architecture

As its name implies, the internet is a collection of networks as shown in Figure 2.1. The networks are connected together by traffic-forwarding devices called routers. You can access the internet through an Internet Service Provider (ISP). In principle, the internet is similar to the postal network. From the network point of view, it is connectionless. In other words, unlike the telephone network, you do not need to establish a physical network connection with the receiver before transmitting information over the internet. Information is carried by packets in the internet. A packet looks like an "electronic parcel." The routers in the internet forward each packet based on the address specified on the packet. In general, only best-effort service is provided. That means that the network itself does not provide a guaranteed

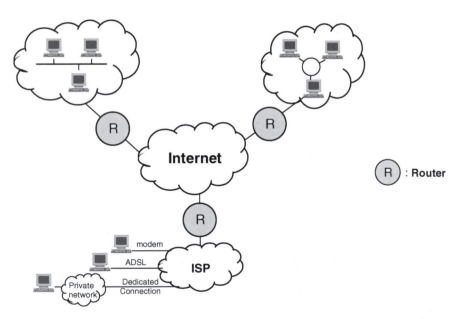

Figure 2.1 Basic network architecture of the internet

service – packets might be duplicated, lost, or delayed for a long time. This best-effort service is often referred to as "Send and Pray" service.

2.1.2 Layered model

The internet is based on a layered model called Transmission Control Protocol/Internet Protocol (TCP/IP). By means of layering, the complex process of transferring packets from one computer to another computer across the internet can be broken into small tasks. This greatly facilitates the design of various protocols for the internet. Layering also creates modularity between the different layers, with clearly defined functions between layers. This allows for independence in implementing each layer. As shown in Figure 2.2, the internet model has four layers: link, network, transport, and application. The link layer is for providing access to the internet; the network layer is for forwarding packets across the internet; the transport layer is for providing end-to-end data transport service; and the application layer is for providing a specific application. Generally speaking, each layer at the sending host communicates with its peer at the receiving host by using a particular protocol. As shown in Figure 2.3 [Stevens, 1994], data is generated from the application layer. Starting from the application layer, each layer adds the required header (and trailer if any) and passes the packet to the lower-lying layer. In other words, each layer is served by the lower lying layer. Packets are forwarded from the originating host through the routers to the destined host as shown in Figure 2.4.

2.1.3 Link layer

The main function of the link layer is to provide access to the network. It addresses the physical characteristics and medium access control. Table 2.1 shows the

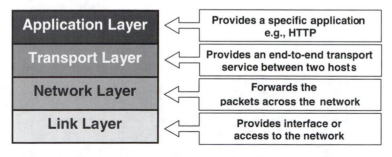

Figure 2.2 Layered model for the internet (See also [Stevens, 1994])

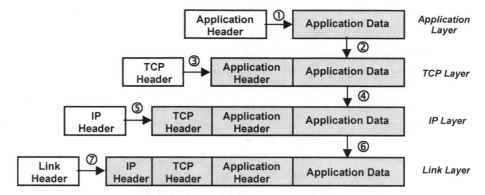

Figure 2.3 Processing at each layer

common way to access the internet [Naik, 1998]. For home users, the most common way to access the internet is by using dial-up modems. With modems, digital data can be turned into analogue signals suitable for transmission over the public switched telephone network. Currently, the maximum data rate that can be supported by a dial-up modem is 56 Kbps. In offices, the most common way to access the internet is through local area networks (LANs). Ethernet is the most popular LAN protocol and it is governed by a medium access control protocol called Carrier Sense Multiple Access with Collision Detection (CSMA/CD). The main challenge of a LAN is to enable computers to share a common channel efficiently. With CSMA/CD, a computer can transmit data at any time if it detects that the channel is free. Should two or more computers want to transmit at almost the same time (causing a collision), the affected computers will retransmit after a random period of time. Currently, there are two commonly used Ethernet standards,

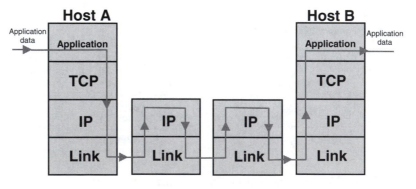

Figure 2.4 Transfer of packets

Table 2.1 Different internet access methods

Access method	Maximum data rate
Telephone modem	56 Kbps
Ethernet (local area network)	10/100 Mbps
Integrated Services Digital Network Basic Rate Interface (ISDN BRI)	112–128 Kbps
Cable modem	30 Mbps (theoretical)
	1.5 Mbps (practical)
Asymmetric Digital Subscriber Line (ADSL)	1.5–9 Mbps (from network to users)
	16–640 Kbps (from users to network)
Wireless local area network (IEEE 802.11)	1–2 Mbps

namely, 10BaseT and 100BaseT with maximum data rates of 10 Mbps and 100 Mbps, respectively. There is also a Gigabit Ethernet standard available running at 1 Gbps.

Besides using dial-up modems, a home user can also access the internet by using the Integrated Services Digital Network (ISDN) Basic Rate Interface (BRI). It provides two barrier (B) channels of 64 Kbps for transmitting voice and data traffic and a data (D) channel of 16 Kbps for transmitting control and signal information. Hence, the maximum access rate is 128 Kbps. Note that for the North American standard, the B channel operates at 56 Kbps only, so the maximum access rate is 112 Kbps in this case. In recent years, both the cable TV companies and the telephone companies also provide high-speed internet access services by using two different technologies. By using cable modems, home users can access the internet via the cable TV networks at a much faster rate than that provided by dial-up modems. Theoretically, the maximum data rate can be as high as 30 Mbps; but practically, only about 1.5 Mbps can be achieved (because of various technical limitations). Telephone companies can also make use of the existing telephone network to provide a high-speed internet access service by using the Asymmetric Digital Subscriber Line (ADSL) technology. The data rate from the network to the users is between 1.5 and 9 Mbps, depending on the distance. The data rate from the users to the network is much lower at about 16–640 Kbps [Naik, 1998]. Hence, this access method is called "Asymmetric." This is particularly useful for the web scenario since the client-to-server communication normally requires less bandwidth than the server-to-client communication. For example, a client may just generate a simple request for getting a large image from the server. Besides accessing the internet through a wired link, we can also access the network through a wireless link. One possibility is through wireless local area networks such as IEEE802.11, which uses a medium access protocol called Carrier Sense Multiple Access with Collision Avoidance. Other wireless access methods include Cellular Digital Packet Data and Code Division Multiple Access [Tanenbaum, 1996].

2.1.4   Network layer

The main purpose of the network layer is to forward packets to their destinations. In principle, this is similar to forwarding a letter through the postal network. Basically, the network layer needs to address two main questions:

- What is the destination?
- How should the packets be forwarded?

In technical terms, the first question is about addressing, and the second question is about routing [Peterson et al., 1996]. The network layer handles these two important issues.

IP address

Just like a "letter," each IP packet has an address called the IP address [Semeria, 1996]. Currently, the most widely used IP is IPv4. In IPv4, each IP address has 32 bits. For ease of reading, each IP address is expressed in the dot-decimal format, e.g. 128.0.0.1 instead of the binary which would read 10000000.00000000.00000000.00000001. Each IP address has two parts: the network number and the host number. Within the same network, all hosts have the same network number. Routers forward packets based on the network number rather than the host number so that they only need to know all the network numbers but not all the host numbers within their areas. There are five classes of IP addresses, namely classes A to E, to cater for different requirements as shown in Table 2.2 [Stevens, 1994; Peterson and Davie, 1996].

Let us further consider the IP address 128.0.0.1. In binary notation, it is 10000000.00000000.00000000.00000001. This is a class B address as it starts with "10." For a class B address, the first 16 bits represent the network number and hence the network number is 128.0.0.0. The possible host numbers are from 128.0.0.1 to 128.0.255.254. Note that 128.0.255.255 is not a valid host number because it is the broadcast address of the network 128.0.0.0.

This addressing scheme is inefficient if a network does not have a sufficient number of hosts to cover the available address space since only a few of the available addresses are utilized. In RFC 950*, a standard method called subnetting is

---

* RFC stands for Request for Comments, which can be viewed as the "internet standards" maintained by the Internet Engineering Task Force (IETF). All the RFCs can be found at www.ietf.org.

Table 2.2   Different classes of IP addresses

Class	Starts with	Network portion	Range of IP addresses	Number of available networks	Main uses
A	0	First 8 bits	0.0.0.0 to 127.255.255.255	2^7	Each network has many hosts
B	10	First 16 bits	128.0.0.0 to 191.255.255.255	2^{14}	Each network has medium number of hosts
C	110	First 24 bits	192.0.0.0 to 223.255.255.255	2^{21}	Each network has a few hosts
D	111	NA	224.0.0.0 to 239.255.255.255	NA	Multicast address
E	1111	NA	240.0.0.0 to 247.255.255.255	NA	Reserved for experimental use

recommended to divide a Class A, B, or C network into sub-networks so that the address space can be utilized more efficiently. In this case, part of the host number becomes the subnet number as specified by a subnet mask, which is used to indicate the network portion of the IP address. For example, a subnet mask 255.255.255.0 (i.e., 11111111.11111111.11111111.00000000 in binary form) means that the first $8 + 8 + 8 = 24$ bits represent the network part. With subnetting, the standard network prefix together with the subnet number identifies the effective network number. Let us look at an example [Semeria, 1996]. Assume that the VBS is given a network number 128.0.0.0 (i.e. a class B network). This means that we can only have hosts ranging from 128.0.0.1 to 128.0.255.254 for this network. Note that 128.0.0.0 and 128.0.255.255 are not valid host IP addresses because they represent the network itself and the broadcast address for the network, respectively. If we apply subnetting by using a subnet mask of 255.255.255.0, the first $8 + 8 + 8 = 24$ bits represent the network part now. That means, the original network number 128.0.0.0 can now be divided into smaller networks (or subnets), i.e., 128.0.0.0, 128.0.1.0, 128.0.2.0, ..., 128.0.255.0. For each subnet, there can be 254 hosts ($2^8 - 2$). For example, for the subnet 128.0.255.0, the possible host numbers are from 128.0.255.1 to 128.0.255.254. Note again that 128.0.255.0 and 128.0.255.255 represent the network itself and the broadcast address for the network, respectively.

Routing

To forward packets across the internet, each router maintains a routing table. In general, each routing table tells the router where a received packet should be forwarded.

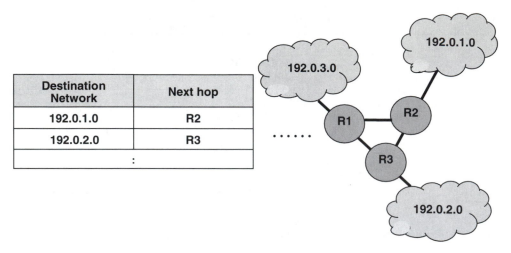

Destination Network	Next hop
192.0.1.0	R2
192.0.2.0	R3
:	

Figure 2.5 A simple routing example

A simple example is shown in Figure 2.5. In this example, there are three networks: 192.0.1.0, 192.0.2.0, and 192.0.3.0 connected by routers R1, R2, and R3. The routing table at R1 shows that to forward a packet destined for 192.0.1.0, the packet should be forwarded to R2, the next-hop router. If a packet is destined for 192.0.2.0, it should be forwarded to R3. The routing tables are updated dynamically based on the traffic situations by using a particular routing protocol. This helps ensure that packets are forwarded through links with less traffic.

The example in Figure 2.5 shows the basic operation of an intradomain routing protocol. In this case, all the networks are in the same autonomous system. This means that each router contains the routing information to reach other networks in the same autonomous system. There are two types of intradomain routing protocols based on two different principles [Peterson *et al.*, 1996; Naik, 1998]. The first one is called the distance vector routing protocol such as the Routing Information Protocol (RIP). In general, each router forwards its routing table to the adjacent routers so as to continuously update the routing table in each router. For the distance vector routing protocol, there is more routing information exchange but less processing at the routers to create and update the routing tables. The second type of intradomain routing protocol is called the link state routing protocol. In this case, each router broadcasts its link states (e.g. traffic loading) to other routers in the autonomous system. Having found the link states of all routers, each router can build a "picture" of the network and use it to construct the routing table. Compared with distance vector routing protocols, less routing information is exchanged but more processing is required to create and update the routing table in each router.

Quite clearly, it is not practical to employ an intradomain routing protocol in a global system because this requires each router to know all the networks in the world. In reality, the internet is divided into many autonomous systems. Within an autonomous system, each router's routing table contains routing information for all networks within the same autonomous system. For forwarding packets across different autonomous systems, the interdomain routing protocol is used. A popular interdomain routing protocol is the Border Gateway Protocol (BGP).

2.1.5 Transport layer

As mentioned earlier, IP provides only best-effort service. That means, packets may not be delivered to their destinations in a reliable fashion. To resolve this issue, we need a transport layer on top of the IP layer to provide end-to-end transport service between the sending and receiving computers. There are two transport protocols for the Internet, namely the User Datagram Protocol (UDP) and Transmission Control Protocol (TCP). UDP (RFC768) is connectionless whose main function is to multiplex data through "ports". As a computer may execute several applications at the same time, ports are used to identify a particular application. In other words, the actual connection between two computers is identified by the source IP address, source port number, destination IP address and destination port number. As specified by the IETF (see RFC 1700), certain port numbers are standardized for internet applications. For instance, port 80 is standardized for HTTP.

Transmission control protocol (TCP) is a connection-oriented protocol for providing a reliable data transport service between two hosts over the internet. To create a TCP connection (see Figure 2.6), the sending and receiving computer each sets up a socket, which is represented by its IP address and a port number [Tanenbaum, 1996]. A TCP connection is set up between two sockets through a three-way handshaking process [Stallings, 1997]. Basically, the sender initiates the connection; the receiver acknowledges the connection request; and finally, the sender acknowledges the receiver's acknowledgment. Having established the connection, the sending TCP process divides the application data into segments and sends them via IP to the receiving TCP process. TCP is byte-based such that each data byte is identified by a sequence number [Peterson and Davie, 1996]. Each segment has a sequence number indicating the first data byte being transmitted. Based on the sequence number, the receiving TCP process can rearrange misordered segments, send acknowledgments to the sending TCP process, and perform flow control. In general, when a receiving TCP process receives a segment, it will return an acknowledgment to the sending TCP process. If the sending TCP process does not receive the acknowledgment for a transmitted segment after a certain period of time called the time-out period, the segment will be retransmitted. To prevent the sender from overloading the receiver,

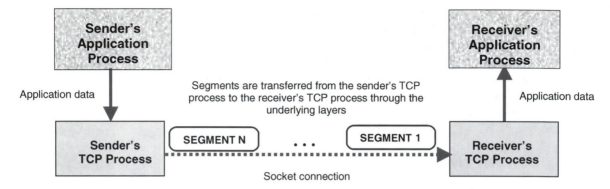

Figure 2.6   Processing by the TCP layer (modified from the work of Peterson and Davie, 1996)

the sending TCP process uses a sliding window mechanism to limit the number of bytes that can be sent to the receiver. The sliding window size is controlled by the receiver's acknowledgment.

2.1.6   Application layer

Making use of the underlying layers, the application layer is for providing a particular application. There are a variety of application layer protocols such as those given in Table 2.3.

     Later in this chapter, we will describe HTTP in detail. This protocol plays an important role in web-based e-commerce systems.

     At this stage, it is important to describe an application called the Domain Name System (DNS), which is defined in RFC1034 and RFC1035. HTTP and other application protocols rely on DNS. While the network processes packets based on the IP addresses, which are binary numbers, for comprehensibility we certainly would like to deal with human language-based names for nodes instead of binary number addresses. For example, we would like to call the VBS server something like

Table 2.3   Common application layer protocols

Protocol	Purpose
Simple mail transfer protocol	Support e-mail services
File transfer protocol	Support file transfer services
Telnet	Allow users to log in remote host
Hypertext transfer protocol	Support communications between a web client and a web server

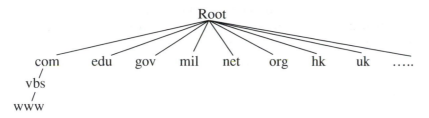

Figure 2.7   Part of the domain naming scheme

www.vbs.com rather than a number like 128.123.123.123. In the previous example, www.vbs.com is referred to as the domain name. Since the network can only understand an IP address, we need a mechanism to translate a host name or domain name to the corresponding IP address. DNS is used to do this translation. Besides providing a hierarchical naming system for identifying domain names, DNS includes a distributed database system for storing domain names, and a mechanism for searching the corresponding IP address of a domain name [Naik, 1998; Tanenbaum, 1996].

Figure 2.7 shows a partial domain naming scheme, which is organized in a tree structure. A name is assigned to each node of the "tree." Except for the "root," each node is connected to a parent node in an upward direction. At the first level of the DNS hierarchy, the major nodes are

com   company

edu   education

gov   government

mil   US military

net   network providers

org   organizations such as IEEE

Furthermore, we also have the country nodes at the first level, such as

hk   Hong Kong

uk   United Kingdom

Each domain name consists of a sequence of terms divided by periods. The first of these is the leaf node and the subsequent ones are the successive parent nodes up till the root. For example, the domain name of our VBS server is www.vbs.com. There are three nodes: www, vbs, and com. www is the leaf node, vbs is the parent node of www, and com is the parent node of vbs.

Generally speaking, this is how the DNS determines the IP address of a domain name. In the internet, there are many DNS servers, which are responsible for handling queries on finding the corresponding IP address for a domain name. Distributed databases are maintained for this purpose. When an application wants to determine the IP address of a domain name, a program known as the Resolver is invoked. The Resolver then makes a query to the associated DNS server. If the DNS server contains the mapping of the domain name and the IP address in its database, the corresponding IP address will be returned to the sender. In many cases, the query may need to propagate through a series of DNS servers in a recursive manner until the corresponding IP address can be returned to the Resolver [see Tanenbaum, 1996].

2.1.7 Next generation internet

The current IP is called IPv4 (i.e. version 4). A new version of IP called IPv6 has been developed for the next generation internet. It has the following main features [Peterson and Davie, 1996]:

- *Use of 128-bit addresses*: IPv4 employs a 32-bit address, which is not sufficient to cope with the rapid growth of the internet. To enlarge the address space, IPv6 uses a 128-bit address, which can support significant more hosts.
- *Support for multicast*: The first generation internet supports only a unicast service. That means, if a packet is to be sent to multiple destinations, multiple packets are transmitted. This is obviously a waste of network resources. In contrast, in a multicast routing protocol, a single packet is transmitted targeted to multiple destinations. Currently, multicast routing protocols are being developed for supporting multicast services on the internet.
- *Support for multimedia application (data flow)*: IPv6 provides better support for multimedia application. In the new IP packet header, there is a "flow label" field for establishing data flows in the network. Furthermore, a resource reservation protocol (RSVP) has been developed to reserve resources in the network in order to provide guaranteed service for real-time multimedia traffic.
- *Better security*: IPv4 does not address security. To address this important issue, an IP Security (IPSec) protocol has been developed for IPv6. This protocol can also be used for IPv4. We will discuss the IPSec protocol in Chapter 8. This protocol can be used to set up virtual private networks over the internet, thus allowing business partners to communicate with each other securely over the internet as if they were connected over a private network.

2.2 *BRIEF HISTORY OF THE WEB*

The invention of the world wide web (www) was not related to e-commerce at all. The story began at the European Particle Physics Laboratory called CERN where physicists around the world gathered to conduct research on nuclear physics [Tanenbaum, 1996; w3c.org]. Due to collaborative research, many documents needed to be exchanged. In 1989, Tim Berners-Lee, a physicist at CERN, proposed the concept of hypertext for linking text-based documents over computer networks and later developed a text-based browser. His work aroused interest around the world to conduct research on web. In 1993, Marc Andreeseen and some students at the University of Illinois developed the world's first graphical web browser called *Mosaic*. In the following year, Marc Andreeseen established Netscape Communications Corporation (Netscape) with James Clark of Silicon Graphics to further develop the web browser. Netscape was listed in NASDAQ in 1995 and provides the dominant web browser in the world. In 1994, the world wide web consortium http://www.w3.org was formed to standardize web-related technologies. Nowadays, the web system together with the internet forms the basic infrastructure for supporting e-commerce.

2.3 *WEB SYSTEM ARCHITECTURE*

Based on the three-tier model as discussed in Chapter 1, Figure 2.8 gives the general architecture of a web-based e-commerce system. Basically, it consists of the following components:

- *Web browser*: It is the client interface. Essentially, it is used for displaying information to the user as well as collecting user's input to the system. Serving as the client, the web browser also interacts with the web server using the HTTP.
- *Web server*: It is one of the main components of the service system. It interacts with the web client as well as the backend system.
- *Application server*: It is the other main component of the service system and it hosts the e-commerce application software.

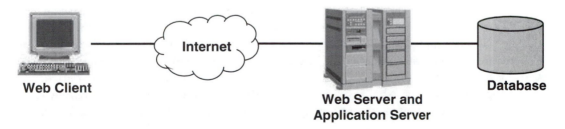

Figure 2.8 The web system architecture

- *Backend system*: It supports the service system for fulfilling the user's request. In many cases, it is a database management system.
- *Internet*: It is the communication platform for the web server and the web client to exchange information with each other.

As the web client and the web server are not connected directly, we need a protocol for them to "talk" or communicate with each other over the internet. This protocol is called the Hypertext Transfer Protocol (HTTP), which will be discussed in Sections 2.5 and 2.6.

2.4 *UNIFORM RESOURCE LOCATOR*

To identify web pages, an addressing scheme is needed. Basically, a Web page is given an address called a Uniform Resource Locator (URL). At the application level, this URL provides the unique address for a web page, which can be treated as an internet resource. The general format for a URL is as follows:

```
protocol://domain_name:port/directory/resource
```

The *protocol* defines the protocol being used. Here are some examples:

- http: hypertext transfer protocol
- https: secure hypertext transfer protocol
- ftp: file transfer protocol
- telnet: telnet protocol for accessing a remote host

The `domain_name`, `port`, `directory` and `resource` specify the domain name of the destined computer, the port number of the connection, the corresponding directory of the resource and the requested resource, respectively.

For example, the URL of the welcome page (main.html) of our VBS may be written as `http://www.vbs.com/welcome/main.html`. In this example, the `protocol` is http, the `domain_name` is www.vbs.com, the directory is `welcome` (i.e., the file main.html is stored under the directory called `welcome`).

Note that in this example, the *port* is omitted because the default port for the protocol is used; that is, formally the URL should be specified as http://www.vbs.com:80/welcome/main.html where 80 specifies the port for HTTP as explained later.

In some protocols (e.g. TELNET) where the user name and password are required, the URL can be specified as follows [Naik, 1998]:

```
protocol://username:password@domain_name:port/directory/resource
```

where *username* and *password* specify the user name and password, respectively.

2.5 *OVERVIEW OF THE HYPERTEXT TRANSFER PROTOCOL*

Let us consider a general overview of HTTP before discussing its details. This protocol is used for the web client and the web server to communicate with each other. Suppose that you access the URL of the VBS http://www.vbs.com/welcome/main.html by clicking the corresponding hyperlink. This is what happens in terms of the interactions between the web browser and the web server according to [Tanenbaum, 1996]. Utilizing the URL of the hyperlink, the web browser (or web client) obtains the IP address of the VBS through the DNS. After receiving the reply, the web client establishes a TCP connection to port 80 of the web server. Note that port 80 is the default port for HTTP. Then it issues a GET command (more specifically, GET/ welcome/main.html) to retrieve the web page "main.html" from the web server. The web server then returns the corresponding file to the browser. In HTTP/1.0, the TCP connection is then closed. In HTTP/1.1, the connection is kept open in order to support multiple requests. The browser then shows the text in the hypertext file. It also obtains the images in the hypertext file from their respective URLs and displays them. This is why you see the text first and the images later, because the images take a longer time to download.

In many companies, a proxy web server is set up for security and other administrative reasons. In this case, users need to access other web servers via the proxy web server. Basically, a user's browser issues a request to the proxy web server first and then the proxy web server retrieves the specific web page on behalf of the user. Having retrieved the web page, it is then returned to the user's browser for display. Essentially, the proxy web server acts as an application gateway (see Chapter 8 for details) for enhancing security. A proxy web server can have both positive and negative effects on web performance. On the positive side, it can be used to keep cache copies of web pages so that if subsequent users require these web pages, they can be returned to the users almost immediately. In other words, the retrieval time can be greatly reduced. However, the proxy web server can also become a bottleneck if the system is not well planned.

2.6   *HYPERTEXT TRANSFER PROTOCOL (HTTP)**

HTTP is a simple application protocol working under a client/server computing environment. Basically, a client issues a request to a server and then the server returns the response. The request is specified in text (ASCII) format, whereas the response is specified in Multipurpose Internet Mail Extensions (MIME) format, which defines different types of content types such as text, image, and audio. The common content types for a server's response are

- text/html – text file in html format
- image/JPEG – image file in JPEG format
- image/GIF – image file in GIF format

JPEG and GIF are different encoding techniques that compress an image for transmitting and storing so as to reduce the number of bytes (size) for representing the image.

At the time of writing, the commonly used version of HTTP is HTTP/1.0, which is defined in RFC1945. A new version of HTTP called HTTP/1.1 is also becoming popular. In order to explain the basic operation of HTTP, we will first give an overview of HTTP/1.0 based on RFC1945. At the end of this chapter, we will give an overview of the enhancements made by HTTP/1.1.

As discussed in the previous section, the basic operation of HTTP is as follows. The web client (e.g. your web browser or even a "robot" program) makes a TCP connection to a web server at port 80. Subsequently, an HTTP request consisting of the specific request, required headers and additional data is forwarded to the web server. After processing the request, the web server returns an HTTP response consisting of the status, additional headers, and the requested resource such as a web page [RFC1945; Hall, 1998].

2.6.1   HTTP request

The general format of the client request is as follows (see RFC1945):

```
Request_method Resource_address HTTP/Version_number
General_header(s)
Request_header(s)
```

---

* This section is based on the information in RFC1945 Naik [1998] and Hall [1998]. In particular, the descriptions of the items in Tables 2.4–2.9 are drawn from the above sources.

Table 2.4 Request methods in HTTP/1.0

Method name	Description
GET	It gets or retrieves a web page.
HEAD	It requests the header information of the web page. In other words, the response is the same as that for GET with the body or the content of the web page removed.
POST	It posts additional data to the web server in the HTTP request message. The additional data is attached after the headers.

```
Entity_header(s)
Blank_line
Entity(Additional_data)
```

As described in Table 2.4, Request_method specifies the request method used. Resource_address is essentially the URL that specifies the location of the requested resource in the web server. HTTP/Version_number tells the web server what HTTP protocol the web client is using. There are three types of headers for passing additional information to the web server, namely, General_header, Request_header, and Entity_header. They are described in Tables 2.5, 2.6, and 2.7, respectively. Finally, the web client can post additional data to the server after the Blank_line. This is used in conjunction with the POST request method. For details on the request methods and the request headers, please refer to RFC1945.

Let us look at the following example of an HTTP request message.

```
GET /vbs.html  HTTP/1.0
Accept:image/gif,image/jpeg,*/*
```

This request message means that the client wants to get a document called "vbs.html" from the server. The document is located at the root directory of the server. Version 1.0 of the HTTP is used. The client can accept any content type as

Table 2.5 General headers in HTTP/1.0

Header name	Description
Date	It specifies when (i.e. date and time) the message was generated.
Pragma	This header is for specifying implementation-specific directives. For example, if the client does not want to receive a cached copy of the requested resource, it will specify Pragma: No-cache.

Table 2.6   Request headers in HTTP/1.0

Header	Description
Authorization	Used with the later WWW-Authenticate response header, it provides authentication information to the web server. HTTP provides a basic authentication scheme by encoding the username and password in Base64 format.
From	This header provides the contact e-mail address. (e.g., the e-mail address of the person who generates the request.)
If-Modified-Since	It asks the web server to provide the requested resource only if it has been modified since the specified time in the header.
Referer	It indicates where (i.e. URL) did the client obtain the current address. By using this header, a web server can trace back the previous link(s), e.g., for maintenance or administrative purposes.
User-Agent	It provides information on the user agent (e.g. web browser) used by the web client.

indicated by "*/*" but for the image content, GIF is preferred to JPEG (see Chapter 3). Note that no additional data can be enclosed in the HTTP request.

2.6.2   HTTP response

Having processed the web client's request, the web server returns a response to the client. The general format of the response is as follows (see RFC1945).

```
HTTP/Version_number status_code Result_message (Status line)
General_header(s)
Response_header(s)
```

Table 2.7   Entity header in HTTP/1.0

Header	Description
Allow	It indicates the request methods (e.g. GET, POST, and HEAD) allowed.
Content-Encoding	It specifies the encoding method (e.g. compression method) applied to the content.
Content-Length	It indicates the length of the content in number of octets.
Content-Type	It indicates the content type or MIME type of the content, e.g., text/html means HTML document in text format.
Expires	It specifies when (i.e. date and time) the content becomes expired.
Last-Modified	It specifies when the content (web page) was last modified.

Table 2.8 Commonly used status codes in HTTP/1.0

Status code	Result message	Meaning
200	OK	This refers to the normal case in which the request is OK or successful.
201	Created	The request is processed and the resource is created as requested.
204	No content	The request is processed but no content is available for the client.
301	Moved permanently	The resource has been moved permanently to the URL as given in the "Location" header.
302	Moved temporarily	The resource has been moved temporarily to the URL as given in the "Location" header. As it is only a temporary relocation, future requests should still be sent to the current URL.
304	Not modified	The requested web page is not returned to the client as it has not been modified since the time as specified in the "If-Modified-Since" header.
400	Bad request	The request is "bad" because it could not be interpreted by the server most possibly because of syntax errors in the request.
401	Unauthorized	Used in conjunction with the WWW-Authenticate header field, it indicates that user authentication is required.
403	Forbidden	Access is forbidden, e.g., the user does not have the access right.
404	Not found	The requested resource is not found, possibly because it has been deleted from the web server.

```
Entity_header(s)
Blank_line
Entity_body (e.g., web page)
```

Again, the HTTP/Version_number indicates the version of HTTP that the server is using. The Status_code indicates the result of the request. The common status codes are given in Table 2.8. The headers General_header(s), Response_header(s), and Entity_header(s) are used to pass additional information to the web client. General_header and Entity_header have been described in Tables 2.5 and 2.7, respectively. Response_header is described in Table 2.9. Following the headers, the response data is enclosed as the Entity_body. Usually this is a hypertext file.

Let us look at an example of a server response. Suppose that the response message was as follows.

Table 2.9 Commonly used response header in HTTP/1.0

Response header	Description
Location	Used with the status code 301 and 302 etc, it provides the new URL for redirection purpose.
Server	It provides information about the server software.
WWW-Authenticate	Used with the unauthorized response message (i.e. status code of 401), it provides the authentication information required for successful authentication.

```
HTTP/1.0 200 OK
Server: Microsoft-IIS/4.0
Date: Sat, 30 Sep. 2000 09:30:00 GMT
Last-Modified: Sat, 30 Sep. 2000 09:00:00 GMT
Content-Type: text/html
Content-Length:600
```

This response message means that the web server is using version 1.0 of HTTP. The request has been processed successfully. The server is Microsoft-IIS/4.0. The current date and time are 30 Sep. 2000 and 09:30:00, respectively. The response document is an HTML file in text format and the file size is 600 bytes. This file has not been modified since 09:00:00 on 30 Sep., 2000.

2.7 GENERATION OF DYNAMIC WEB PAGES

So far, we have talked about how to get a static web page from a web server by using the GET command. In many cases, the returned web page is user-dependent, i.e., it is dynamic rather than static. For example, a user may want to use the search engine of our VBS to search for books about e-commerce. In this case, the returned web page will be dependent on the user's search criteria. Therefore, we need a method for the web client to pass additional data to the web server. One simple way to do this is to attach the data at the end of the URL by using the following format [Hall, 1998]:

```
?name₁=value₁&name₂=value₂&...&nameₙ=valueₙ
```

where $name_1$, $name_2$, ..., $name_N$ specify the names of the input elements and $value_1$, $value_2$, ..., $value_N$ specify the corresponding values.

For example, if a user wants to search for all books on ecommerce published in the year 2000, he can append the search criteria after the URL as shown in the following:

```
http://www.vbs.com/servlet/booksearch?title=ecommerce&year=2000
```

where $name_1$ is "title" and the corresponding value is "ecommerce" and $name_2$ is "year" and its value is "2000."

By entering these, the web browser will issue the following GET command:

```
GET /servlet/booksearch?title=ecommerce&year=2000 HTTP/1.0
```

in the HTTP request message.

In this case, the request is not just for a static web page. Instead, we invoke a program called "booksearch" in order to generate the search result and then return it to the user. The program "booksearch" is a servlet program stored under the logical directory "servlet" of the host www.vbs.com. We will deal with servlets when discussing server-side programming later in the book. At the moment, our concern is how to pass the search criteria to the web server. In some cases, we may need to pass some special characters to the web server as well. The default encoding method is called "application/x-www-form-urlencoded." In this encoding method, the following rules are used [Hall, 1998]:

- a space becomes a "+"
- a nonalphanumeric character becomes a hexidecimal code preceded by a %

For example, ?Input=%2F%7Ehenry%2Flecture2%2Dnotes.html is equivalent to attaching a name called "Input" with value

```
/~henry/lecture2-notes.html
```

to the URL because %2F is "/", %7E is "~" and %2D is "-".

An alternative way to pass data to the web server is by using the POST command. In this case, data is appended after the headers in the HTTP request message. For example, if we use the POST command to pass data to the above "booksearch" program, you will find the following in the HTTP request message:

```
POST /servlet/booksearch HTTP/1.0
Accept */*

title=ecommerce&year=2000
```

Note that data is appended after a blank line following the header. In this example, there is only one header called "Accept */*." It specifies that the web client is willing to accept any content type.

2.8 *COOKIES*

HTTP is a stateless protocol. That means, the web server will not keep user's state or user's information. For example, when a web server receives an HTTP request, it does not know whether this request comes from a previous client or a new client. In other words, there is no way to tell whether or not the current request is related to a previous request. In many e-commerce applications, knowing the user's state is an important requirement. For example, in a shopping cart application, the server needs to know the content of the user's shopping cart in order to display the items to the user correctly. To address this important issue, Netscape proposed a method called "cookies" for a web server to save state data at the web client. The original specification is stored at http://www.netscape.com/newsref/std/cookie_spec.html, and it has now been standardized in RFC2109. A maximum of 20 cookies are allowed at each domain and each cookie is limited to 4 Kb to prevent overloading the memory of the client's computer [RFC2109; Hall, 1998].

If a web server wants a web client to save "cookie," it will send the Set-Cookie header in the HTTP response. The Set-Cookie header is of the form

```
Set-Cookie: Name=Value
```

where `Name` and `Value` are the name and value of the cookie, respectively. Whenever required, the client will include the cookie in the HTTP request header using the following format:

```
Cookie: Name=Value
```

This allows the user's information to be passed to the server.

Let us look at how cookies can be used to implement a simple shopping cart for our VBS. Suppose that there are already two items in the shopping cart. The first item (Item1) has a product code of 11111 and the second item (Item2) has a product code of 22222. When the client sends a HTTP request to put another item (say an item with product code 33333) into the shopping cart, the server can set a cookie by including the following cookie header:

```
Set-Cookie: Item3=33333
```

It means that the third item has a product code of 33333. In the next HTTP request, the user needs to send to the server the following cookie headers:

```
Cookie: Item1=11111
Cookie: Item2=22222
Cookie: Item3=33333
```

By reading the cookies, the server knows the content of the shopping cart so that it can be displayed in the returned web page accordingly.

Besides the Set-Cookie header, the following are extra information that can be provided for the cookie(s) (see RFC2109 and Hall [1998]). They can be added on the Set-Cookie header as shown in the later example*.

- *Comment* – provides information on the cookie (e.g. its use)
- *Domain* – specifies in which domain the cookie is effective
- *Expires* – specifies when the cookie will expire
- *Max-age* – specifies the cookie's lifetime in seconds
- *Path* – specifies the URLs to which the web client should return the cookie(s)
- *Secure* – specifies that the cookie is returned only if the connection is secure (e.g., SSL is enabled, see Chapter 8)

Here is a simple example based on similar examples in [Hall, 1998]. Suppose that the VBS web server wants to create a cookie called Credit=111 in order to remember the user's credit. The Set-Cookie header is

```
Set-Cookie: Credit=111; secure; expires=Thursday,
07-Dec-2000 10:00:00 GMT; domain=.vbs.com; path=/
```

It means that the cookie Credit=111 will be returned only to a SSL-enabled server. The expiry date of the cookie is 07-Dec-2000, 10:00:00 GMT. The cookie is effective under the domain name vbs.com. Note that "path=/" means that the cookie applies to any directory under the root directory of the server.

2.9 *HTTP/1.1*

In HTTP/1.1, many enhancements are included to improve the performance of HTTP, to enhance its functionality, and to eliminate the limitations of HTTP/1.0. Generally speaking, HTTP/1.1 works in a similar manner to HTTP/1.0 except that many additional headers are added so HTTP/1.1 is upwardly compatible with HTTP/1.0. Some

---

* We consider the headers in both RFC2109 and the original specification.

of the major enhancements are summarized as follows according to [Krishnamurthy, Mogul, and Kristol, 1999]:

- *Persistent connections and pipelining*: In HTTP/1.0, a connection is released after a request is served. Obviously this is inefficient because a web client may want to retrieve other web pages from the same web server. In HTTP/1.1, a connection is kept open such that the web client can send multiple requests over the same connection. For example, after accessing the home page of the VBS, the customer may want to read the company information by getting the corresponding web page from the web server. Instead of opening a new connection for this request, it can be sent along the same connection. Furthermore, a web client can send the next request without waiting for the response to the previous request. In other words, HTTP/1.1 allows pipelining of requests and responses. If a web client wants to close a connection, it can specify a "close" option in the Connection request header, i.e., Connection: close.

- *Efficient use of IP addresses*: Currently many small organizations use a web hosting service from ISPs. For example, we may put the VBS in an ISP's web server such that we do not need to set up and look after a web server ourselves. In HTTP/1.1, a Host header must be included in the HTTP request message to specify the host name in the web server. This enables different organizations to share the same IP address of the web server thus allowing the efficient use of IP addresses.

- *Range request*: HTTP/1.1 allows a web client to retrieve part of the file by using the Range header. For example, if the connection is broken while the web client is receiving a large file, it can request the web server to send the file from the "break point." Furthermore, the range request function is useful when the web client wants only a portion of a large file.

- *Cache control*: The purpose of caching is to shorten the retrieval time of web pages. It is done by maintaining a cache copy of the previous responses in the web browser or the proxy server so that future requests can be served by the cache copies rather than by the original servers. HTTP/1.0 only supports basic cache control. For example, by using the Expires header, the original server can tell the proxy server when a cache copy should be removed. Furthermore, the web client can tell the proxy server that it does not want a cache copy of the response by using the "Pragma: No-cache" header. In HTTP/1.1, a "Cache-Control" header is included to provide better cache control and cache functions.

- *Support for proxy authentication*: HTTP/1.1 provides the Proxy-Authentication and Proxy-Authorization headers for enabling proxy authentication. In principle, they work in a similar manner to the WWW-Authentication and

EXAMPLE   **51**

Table 2.10 Additional request methods in HTTP/1.1

Method name	Description of the request
PUT	Put the specified resource to the web server.
DELETE	Delete the specified resource from the web server.
OPTIONS	Return the options available from the web server.
TRACE	"Loop back" a request, e.g., for diagnostic purposes.

Authorization headers in HTTP/1.0, respectively. However, the Proxy-Authentication and Proxy-Authorization headers are used on a hop-by-hop basis.

- *Better support for data compression*: HTTP/1.1 provides better support for data compression. In particular, a web client can specify the encoding method such as the compression scheme(s) that is/are supported and preferred by using the Accept-Encoding header.

- *Better support for language(s)*: In HTTP/1.1, a web client can specify the language(s) that is/are acceptable and preferred.

- *Support for content integrity*: In HTTP/1.1, content integrity can be supported by the Content-MD5 header.

- *Additional request methods*: Four additional request methods are added as described in Table 2.10. However, they are less commonly-used than the GET, POST, and HEAD request methods.

2.10 *EXAMPLE*

Let us summarize these web technologies in the context of building the VBS. To build the VBS, we need to set up a web server. This web server interfaces with the web client as well as the backend system. Customers access the VBS through their web browsers (web clients). Basically, when the URL of the VBS is accessed, the web client makes a TCP connection over the internet to port 80 of the VBS web server. The web client then uses the HTTP GET command to retrieve the homepage of the VBS from the web server. After receiving the request, the VBS web server will return the homepage in the HTTP response message. The homepage will then be displayed to the customer. In the next chapter, we discuss how to build the homepage by using the hypertext markup language. In many cases, the customer may want to search for some books. In this case, he generates another HTTP request to the VBS web server.

This time, additional data about the search criteria will be passed to the web server. This can be done by using the HTTP GET or POST command. In the former case, the additional data is appended at the end of the URL. In the latter case, the additional data is embedded in the HTTP request message. Having received the search request, the web server will process it accordingly with the help of other servers and the backend system. We will discuss this in the chapter on server-side programming. The book search result will be returned to the customer. Unlike the previous homepage, this web page is generated dynamically, based on the customer's input. In order to keep the customer's information, the Cookie method can be used. In particular, this can be used to implement the shopping cart application.

2.11 *SUMMARY*

In summary, the internet is a collection of networks interconnected by routers. It is based on a layered model consisting of four layers, namely, link layer, network layer, transport layer, and application layer. In a web-based e-commerce system, there are four main components. They are the web client, the web server, the application server, and the backend system. The web client and the web server communicate with each other based on a request/response protocol called HTTP. Basically, a web client passes an HTTP request to the web server with some headers and optional data. The web server then returns a response to the web client with some headers and the requested resource such as the requested web page. The web client can also pass additional data to the web server by appending it after the URL or embedding it inside the HTTP request message. This can be used to generate dynamic web pages. As the HTTP is stateless, a "Cookie" method can be used to keep track of a user's state. This is important for many e-commerce applications such as building a shopping cart.

REFERENCES

Hall, M., *Core Web Programming*, Prentice-Hall, Upper Saddle River, NJ, 1998.

Krishnamurthy, B., Mogul, J. C., and Kristol, D. M., "Key differences between HTTP/1.0 and HTTP/1.1," *Computer Networks* **31** (1999) 1737–1751.

Naik, D. C., *Internet Standards and Protocols*, Microsoft Press, 1998.

Peterson, L. L. and Davie, B. S., *Computer Networks: A System Approach*, Morgan Kaufmann, San Francisco, CA, 1996.

Semeria, C., "Understanding IP addressing: Everything you ever wanted to know," (available at http://www.3com.com/nsc/501302.html; accessed in 1996).

Stallings, W., *Data and Computer Communications*, 5th edn., Prentice-Hall, Upper Saddle River, NJ, 1997.

Stevens, W. R., *TCP/IP Illustrated Vol. 1*, Addison-Wesley, Reading, MA, 1994.

Tanenbaum, A. S., *Computer Networks*, 3rd edn., Prentice-Hall, Upper Saddle River, NJ, 1996.

RECOMMENDED READING

There are many good books on computer networks in general and the internet in particular.

Naik, D. C., *Internet Standards and Protocols*, Microsoft Press, 1998.

This book gives a good overview on internet standards.

Tanenbaum, A. S., *Computer Networks*, 3rd edn., Prentice-Hall, Upper Saddle River, NJ, 1996.

Stallings, W., *Data and Computer Communications*, 5th edn., Prentice-Hall, Upper Saddle River, NJ, 1997.

Peterson, L. L. and Davie, B. S., *Computer Networks: A System Approach*, Morgan Kaufmann, San Francisco, CA, 1996.

These are some popular textbooks on computer networks.

Stevens, W. R., *TCP/IP Illustrated Vol. 1*, Addison-Wesley, Reading, MA, 1994.

Stevens, W. R., *TCP/IP Illustrated Vol. 2*, Addison-Wesley, Reading, MA, 1995.

These are classic references to explore further about TCP/IP protocols.

Krishnamurthy, B., Mogul, J. C., and Kristol, D. M., "Key differences between HTTP/1.0 and HTTP/1.1," *Computer Networks* **31** (1999) 1737–1751.

This provides a good comparison between HTTP/1.0 and HTTP/1.1.

Hall, M., *Core Web Programming*, Prentice-Hall, Upper Saddle River, NJ, 1998.

This book gives a good overview of HTTP and cookies. It also provides some Java programs to build a simple web server.

Semeria, C., "Understanding IP addressing: Everything you ever wanted to know," (available at http://www.3com.com/nsc/501302.html; accessed in 1996).

This is a very good paper on IP addressing.

The RFCs for internet standards are maintained in the IETF homepage at www.ietf.org. In particular, the standards for HTTP/1.0 and HTTP/1.1 are given in RFC1945 and RFC2616, respectively. There is also a good TCP/IP tutorial in RFC1180. Web-related technologies and standards can be found at the W3 homepage at www.w3.org.

3

Client-Side Programming

3.1 Important Factors in Client-Side or Web Programming

3.2 Web Page Design and Production

3.3 Overview of HTML

3.4 Basic Structure of an HTML Document

3.5 Basic Text Formatting

3.6 Links

3.7 Images

3.8 ImageMap

3.9 Tables

3.10 Frames

3.11 Form

3.12 Cascading Style Sheets

3.13 JavaScript

3.14 Summary

References

Recommended Reading

In Chapter 2, it was explained that the web browser downloads the required information and provides the basic display on the client site. To do this, it downloads web pages including Hypertext Markup Language (HTML) codes and other web page elements (e.g. Java Applets) from the respective server(s). For example, a customer may access the URL of our VBS through his web browser. After receiving the request, the web server of our VBS will return the web page to the customer. The web page contains information on the VBS as well as other forms of input elements. Essentially, it provides the user interface. Hence, we need to create the web site so that when the browser accesses it, the required user interface can be displayed to the client. This process of setting up the web pages or programs at the web sites for clients to see the required display is referred to in this book as client-side programming. In general, this is different from setting up the user interface in conventional client–server architecture. In that case, the user interface programming code actually resides at the client side (i.e., it is not downloaded and displayed within a browser). This is the reason that client-side programming in e-commerce is sometimes referred to as web Programming. This is a very important distinction in client-side programming, as carried out in e-commerce systems.

Besides static web pages, one could also create interactive or dynamic web pages by downloading program codes written in an appropriate language such as JavaScript or Java. In addition, multimedia elements such as image, video, animation, and sound could be included on the web pages.

In terms of e-commerce applications, client-side programming is mainly used for processing a sale transaction, providing information on your business, and updating information in the backend system (e.g. a database). This involves disseminating information or carrying out interactions with the server side over the internet.

3.1   *IMPORTANT FACTORS IN CLIENT-SIDE OR WEB PROGRAMMING*

To carry out client-side programming in e-commerce applications, there are several different ways, which include using HTML, JavaScript, Java Applets, and ActiveX controls. Furthermore, one could also use plugins, which are applications of different sorts that are embedded in a web page for performing special functions (e.g. showing animations). In this chapter, we will focus on HTML because it forms the basis of nearly all the client-side programming techniques. Furthermore, we will give an overview of JavaScript towards the end of this chapter. It enhances the functions of HTML and makes a web page more interactive and dynamic. While there are many client-side programming techniques available, HTML and JavaScript are currently the most commonly used programming techniques for building the user interface at the client side.

A very important factor in client side programming for e-commerce applications is downloading time. This is the time required to download a web page and its associated elements from the server side to the client side over the internet. This depends on many factors, including the quality of the network and the type of connection to the network. For B2C applications, many clients are likely to access the internet using dial-up modems, working at 56.6 Kbps or below. In B2B applications, most of the clients could access the internet through Ethernet connections or leased lines with a much higher data rate.

In general, the downloading time should be kept within 15 s, otherwise it may become unacceptable from the client's point of view. This limits or greatly influences the choice of web programming techniques. Generally speaking, the downloading time for Java Applets is much higher than that of HTML or JavaScript. For this reason, while early e-commerce applications may have sometimes utilized Java Applets, they are now only very sparingly utilized, if at all, to address special requirements. In fact, JavaScript can perform many interactions at the client side already.

Data validation is another important factor to be considered when developing a user interface. It can involve several aspects and includes

1. type checking (e.g., integer)
2. range checking (e.g., between two numbers, say n_1 and n_2)
3. sequence checking (e.g., one cannot initiate an event in the past retrospectively)
4. business requirements checking

Generally speaking, points 1–3 can be validated at the client side by embedding programming code such as JavaScript within the HTML document, as discussed later in this chapter. For point 4, it is often performed at the server side because it frequently requires additional information from the backend system (e.g. database).

It is important to note that in an e-commerce system, a client is likely to be at a physically different location from the e-commerce application servers and hence technical support. In fact, he could be on the other side of the world. Thus, the "usability" of a client interface has to be kept at a very high standard.

The *usability* of a computer software "is measured by how easily and how effectively it can be used by a specific set of users, given particular kinds of support, to carry out a defined set of tasks, in a defined set of environments" [Shackel, 1981].

There is a large body of literature on the factors that make up a usable user interface. Molich and Nielson [1990] and Bevan and Macleod [1994] have all identified factors based on different empirical studies. A study of the literature indicates that the following list of factors would give a comprehensive coverage of the notion of usability. These factors include

1. system feedback
2. consistency
3. error prevention
4. performance/efficiency
5. user like/dislike
6. error recovery

System feedback: The purpose of system feedback is to inform the users what is going on in the system at any time. A well-designed system should always provide users with appropriate feedback, including immediate system feedback, acknowledgements, follow-ups, and indications that an action request has been carried out.

System feedback is characterized by several aspects in particular to address the following issues:

- Where does the error occur (i.e. error localization)?
- If an action is not allowed, does the system give the reason?
- Does the system give prompts on how to proceed?
- Does the system let one know where one is?
- Does the system explain why an action cannot be performed?
- Does the system acknowledge that an action requested has been carried out?

Inadequate system feedback has several components and these include

- number of times dialogue/feedback is missing
- number of times dialogue/feedback is unnecessary
- number of times system feedback confuses the user
- number of messages that are irrelevant
- number of actions taken which lead to repeated feedback message
- number of times the user makes the wrong choice of action due to improper system feedback

Consistency: The interface should be consistent in terms of the look, feel, and behavior throughout the application and with other applications in the same domain. Most guidelines seek to fulfill this important goal. This consistency should be maintained across a variety of issues such as message display methods, color use, key definition, data entry methods, etc. If the user interface is consistent, it reduces the amount of uncertainty that the user faces when using the interface. It is also likely to reduce the number of erroneous interpretations or actions that the user makes. Consistency of the interface has a number of components and these include consistency with respect to the following:

1. Message display methods (prompts, warnings, helps)
2. Color use (entry form, menu and submenu, foreground/background)
3. Keys definition

4. Data entry method

5. Menu, dialogue, and window display methods

6. Menu hierarchy that is consistent with the real world

7. Terminology used is the same as in real life in that domain

8. Menu options have to be consistent with Menu Title

The issue of consistency with other applications in the same domain is very important for e-commerce applications, particularly B2C applications as the user is unlikely to remember what different things meant between one visit and another.

Error prevention: Error prevention is an important goal of the design of the client user interface. If the user interface specifically helps the user to avoid making errors, it increases his efficiency. It will also reduce the level of frustration the user is likely to experience with the user interface and therefore bring about greater acceptance of the user interface by the user. There are several aspects that need to be taken into account in error prevention and these include

- number of errors encountered during task
- number of wrong key strokes/press causing error messages
- number of times the same key is pressed without the desired response
- number of extra key presses that are unnecessary
- number of times the same error encountered
- number of steps missing compared with real-world execution

Performance/efficiency: Performance or efficiency is a quality of the user interface that determines how effectively or efficiently the user can complete his tasks. Performance and efficiency have a number of components and these are as follows:

1. number of goals/tasks not achieved

2. time taken for task completion

3. unproductive period

4. percentage of tasks not completed

Like/dislike: Unlike the aforementioned factors, which characterize the manner in which the user interface facilitates user effectiveness or efficiency, the like/dislike factor measures user preference. This essentially indicates the level of satisfaction that the user feels with the system and the user interface.

Error recovery: Error recovery is that quality of the system of the user interface which allows the user to exit from a situation that the user did not intend to be in.

Users frequently choose the wrong option or enter the wrong data and they are likely to find themselves in an error state from which they need to recover. The manner in which the system facilitates this recovery from error could reduce the time the user spends recovering from this error state. Recovery from error consists of a number of components and these include

- number of times the user has to redo the task
- number of times the user did not continue
- number of actions taken that do not solve the problem
- number of minutes (hours) spent on one error recovery
- percentage of all time spent on error recovery
- number of times the user has to re-robot/start again

In addition to these factors, one also needs to add the following four in the case of client-side programming on the internet, namely

- browser compatibility
- attractiveness
- suitable navigational structure
- a site search engine

Browser compatibility relates to the fact that the appearance of a web page may change depending on the browser the client is using. The reason for this is that the HTML code and tags merely provide information on the type of information to the browser, e.g., a heading, paragraph, etc., in order to allow the browser to lay out the information. However, the manner in which the browser actually lays out the information is dependent on the browser itself.

The attractiveness of the layout of web pages is an important issue. This is true for the whole web site and even more so for the homepage. This arises from the fact that the web display seen by a customer in an e-commerce site is not only a software user interface in the traditional sense but also a marketing tool for the company to the client. Thus, the homepage and entire web site should be designed to project a specific image that is compatible with one that the company is trying to project. Several of the issues related to this will be discussed in Chapter 14 on Web Publishing and Advertising.

The creation of a navigational structure through the web site, which suits the particular audiences who visit that site, is of considerable importance and is discussed in detail in a later section.

It is important that there be, if possible, a site search engine that allows one to find information required, e.g., particular products using keyword search.

Last but not least, it is important that the design and architecture of the web site be such that it allows for evolution and change. As further changes and developments always take place, the initial design should allow for easy integration.

3.2 *WEB PAGE DESIGN AND PRODUCTION*

Before one begins programming a web site or the client-side of an e-commerce application, it is important to develop a careful design. These are briefly discussed here and in much greater detail in Chapter 14. In general, the steps in web site design and production can be described as follows.

3.2.1 Define the audiences and the information requirements

An effective web site should adopt an audience-centered design. Each web site may have many different types of audience, each having a different requirement. For example, a repeat customer may want to reorder something from the web site, but a new customer may want to learn more about the company. Having decided different types of audience, we should then formulate the information requirements for each type of audience accordingly.

3.2.2 Develop the logical design of the web site

Technically, the logical design of the client-side user interface involves the identification of abstract user interface objects and their interaction with other abstract user interface objects as well as other objects in the system such as domain objects or data management objects. The abstract user interface objects specify *what* the user interface does, not *how* the user interacts with the system to perform his/her tasks.

The logical design involves, among other things, characterization of the *flow of interaction*. The flow of interaction requires an understanding of the possible sequences involved in the interaction between the application and the software. This is frequently embedded in the user's perception of how the tasks should be carried out. It could be considered as a delegation/monitoring/control paradigm of the task to the machine. The dynamics of the interaction are determined by this aspect of the user's model of the task.

Among other things, the logical design should give one

- the site architecture
- the navigational structure
- the data input, data displayed, and actions that can be taken from each page

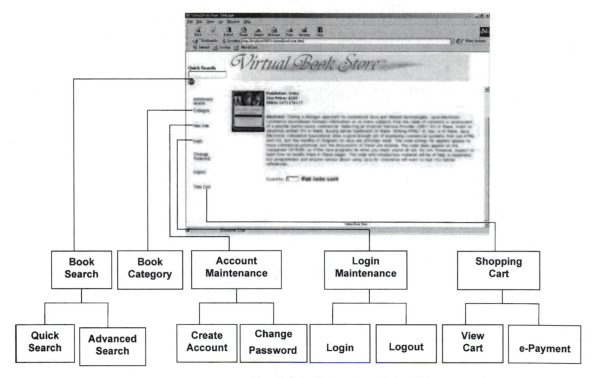

Figure 3.1   Homepage of the VBS

An example of the site architecture for the VBS is given in Figure 3.1. To do the design, one needs a mechanism for representing the abstract user interface objects and the flow of interaction using FINs. These are discussed in greater detail in Chapter 14.

3.2.3   Develop the perceptual design

The perceptual level of the design involves the choice of user interface widgets and the appearance of each particular page and its constituent parts. The user interface widgets employed in a particular user interface are sometimes referred to as *concrete user interface objects*. They define the actual items the user sees and interacts with on the screen such as buttons, pop-up menus, dialogue boxes, check boxes, entry forms, list boxes, etc. Therefore, they define *how* the user interacts with the system. In addition to actually choosing these concrete user interface objects, the actual arrangement of these on a two-dimensional surface must be specified during perceptual design. This is known as the layout of the page.

The outputs of the perceptual design should be the layout, the choice of graphics, images, etc. for the display of information, and the choice of colors, sizes, posters, etc.

3.2.4 Content creation

Having developed the logical design and the perceptual design of the web site, we need to create the content in accordance with the information requirements as defined in the first step.

3.2.5 Programming

This involves putting the content and other elements of the web pages together. As mentioned, we will discuss HTML and JavaScript later in this chapter. During the programming stage, it is important to evaluate the usability of the web pages and make enhancements accordingly. Usability evaluation consists of getting a set of prospective users to carry out a designated set of tasks on the client-side interface and the monitoring and evaluation of them to determine

1. the user acceptance of the interface
2. user efficiency in carrying out the task

It also helps identify specific deficiencies in the design of the pages, which can then be rectified.

It is useful to prototype an initial set of client-side screens using a rapid development tool such as Cold Fusion, Dreamweaver, or Front page and get user criticism and evaluation. This permits the screens to be changed without a great deal of effort. Once the final layout of the screens and the underlying web pages have been determined, one can proceed to code them using HTML or JavaScript or some combination of these or build them using the software tools such as those referred to earlier.

The overall structure of the client-side design is shown in Figure 3.2.

3.2.6 Posting and hosting the site

Finally, the web sites will be set up accordingly. Basically, we can either host the web site in a private web server or use a third-party's web hosting service.

3.3 OVERVIEW OF HTML

The rest of this chapter is about building the user interface using HTML. We only give an overview of HTML. This is similar to several other books including Ray and Ray [1997] Lemay [1999] Zakour *et al.* [1997] and Deitel *et al.* [2000]. For readers

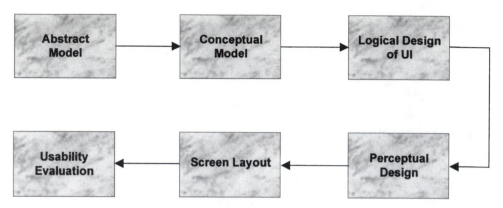

Figure 3.2 The proposed user interface design process

who are interested in a more detailed discussion of HTML, the books by Ray and Ray [1997] and Lemay [1999] are highly recommended. Furthermore, we will also give an overview of JavaScript. HTML is the commonly used markup language for web publishing, and JavaScript is often used to enhance the functionality of HTML. At the time of writing, HTML 4.0, is the most updated version. We will give an overview of HTML 4.0, in particular the most commonly used elements for building an e-commerce system.

HTML is a markup language for telling a Web browser how to format and display a Web page. It can be viewed as a subset of the Standard Generalized Markup Language (SGML), which is for defining general document format [Tanenbaum, 1996]. Predefined tags are employed to describe the format of a document. For example, by putting the word "Italics" inside the `<I></I>` tag pair (i.e., `<I> Italics </I>`), the word "Italics" will be displayed by the Web browser in Italics form. Most tags have a "start tag" and an "end tag" (also called container tags) and the content is embedded between the two tags. Some tags are standalone only without any content [Naik, 1998]. An example is the <HR> tag, which adds a horizontal rule. For most tags, one can also specify its attributes so as to define additional properties about the tag [Ray and Ray, 1997]. For example, one can change the font face by applying the FACE attribute of the <FONT> tag as shown below:

```
<FONT FACE="Arial"> The font face is Arial.</FONT>
```

3.4 BASIC STRUCTURE OF AN HTML DOCUMENT

Basically, the structure of an HTML document is defined as follows [Naik, 1998]

```
<!DOCTYPE HTML PUBLIC "-//W3C//DTD HTML 4.0 Final//EN">
<HTML>
<HEAD>
<TITLE>
<! - - Put the VBS homepage title here - ->
</TITLE>
</HEAD>
<BODY>
<! - - Put the VBS homepage here - ->
</BODY>
</HTML>
```

The `<!DOCTYPE>` tag specifies the version of the HTML document and other related information. `<HTML>` and `</HTML>` tags define the start and the end of an HTML document, respectively. Within the `<HTML>` tag pair, there are two main sections namely the HEAD section as included inside the `<HEAD></HEAD>` tag pair and the BODY section as included inside the `<BODY></BODY>` tag pair. The HEAD section provides information (e.g. the document title) for the web browser to process the document but the information is not displayed. The web browser only displays the information within the `<BODY></BODY>` tag pair. In an HTML document, users can also insert comments inside the comment tag pair: `<!- -` and `- ->`. The comments are not displayed by the web browser. In the above example, comments are used to tell you what should be put inside the respective tags.

The common attributes of the `<BODY>` tag are given as follows:

Attribute	Meaning
BACKGROUND	Specifies the URL of the background image
BGCOLOR	Specifies the background color to be used
TEXT	Specifies the default color of the text in the Web page
LINK	Specifies the color of the hyperlinks that have not been visited
ALINK	Specifies the color of the active hyperlinks
VLINK	Specifies the color of the visited hyperlinks

In conventional HTML, colors are represented by a hexidecimal code. For example, black and white colors are represented by the codes `"#000000"` and `"#FFFFFF,"` respectively.

3.5 *BASIC TEXT FORMATTING*

Let us first look at a simple example that shows most of the basic formatting features. The corresponding web page is shown in Figure 3.3.

```
<HTML>

<HEAD>
<TITLE>A simple web page</TITLE>
</HEAD>

<BODY>
<H1 ALIGN="center">First level heading</H1>
<H2>Second level heading</H2>
<P><FONT FACE="Courier" SIZE="4">The font face is Courier and
   the font size is 15pt.</FONT></P>
<P><FONT COLOR="\#FF0000">The font color is red.</FONT></P>
<P><EM>The text is in italic form.</EM></P>
<P><U>The text is underlined.</U></P>
<P><STRONG>The text is expressed in bold face.</STRONG></P>
<P>This is<SUP>superscript</SUP>and this
   is<SUB>subscript.</SUB></P>
<P><BLINK>This text is blinking.</BLINK></P>
<HR>

<P>This is a simple bullet list:

<UL>
  <LI>First item</LI>
  <LI>Second item</LI>
</UL>

<P>This is a simple numbered list:

<OL>
  <LI>First item</LI>
  <LI>Second item</LI>
</OL>
</BODY>
</HTML>
```

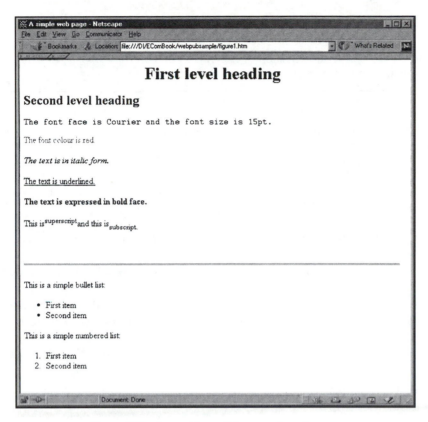

Figure 3.3   A snapshot of the sample web page

3.5.1   Heading

The heading tags `<H1>` and `<H2>` are used to create a first and second level heading, respectively. Altogether there are six levels of headings: `<H1>,<H2>,...,<H6>`. The `ALIGN` attribute specifies the alignment method. Possible options are `LEFT`, `CENTER`, and `RIGHT`. For instance, in the earlier example, the first level heading is aligned to the center whereas the second level heading is aligned to the left because no attribute is specified, so the default alignment method is used.

3.5.2   Paragraph

You can define the start and the end of a paragraph by using the `<P>` and `</P>` tags, respectively. Similar to the heading tag, the `ALIGN` attribute can be used to specify the alignment method.

3.5.3 Font

As shown in the example, the <FONT> tag is used to define the font properties. Its common attributes are as follows:

Attribute	Meaning
COLOR	Defines the font color (i.e. color of the text)
FACE	Defines the font style listed in order of preference. For example, "Arial, Courier" means that Arial is preferred to Courier (i.e., Courier is used if Arial is not supported.)
SIZE	Defines the default font size (an absolute scale of 1–7 can be used)

3.5.4 Other special tags for formatting text

We can also set the text in italics by using either the <EM> or <I> tag. For underlining the text, the <U> tag can be used. The <STRONG> tag can be used to display the text using bold face. Alternatively, the <B> tag can be used for the same purpose. The <SUB> and <SUP> tags are for displaying text as subscript and superscript, respectively. To create blinking text, we can put the text between the <BLINK> and </BLINK> tags.

3.5.5 Horizontal rule

To insert a horizontal rule, the <HR> tag is used. Its common attributes are as follows:

Attribute	Meaning
ALIGN	Defines the alignment method: LEFT, CENTER, or RIGHT
NOSHADE	Display the rule using solid color (black)
SIZE	Sets the thickness in pixels
WIDTH	Sets the width

Note that the width of an horizontal rule can be set in terms of pixels or a percentage of the web page width.

3.5.6 Lists

To format text using a list for ease of reading, the <OL> or <UL> tag can be used. <OL> and <UL> are for creating an ordered list and unordered list, respectively. After creating the list tag, the list items are specified by the <LI> tag.

The TYPE attribute of the <OL> tag specifies the numbering style of the list. The available ones are [Ray and Ray, 1997; Lemay, 1999]

- TYPE=1 – Arabic numerals starting from 1
- TYPE=a – alphabatical order starting from a (i.e. small letters are used)
- TYPE=A – alphabatical order starting from A (i.e. capital letters are used)
- TYPE=i – lowercase Roman numerals starting from i
- TYPE=I – uppercase Roman numerals starting from I

To specify the starting value of the ordered list, we can use the START attribute of the <OL> tag. For example, <OL TYPE=1 START=6> means that the first item of the list starts at 6.

For the <UL> tag, the TYPE attribute specifies the bullet shape. The available ones are

- TYPE=CIRCLE – the bullet type is a circle
- TYPE=DISC – the bullet type is a disc
- TYPE=SQUARE – the bullet type is a square

The <LI> tag has the same attributes as the corresponding <OL> or <UL> tag. Therefore, we can override the original attribute by applying the new attribute in the respective <LI> tag. Furthermore, for the <LI> tag of the ordered list, we can assign a new value with the VALUE attribute. For example, <LI TYPE=1 VALUE=11> specifies that the respective item is assigned as the 11th item irrespective of the previous order [Ray and Ray, 1997].

3.6 LINKS

Links (or hyperlinks) are the most powerful feature of an HTML document. They are used to link web pages. For example our VBS web page can be linked to a publisher's web page. The two web pages can be situated in two different web servers that may be distant from each other. The computer screen is two-dimensional but the internet space is infinite because the hyperlinks give HTML files an infinite depth. The following gives an overview of hyperlinks. More details can be found in the book by Ray and Ray [1997].

Links are defined by the anchor tag pair: <A> and </A>. For example, a basic hyperlink looks like the following:

```
<A HREF=http://www.vbs.com/Books/Art.html>Art</A>
```

In this example, the word "Art" is underlined and colored. When it is clicked, the browser links to the URL http://www.vbs.com/Books/Art.html as specified by the HREF attribute. Recall that in the URL, "http" stands for the hypertext transfer protocol; "www.vbs.com" is the server name; "Books" is the directory; and, "Art.html" is the HTML file.

We can also set up an email link with the <A> tag. It is widely supported by most browsers such as Netscape and Internet Explorer. For example, we can set up the following email link for customers to send emails to the Webmaster of our VBS:

```
<A HREF=mailto:webmaster@vbs.com>Please send any question to the
Webmaster</A>
```

A URL can be relative or absolute. For a relative URL, the location of the requested web page is relative to the current web page. For example, if the current web page "Art.html" contains a hyperlink say

```
<A HREF=Science.html>Science</A>,
```

the file "Science.html" will be accessed under http://www.vbs.com/Books, i.e., at the same directory as the current document "Art.html." For an absolute URL, the full address is specified just like the full address specified in the above example.

If a file such as "Welcome.html" is at the server root, we can also specify the link as <A HREF=/Welcome.html></A> where "/" denotes the server root. To access documents at another directory, we can use "../" to go back one directory, "../../" to go back two directories, and so on. For example, the following hyperlink <A HREF=../Welcome.html></A> means that to get the web page "Welcome.html," we need to go back one directory relative to the current web page. It is worth mentioning that it is possible to link to a file in a local disk as well. For example, if we want to link to a file called *"thefile"* stored under *"c:\directory\subdirectory"* in a local disk, the URL is

```
file:///c|/directory/sub-directory/thefile
```

Note that an additional backslash ("/") is used to replace the normal host name.

With HTML 4.0, it is possible to link to different locations within the same web page by using the anchor tag. It can best be explained with an example. Suppose that in "Science.html," we want to identify a section called "Computing" such that we can link to this section from other parts of the web page. We can define the name anchor by specifying the name attribute in the <A> tag as follows:

```
<A NAME="Computing">Books on computing</A>.
```

Note that unlike the hyperlinks, the words `"Books on computing"` will still appear as normal text (i.e., it will not be underlined and colored). Within the same web page (i.e. `Science.html`), we can link to the `"Computing Section"` by using the following tag:

```
<A HREF="#Computing">
```

In general, we can link to the `"Computing Section"` by specifying the following URL within the `<A>` tag as follows:

```
<A HREF="http://www.vbs.com/books/science.html#Computing">
Computing Section</A>
```

Finally, let us discuss a major advantage of using relative URLs concerning movement and change. Sometimes we need to move documents between servers. Suppose that we need to migrate all the files from `www.vbs.com` to another server say `www.xyz.com`. If all the links are specified using relative URLs and the directory structure remains unchanged, basically we do not need to update the hyperlinks inside the files. However, if the links are specified using their absolute addresses, they have to be updated with the new server name. Of course, the absolute URL approach must be used for accessing documents in other external servers.

3.7 IMAGES

Currently, there are two major image formats for the web, namely, Graphics Interchange Format (GIF) and Joint Photographic Experts Group (JPEG) [Ray and Ray, 1997; Lemay, 1999]. They are used to store images in compressed form so that the file size can be reduced. In general, GIF is more commonly used for a number of reasons. First, the compression method (called LZW) employed by GIF is lossless. This means that images can be compressed while preserving the data (i.e. no loss). Second, by using special image-editing tools (e.g. Paint Shop Pro), animated GIF files can be created for presenting simple animation effects on a web page. Third, a GIF image can be made to look transparent in a web page by specifying its background color to match with that of the web page. However, GIF works well only for simple images such as logos but not for complex images such as photographs because it only provides 256 colors. In contrast, JPEG employs a lossy compression method. While the file size can be reduced further, some data are lost during compression. In general, JPEG is well-suited for photographs because it provides significantly more colors than GIF. GIF is used for general purpose images.

The <IMG> tag is used for including images in a web page. Its common attributes are as follows [Zakour *et al.*, 1997]:

Attribute	Meaning
ALIGN	Defines the alignment method (i.e., LEFT, RIGHT, TOP, MIDDLE, or BOTTOM)
ALT	Gives a description of the image, which is displayed when the image is not available (e.g. during loading)
BORDER	Sets the border size in pixels
HEIGHT	Fixes the height of the image in pixels
HSPACE	Specifies the additional horizontal space to be added
SRC	Specifies where (i.e., the URL) to load the source image
VSPACE	Specifies the additional vertical space to be added
WIDTH	Fixes the width of the image in pixels

Here is an example of inserting the image of our VBS Logo (VBS.gif):

```
<IMG SRC="VBS.gif" HEIGHT="100" WIDTH="100" ALIGN="LEFT"
BORDER="1" ALT="VBS">
```

It means that the height and width of the image is of 100 pixels each, the alignment is to the left, and the border width is 1 pixel. When the image is not available (e.g., when the browser is getting the image), the text "VBS" is displayed.

One can also create an image link by embedding the <IMG> tag inside the <A></A> tag pair. For example, for creating an image link using the VBS logo, one can write it as

```
<A HREF="main.html"><IMG SRC="VBS.gif"></A>
```

3.8 *IMAGEMAP*

Apart from using hyperlinks, we can also create an ImageMap for linking to different URLs. There are two types of image maps, namely, server-side and client-side image maps. As the latter is more commonly used, we will focus on client-side image maps in this book.

A client-side image map (referred to as image map hereafter) is defined by using the <MAP></MAP> tag pair as follows [Lemay, 1999]:

```
<MAP NAME="map_ID">
  <AREA SHAPE="CIRCLE/RECT/POLY" COORDS="..." HREF="URL">
```

```
<AREA SHAPE="CIRCLE/RECT/POLY" COORDS="..." HREF="URL">
                                   .
                                   .
                                   .
<AREA SHAPE="CIRCLE/RECT/POLY" COORDS="..." HREF="URL">
</MAP>
```

Between the `<MAP>` and `</MAP>` tags, the `<AREA>` tag is used to define the areas for the image map. As specified by the SHAPE attribute, each area can be a circle (`CIRCLE`), a rectangle (`RECT`), or a polygon (`POLY`). Depending on the shape of the area, the boundary is specified by the respective coordinates as follows:

- *Circle*: SHAPE="CIRCLE" COORDS="x,y,r" where (x,y) defines the center and r is the radius of the circle.
- *Rectangle*: SHAPE="RECT" COORDS="xL,yL,xR,yR" where (xL,yL) and (xR,yR) define the top-left corner and bottom-right corner of the rectangle, respectively.
- *Polygon*: SHAPE="POLY" COORDS="$x1,y1,x2,y2,\ldots, xi,yi$" where $(x1,y1)$, $(x2,y2),\ldots,$ (xi,yi) specifies the *i*-th corners of the polygon.

Note that $(0,0)$ is the co-ordinate of the top-left corner of the web page. The destined URL is defined by the HREF attribute.

Having defined the image map, the respective image can be put into the web page using the `<IMG>` tag as follows:

```
<IMG SRC="image_file" USEMAP="#map_ID">
```

where `"image_file"` specifies the source of the image file and `"#map_ID"` gives the corresponding image map (i.e., the one defined earlier). Note that the `"#"` symbol indicates that the image map is situated in the current web document rather than the web server.

3.9 TABLES

Tables are typically used to organize information in a structural manner for ease of reading. In addition, they are commonly used for facilitating the layout of web page components. For instance, we can format a web page in a two-column format using a borderless table and then place the navigation buttons and the content into the left and right column, respectively. Note, however, that unlike using frames, the navigation buttons and the content are contained in the same web page. Basically, a table is created by using the following tags:

```
<TABLE>
    <TR>
        <TH>Heading cell (first row, first column)</TH>
        <TH>Heading cell (first row, second column)</TH>
    </TR>
    <TR>
        <TD>Data cell (second row, first column)</TD>
        <TD>Data cell (second row, second column)</TD>
    </TR>
</TABLE>
```

The `<TABLE> </TABLE>` tag pair specifies the beginning and the end of a table, respectively. The `<TR></TR>` tag pair defines a table row and the `<TD></TD>` tag pair defines a data cell. Therefore, this table has two columns and two rows because there are two `<TR></TR>` tag pairs and each row contains two data cells. In the first row, the `<TH></TH>` tag pair specifies the heading cell.

The common attributes of the `<TABLE>` tag are given as follows. They are used for formatting a table [Zakour *et al.*, 1997].

Attribute	Meaning
ALIGN	Specifies the alignment method (LEFT, CENTER, or RIGHT), e.g., ALIGN = CENTER means that the table is aligned to the center of the document
BGCOLOR	Specifies the background color for the table
BORDER	Sets the border thickness in pixels (Note: BORDER = 0 means that there is no border)
CELLPADDING	Sets the padding (in pixels) between the cell border and content, e.g., CELLPADDING = 2 means that a cell padding of 2 pixels is used
CELLSPACING	Sets the spacing (in pixels) between data cells, e.g., CELLSPACING = 3 means that a cell spacing of 3 pixels is used
COLS	Specifies how many columns the table has
WIDTH	Defines the table width (in terms of a percentage of the document width or pixels), e.g., WIDTH = 50 means that the table width is 50 pixels.

After setting up the basic structure of a table, the `<TR>`, `<TH>`, and `<TD>` tags are used to construct the rows, the heading cells, and the data cells, respectively. If we specify an attribute for the `<TR>` tag, it will be applied to all the data cells of that row.

For changing the attribute of a data cell or a heading cell, we can override the original attribute with a new attribute in the respective <TH> or <TD> tag. If we do not specify any attribute, the web browser will use the default attributes. The common attributes for these tags are given as follows.

Attribute	Meaning
ALIGN	Defines the cell alignment method (LEFT, CENTER, RIGHT, JUSTIFY, or CHAR), e.g., ALIGN = CENTER means that the text is aligned to the center of the cell.
BGCOLOR	Specifies the background color.
COLSPAN*	Specifies the number of columns spanned by the data cell, e.g., COLSPAN = 2 means that the data cell covers two columns.
ROWSPAN*	Specifies the number of rows spanned by the data cell, e.g., ROWSPAN = 2 means that the data cell covers two rows.
VALIGN	Defines the vertical alignment method (TOP, MIDDLE, BOTTOM), e.g., VALIGN = MIDDLE means that the vertical alignment method is middle.
WIDTH*	Sets the cell width in terms of the table width percentage or pixels, e.g., WIDTH = 20 means that the cell width is 20 pixels.

Figure 3.4 shows an example of a simple table incorporating the table tags and the common attributes.

3.10 *FRAMES*

Very often, a company wants to display multiple Web pages on a browser. In HTML, frames are available for satisfying this requirement. For example, a company may set up a LEFT frame and a RIGHT frame for displaying the navigation buttons and the content, respectively. The navigation buttons and the content can be written in two different HTML files. To set up frames, we need to use the <FRAMESET> tag to define the frame format and then use the <FRAME> tag to define the frame content.

The common attributes of the <FRAMESET> tag are:

```
COLS="c₁, c₂ .... cₚ" (i.e. there are   p columns)
ROWS="r₁, r₂ .... rₘ" (i.e. there are   m rows)
```

where c_x and r_x and are the sizes of the x-th column and row, respectively. The units are expressed in terms of a percentage of the document width or pixels. Furthermore,

---

* These attributes are for <TD> and <TH> only.

Title		
Heading		
Data	Data	
	Data	
		Data

```
Source of file ///C/WINDOWS/Desktop/table.htm - Netscape                                          _ 回 ×
<html>
<head>
<title></title>
</head>
<body>
<table width="50%" align="CENTER" border="2"
bordercolor="#FF0000" background="Logo.jpg">
  <caption valign="top"><b>Title</b></caption>
  <tr>
    <td align="CENTER" valign="MIDDLE"
    colspan="2" width="50%" >Heading </th>
  </tr>
  <tr>
    <td rowspan="3">Data</td><td>Data</td>
  </tr>
  <tr>
    <td align="CENTER">Data</td>
  </tr>
  <tr align="RIGHT">
    <td valign="TOP">Data</td>
  </tr>
</table>
</body>
</html>
```

Figure 3.4   Table example

we can use * to tell the browser how to allocate the available space. Let us look at a few examples. <FRAMESET COLS="*, *"> can be used to set up two column frames (left and right) with equal width. If we use 3* instead of * for the right frame (i.e., <FRAMESET COLS="*, 3*">), this will set the right frame three times the size of the left frame. What does <FRAMESET ROWS="20%, *, 3*"> mean? It means that there are three row frames. Starting from the top of the browser, the first frame is 20% of the browser window in height. For the last two frames, the third one is three times the size of the second one.

After defining the frame layout using the <FRAMESET> tag, we need to specify the frame content by using the <FRAME> tag. The common attributes of the <FRAME> tag are as follows:

Attribute	Meaning
FRAMEBORDER	Indicates whether a frame border is used (1) or not used (0)
HEIGHT	Sets the frame height
MARGINHEIGHT	Specifies the top and bottom margins
MARGINWIDTH	Specifies the left and right margins
NAME	Specifies a name for identification purpose
NORESIZE	Does not allow users to change the size of the frame
SCROLLING	Indicates whether a scrollbar is used (YES, NO, or AUTO)
SRC	Specifies the URL of the initial HTML file to be loaded
WIDTH	Sets the frame width

Again let us look at some examples. If we want to specify three column frames (called, say, LEFT, MIDDLE, and RIGHT) of equal width, the corresponding HTML code is as follows:

```
<FRAMESET COLS=*,*,*>
    <FRAME NAME=LEFT SRC=Left.html>
    <FRAME NAME=MIDDLE SRC=Middle.html>
    <FRAME NAME=RIGHT SRC=Right.html>
</FRAMESET>
```

where SRC specifies the initial HTML file for the frame.

Many companies like to divide their web pages into three frames: a banner frame, for displaying the company banner; an index frame, for showing the navigation buttons; and a content frame, for presenting the content. This can be done using nested frames as follows and Figure 3.5 shows the corresponding web page.

```
<HTML>
<FRAMESET ROWS="20%,80%">
    <FRAME NAME="BANNER_FRAME" SRC=BANNER.html>
    <FRAMESET COLS="30%,70%">
      <FRAME NAME="INDEX_FRAME" SRC=INDEX.html>
      <FRAME NAME="CONTENT_FRAME" SRC=CONTENT.html>
    </FRAMESET>
</FRAMESET>
</HTML>
```

When a hyperlink is clicked, the TARGET attribute of the <A> tag determines in which frame the corresponding HTML page is opened. For example, suppose that

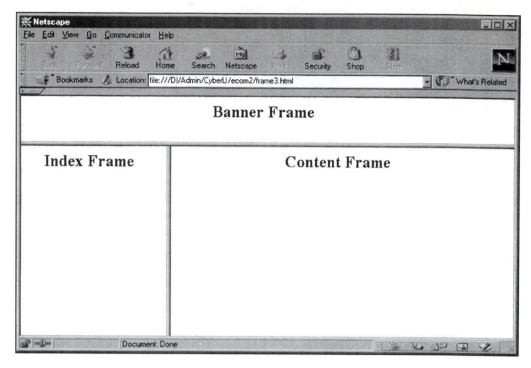

Figure 3.5   A snapshot of banner, index, and content frames

there are two frames, namely,

```
<FRAME NAME="left" SRC="left.html">
<FRAME NAME="right" SRC="right.html">
```

If a hyperlink is defined as follows:

```
<A HREF="page.html" TARGET="left">Choice</A>
```

the web page "page.html" will be opened in the left frame.
    Other target attributes include the following:

- _blank: display the HTML page in another browser window
- _self: display the HTML page in the originating frame
- _top: display the HTML page in the full browser window without any frame (i.e., eliminate the previous frames)

You can also specify the default target attribute in the `<BASE>` tag within the `<HEAD>` section of the HTML document. For example, `<BASE TARGET="CONTENT">` means that unless otherwise specified, all documents should be displayed in the frame named `"CONTENT."`

While frames provide many advantages, they should be used with caution. Some older browsers do not support frames, so it is a good practice to include the `<NOFRAMES></NOFRAMES>` tag pair to cater for this situation. For example, you can include a statement like this:

```
<NOFRAMES>
Sorry. You cannot view this web page because your browser does
not support frames.
Please choose the nonframe version.
</NOFRAMES>
```

Furthermore, a framed web page may be displayed differently if a different browser is used or the screen resolution is changed; so framed web pages should be tested more carefully. It is also a common practice to provide a "nonframe" version in case the user encounters difficulties in displaying the framed web pages.

3.11 *FORM*

Forms are generally used to obtain data from the client for submission to the server. Typically, a program in the server is invoked to process the data, possibly with the assistance of the backend system. The result (in most cases, an HTML file) will then be passed to the web client by using the HTTP.

In general, an HTML form has the following format [Naik, 1998]:

```
<FORM ACTION="Program URL" METHOD="GET or POST">
    <! -- Put form input elements here -->
</FORM>
```

The `ACTION` attribute provides the URL of the program for processing the form data, and the `METHOD` attribute specifies the method for passing data to the server (i.e., by using `GET` or `POST`). Recall that if `GET` is used, data is attached to the destined URL using a query string ([Hall, 1998]). If `POST` is used, data will be embedded inside the HTTP request message.

Between the `<FORM>` and `</FORM>` tags, different form input elements can be included. Most of them are defined by the `<INPUT>` tag. The common attributes of the `<INPUT>` tag are as follows:

- `TYPE`: the type of the input such as `"TEXT"` and `"CHECKBOX"` as described later
- `NAME`: the name of the input
- `VALUE`: the value of the input

3.11.1 Textbox

A textbox is used to collect simple text input. The length of the textbox is specified by the `SIZE` attribute. We can also use the `MAXLENGTH` attribute to specify the maximum number of characters that can be entered into a textbox. Here is an example of a simple textbox:

```
<INPUT TYPE="TEXT" NAME="InputName" SIZE="15">
```

It means that the textbox is 15 characters long, the NAME of the input is called "InputName" and its value is the data entered in the textbox.

3.11.2 Password textbox

Password textbox is a special textbox for entering a password. It is almost the same as the textbox except that the entered characters appear as * so that they cannot be seen by others. Here is an example:

```
<INPUT TYPE="PASSWORD" NAME="InputName" SIZE="20">
```

3.11.3 Checkbox

Checkbox is for making a choice out of a number of items. It is defined by `TYPE="CHECKBOX."` If a checkbox is checked, the specified `NAME` and the corresponding `VALUE` will be passed to the server for processing. If you want to set a checkbox by default, you can set the `CHECKED` attribute within the `<INPUT>` tag. By setting this attribute, the checkbox will appear as checked, otherwise the checkbox will remain blank. In the following example, the checkbox is checked by default. If the user chooses this default choice, the parameter `"InputName=InputValue"` will be passed to the server for processing.

```
<INPUT TYPE="CHECKBOX" NAME="InputName" VALUE="InputValue" CHECKED>
```

3.11.4 Radio button

Radio button functions like the checkbox. An example is shown below.

```
<INPUT TYPE="RADIO" NAME="InputName" VALUE="InputValue" CHECKED>
```

3.11.5 Submit button

A submit button is for submitting a form to the web server. That means, when a submit button is clicked, the input data (i.e., all the NAME/VALUE pairs in the form) will be sent to the server using the METHOD specified in the <FORM> tag. The following is a simple example of the submit button. Users will see the word "Submit" on the button. When the button is clicked, the input data on the form as well as the parameter "InputName=Submit" will be passed to the server for processing.

```
<INPUT TYPE="SUBMIT" NAME="InputName" VALUE="Submit">
```

3.11.6 File input field

The file input field is for uploading a file (e.g. an image file) to the server. It is defined by TYPE="FILE." The name of the file is specified by the NAME attribute. The length and maximum size of the field is defined by the SIZE and MAXLENGTH attributes, respectively.

Furthermore, the allowable file type(s) can be set with the ACCEPT attribute. Here is an example:

```
<INPUT  TYPE="FILE"  NAME="BOOK1"  ACCEPT="image/gif"
MAXLENGTH="40"  SIZE="15">
```

It means that the name of the file is BOOK1, the length of the input field is 15 characters, and only a maximum of 40 characters can be entered. The uploaded file must be an image file in GIF format.

3.11.7 Hidden form field

Hidden form fields are hidden (i.e. not displayed). They are used mainly to pass additional data to the server. For example, they can be used to pass user's state to the server like cookies do. An hidden field is defined by TYPE="HIDDEN." An example is given below.

```
<INPUT TYPE="HIDDEN" NAME="User_ID" VALUE="123456">
```

In this example, the hidden form field is used to tell the server that this request is from User_ID=123456.

3.11.8 Textarea (Comment box)

Textarea is not defined by the <INPUT> tag but by the <TEXTAREA> tag. It is typically used for collecting customer's comments. The ROWS and COLS attributes specify the number of rows and columns for the textarea, respectively. For example, the following TEXTAREA has six rows and ten columns.

```
<TEXTAREA NAME="InputName" ROWS="6" COLS="10"></textarea>
```

3.11.9 Select menu

A select menu allows users to choose one or more choice(s). It is defined by the <SELECT> tag as shown below. The SIZE attribute inside the <SELECT> tag defines how many field(s) in the select menu is/are displayed. Within the <SELECT></SELECT> tag pair, the <OPTION> tag is used to define the options available for selection. Here is an example:

```
<SELECT NAME="InputName" SIZE="1">
  <OPTION VALUE="Value1">Value 1</OPTION>
  <OPTION VALUE="Value2">Value 2</OPTION>
</SELECT>
```

In this example, the select menu has only two fields. As the SIZE attribute is "1", only the first one is displayed. We need to scroll down the select menu in order to select the second item.

3.12 *CASCADING STYLE SHEETS*

In general, a web page has three main components, namely "presentation structure" (referred to as structure for simplicity), "style," and "content." In the early HTML versions, the structure and style are integrated. Let us look at the following example:

```
<P ALIGN=CENTER>This is a paragraph<P>
```

In this example, the structure is defined by the `<P>` tag (it defines that this is a paragraph), the style is given by the attribute inside the `<P>` tag and the content is the sentence `"This is a paragraph."`

In HTML 4.0, Cascading Style Sheet (CSS) is available to separate the style from the structure. Hence, it enables web designers to control the style of a web page in a more flexible manner. For example, by using CSS, a single style sheet can be applied to different web pages that require the same style (i.e., to fulfill the consistency requirement as discussed earlier). There are three types of CSS, namely

- external style sheets
- embedded style sheets
- inline style sheets

Lemay [1999] gives a very good and detailed explanation of stylesheet. Here we give an overview based on Lemay's approach.

3.12.1 External style sheets

For external style sheets, the style definitions are stored in a separate file with a file extension of `".css."` Using external style sheets, our VBS can maintain a consistent style by applying the same style sheet to all the HTML files.

To create an external style sheet for an HTML file, there are two basic steps:

- *Step 1*: Create the following `<LINK>` tag in the HEAD section of the HTML file:

```
<LINK REL="stylesheet" HREF="external_stylesheet.css">
```

where REL specifies that a style sheet is to be used and HREF specifies the URL of the external style sheet.
- *Step 2*: Create the external style sheet and save it as the specified file.

Let us create an external style sheet called `"style1.css"` as follows:

```
BODY { font-color: blue; font-family: Times New Roman;
font-size: 20 pt}
A:link { color: red }
H1 { font-weight: bolder }
H2 { font-weight: bold }
```

In this example, the external style sheet specifies the font color of the BODY section to be "blue", the default font to be "Times New Roman," and the default font size to be 20 pt. For the reference links, the default color is "red". The font-weight of the first and second level headings is set to be bolder and bold, respectively.

Besides the background color, font style, and font properties, a web designer can also apply the following style properties to a web page:

- Page layout properties on the page margin:
  ```
  margin-x
  ```
  where "x" is the attribute including left, right, top, or bottom.
- Other background properties:
  ```
  Background-x
  ```
  where "x" is the attribute including color or image.
- Font properties:
  ```
  font-x
  ```
  where "x" is the attribute including style, family, size, or weight.
- Border properties:
  ```
  border-x
  ```
  where "x" is the attribute including style, width, or color.

Details of the CSS formatting styles and rules can be found in W3C CSS homepage: `http://www.w3.org/Style/`.

3.12.2 Embedded style sheets

Instead of using an external style sheet, we can also embed the style definitions inside the HEAD section of the HTML file. This is called embedded style sheets.

In this case, the style definitions are put between the <STYLE> and </STYLE> tags within the HEAD section of the HTML file as shown below:

```
<HEAD>
...
<STYLE TYPE="text/css">
<!---
    Put the style definitions here
-->
</STYLE>
</HEAD>
```

The TYPE attribute specifies the content (MIME) type of the style. In most cases, it is "text/css." As you can see, all the style definitions are embedded within the comment tags "<--" and "-->." This allows browsers that cannot support CSS to ignore the style definitions by processing them as comments.

The previous style sheet can be embedded within the HEAD section as follows to create the same style.

```
<HEAD>
<TITLE>VIRTUAL BOOKSTORE (VBS): WELCOME</TITLE>
      <STYLE TYPE="text/css">
      <!--
      BODY { font-color: blue; font-family: Times New Roman;
      font-size: 20 pt}
      A:link { color: red }
      H1 { font-weight: bolder }
      H2 { font-weight: bold }
      -->
      </STYLE>
</HEAD>
```

In general, if we want to create a set of web pages with the same style, the external style sheet should be used. On the other hand, if we want to design a web page with a unique style, the embedded style sheet provides a better solution.

3.12.3 Inline style

In some situations, we may want to apply a style rule to part of a web page (e.g., a paragraph). In this case, the inline style can be used. Suppose we want to set the style of a heading, this can be done by the <STYLE> attribute as follows:

```
<H1 STYLE="font-family: Helvetica, sans-serif; font-size: 18pt">
The specific style for this heading.</H1>
```

By doing so, the content between the <H1> and </H1> tags is reformatted using the style rule as defined by the STYLE attribute.

Apart from using the STYLE attribute, users can also create the same effect by using the CLASS attribute. This can be used in an external style sheet as well as in an embedded style sheet. By using the CLASS attribute, the defined style rule can be reused elsewhere in a web page. It is best to explain with an example. In this example, a user can specify two different styles for the `<H1>` tag using embedded style sheet as shown below:

```
<STYLE TYPE="text/css">
<!--
H1 {font-family: Helvetica; font-style: normal}
H1.italic {font-family: Helvetica; font-style: italic}
-->
</STYLE>
```

The first one and the second one give the default style and the style for the first level heading requiring italic display, respectively. If we want to display a first level heading in italic, the `CLASS` attribute can be specified as follows:

```
<H1 CLASS="italic">
The words will be displayed in italic.
</H1>
```

The `STYLE` and `CLASS` attributes work fine for text within container tags (i.e., those with open and close tags). For noncontainer tags, we can use the `<DIV></DIV>` tag pair to apply the style as follows:

```
<DIV STYLE="...">...          </DIV>
<DIV CLASS="NameOfClass">...</DIV>
```

In the first case, a user can specify the required inline style for the text between the `<DIV>` and `</DIV>` tags. In the second case, the style as defined by the `"NameOfClass"` will be applied to the content between the `<DIV>` and `</DIV>` tags. Alternatively, we can use the `<SPAN></SPAN>` tag pair for the same purpose.

3.13 JAVASCRIPT

3.13.1 What is JavaScript?

JavaScript is a scripting language proposed by Netscape to enhance the functions of HTML (e.g. form validation). It is often called an object-oriented (OO) scripting language with syntax looking like Java. In particular, it can be used to make a web page more interactive and dynamic. It is supported by most commonly used browsers including Microsoft's Internet Explorer and Netscape's Navigator. Unlike the server-side programs, a JavaScript code is included in an HTML document and executed on the client side. In this section, we will give an overview of JavaScript by using some examples. For the detailed documentation and the latest developments of JavaScript, please refer to Netscape's site on JavaScript (`http://developer.netscape.com/docs/manuals/index.html`).

3.13.2 Basic structure of JavaScript

A JavaScript code is embedded between the `<SCRIPT>` and `</SCRIPT>` tags as follows [Lemay, 1999]:

```
<HTML>
<HEAD>
<TITLE>HTML file with JavaScript code</TITLE>
<SCRIPT LANGUAGE="JavaScript">
<!---
      Put the JavaScript code here.
//-->
</SCRIPT>
</HEAD>
</HTML>
```

In the example, the LANGUAGE attribute specifies that JavaScript is used. Other scripting languages such as VBScript can also be used. The JavaScript code is put between the comment tag pair, i.e., "`<!--`" and "`//-->`" so that if the browser does not support JavaScript, the code will just be processed as a comment rather than an error. For complex JavaScript codes, they can be stored in a separate file with a file extension of "`.js.`" In this case, the JavaScript code(s) can be linked to the HTML file by using the `SRC` attribute of the `<SCRIPT>` tag as follows:

```
<SCRIPT LANGUAGE="JavaScript" SRC="JavaScript_URL">
```

where `JavaScript_URL` specifies the URL of the JavaScript code.

3.13.3   A simple JavaScript example

In JavaScript, there are three main objects, document, form, and location, as described briefly here [Lemay, 1999]:

- *Document object* – for providing information on the document, such as page characteristics, links, etc.
- *Form object* – for providing information on the form(s) used in the current web page, such as information on a particular form element.
- *Location object* – for providing location related information for the current web page, such as URL, host name, directory path, etc.

In many cases, a JavaScript code is invoked when a certain event occurs (e.g., when a form is submitted or the mouse is clicked). JavaScript provides a number of "event handlers" for handling this requirement. Some common event handlers are as follows:

- onClick – indicates that the mouse is clicked
- onMouseOver – indicates that the mouse is moved over a specific element
- onSubmit – indicates that the form is submitted
- onKeyPress – indicates that a key is pressed

Let us first look at a simple JavaScript example for displaying a welcome message, the URL of the current web page, and the current date. The JavaScript code is as shown below:

```
<HTML>
<HEAD>
<TITLE>JavaScript Hello World</TITLE>
<SCRIPT LANGUAGE="JavaScript">
<!--
document.write("<HR ALIGN='left' WIDTH=80%><BR>");
document.write("<H1>JavaScript : Hello World!!</H1><BR>");
document.write("<HR ALIGN='left' WIDTH=80%><BR>");
document.write("Current URL is:");
document.write(location.toString( ));
document.write("<BR>Current time is:");
document.write(Date( ));
//-->
</SCRIPT>
```

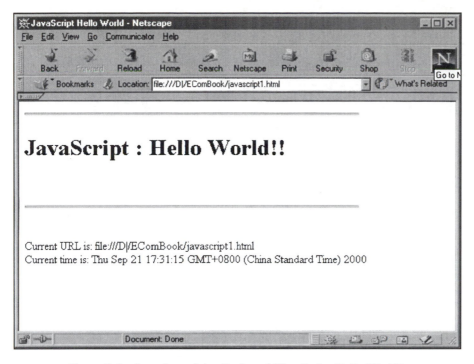

Figure 3.6 Snapshot of the display of "JavaScript Hello World"

```
</HEAD>
<BODY>
</BODY>
</HTML>
```

Figure 3.6 gives a snapshot of the display when the web page is loaded by a browser.

In this example, the `"write"` method of the `"document"` object is used to write the HTML file using the standard HTML tags. By using the `toString()` method of the `"location"` object, the current URL can be displayed. Furthermore, we can print out the current time by using the `built-in Date()` method or function.

3.13.4 Form validation using JavaScript

An important application of JavaScript is for form validation. In this section, we present a simple form validation example. Suppose that a form is created as follows:

```
<FORM ACTION="/servlet/vbs.processform" METHOD="POST"
 onSubmit="return validation(this)">

   <P>Name :<INPUT TYPE="text" NAME="name" size="32"></P>
   <P>
     Registered:
     <INPUT TYPE="radio" NAME="register" VALUE="yes">
     Not registered:
     <INPUT TYPE="radio" NAME="register" VALUE="no">
   </P>
   <P>
     Date of birth:
     Year <INPUT TYPE="text" NAME="year" size="3">
     Month <INPUT TYPE="text" NAME="month" size="3">
     Date <INPUT TYPE="text" NAME="date" SIZE="3">
   </P>
   <P>Email: <INPUT TYPE="text" NAME="email" SIZE="32"></P>
   <INPUT TYPE="SUBMIT" NAME="Submit" VALUE="Submit">
</FORM>
```

As you can see, this form is used to collect the name, registration status, date of birth, and e-mail address of a customer. To validate the input data, we need to check that the `"Name"` field is not empty, one of the radio buttons is selected, the `"e-mail"` field contains the character `"@"` and the `"Date"` field contains a valid date. These are the commonly used form validation procedures. The corresponding JavaScript code is shown in Figure 3.7. Let us explain the key points as follows.

The form is validated by a function called `"validation"` and the input argument is called `"qform."` The value of the `"Name"` field is identified by `"qform.name.value."` Hence, if it is empty, an alert message will be displayed by using the alert function. Note that the alert function is provided by JavaScript and the input argument is the alert message. Following Lemay's [1999] approach, for the radio buttons, `"qform.register[i].status"` ($i=0,1$) can be used to determine whether the $(i+1)$-th radio button is checked. If it is not checked, the status will be `"false."` By checking the status of the radio buttons, we can determine whether the customer has been registered. If not, an alert message will be displayed accordingly.

To check whether a valid date is entered for the `"Date of birth"` field, we can combine the field elements (i.e., `qform.year`, `qform.month`, and `qform.day`) into a date variable using the `Date()` method as follows

```
var datefield=new Date(qform.year.value,qform.month.
value,qform.day.value);
```

Then we can check whether the `"datefield"` is valid or not using the `"isNaN()"` method as follows:

```
<SCRIPT LANGUAGE="JavaScript">
<!--
function validation( qform ) {
  //Check name
  if(qform.name.value==""){
    alert("Please input your name!");
    return false;
  }

  // Check registration
  if(qform.register[0].status==false && qform.register[1].status==
    false){
    alert("Please indicate your registration status!");
    return false;
  }

  // Check date, month and year
  var datefield = new Date(qform.year.value,qform.month.value,
  qform.day.value);
  if(is NaN(datefield.valueOf())){
    alert("Please enter a valid date!");
    return false;
  }

  //Check Email address
  if(qform.email.value.indexOf('@')==-1){
    alert("Please enter a valid email address!");
    return false;
  }
}
  return true
}
//-->
</SCRIPT>
```

Figure 3.7 JavaScript for form validation

```
if(isNaN(datefield.valueOf( ))){
    alert ("Please enter a valid date!");
    return false;
}
```

If it is invalid, the results will be "NaN." In this case, an alert message will be displayed accordingly.

To check whether the `"e-mail"` field contains the character `"@,"` we can use the `"indexof"` method as follows:

```
qform.email.value.indexof("@")==-1
```

If this statement is true, it means that the e-mail field does not contain the character `"@,"` so the corresponding alert message should be displayed.

In the `<FORM>` tag, we need to activate the validation function as follows:

```
<FORM ACTION="/servlet/vbs.processform" METHOD="POST"
onSubmit="return validation(this)">
```

It means that when the form is submitted (as detected by the onSubmit event handler), the `"validation"` function is triggered to validate the form. Note that the `"this"` parameter refers to the current form object. If the validation result is `"false"` (i.e., the validation fails), the submission will not be proceeded, otherwise the form will be submitted to the server for processing by the program `"vbs.processform"` stored under the `"servlet"` directory.

The above is a simple but a commonly used example to show how JavaScript can be used for form validation. In fact, a complete form validation library using JavaScript can be found in the Netscape JavaScript developer web site (`http://developer.netscape.com/docs/examples/JavaScript/formval/overview.html`).

3.14 *SUMMARY*

In this chapter, we have given an overview of the web page design process as well as HTML 4.0 and JavaScript for client-side programming or web publishing. HTML makes use of tags to format a document. For most tags, additional attributes can be defined. Basically, HTML can be used to format text, to link documents, to add images, and to construct tables. In addition, frames are often used to display multiple web pages in the same browser window. With HTML 4.0, web page designers can control the styles of web pages more effectively by using CSSs. Besides formatting web pages, HTML provides various form input elements for collecting user's input. By submitting a form to the server, a server-side program can be invoked to process the user's request with the input data. We will describe server-side programming techniques in the next chapter. JavaScript can be used to enhance the functionality of HTML in particular to make a web page more dynamic and interactive. A typical application of JavaScript is form validation.

REFERENCES

Bevan, N. and Macleod, M., *Usability Measurement in Context*, Behaviour and Information Technology, 1994, 132–145.

Deitel, H. M., Deitel, P. J., and Nieto, T. R., *Internet and World Wide Web – How to Program*, Prentice-Hall, Upper Saddle River, NJ, 2000.

Hall, M., Core Web Programming, Prentice-Hall, Upper Saddle River, NJ, 1998.

Lemay, L., *Teach Yourself Web Publishing with HTML4*, Sams Publishing, 1999.

Molich, R. and Nielsen, J., (1990), "Heuristic evaluation of user interfaces," in *Proceedings of ACM Human Factors in Computing Systems CHI'90*, vol. 4, 249–256.

Naik, D. C., *Internet Standards and Protocols*, Microsoft Press, 1998.

Ray, D. S. and Ray, E. J., *Mastering HTML 4.0*, Sybex Inc., 1997.

Shackel, B., "The concept of usability," in *Proceedings IBM Software and Information Usability Symposium*, Poughkeepsie, NY, Sept. 1981.

Tanenbaum, A. S., *Computer Networks*, 3rd edn., Prentice-Hall, Upper Saddle River, NJ, 1996.

Zakour, J., Foust, J., and Kerven, D., *HTML4 How-To*, Waite Group Press, 1997.

RECOMMENDED READING

Tanenbaum, A. S., *Computer Networks*, 3rd ed., Prentice-Hall, Upper Saddle River, NJ, 1996.

   This book provides a good introduction to HTML.

Ray, D. S. and Ray, E. J., *Mastering HTML 4.0*, Sybex Inc., 1997.

Lemay, L., *Teach Yourself Web Publishing with HTML4*, Sams Publishing, 1999.

Deitel, H. M., Deitel, P. J., and Nieto, T. R., *Internet and World Wide Web – How to Program*, Prentice-Hall, Upper Saddle River, NJ, 2000.

Zakour, J., Foust, J., and Kerven, D., *HTML4 How-To*, Waite Group Press, 1997.

   These books, particularly the first two, give an in-depth overview of the standards concerning HTML 4.0 and JavaScript. They are highly recommended. The last book includes a good HTML quick reference table in the appendix.

Chang, E. and Dillon, T., "Use of perspectives for design of user interfaces," in *Int'l Conference on Object Role Models*, Magnetic Island, Australia, 1993.

Chang, E. and Dillon, T., "The navigational aspects of the logical design of user interfaces," in *1st IEEE Int. Symp. on Object-oriented Real Time Distributed Computing ISORC*, Kyoto, 1998, 425–430.

Chang, E. and Dillon, T., "Audience centred web based design," in *Proceedings of the IEEE Conference on Systems, Men and Cybernetics*, Tokyo, Japan, October 1999.

De Troyer, O. and Leune, C., "WDSM: A user centred design method for web sites," in *Proc. 7th Int'l World Wide Web Conference* (H. Ashman and P. Thistlewaite, eds.) Elsevier, Amsterdam, 1998, 85–94.

De Troyer, O., "Designing well-structured web sites: Lessons to be learned from database schema methodology," in *Proceeding of the ER-Conference 98*, Springer-Verlag, Berlin, 1998. Lectures Notes in Computer Science.

Garzotto, F., Paolini, P., and Schwabe, D., "A model-based approach to hypertext application design," *ACM Transactions on Information Systems* **11** (1) (1993), 1–26.

Greenspun, F., *Greenspun's, Database Backed Web Sites: The Thinking Person's Guide to Web Publishing*, SD Press, 1997.

Isakowitz, T., Stohr, E. A., and Balasubramanian, P., "A methodology for structured hypermedia design," *Communications of the ACM* **38** (8) (1995) 34–43.

Sterling, G., Chang, E., and Dillon, T. S., "Semantics of a multimedia database for support within synthetic environments for multiple sensor systems," in *Database Semantics in Semantic Issues in Multimedia Systems* (R. Meesnau, E. Tari, and S. Stevens, eds. Kluwer, Boston, 1999, Chapt. 23, 413–434.

The HTML specification and its latest development can be found at the www.w3.org. This web site also includes a short tutorial on HTML 4.0.

4

Server-Side Programming I: Servlet Fundamentals

4.1   Revisiting the Three-Tier Model

4.2   Common Gateway Interface (CGI)

4.3   Active Server Page (ASP)

4.4   Overview of Java Servlet

4.5   Java Servlet Architecture

4.6   Overview of the Servlet API

4.7   Building the Virtual Bookstore – Step by Step

4.8   Your First Servlet – Welcome to VBS

4.9   Compile and Run WelcomeVBS

4.10 An Interactive Servlet Program Example: Topics of Interest

4.11 Topics of Interest: Cookie Approach

4.12 Summary

      References

      Recommended Reading

In the last chapter, we explored how to build the web system using various client-side programming and web publishing techniques. However, in e-commerce applications, client–server programming is of the utmost importance. The facilities provided range from simple electronic form submission systems to more sophisticated shopping cart systems in an interactive cyber store. When designing server-side applications, we need to consider many different factors such as efficiency, security, cost-effectiveness, and compatibility. Traditional Common Gateway Interface (CGI) programming techniques may become deficient under these considerations.

In this chapter, we initially discuss common server-side programming techniques. In particular, we will introduce Java Servlets – an effective programming technology that extends the functionality of Java to the server-side. We will also explain the advantages of servlets over other techniques for developing web-based e-commerce applications. We also discuss the basic framework of the servlet model and how it can be integrated with other technologies to implement e-commerce applications. Finally, we will present two simple Java Servlet programs.

4.1   REVISITING THE THREE-TIER MODEL

In previous chapters, we introduced the "three-tier model" for building e-commerce applications. As an introduction to server-side programming, let us revisit the three-tier model before discussing various server-side programming techniques.

To achieve the purposes of modular design and platform independence, web-based e-commerce applications are usually developed based on the three-tier model as shown in Figure 4.1. By means of the three-tier model, we can separate the business logic of the web applications from the "frontend" (i.e. web client) and the "backend" (i.e. database systems). This gives us a more flexible and scaleable system.

In summary, the three-tier model has the following components:

1. *The first tier – Web client:*   The first tier provides a web-based Graphical User Interface (GUI) displayed through a web browser in the client computer. Implementation of the web client in the web application is usually referred to as "Web publishing" and "Client-side programming," which has been extensively discussed in Chapter 3.

2. *The second tier – Server-side application (SSA):*   The second tier consists of server-side applications that run on a web server or a dedicated application server. In general, these applications implement the business logic of the web system. In this chapter, we will give an overview of the following server-side programming techniques:

   • Common Gateway Interface (CGI)
   • Active Server Page (ASP)
   • Java Servlets

   We will compare their advantages and shortcomings. As an example, we will use Java Servlets as the server-side programming tool throughout the book.

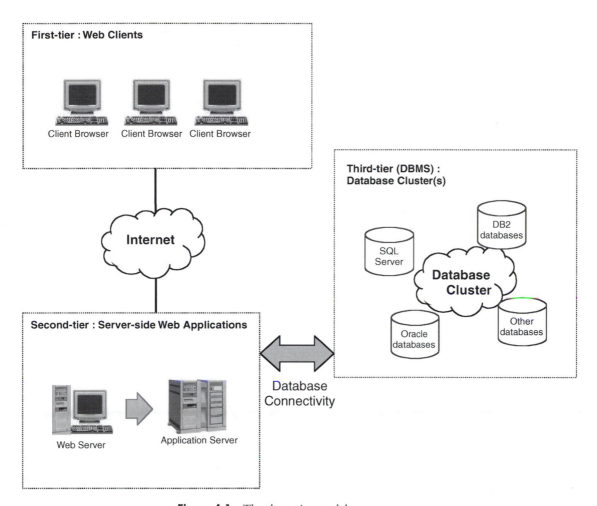

Figure 4.1 The three-tier model

3. *The third tier – Database management systems (DBMS):* The third tier provides data storage/retrieval services for the second tier so that dynamic web pages can be created. Depending on the system requirements, the third tier may consist of one database or a group of databases (i.e. database cluster). To "bridge" the second tier server-side applications and the "backend" DBMS, there are numerous ways to provide the database connectivity. A popular method is by means of JDBC such as a JDBC–ODBC (Java Database Connectivity–Open Database Connectivity) bridge. Alternatively, other techniques such as Proprietary Network Protocol drivers and Native API drivers can also be used. To facilitate communication with a database, the Structural Query Language (SQL) is often used. This will be discussed in Chapter 5.

In general, the three-tier model has the following advantages over the traditional single-tier or two-tier model, especially for web applications:

- Its modular design or layered architecture facilitates the change or replacement of one tier without affecting the other tiers.
- Using browsers as the web clients allows different applications to share the same look and feel.
- As web browsers can be found in almost all computers, web applications can be accessed from almost anywhere.

Another important requirement in e-commerce applications is "state tracking," or "session tracking." As HTTP is a *stateless* protocol (i.e., it does not keep track of the user's state), session tracking and management techniques are required for supporting many e-commerce application functions such as user login and shopping carts. In Chapter 6, we will discuss different types of session tracking techniques for building e-commerce applications. These include

- Hidden form fields
- Cookies
- URL rewriting
- HTTP user authorization

We will compare their advantages and disadvantages in terms of usability and ease of implementation. We also explore the Java Servlet Session Tracking API – a platform-independent Java Servlet library for supporting session tracking. We discuss how it works and why it is more effective than other session tracking techniques. In particular, we will use a simple shopping cart example to illustrate how the Java Servlet Session Tracking API can be used in the three-tier model for building interactive e-commerce applications.

4.2 COMMON GATEWAY INTERFACE (CGI)

4.2.1 CGI fundamentals

Early web pages were "static." In other words, a client could request only a static HTML document from the web server as shown in Figure 4.2. Later, CGI programming techniques were introduced to eliminate this constraint. CGI programming allows a web client to pass data to a server-side application so that a dynamic web page can be returned to the client according to the input data.

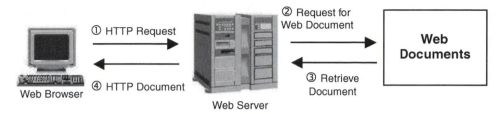

Figure 4.2 Static web page retrieval

Figure 4.2 explains the retrieval of a static web page. When the web browser receives a client request, it goes to the designated URL on a specific web server to retrieve the required static HTML document. Note that the content is independent of the request, in the sense that everyone who makes a request of that particular URL gets the same document.

If we are to allow interactivity between the web client and the web server, one needs a server-side programming technique to generate dynamic web pages. Such interactivity is of particular importance in e-commerce systems for purposes such as order submission or data input. CGI programming provided one of the first techniques that was utilized for this interactivity (Figure 4.3).

In a typical CGI-based web application, to provide this interactivity, a client invokes a CGI script to perform a specific action on the server side. For example,

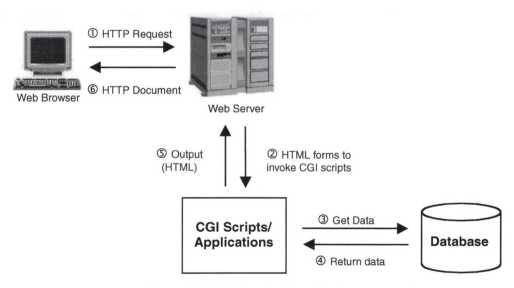

Figure 4.3 CGI-based web application

a `"visit counter"` can be included for displaying the number of visits to a particular web page, which can be done with the following image tag:

```
<IMG SRC="/cgi-bin/visit_counter">
```

This causes the web browser to start a CGI script on the server side on encountering the `<IMG>` tag. This CGI script updates the counter value and returns the current counter value to the client in the form of a GIF image.

Another common approach to invoke a CGI program is by using an HTML form. As discussed in Chapter 3, we can invoke a server-side program by using the ACTION attribute in an HTML form. To pass data from the web client to the web server for data processing using HTML forms, one can include the CGI program called `"order.pl"` in the `<FORM>` tag as follows:

```
<FORM METHOD="POST" ACTION="/cgi-bin/order.pl">
```

Note that the ACTION attribute specifies the server-side application or script to be invoked. In this case, it is a Perl script called `"order.pl"` stored under the `"cgi-bin"` directory of the web server.

The METHOD attribute of the `<FORM>` tag (i.e. POST) tells the browser how to send the information to the server. In this case, the data is embedded in the HTTP request message. If one uses the METHOD attribute GET instead, the data will be appended to the end of the URL.

4.2.2 CGI languages

CGI languages can be interpreted scripted languages (e.g., Perl, Apple Script, Unix Shell Scripting, and TCL) or compiled languages (e.g., C, C++, and Visual Basic). Perl (Practical Extraction and Report Language) has evolved to become a web programming language and is one of the most widely used CGI interpreted scripting languages. Running a script requires an interpreter to interpret the script before performing the required tasks. This makes for slow execution. However, scripts are easier to learn. Compiled languages produce a compact binary executable code from the source CGI code, and execution of this binary executable code leads to faster execution.

4.3 *ACTIVE SERVER PAGE (ASP)*

To develop interactive web applications, Microsoft introduced a server-side programming tool called Active Server Page (ASP). ASP is a "scripting" technique that runs on web servers rather than web clients. This contrasts with VBScript and JavaScript,

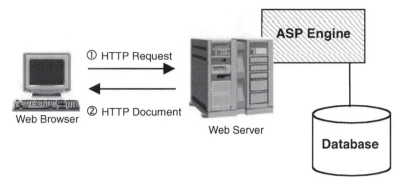

Figure 4.4 ASP model

which run on web clients. It basically generates dynamic HTML documents for the web client. Execution of the ASP code by the server returns the corresponding HTML document to the client. The server-side code written in ASP can be embedded in the HTML document, which allows one to insert it into web pages even though it is executed on the server. As ASP is a Miscrosoft product, it can easily be integrated with other Microsoft web development tools and ActiveX controls. Figure 4.4 shows the schematic diagram of the ASP model.

However, ASP has two disadvantages. Firstly, it is not a formal programming language, so debugging can be more difficult. Secondly, it is not object-oriented. In the next section, we will introduce an effective server-side programming technique called Java Servlet. As it is an object-oriented programming technique based on Java, it has a number of advantages over the other server-side programming techniques.

4.4 OVERVIEW OF JAVA SERVLET

Java was originally introduced by Sun Microsystems Inc. with the aim of enhancing interactivity in the web, particularly on the client side. To accomplish this, Sun developed a small client-side application called Applet ("App" means applications and "let" means small). Although applets can enhance client-side interactivity, this is done at the expense of long downloading time; hence, they are not attractive for most e-commerce applications. Furthermore, in many e-commerce applications, a client's request is often required to be processed in conjunction with the backend databases. For example, a customer may want to look up a particular product from the backend database. Obviously, it is not effective to download the whole database to the client side for processing. Hence, there is a strong need for server-side Java to cater for these requirements.

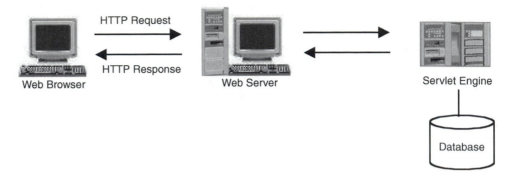

Figure 4.5   A typical web-based servlet interaction

A servlet is a small piece of server-side application, which can be viewed as the server-side analog of an applet. In a typical servlet application, a servlet-enabled web server receives an HTTP request from the client (see Figure 4.5). It then forwards the request to the servlet engine for performing the necessary operations as specified by the program. Finally, it returns a response (e.g. HTML document) to the client via the web server.

Let us look at a simple book ordering system for our VBS based on Java Servlet. The servlet is invoked by using an HTML form. The main steps are described as follows:

1. Using his browser, the customer accesses our VBS web server through HTTP.
2. The book ordering form is forwarded to the customer's browser.
3. The customer fills in the book ordering form (electronically) and sends the form to the server by pressing the "Submit" button.
4. This HTTP request is forwarded to the servlet engine by the VBS web server.
5. The servlet processes the request by performing the necessary operations, e.g. updating the order transaction database and invoking the payment gateway for the internet payment, etc.
6. After processing, the corresponding response is returned to the client via the web server.

Compared to other server-side programming techniques, particularly traditional CGI programming, Java Servlet has the following advantages:

- As it is a formal programming language, debugging is easier. Furthermore, its object-oriented features can greatly facilitate program design.

- Each servlet can handle multiple requests. In other words, once a servlet is invoked, it will remain in the system and can be used by different requests requiring the same servlet.

- Traditional CGI programming techniques such as Perl are usually platform-dependent. Java Servlets, on the other hand, are based on the philosophy "written once, run everywhere."

- As part of the Java family, servlets can use the Java security APIs if necessary and can be easily integrated with other Java-based programming techniques such as CORRA, RMI, JDBC, and JCA (Java Cryptography Architecture) to build a comprehensive e-commerce system.

However, compared with other server-side scripting techniques such as Perl and ASP, the writing of servlets generally requires more programming effort and hence longer development time.

4.5 JAVA SERVLET ARCHITECTURE

A servlet is a server-side Java program running inside a Java Virtual Machine (JVM). Through the servlet engine, it can interact with the server and also the HTTP. Like other CGI applications, a servlet is invoked by a client from the client browser (e.g. via an HTML form). It may also be invoked by other servlets or Java programs. As mentioned earlier, unlike traditional CGI applications, which need to set up multiple processes for handling multiple requests, a servlet can handle multiple requests under different threads. Therefore, servlets provide a solution that is more scaleable. Furthermore, servlets can interact closely with the server to do things that may be performed easily with the traditional CGI programming techniques.

To run servlets, there are basically two alternatives. The first one is to use a servlet-enabled web server, i.e., a web server that can support the servlet APIs directly. The second solution is to use a "plug-in" servlet engine in a nonservlet-enabled web server. Tables 4.1 and 4.2 give some examples of the commonly used servlet-enabled web servers and the "plug-in" servlet engines [Moss, 1998; Hunter and Crawford, 1998].

4.6 OVERVIEW OF THE SERVLET API

The life cycle of a servlet looks like this. Upon receiving a request to invoke a servlet, the server will create the servlet, call the `init()` method, and then the `service()` method of the servlet. The `init()` method is for performing initialization actions. If a

Table 4.1   Example of servlet-enabled web servers

Vendor	Product	URL
Apache	Apache web Server	http://www.apache.com/pws1410.php3
Lotus	Domino Go web Server	http://www.lotus.com/home.nsf/ welcome/domino
IBM	Internet Connection Server	http://www.as400.ibm.com/developer/ ebiz/protocols/http_v4r1.html
IBM	Visual Age WebRunner	http://www.ibm.com/software/ad/ webrunner/
Netscape	Netscape Enterprise Server	http://home.netscape.com/ enterprise/v3.6/index.html
O'Reilly	Website Professional	http://www.oreilly.com/catalog/webpro2/
Sun Microsystems	Sun web Server	http://www.sun.com/products-n- solutions/software/internet-intranet/ index.html
Sun Microsystems	Java Web Server	http://www.sun.com/software/jwebserver /index.html
W3C	Jigsaw HTTP Server	www.w3.org/Jigsaw/
Web Easy	WEASAL	http://www.webeasy.com/products/ weasel.htm
Zenus Technology	Zenus Web Server	http://www.zenus.com/pr.html

servlet has been invoked before, it can be reused. In this case, the service() method will be called directly for processing the request. Finally, if a servlet is to be removed, the destroy() method is called before removing it. In this book, we will only cover the servlet basics, in particular how servlets can be used to build the VBS. For details on servlet programming, please refer to the references at the end of this chapter.

There are two main packages in the Servlet API, namely javax.servlet and javax.servlet.http. They can be downloaded from http://java.sun. com/products/servlet as part of the Java Servlet Development Kit (JSDK). The two packages are for developing generic servlets and servlets for the HTTP (i.e., under

Table 4.2   Example of third-party middleware servlet engines

Vendor	Product	URL
IBM	WebSphere Application Server	http://www-4.ibm.com/software/webservers/appserv/
Live Software	JRun	http://www.jrun.com/Products/Jrun/

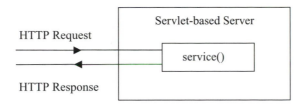

Figure 4.6 A generic servlet model (based on the work of Hunter and Crawford [1998])

the web environment), respectively. The `javax.servlet` and `javax.servlet.http` packages include two main classes, namely GenericServlet and HttpServlet, whereby the latter is extended from the former. Each servlet request is processed by the `service ()` method first and so you must implement this method if you extend the GenericServlet class. `GenericServlet.service()` is an abstract method as defined below:

```
public abstract void service(ServletRequest req,
ServletResponse res) throws ServletException, IOException;
```

As shown here, there are two object parameters, namely ServletRequest and ServletResponse. The former object is related to the request to the servlet program (e.g., it contains the client's information). On the other hand, the ServletResponse object is used to handle the response returned to the client via the server. This is shown in Figure 4.6.

For HTTP servlets, the `service()` method passes the requests to the corresponding `doREQ()` method where REQ is the HTTP request command. In particular, the `doGet()` and `doPost()` methods are invoked by the HTTP GET and POST commands, respectively. For HTTP servlets, it is preferable to override the `doREQ()` methods rather than the `service()` method. This allows actions to be taken based on the type of HTTP request received. A schematic overview of the HTTP servlet model is shown in Figure 4.7.

Besides the `doGet()` and `doPost()` methods, a variety of methods corresponding to different HTTP commands are available as shown in Table 4.3. Essentially, these methods allow a servlet to perform actions according to the type of HTTP request received. The most commonly used methods are `doGet()`, `doPost()`, and `doHead()`.

4.7 BUILDING THE VIRTUAL BOOKSTORE – STEP BY STEP

Throughout this book, we will demonstrate how to build a simple Virtual Bookstore (VBS) by using Java Servlets as the core server-side programming tool. We

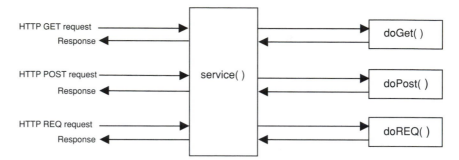

Figure 4.7   An HTTP servlet model (based on the work of Hunter and Crawford [1998])

will illustrate how to build this dynamic web-based application using the following programming techniques:

- Client-side programming using HTML and JavaScript (Chapter 3).
- Server-side programming using Java Servlets (this chapter and chapters 5 and 6).
- JDBC programming with servlets to implement database connectivity (Chapter 5).
- Session tracking technique using the servlet session tracking API to implement user login and shopping cart applications (Chapter 6).

Table 4.3   A summary of methods used to create a functional HTTP servlet

Method	Description
service( )	This method is invoked for all generic servlets when the server receives a request. In case of HTTP servlets, this method will usually be overridden by one of the following methods associated with various HTTP requests (e.g. POST or GET).
doGet( )	This method is invoked when the server receives an HTTP GET command.
doPost( )	This method is invoked when the server receives an HTTP POST command.
doPut( )	This method is invoked when the server receives an HTTP PUT command.
doDelete( )	This method is invoked when the server receives an HTTP DELETE command.
doTrace( )	This method is invoked when the server receives an HTTP TRACE command.
doOptions( )	This method is invoked when the server receives an HTTP OPTIONS command.

In order to provide a step-by-step illustration of different techniques, and how they are integrated to build the VBS, all the program examples presented in this chapter and the following chapters will be component modules of the VBS application. It is anticipated that once you have gone through the programming examples, you should be able to build a VBS similar to Amazon.com or other B2C e-commerce systems. Towards the end of the book, there is a step-by-step exercise for building the VBS. Suggested answers are also provided via the book web site.

4.8 *YOUR FIRST SERVLET – WELCOME TO VBS*

Like learning other programming languages, let us first show you how to print a simple `"Welcome to VBS"` message. This programming example shows you how to display a simple message "Welcome to VBS" on the client browser using a servlet program called `"WelcomeVBS.java."` The program listing is given in Figure 4.8.

Figure 4.9 shows a simple HTML file `"WelcomeVBS.html"` to invoke the servlet called WelcomeVBS. As indicated in the package statement inside the program, this servlet is stored under the directory `"/vbs/servlet1/."`

Before studying the servlet program in detail, let us briefly look at the caller file, `WelcomeVBS.html`. It is a very simple HTML form. In the FORM tag, the URL of the servlet file "WelcomeVBS" is specified using the Unix naming convention. In this case, `"/servlet/"` is used to inform the web server that the file WelcomeVBS is a servlet program. It is a logical directory in the server. In the HTML form, a "Submit" button is provided for the user to invoke the servlet program by using the GET method. In later examples, we will use multiple buttons to handle multiple actions.

The servlet program `"WelcomeVBS.java"` contains only the `"doGet()"` method. When a user clicks the "Submit" button on the form, an HTTP GET request will be sent to the web server. By reading the ACTION attribute of the HTML form, the web server knows that a servlet program is to be invoked so the request is passed to the servlet engine accordingly. The doGet() method of the corresponding servlet will be invoked as this is an HTTP GET request. Moreover, two object parameters, namely HttpServletRequest and HttpServletResponse will be created.

In general, data sent by the client, including the corresponding HTTP request information is provided by the HttpServletRequest object. As shown in later examples, this object can be used to generate dynamic web pages based on the client's input data, which is important for e-commerce applications.

```
package vbs.servlet1;
import java.io.*;
import javax.servlet.*;
import javax.servlet.http.*;

public class WelcomeVBS extends HttpServlet{
  public void doGet(HttpServletRequest req, HttpServletResponse resp)
  throws ServletException, IOException
  {

  //Specify the content type
    resp.setContentType("text/html");

  //Get the PrintWriter object for writing the response
    PrintWriter out=resp.getWriter();

  //Print the response
    out.println("<html>");
    out.println("<head><title>Welcome to VBS: Servlet Approach </title></head>");
    out.println("<h2>Welcome to VBS: Servlet Approach.<h2>");
    out.println("</html>");
  }
}
```

Figure 4.8 Program listing of WelcomeVBS.java (based on the HelloWorld program in JSDK)

On the other hand, the HttpServletResponse object provides information for generating the HTTP response to the client. In this example, a simple message "Welcome to VBS" (in HTML format) is returned to the client via the HttpServletResponse object. To do this, two basic steps are involved. Firstly, the program needs to "notify" the web server that an HTML file (in text format) will be sent. This is done by using the "setContentType" method as follows:

```
resp.setContentType("text/html");
```

Secondly, a PrintWriter object named "out" is created to write the response to the client as follows:

```
PrintWriter out=resp.getWriter();
```

After setting up the PrintWriter object, the "println" method can be used to write the response on a line-by-line basis. With the output stream "out"

```
<html>
<head>
<title>Welcome to VBS : SERVLET APPROACH</title>
</head>

<body>
<form action="/servlet/vbs.servlet1.WelcomeVBS" method="GET">
<h2><center>Welcome to VBS: Servlet Approach</center></h2>
<hr>
<p>Press the button to invoke the servlet for displaying the welcome message
</p>
<br><br>
<center>
<input name="Test" type="submit" value="Start Servlet">
</center>
<br>
<hr>
</form>
</body>
</html>
```

Figure 4.9   Program listing of Welcome.html

and the `"println"` method, the simple message: `"Welcome to VBS - Servlet Approach"` can be written to the client in HTML format.

4.9   COMPILATION AND EXECUTION OF SERVLETS

Basically, there are three alternative methods for compiling a servlet program. The simplest way is to download the JSDK from Sun (`http://java.sun.com/products/Servlet/`). The latest version at the time of writing is version 2.2. However, it provides only a text-based interface for developing servlets. Apart from JSDK, many other third-party Java development software tools, such as Borland JBuilder™ from Borland Corporation or IBM VisualAge™ from IBM Corporation, also support servlet programming. All of them provide a GUI, which is user-friendly. You can also install a servlet engine, which is listed in Tables 4.1 and 4.2. Most of them provide tools for compiling servlet programs.

There is a program called `"startserver"` in the Sun JSDK (version 2.0 or above), which will enable you to "emulate" a servlet-enabled web server using the local computer. This is the simplest way to test your servlets and it is free of

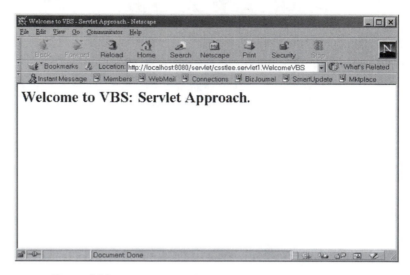

Figure 4.10   A snapshot of the servlet WelcomeVBS output

charge. Once you have started the `"startserver"` program, you can invoke a servlet (say `ServletProgram`) by referring to its URL such as `http://localhost:8080/servlet/ServletProgram`. In the previous example, according to the package, the URL is `http://localhost:8080/servlet/csstlee.servlet/.WelcomeVBS`. A snapshot of the result after running the servlet is shown in Figure 4.10. Of course, if you have a servlet-enabled web server, you can run the servlet in the web server.

4.10 AN INTERACTIVE SERVLET PROGRAM EXAMPLE: TOPICS OF INTEREST

In the previous program, the response is static such that everyone gets the same welcome message from the servlet. Furthermore, no data is passed from the client (i.e., the user browser) to the servlet for processing. In this example, we enhance the `WelcomeVBS.java` program to make it interactive. In the enhanced program, a user can input three topics of interest and submit them to the server. The server then reads the user's input and returns the topics of interest to the user in an HTML file. In the next section, we will store the topics of interest using cookies.

In the new HTML file, the following textboxes are included for a user to enter the three topics of interest.

```
First  topic: <input TYPE="TEXT" NAME="Topic1_name" size="20">
Second topic: <input TYPE="TEXT" NAME="Topic2_name" size="20">
Third  topic: <input TYPE="TEXT" NAME="Topic3_name" size="20">
```

```
<html>

<head>
<title>Welcome to VBS: Topics of Interest</title>
</head>

<body>

<form action="/vbs.servlet1.TopicsOfInterest"method="GET">
 <div align="center"><center><h2>Welcome to VBS: Topics of Interest</h2>
 </center></div><hr>
 <p>Please input your topics of interest<br>
 First topics:   <input type="TEXT" name="Topics1_name" size="20"><br>
 Second topics: <input type="TEXT" name="Topics2_name" size="20"><br>
 Third topics:  <input type="TEXT" name="Topics3_name" size="20"></p>
 <div align="center"><center><p><input name="Test_name" type="submit"
  value="Enter"><br>
 </p>
 </center></div><hr>
</form>
</body>
</html>
```

Figure 4.11   Program listing of TopicsOfInterest.html

Figure 4.11 shows the complete HTML file `TopicsOfInterest.html`.
`TopicsOfInterest2.java` is similar to the previous program in Figure 4.8 except that we need to extract the three topics of interest from the `HttpServlet Request` object `req`. This is done by using the `getParameter()` method as follows:

```
String Topic1_value=req.getParameter("Topic1_name");
String Topic2_value=req.getParameter("Topic2_name");
String Topic3_value=req.getParameter("Topic3_name");
```

As shown here, the values extracted from the `req` object are stored in the respective string variables so that they can be displayed later. In fact, both the `getParameter()` and `getParameterValues()` methods can be used for extracting the values. The difference is that `getParameter()` returns a single string value, while `getParameterValues()` returns an array of strings. Figure 4.12 shows the program listing of `TopicsOfInterest.java`. A snapshot of the result after executing the program is shown in Figure 4.13.

Besides `getParameter()` and `getParameterValues()` methods, the Java Servlet API includes many other methods for acquiring various types of information

```java
package vbs.servlet1;
import java.io.*;
import javax.servlet.*;
import javax.servlet.http.*;

public class TopicsOfInterest extends HttpServlet{
  public void doGet(HttpServletRequest req, HttpServletResponse resp)
  throws ServletException, IOException
  {

   //Specify the content type
   resp.setContentType("text/html");

   //Get a PrintWriter object for writing the response
   PrintWriter out=resp.getWriter();

   //Get customer's topics of interest
   String Topics1_value = req.getParameter("Topics1_name");
   String Topics2_value = req.getParameter("Topics2_name");
   String Topics3_value = req.getParameter("Topics3_name");

   //Write the HTML response
   out.println("<html>");
   out.println("<head><title>Welcome to VBS</title></head>");
   out.println("<h2>Welcome to VBS </p>");
   out.println("<h3>Your topics of interest: <b></h3>");
   out.println("<ul><li>" + Topics1_value +"</li>");
   out.println("<li>" + Topics2_value +"</li>");
   out.println("<li>" + Topics3_value +"</li></ul>");
   out.println("</html>");
  }
}
```

Figure 4.12   Program listing of TopicsOfInterest.java

from a client request. Table 4.4 gives a summary of the commonly used HTTP servlet methods. For details, please refer to `http://java.sun.com/products/Servlet` and also the books by Moss [1998] and Hunter and Crawford [1998].

Again, the HttpServletResponse object `resp` is used to pass an HTML document back to the client as follows:

```java
resp.setContentType("text/html");
PrintWriter out=resp.getWriter();
```

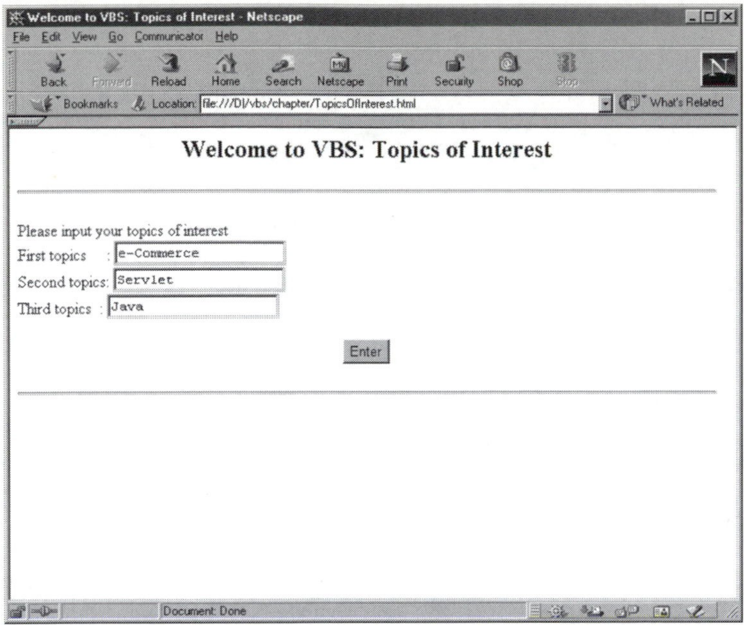

(a)

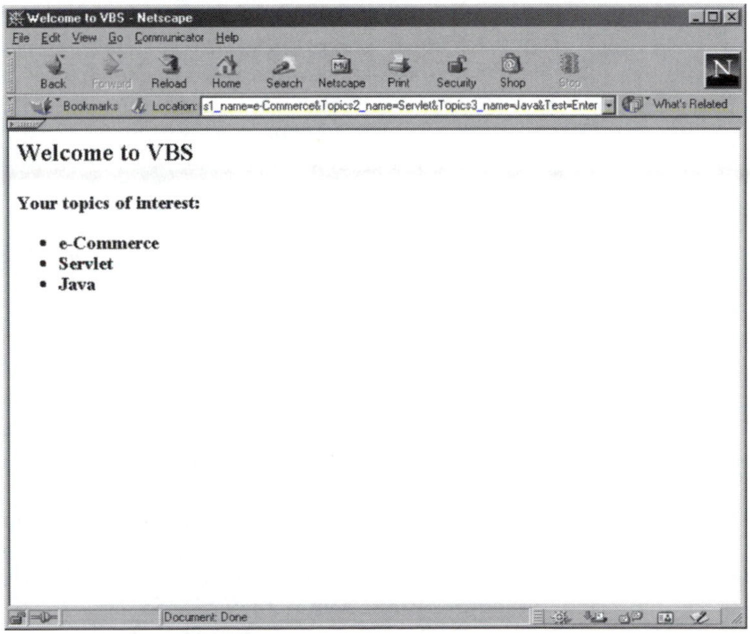

(b)

Figure 4.13 A snapshot of the input to output screens of TopicsOfInterest program (a) the HTML input file (b) the output screen showing the topics of interest

Table 4.4   Summary of commonly used HTTP servlet/general servlet request methods

Method	Returned value/object	Return type
HTTP servlet request methods		
getAuthType( )	Authentication type associated with the request (null if none)	String
getDateHeader(String)	Value of the date header fields	Long integer
getHeader(String)	Value of the specified header field (null if not found)	String
GetHeaderNames( )	An enumeration of the header names	Enumeration
getIntHeader(String)	Integer value of the specified request header	Integer
getMethod( )	HTTP method (e.g. GET or POST) used for this request	String
getPathInfo( )	Extra path information associated with the request	String
getQueryString( )	Query string of the request	String
getRemoteUser( )	Identity of the user initiating this request.	String
getSession(boolean)	Current session object corresponding to this request(null if there is none) (Note: If there is no session object, a new one will be created if the input parameter is "True")	HttpSession
Generic servlet request methods		
getContentLength( )	Length of the content (in bytes) in this request (−1 if unknown)	Integer
getContentType( )	Content type of the data (null if unknown)	String
getInputStream( )	Input stream for retrieving binary data	Servlet-InputStream
getParameter(String)	Value of the specified parameter (null if it does not exist)	String
getParameterNames( )	An enumeration of the names of all the parameters in this request	Enumeration
getParameterValues( )	Values of the specified parameter expressed as an array of String objects (null if it does not exist)	String[ ]
getProtocol( )	Protocol being used by this request	String

Table 4.4 *(Cont.)*

getRemoteAddr( )	IP address of the client sending this request	String
getRemoteHost( )	Name of the client sending this request	String
getServerName( )	Host name of the server that received this request	String
getServerPort( )	Server port number on which this request was received	Integer

Besides setting the content type (i.e. MIME type) as `"text/html,"` which means a text-based HTML document, other possible alternatives are

- `text/plain`: Plain ASCII text without HTML tags
- `image/gif`: GIF image
- `image/jpeg`: JPEG image

Using the `println()` method of the PrintWriter object, the HTML document can be written to the client on a line-by-line basis. If we need to return binary data to the client, we can use the `getOutputStream()` method to set up an output stream. Besides the `setContentType` method, other commonly used response methods are summarized in Table 4.5. For details, please refer to `http://java.sun.com/products/servlet` and also the books by Moss [1998] and Hunter and Crawford [1998].

4.11 *TOPICS OF INTEREST: COOKIE APPROACH*

The servlet API also provides support for using cookies through the interface `javax.Servlet.http.Cookie`. As an extension of the previous program, we can make use of this interface to store the three topics of interest as cookies in the client computer. For example, we can set a cookie called `ckTopic1` and add it to the response through the `addCookie()` method as follows:

```
Cookie ckTopic1=new Cookie("Topic1_name", Topic1_value);
            resp.addCookie(ckTopic1);
```

where `resp` is the `HttpServletResponse` object. Here, the cookie `ckTopic1` is assigned a name `"Topic1_name"` and a value `"Topic1_value."` Note that the

Table 4.5 Summary of commonly used HTTP servlet/genral servlet response methods

Method	Description	Return type
HTTP servlet response methods		
sendError(int)	Return an error code to the client as specified in the parameter	Void
sendError(int, String)	Return an error code and an error message to the client as specified in the parameters	Void
containsHeader(String)	Indicate whether the response contains the specified header	Boolean
addCookie(Cookie)	Add the specified cookie in the HTTP response	Void
setDateHeader(String, long)	Set the Date header in the HTTP response with a particular date value.	Void
setHeader(String, String)	Set the HTTP response header (as defined by the first parameter) with the specified value (as defined by the second parameter)	Void
setIntHeader(String, int)	Set the HTTP response header (as defined by the first parameter) with the specified integer value (as defined by the second parameter)	Void
setStatus(int)	Set the response status code	Void
setStatus(int, String)	Set the response status code together with a status message	Void
Generic servlet response methods		
setContentType(String)	Set the associated content type	Void
setContentLength(int)	Set the associated content length	Void
getWriter( )	Get a PrintWriter object for writing the response	PrintWriter
getOutputStream( )	Get an output stream for returning a stream of binary response data	ServletOutput-Stream

value `"Topic1_value"` is what the user enters in the respective textbox in this example. Similarly, we can also store the other topics of interest as cookies. After adding the cookies to the response object `resp`, they will be included in the HTTP response accordingly. To obtain the cookies sent by the client, a servlet can use the getCookies() method of the HttpServletRequest object as follows:

```
Cookie cookies[]=req.getCookies();

  if (cookies!=null) {

  while(i<cookies.length){
   if(cookies[i].getName().equals("Topic1_name")){
     Topic1_value=cookies[i].getValue();
   }else if (cookies[i].getName().equals("Topic2_name")){
     Topic2_value=cookies[i].getValue();
   }else if (cookies[i].getName().equals("Topic3_name")){
     Topic3_value=cookies[i].getValue();
   }
   i++;
   }
   }
```

The getCookies( ) method returns an array of cookies (cookies[ ]) because the browser may return a number of cookies to the server. To retrieve the cookie named "Topic1_name," one can use the "getName( )" method to get the cookie name from

```
<html>
<head>
<title>Set Cookie - Servlet Approach</title>
</head>
<body>
<form action="/servlet/vbs.servlet1.SetCookie"  method="GET">
<h2><center>Welcome to VBS - Set Cookie</center></h2><hr>
<p>Press the button to save your topics of interest using cookie.<br><br>
<p>Please input your topics of interest<br>
 First topics:   <input type="TEXT" name="Topics1_name" size="20"><br>
 Second topics: <input type="TEXT" name="Topics2_name" size="20"><br>
 Third topics:   <input type="TEXT" name="Topics3_name" size="20"></p>
 <div align="center"><center><p><input name="Test" type="submit" value=
  "Enter"><br>
 </p>
 </center></div><hr>
</form>
</body>
</html>
```

Figure 4.14 Program listing of SetCookie.html

```java
package vbs.servlet1;
import java.io.*;
import javax.servlet.*;
import javax.servlet.http.*;

public class SetCookie extends HttpServlet{
  public void doGet(HttpServletRequest req, HttpServletResponse resp)
  throws ServletException, IOException
  {

   //Specify the content type
   resp.setContentType("text/html");

   //Get a PrintWriter object
   PrintWriter out=resp.getWriter();

   //Get customer's topics of interest
   String Topics1_value = req.getParameter("Topics1_name");
   String Topics2_value = req.getParameter("Topics2_name");
   String Topics3_value = req.getParameter("Topics3_name");

   //Set cookies to client machine
   Cookie ckTopics1 = new Cookie("Topics1_name", Topics1_value);
   Cookie ckTopics2 = new Cookie("Topics2_name", Topics2_value);
   Cookie ckTopics3 = new Cookie("Topics3_name", Topics3_value);
   resp.addCookie(ckTopics1);
   resp.addCookie(ckTopics2);
   resp.addCookie(ckTopics3);

   //Write the response
   out.println("<html>");
   out.println("<head><title>Set Cookie </title></head>");
   out.println("<h2>Cookies have been created to store your topics of interest</h2>");
   out.println("</html>");
  }
}
```

Figure 4.15 Program listing of SetCookie.java

(a)

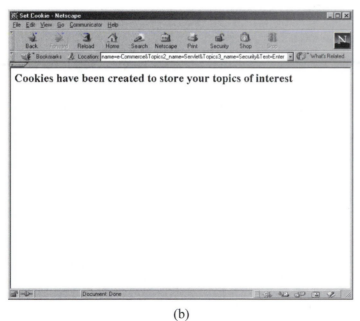

(b)

Figure 4.16 Screen output of the SetCookie Servlet (a) the HTML input file (b) response page from SetCookie program

```html
<html>
<head>
<title>Topics of Interest using Cookie Technique</title>
</head>
<body>
<form action="/servlet/vbs.servlet1.TopicsOfInterest2" method="GET">
<h2><center>Topics of Interest using Cookie Technique</center></h2>
<hr>
<p>Press the button to display your topics of interest. </p>
<br>
<center>
<input name="Test" type="submit" value="Enter">
</center>
<br>
<hr>
</form>
</body>
</html>
```

Figure 4.17   Program listing of TopicsOfInterest2.html

```java
package vbs.servlet1;
import java.io.*;
import javax.servlet.*;
import javax.servlet.http.*;
public class TopicsOfInterest2 extends HttpServlet{
  public void doGet(HttpServletRequest req, HttpServletResponse resp)
  throws ServletException, IOException
  {
   //Specify the content type
   resp.setContentType("text/html");

   String Topics1_value = "";
   String Topics2_value = "";
   String Topics3_value = "";

   //Get the PrintWriter object
   PrintWriter out=resp.getWriter();

   int i=0;

   Cookie cookies[] = req.getCookies();
```

Figure 4.18   Program listing of TopicsOfInterest2.java

```
if (cookies != null) {

while (i<cookies.length){
 if (cookies[i].getName().equals("Topics1_name")){
    Topics1_value = cookies[i].getValue();
 }else if (cookies[i].getName().equals("Topics2_name")){
    Topics2_value = cookies[i].getValue();
 }else if (cookies[i].getName().equals("Topics3_name")){
    Topics3_value = cookies[i].getValue();
 }
 i++;
 }
 }
 //Write the response in HTML format
 out.println("<html>");
 out.println("<head><title>Welcome to VBS</title></head>");
 out.println("<h2>Topics of Interest: Cookie Technique </p>");
 out.println("<h3>Your topics of interest: <b></h3>");
 out.println("<ul><li>" + Topics1_value +"</li>");
 out.println("<li>" + Topics2_value +"</li>");
 out.println("<li>" + Topics3_value +"</li></ul>");
 out.println("</html>");
 }
}
```

Figure 4.18 (*Continued*)

the cookies array. Once it is found, we can then obtain its value by using the
getValue() method.

In the following example, we slightly modify the previous example into two servlets: SetCookie.java and TopicsOfInterest2.java. The program SetCookie
generates a form for a user to enter three topics of interest, which are passed to
the server as three text strings, namely "Topic1_value," "Topic2_value," and
"Topic3_value." The program then generates three cookies to store the topics accordingly. After receiving the response, the cookies are stored in the client computer.
Program listing of SetCookie.java, the corresponding HTML file and sample
screens are shown in Figures 4.14–4.16. The program TopicsOfInterest2.java
retrieves these three cookies from the client machine and returns their values to the
client browser.

The servlet program TopicsOfInterest2.java is invoked by the HTML document TopicsOfInterest2.html as shown in Figures 4.17–4.19.

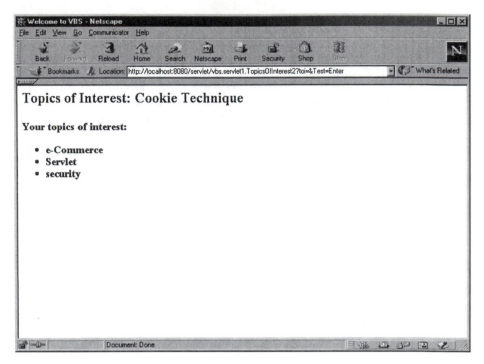

Figure 4.19   Screen output of the TopicsOfInterest2 servlet program

4.12 *SUMMARY*

In this chapter, we introduced the Java Servlet – an effective server-side programming technique. We compared it with other server-side programming tools such as CGI. We also discussed the three-tier model, and how it can be implemented with the support of the Java Servlet.

Throughout the book, we will use a case study of the VBS to demonstrate how to build an e-commerce application. More importantly, we will illustrate how to integrate different web programming techniques to achieve this goal.

In the last part of this chapter, we presented a simple "VBS Welcome page" program illustrating the basic structure of a servlet program. We also discussed how to build a simple interactive servlet program and how to make use of the cookie technique to store simple data objects.

In the following chapters, we will demonstrate the other components of the Java Servlet for building the VBS.

REFERENCES

Hunter, J. and Crawford, W., *Java Servlet Programming*, O'Reilly & Associates, Inc., 1998.

Moss, K., *Java Servlets*, McGraw-Hill, New York, 1998.

RECOMMENDED READING

Jardin, C. A., *Java Electronic Commerce Sourcebook*, John Wiley & Sons, New York, 1997.

  This is a good book for readers who are interested in knowing more about how CGI can be used in e-commerce applications.

Hunter, J. and Crawford, W., *Java Servlet Programming*, O'Reilly & Associates, Inc., 1998.

Callaway, D. R., *Inside Servlets: Server-Side Programming for the Java Platform*, Addison-Wesley, Reading, MA, 1999.

Moss, K., *Java Servlets*, McGraw-Hill, New York, 1998.

  These books provide for an in-depth explanation of Java Servlet programming. They are highly recommended.

Hall, M., *Core Web Programming*, Prentice-Hall, Upper Saddle River, NJ, 1998.

  This book gives an overview of different web programming techniques, ranging from JavaScript and Java Applets for client-side programming, to CGIs and Java Servlets for server-side programming.

Berlin, D., *CGI Programming Unleashed*, Sams Publishing, 1996.

Boutell, T., *CGI Programming in C and Perl*, Addison-Wesley, Reading, MA, 1996.

  For readers who are interested in CGI programming, these two books provide an elaboration of CGI programming using Perl and other programming languages.

Zukowski, J., *Mastering: Java 1.2*, Sybex Inc., 1998.

Naughton, P., *Java 2: The Complete Reference*, Osborne/McGraw-Hill, Berkeley, CA, 1999.

  These can be referred to for a complete reference on Java programming.

Deitel, H. M. and Deitel, P. J., *Java: How to Program*, 3rd edn., Prentice-Hall, Upper Saddle River, NJ, 1999.

  This book is good for newcomers to Java programming.

The Java Servlet specification [JSDK] can be downloaded from http://java.sun.com/products/servlet/.

5

Server-Side Programming II: Database Connectivity

5.1 Introduction

5.2 Relational Database Systems

5.3 JDBC Perspectives

5.4 A JDBC Program Example: Simple Servlet Book Query

5.5 An Advanced Book Query: ServletBookquerymulti

5.6 Advanced JDBC Servlet: VBS Advance Book Search Engine

5.7 Summary

References

Recommended Reading

5.1 INTRODUCTION

In most e-business solutions, connectivity to the backend database engines becomes a necessary and important requirement. As most of these databases are relational, the Structured Query Language (SQL) plays an important role in web-based database interactions in these e-commerce applications.

In the previous chapter, we discussed basic server-side programming techniques to support e-commerce applications, ranging from traditional CGI to the contemporary Java Servlets approach. In this chapter, we will explore in detail how database connectivity can be achieved in the internet environment.

All types of e-commerce applications, ranging from B2C applications such as e-shopping to B2B applications such as virtual marketplace, require one to connect to and access information from the back-end database system.

For instance, in an e-shopping scenario such as purchasing books in our VBS, we may need to access the back-end database systems in numerous cases, which include

- searching for books according to certain criteria such as the name of the author, publisher, book title, etc.
- obtaining the purchase history of a given customer over a prespecified period.
- updating and checking the book inventory and delivery information database when an order is received.
- updating of the sales transaction database and the accounts receivable (A/R) database during invoicing and payments.

An Application Program Interface (API) is a useful piece of middleware, which provides an interface that allows one to access the necessary functionality for that application. Java provides an API, the JDBC (Java Database Connectivity), to allow one to develop web applications that can access and update backend database systems. These allow one to integrate servlet-based programming techniques described in the last chapter, with the backend database systems. An important feature of JDBC is that the API is database independent. Thus, a JDBC-enabled web application can be used with a different database system without the need to modify the program statements and SQL commands, and only the JDBC driver needs to be replaced. In other words, it is exactly the "three-tier model" discussed in the last chapter.

In this chapter, we initially give only a brief introduction to relational database systems, and explain some basic SQL commands and their usage. Secondly, we will discuss the basic concept of the JDBC infrastructure, the main mechanisms, together with an example of a simple Java program using JDBC components. Lastly, we will discuss how to integrate the JDBC API with servlet technology to build an interactive server-side database accessor program. Throughout this chapter, we will make use of the VBS as an example. In particular, we will discuss how to develop the Advance Search Engine by using the JDBC servlet programming technique – a vital aspect of the VBS project.

5.2   RELATIONAL DATABASE SYSTEMS

5.2.1   What is a relational database?

Generally speaking, a "database" can be considered as a shared collection of interrelated data in a structured form, which provides useful information to an organization.

Before E. F. Codd proposed the relational database model in 1970, there were numerous database models being used, such as hierarchical and network models. Since then, the relational database has dominated the database market all over the world.

A "relational database" essentially uses relations to represent entities and relationships (the E–R relationship). There is a schema that describes the structure of the database. The relations are essentially "tables." These tables can be accessed or updated, or rows within them created or deleted using SQL.

SQL statements can be used in conjunction with general purpose programming languages such as Java, C++, or Basic. Alternatively, a call-level API helps to provide a platform-independent approach to accessing and manipulating the information in the database. Basically, this call-level API passes the SQL statements onto the database engine. JDBC constitutes such a call-level API. Relational databases can be accessed by different applications at the same time.

In this section, we will briefly discuss relational databases and SQL statements.

5.2.2 A brief overview of relational databases: an example of book ordering

A relation (or table) in the relational database can be thought of as a two-dimensional collection of data with rows and columns. An important concept in relational databases is the notion of a primary key, which is used to uniquely identify each row in the table, so that the rows will not contain any duplicates of each other. The key is a specially designated field(s) (column(s)) of the table. A useful feature of a relational database is that the underlying "tables" can be linked up together using the "key field(s)" in another table as a "foreign key." This provides a meaningful relationship between different parts of the data. An example of a BOOK database can be found in Figure 5.1.

The BOOK database system demonstrates part of a typical database model for capturing a sale transaction that might be found in a B2C e-shopping system.

This database consists of three tables, namely Customer table, Transaction table, and sbook table. The Customer table stores all the customer records, and each record contains fields such as "Lastname," "Firstname," "Tel. No.," etc. "Customer_ID" is used as the "primary key." The Transaction table contains all the book order transactions and uses "Transaction_No" as the "primary key." It includes other fields such as "Date," "Customer_ID," "ISBN," number of books being purchased ("Qty"), and the total price ("Total"). The sbook table contains the book inventory. In this example, we are using a simplified book inventory that contains only 13 book records. The sbook table has fields such as book ISBN number ("ISBN"), book name ("Name"), "Author," publisher name ("Publisher"), year of publication ("Year"), and "Price." "ISBN" is used as the "primary key" for the sbook table.

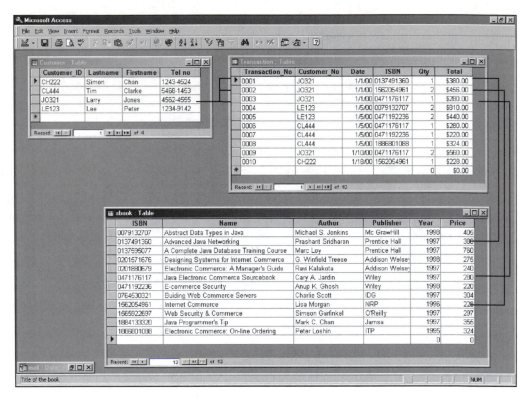

Figure 5.1 A snapshot of BOOK database (Book.mdb) under Ms. Access environment

Note that in Figure 5.1, both the `Customer` table and the `Transaction` table can be "linked" together based on the `"Customer_No"` field. On the other hand, the `Transaction` table and the `sbook` table can be "linked" together by using the `"ISBN"` field, from which we can extract detailed information of the books being purchased (such as the title of the book, the publisher, etc.) for each sale transaction. Figure 5.1 also shows an example of how to extract and link up all the information for the book being purchased by Larry Jones on 1/1/2000 by using the relational database functionality.

5.2.3 Basic SQL statements

In this section we will provide a brief overview of SQL using the BOOK database as an example of how to manipulate a relational database based on SQL commands. This is only a brief discussion to facilitate an understanding of the three-tier e-commerce system.

There are four different basic SQL statements. They are

- SELECT statement
- INSERT statement
- UPDATE statement
- DELETE statement

The SELECT *statement*

The SELECT command produces a "query" to the database table(s) in the sense that according to the user specified "condition(s)," it will "select" the matched records and display them on the output device (e.g. user screen). A typical form of the SELECT statement is given by

SELECT fields **FROM** table **WHERE** criteria

This will select all rows from the table specified that satisfy the criteria and display the fields given in the SELECT part for these rows. An example of a conditional SELECT query on the "sbook" table is shown below:

SELECT ISBN, Name **FROM** sbook **WHERE** Publisher="Wiley"

It retrieves all the records with publisher name "Wiley," and the records will contain only the fields (ISBN, Name) as shown in Figure 5.2.

As described previously, the power of the relational database lies in its ability to link different tables during a query. A composite SQL statement using the "cross-linkage" SELECT query on customer Larry Jones of the BOOK database is shown in the following example:

```
SELECT Customer.Customer_ID, Customer.Firstname,
  Transaction.Transaction_No,
Transaction.ISBN  FROM Customer, Transaction WHERE
  Customer.Customer_ID =
Transaction.Customer_No AND Customer.Customer_ID="JO321"
```

A snapshot of the query result is shown in Figure 5.3.

ISBN	Name
0471176117	Java Electronic Commerce Sourcebook
0471192236	E-commerce Security

Figure 5.2 A conditional query on sbook table

Customer_ID	Firstname	Transaction_No.	ISBN
JO321	Jones	0001	0137491360
JO321	Jones	0002	1562054961
JO321	Jones	0003	0471176117
JO321	Jones	0009	0471176117

Figure 5.3   A composite query on Customer and Transaction tables

In this composite query example, all the transactions for customer Larry Jones are extracted by linking both the `Customer` and `Transaction` tables. Note that in the condition clause, we have to specify the "linkage" or join between the two tables. In this case, they are `"Customer_ID"` from the Customer table and `"Transaction_No"` from the `Transaction` table. This approach for linking tables is known as a "join."

Generally, linking too many tables is likely to slow down the query, and care must be taken when doing this.

The INSERT statement

The `SELECT` statement will only retrieve information but it will not modify the information stored in the database. In order to modify the data, we need to use other SQL commands.

The `INSERT` statement is used to add new rows to a table. In general, it comes in two different forms:

* allows the user to insert only a single new row; and
* allows the user to insert a set of rows to a table using information from another table.

INSERT statement to add a new row.   The typical form of this SQL `INSERT` is

```
INSERT INTO table
(field_name1, field_name2,...,field_nameN)
VALUES (field_value1, field_value2,...,field_valueN)
```

where "`field_name1,..., field_nameN`" and "`field_value1,..., field_valueN`" forms the list of field names and their corresponding values that are being inserted into the table. In case there are more fields in the table than specified in the `INSERT` statement, null or default values are usually entered into the unspecified fields. Note that the `"NOT NULL"` fields must be specified within the `<field list>` of the `INSERT` statement.

Customer_ID	Lastname	Firstname	Tel. No.
CH222	Simon	Chan	1243-4524
CL444	Tim	Clarke	5468-1453
JO321	Larry	Jones	4562-4555
LE123	Lee	Peter	1234-9142
HU133	**Tommy**	**Hunter**	**2478-4699**

Figure 5.4   Effect of INSERT statement to add new record

We can insert an extra row by using the following SQL statement in the Customer table:

```
INSERT INTO Customer
(Customer_ID, Lastname, Firstname, "Tel. No.")
VALUES ("HU133", "Tommy", "Hunter", "2478-4699")
```

We can then display the customer list by using the `"SELECT * from Customer"` statement as shown in Figure 5.4.

INSERT statement to populate a table with records from another table.   As mentioned earlier, another type of the INSERT statement allows one to add rows to a table based on information from another table (see Figure 5.5).
   The typical format is as shown below:

```
INSERT INTO to_table
(field_name1, field_name2,...,field_nameN)
SELECT (field_name1, field_name2,...,field_nameN)
FROM from_table
[WHERE <condition>]
```

Here, `"from_table"` and `"to_table"` represent the source and destination tables for data insertion, respectively. The condition for data insertion is specified in the WHERE clause.
   In the following examples, we take information from the Customer table and insert it as rows in an empty table called BkCustomer in the BOOK database.

Customer_ID	Lastname	Firstname	Contact
CH222	Simon	Chan	1243-4524
CL444	Tim	Clarke	5468-1453
CR443	Jane	Craw	4875-2222

Figure 5.5   Using INSERT statement to populate BkCustomer table from Customer table

Let us assume that the BkCustomer table has the following schema:

```
TABLE BkCustomer
(Customer_ID CHAR(8) NOT NULL,
Lastname CHAR(15) NOT NULL,
Firstname CHAR(15) NOT NULL,
Contact CHAR(15))
```

It can be created with a CREATE statement. The "NOT NULL" fields must contain values for every single row of the table. We can now use the following INSERT statement:

```
INSERT INTO BkCustomer
(Customer_ID, Lastname, Firstname, Contact)
SELECT Customer_ID, Lastname, Firstname, "Tel. No."
FROM Customer
WHERE Firstname LIKE "C%"
```

Note that the field names need not be the same in the two tables. For example, the "Tel. No." field is replaced by the "Contact" field in the BkCustomer table. Secondly, we make use of the LIKE statement in the condition clause, with the "%" used to indicate one or more unknown characters. Thus, only rows with "Firstname" starting with character "C" are inserted into the BkCustomer table.

The UPDATE *statement*

The UPDATE statement is used to update/modify the data within a table. The typical format is

```
UPDATE table
SET field_name1 = field_value1, field_name2 = field_value2,...,
field_nameN = field_valueN
[WHERE <condition>]
```

Using the UPDATE statement, we can also modify the specified record(s) by means of some calculations. For instance, using the Transaction table of the BOOK database, we can update the transaction to (say) "0010" for buying 2 books instead of 1 book and recalculate the total amount as well:

```
UPDATE Transaction
SET Qty = 2, Total = Total * 2
WHERE Transaction_No = "0010"
```

A snapshot of the updated Transaction table is shown in Figure 5.6.

Transaction_No	Customer_No	Date	ISBN	Qty	Total
0001	JO321	1/1/00	0137491360	1	$380.00
0002	JO321	1/1/00	1562054961	2	$456.00
0003	JO321	1/1/00	0471176117	1	$280.00
0004	LE123	1/5/00	0079132707	2	$810.00
0005	LE123	1/5/00	0471192236	2	$440.00
0006	CL444	1/5/00	0471176117	1	$280.00
0007	CL444	1/5/00	0471192236	1	$220.00
0008	CL444	1/5/00	1886801088	1	$324.00
0009	JO321	1/10/00	0471176117	2	$560.00
0010	**CH222**	**1/18/00**	**1562054961**	**2**	**$456.00**

Figure 5.6   Using UPDATE statement to modify data in the Transaction table

The DELETE *statement*

The DELETE statement is used to remove a record or a series of records from a table under the specified condition. The typical form of it is given by

```
DELETE
FROM table
[WHERE <condition>]
```

Using the Customer table as an example, we can delete all the records with Lastname(s) containing the character "i" by using the following statement:

```
DELETE
FROM Customer
WHERE Lastname LIKE "%i%"
```

In this example, two records with lastnames "Tim" and "Sim" will be deleted from the table, and the resulting Customer table is shown in Figure 5.7.

Customer_ID	Lastname	Firstname	Tel. No.
CH222	Chan	Simon	1243-4524
CR443	Jane	Craw	4875-2222
JO321	Larry	Jones	4562-4555
HU133	Tommy	Hunter	2478-4699
LE123	Lee	Peter	1234-9142

Figure 5.7   Customer table after the DELETE operation

5.3 *JDBC PERSPECTIVES*

5.3.1 What is JDBC?

JDBC (Java Database Connectivity) is an API specification that provides a set of interfaces and classes to perform database-related operations developed by JavaSoft. The JDBC specification can be obtained from JavaSoft at `http://java.sun.com/products/jdbc/index.html`.

Java Programs, Java Servlets, and Java Beans applications can, through integration with JDBC, execute SQL statements to access, display, and modify the backend database systems; that is, the primary purpose of JDBC is to provide connectivity with a database in a layered fashion. Provided a database is JDBC enabled (i.e., it has JDBC drivers provided), replacement of one database by another does not require reprogramming of the application.

Thus, JDBC allows one to develop portable database-related applications. This is useful if the development of a prototype is frequently carried out on one platform and then migrated to another platform on a corporate server.

5.3.2 Layered infrastructure of JDBC

To understand the manner in which JDBC-based programs interact with a database system, let us take a look at the schematic diagram of the JDBC infrastructure as shown in Figure 5.8. This reveals the layered approach used in the JDBC infrastructure. At the highest layer, Java applications access and execute SQL statements via the JDBC APIs, in the `java.sql` package. The java.sql package contains only interfaces to the actual SQL-level implementations supplied by third-party database vendors and does not provide the actual implementations.

The application accesses the database system via the JDBC "Driver Manager," which is the next lower layer. This provides a connection to the specific JDBC drivers for the particular database system that implements the java.sql.Driver interface. Note that the JDBC API specification sets out the requirements for the drivers. Most of the popular RDBMS systems, such as Oracle, Sybase, and Informix, provide a JDBC driver, which comes with the database engine, or is an integrated part of their application servers.

5.3.3 The JDBC drivers

Generally, one can distinguish between four different types of JDBC drivers, and they are [Moss, 1998; Hunter and Crawford, 1998]

- *Type 1*: JDBC–ODBC bridge

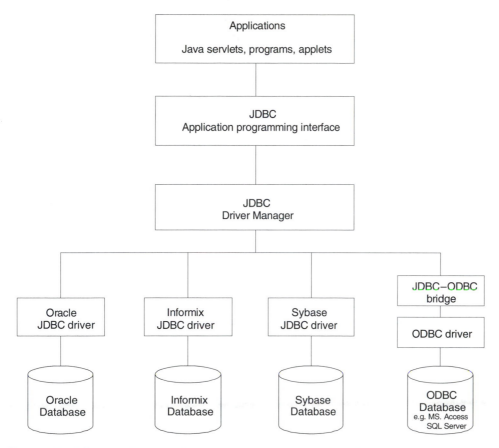

Figure 5.8 Schematic diagram of JDBC infrastructure (based on the works of Moss [1998] and Callway [1999])

- *Type 2*: Native API partly technology enabled driver
- *Type 3*: Pure Java driver for database middleware
- *Type 4*: Direct to database pure Java driver

The JDBC–ODBC bridge provides connectivity between the JDBC API and the Microsoft's ODBC drivers. This allows one to access ODBC-enabled databases such as MS-Access and MS-SQL server. It is included with the Java Development Kit (from version 1.1). The JDBC–ODBC bridge has the following advantages [Moss, 1998; Williamson, 1999], namely, it provides simple, low-cost connectivity particularly for systems that provide an ODBC driver but not a JDBC one. On the other hand, the approach depends on the reliability and performance of the ODBC driver and "inherits" some of the problems of the existing ODBC drivers, namely "limited and unstable" concurrent access functionality. Generally speaking, it is more useful for prototyping than building full-blown industrial strength applications.

Type 2 JDBC driver integrates a thin layer of Java code with the proprietary native codes (mainly C, C++, or assembly code) provided by the database manufacturers. This type of driver is faster than the JDBC–ODBC bridge. However, it still suffers from the shortcomings "inherited" from the native code. Thus, defects in the driver native code create a risk of crashing the whole system.

Unlike the Type 2 JDBC drivers which make use of native code for driver programming, the Type 3 JDBC drivers use 100% Java code for database connection using a "middleware" technology approach. These frequently use propriety network protocols specified by the driver developer.

The Type 4 JDBC drivers are also written in 100% pure Java code. Using their native protocols, Type 4 JDBC drivers communicate directly with the database. This is unlike Type 3 JDBC drivers which are integrated with the Java middleware. Among the four types of drivers, Type 4 JDBC drivers usually provide the best performance, since no middleware is involved. However, due to the propriety nature of Type 4 JDBC drivers, they may not provide a portable solution (i.e., when the database is changed, a new driver may be needed).

5.3.4   JDBC API

Basically, there are four fundamental classes in the JDBC API, namely [Williamson, 1999]

1. java.sql.DriverManager
2. java.sql.Connection
3. java.sql.Statement
4. java.sql.Resultset

The first two classes, `java.sql.DriverManager` and `java.sql.Connection`, are mainly for loading the database driver and making the database connection. The class `java.sql.Statement` is for creating a statement for processing the database query, and the class `java.sql.Resultset` is for storing the query results. Making use of these classes, the JDBC operation is almost the same whether we use a standalone Java program, an applet in a browser, or a servlet on a server. To demonstrate the JDBC operation, we will create a simple book search engine for our VBS. In Section 5.4, first of all, we will present a simple book query example to demonstrate the integration of servlet and JDBC using the JDBC–ODBC bridge and Microsoft Access. In most e-commerce systems, search results are presented in multiple pages. In Section 5.5, we will extend the example from Section 5.4 to present the search results in multiple pages. Finally, we will present an overview of the Advanced Book Search Engine for our VBS.

5.4 A JDBC PROGRAM EXAMPLE: SIMPLE SERVLET BOOK QUERY

5.4.1 Preparing for your first JDBC program

In this section, we will start with a JDBC programming illustration with a simple servlet book query Java program. We will still make use of the BOOK database (a simple MS Access database) to send a SELECT SQL statement to the sbook table (a simple book inventory that contains less than 20 books, see Figure 5.9) in order to display the book list on the browser. Throughout the program, we will make use of a JDBC–ODBC bridge and demonstrate the whole workflow involved in creating the database, setting up the ODBC links in your backend Web server, and programming the interactions for this example.

To start with, we need to do the following:

- create a Microsoft (MS) Access database;
- create an ODBC link; and
- compile and execute the Java JDBC servlet.

ISBN	Name	Author	Publisher	Year	Price
0079132707	Abstract Data Types in Java	Michael S. Jenkins	Mc GrawHill	1998	405
0137491360	Advanced Java Networking	Prashant Sridharan	Prentice Hall	1997	380
0137595077	A Complete Java Database Training Course	Marc Loy	Prentice Hall	1997	760
0201571676	Designing Systems for Internet Commerce	G. Winfield Treese	Addison Welsey	1998	275
0201880679	Electronic Commerce: A Manager's Guide	Ravi Kalakota	Addison Welsey	1997	240
0471176117	Java Electronic Commerce Sourcebook	Cary A. Jardin	Wiley	1997	280
0471192236	E-commerce Security	Anup K. Ghosh	Wiley	1998	220
0764530321	Buiding Web Commerce Servers	Charlie Scott	IDG	1997	304
1562054961	Internet Commerce	Lisa Morgan	NRP	1996	228
1565922697	Web Security & Commerce	Simson Garfinkel	O'Reilly	1997	297
1884133320	Java Programmer's Tip	Mark C. Chan	Jamsa	1997	355
1886801088	Electronic Commerce: On-line Ordering	Peter Loshin	ITP	1995	324

Figure 5.9 The sbook table

Step 1: Create the BOOK database

Create an Access database, namely `"sbook.mdb"` Create a table, namely `"sbook"` and create the table structure as follows:

- ISBN: Text [10] (primary field) – Book ISBN
- Name: Text [50] – Book name
- Author: Text [50] – Author name
- Publisher: Text [30] – Publisher name
- Year: Number – Year of publication
- Price: Number – Book price

Type the content of the book information as given in Figure 5.9.

Step 2: Create the ODBC link

In order to create an ODBC link, one can invoke the ODBC administration program from the control panel. It is essential to select a new data source and link it to an MS Access database by selecting the appropriate ODBC driver and naming and selecting the required database. The steps involved once ODBC administration has been invoked are

1. Click Add button.
2. Click on MS Access driver.
3. Input `"Data Source Name"` and `"Description"` (see Figure 5.10).
4. Select the `"sbook.mdb"` database you have created in Step 1.
5. Click on OK button and finish the setup.

This will complete the creation of the ODBC link.

Step 3: Compile and run the program

- Compile the program listed in the next section.
- Study the program carefully and learn the program logic flow.
- Test the program on your local computer and see the result.

5.4.2 Simple Book Query – ServletBookquery

From the programming point of view, the usage of the servlet JDBC is a simple and straightforward combination of the programming techniques that you have already

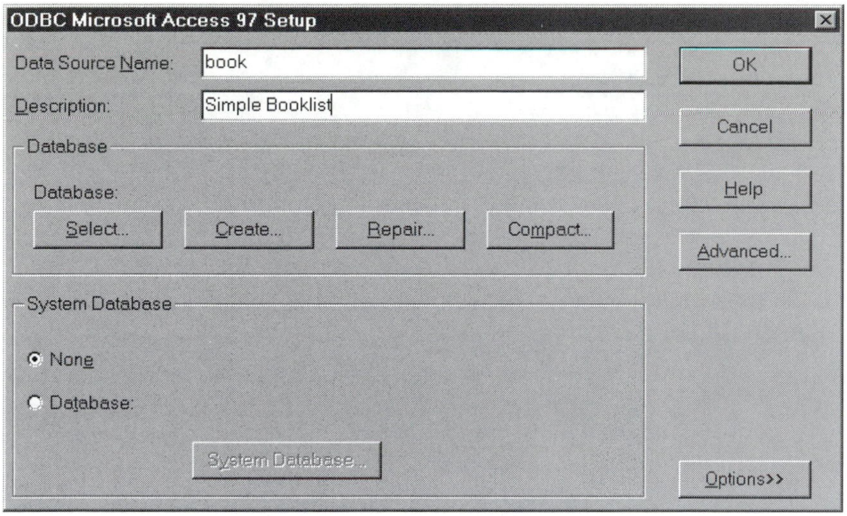

Figure 5.10   The ODBC setup screen

learnt previously, including

• HTML form;
• servlet programming technique;
• SQL statement generation; and
• JDBC programming method.

The whole program listing of your first Java JDBC servlet – `ServletBook-query.java` is listed in Figure 5.11.

Let us go through the main points of the program. First, we need to set up a database connection. This involves the creation of a driver object as follows:

```
Class.forName("sun.jdbc.odbc.JdbcOdbcDriver").newInstance().
```

Then we need to set up a database connection by using the following statement:

```
Connection connection = DriverManager.
  getConnection("jdbc:odbc:mall"):
```

Each JDBC connection is specified by a URL with the following format:

```
jdbc: [subprotocol]:[subname].
```

```java
package vbs.chapter; // use your own package instead
import javax.servlet.*;
import javax.servlet.http.*;
import java.sql.*;
import java.io.*;

public class ServletBookquery extends HttpServlet
{

  public void doGet(HttpServletRequest req, HttpServletResponse
    resp) throws ServletException, IOException
  {

    // Specify the content type
    resp.setContentType("text/html");

    // Get a PrintWriter object for writing the response
    PrintWriter out = resp.getWriter();

    // Create a SQL query
    String sqlQuery = "SELECT Name, Author, ISBN, Price FROM sbook";

    try{

    // Create a database driver
    Class.forName("sun.jdbc.odbc.JdbcOdbcDriver").newInstance();

    // Create a database connection
    Connection connection = DriverManager.
      getConnection("jdbc:odbc:book");

    // Create a statement object for handling SQL query
    Statement statement = connection.createStatement();

    // Execute the query
    ResultSet resultSet = statement.executeQuery(sqlQuery);

    // Display the results

    out.println("<html><head>");
    out.println("<title>Book query</title></head>");
```

Figure 5.11   Program listing of ServletBookquery.java

```java
out.println("<img src=\"/vbs/chapter/vbsbanner.jpg\">");
out.println("<br><body>");

String fcolor = "";
int record_no = 0;

while (resultSet.next()) {
 record_no++;
 // Use alternative color for displaying the table rows
 if ((record_no % 2) == 0){
  fcolor ="#0000FF";
 }else{
  fcolor ="#000000";
 }

// Display the book record
out.println("<p><font face=\"Arial\" size=\"3\"><strong>
  <font color=\""+fcolor+"\">"+record_no+".
  "+resultSet.getString(1)+"</font></strong><br>");

// Display the author name
out.println("<font face=\"Arial\" size=\"2\"><font
  color=\""+fcolor+"\"><em>    by
  "+resultSet.getString(2)+"</em><br>");

// Display the ISBN
out.println("    ISBN No:
  "+resultSet.getString(3)+"<br>");

// Display the price
out.println("    Our Price:$
  "+resultSet.getString(4)+"<p>");
}

out.println("</body></html>");

// Close the following objects
resultSet.close();
statement.close();
connection.close();
out.flush();
out.close();
}
```

```
catch (ClassNotFoundException e){
System.out.println("JDBC-ODBC bridge cannot be loaded!");
}
catch (SQLException e){
System.out.println("SQL exception error!");
}
catch (Exception e){
// Print the exceptions
e.printStackTrace(out);
}
}
}
```

Figure 5.11   (*Continued*)

The `"subprotocol"` specifies the subprotocol used for the database connection (e.g., ODBC in our example) and the `"subname"` refers to the name of the database connection (in our case this is the ODBC link, namely `"book"`).

Having established the database connection, we need to create a `Statement` object as follows:

```
Statement statement = connection.createStatement();
```

The next step is to execute the SQL query and store the results in the `ResultSet` object as shown below:

```
ResultSet resultSet = statement.executeQuery(sqlQuery):
```

In this example, `"sqlQuery"` is the SQL statement for the query that is invoked by using the `executeQuery()` method of the Statement object.

Note that we have used the Statement object and the `createStatement()` method to bind and execute the SQL statement. Alternatively, one can use a prepareStatement object and the `prepareStatement()` method. This can speed up the execution time of the SQL statement as the prepareStatement is precompiled.

It is important to note that when using SQL statements, such as `"INSERT,"` `"DELETE,"` or `"UPDATE"` commands, we need to invoke the `executeUpdate()` method (i.e., `statement.executeQuery(query)`). In this case, the system will return a value only for the number of records (rows) being operated on by the SQL statement rather than returning a query table.

In the program, the query results returned are in the form of a table, which is "serialized" and "contained" in the `resultSet` object. We can use the `getString()`

method to retrieve the query result. In our example, the result table has four columns (data fields). We can use a `"while-loop"` to retrieve all the table contents. For each table row, a series of `resultSet.getString()` methods are used to extract all the data fields (including book title, author name, ISBN number, and price). After that, the `resultSet.next()` method is invoked to advance to the next record, until all the records in the query result table have been retrieved.

Finally, we need to close the objects accordingly as follows:

```
resultSet.close();
statement.close();
connection.close();
```

Furthermore, we also need to handle possible exceptions.

It is worth mentioning that if we want to present the search results in a table, we can make use of the `ResultSetMetaData` object to obtain the number of columns and header names of the query results. First, we set up a `ResultSetMetaData` object as follows:

```
ResultSetMetaData rsMetaData = resultSet.getMetaData();
```

Second, we can find out the number of columns by using the `"getColumnCount"` method, that is

```
int column_no = rsMetaData.getColumnCount();
```

The header field for the *i*th column can then be obtained by the `getColumnLabel` method as follows:

```
rsMetaData.getColumnLabel(i);
```

By using a `for-to-loop`, the header fields can then be printed. Finally, the data for the table can be printed using the `"getString"` method similar to above.

The `ResultSetMetaData` object is particularly useful in a complex database schema scenario because it provides a "generic" method for displaying data.

5.4.3 ServletBookquery – Program summary

To summarize, this program makes use of the "general" structure for building a servlet program and for construction of the servlet class `ServletBookquery`, which is an extended class from the `"HttpServlet"` class. Secondly, we make use of the

PrintWriter object "out" to drive the data via the HttpServletResponse object "resp" in the program.

For displaying the results, we make use of the getString() method within the do-while loop to print out all the query output:

```
//Display record no and book title
out.println("<p><font face=\"Arial\" size=\"3\"><strong>
  <font color=\""+fcolor+"\">"+record_no+".
"+resultSet.getString(1)+"</font></strong><br>");
//Display author name
out.println("<font face=\"Arial\" size=\"2\">
  <font color=\""+fcolor+"\"><em>   by
"+resultSet.getString(2)+"</em><br>");
//Display ISBN
out.println("   ISBN No:"+resultSet.getString(3)
  +"<br>");
//Display price
out.println("   Our Price:$"+resultSet.getString(4)
  +"<p>");
```

Furthermore, for ease of reading, we print out the even number rows and the odd number rows in different colors. This is done by setting a different font color (fcolor) for each table row as follows:

```
if ((record_no % 2) == 0){
    fcolor ="#0000FF";
}else{
    fcolor ="#000000";
}
```

where record_no is the row number.

The output generated by execution of the ServletBookQuery program is displayed in Figure 5.12.

5.5 *AN ADVANCED BOOK QUERY: SERVLETBookquerymulti*

As mentioned, nearly all search engines present query results in multiple pages (e.g., with each page containing 6–10 items). A customer can access a page by clicking the respective "page pointer" at the bottom of each page. As an extension of the previous program, the following program ServletBookquerymulti.java in Figure 5.13 provides this useful function.

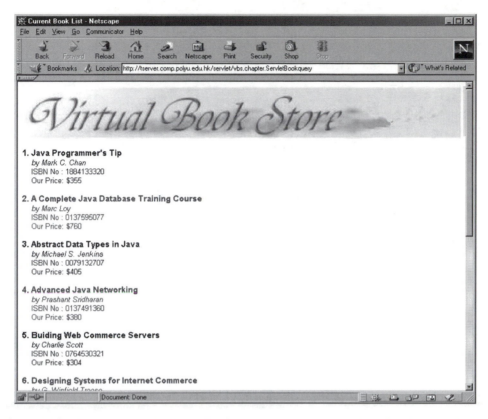

Figure 5.12 A snapshot of the ServletBookquery program output (Note that the records are for illustration only)

In this program, we make use of a book list containing more than 40 records – the bookstore table in the `BOOK.mdb` database. To control the listing of books, we need to keep track of the books already listed. We use a hidden form field called `prevISBN` for this purpose. In general, this hidden form field stores the `ISBN` number of the book listed in the previous HTML query table. This is based on a similar approach used by Moss [1998], but our program provides multiple page pointers.

In order to do this, firstly, we have to retrieve the `prevISBN` field by using the `getParameter("prevISBN")` method:

```
String prevISBN = req.getParameter("prevISBN");
```

In the enhanced program, two methods called `"booksearch"` and `"display-Results"` are written to handle the book search and to display the search results,

```java
package vbs.chapter;

import javax.servlet.*;
import javax.servlet.http.*;
import java.sql.*;
import java.io.*;
import java.util.*;

public class ServletBookquerymulti extends HttpServlet
{

  public void doGet(HttpServletRequest req, HttpServletResponse
    resp)
  throws ServletException, IOException
  {
      // Get the previous ISBNdisplayed
      String prevISBN = req.getParameter("prevISBN");

      // Set prevISBN="0" initially
      if (prevISBN == null)
      {
       prevISBN = "0";
      }

      // Specify the content type
      resp.setContentType("text/html");

      // Get a PrintWriter object
      PrintWriter out = resp.getWriter();

      // Set up the SQL query (sorted by ISBN in ascending order)
      String sqlQuery = "SELECT Name, Author, ISBN, Price FROM
        bookstore order by ISBN";

      // Process the query
      booksearch(prevISBN, out, sqlQuery);

      // Close stream
      out.flush();
      out.close();
  }
```

Figure 5.13   Program listing ServletBookquerymulti.java

```java
public void doPost(HttpServletRequest req, HttpServletResponse
    resp)
throws ServletException, IOException
{
    // Call doGet
    doGet(req, resp);
}


// Process the query
private void booksearch(String prevISBN, PrintWriter out,
    String sqlquery)
{
        try{
            // Create a JDBC_ODBC driver
            Class.forName("sun.jdbc.odbc.JdbcOdbcDriver").
                newInstance();

            // Create a database connection.
            Connection connection = DriverManager.
             getConnection("jdbc:odbc:book");

            // Create a statement object for processing the query
            Statement statement = connection.createStatement();

            // Process the SQL query
            ResultSet resultSet = statement.executeQuery(sqlquery);

            // Display the results
            displayResults(prevISBN, out, resultSet);

            // Close resultSet, statement and connection objects
            resultSet.close();
            statement.close();
            connection.close();
}
catch (ClassNotFoundException e){
 System.out.println("JDBC-ODBC bridge cannot load!");
}
catch (SQLException e){
 System.out.println("SQL exception error!");
}
```

```
        catch (Exception e){
                // Print the exceptions
                e.printStackTrace(out);
        }
}
// Display the results
private void displayResults(String prevISBN, PrintWriter out,
  ResultSet resultSet)
throws Exception
{
  Vector isbn = new Vector();
  String currentISBN ="";
  int maxRows = 6, sizeCount = 0;

  //The ISBN for the 1st page is 0
  isbn.addElement("0");

  // Display the results
  int record_no = 0;
  String fcolor ="";

  // Write the response
  out.println("<html><head>");
  out.println("<title>Book query</title></head>");
  out.println("<img src=\"/vbs/chapter/vbsbanner.jpg\">");
  out.println("<br><body>");

  while (resultSet.next()) {
    record_no++;
    // Use alternative color for the table rows
    if ((record_no % 2) == 0){
       fcolor ="#0000FF";
    }else{
       fcolor ="#000000";
    }

    // Get current ISBN
    currentISBN = resultSet.getString(3);

    //Display the records after the prevISBN and up to the
      maximum number of rows
    if(currentISBN.compareTo(prevISBN)>0&&sizeCount<maxRows)
```

Figure 5.13   *(Continued)*

```
        sizeCount++;

        // Display book records
        // Display record number and book title
        out.println("<p><font face=\"Arial\" size=\"3\"><strong>
          <font color=\""+fcolor+"\">"+record_no+".
          "+resultSet.getString(1)+"</font></strong> ");

        // Display author's name
        out.println("<font face=\"Arial\" size=\"2\">
         <font color=\""+fcolor+"\"><em>by
          "+resultSet.getString(2)+"</em><br>");

        // Display ISBN
        out.println("   ISBN No:
          "+currentISBN+"<br>");

        // Display price
        out.println("    Our Price:
          "+resultSet.getString(4)+"<p>");
    }

    //Store the ISBN of the "boundary page" for building the
      index later
    if(record_no%maxRows == 0){
      isbn.addElement(currentISBN);
    }
  }

  // Display the index (page pointers)
  out.println("<br><hr>Go to page:");
  out.println("<center><table border=0><tr>");

  for(int i=0;i<isbn.size();i++){
        out.println("<td><form name=index"+(i+1)+"method=POST
action=/servlet/vbs.chapter.ServletBookquerymulti>");
        out.println("<input type=hidden name=prevISBN value="
          +isbn.elementAt(i)+">");
        out.println("<a href=\"/\"onclick=\"document.index"+(i+1)
          +".submit(); return false;\">"+(i+1)+"</a>");
        out.println("</form></td>");
  }
```

```
out.println("</tr></table></center>");
out.println("</body></html>");
}
}
```

Figure 5.13   (*Continued*)

respectively. The `"prevISBN,"` `"out"` object, and the SQL query statement are passed to the `"booksearch"` method for processing. After searching, the `"displayResults"` method prints a record only if the corresponding ISBN is greater than the previous ISBN and the number of records has not exceeded the limit.

We also need page pointers to keep track of the different pages of the query results. A vector object `"isbn"` is used to store the `"boundary isbn"` for each page. For example, isbn(2) stores the ISBN of the last book in page 1. Note that isbn(1) is zero.

Finally, in the `"displayResults"` method, the prevISBN data will pass as HTML output using the `"Hidden Form Field"` element, whereas the list of "page pointers" is generated accordingly within the `"for"` loop as follows:

```
for(int i=0;i<isbn.size();i++){
out.println("<td><form name=index"+(i+1)+"method=POSTaction=
  /servlet/vbs.chapter.ServletBookquerymult>");
out.println("<input type=hidden name=prevISBN value="+isbn.
  elementAt(i) +">");
out.println("<a href=\"/\"onclick=\"document.index"+(i+1)+".
  submit(); return false;\">"+(i+1)+"</a>");
out.println("</form></td>");
}
```

Basically, there are *i* forms each corresponding to a page. The forms for the 1st, 2nd pages, etc. are called index1, index2, etc. By using the `"onclick"` command, it can be determined which form, and hence which page, is selected. Note that the $(i+1)$th element of the `"isbn"` vector gives the ISBN of the last book at the *i*th page (i.e. the previous page). Hence, it can be used to determine the first book on the next page. The detailed mechanism is shown in the program.

A snapshot of the program output is shown in Figure 5.14.

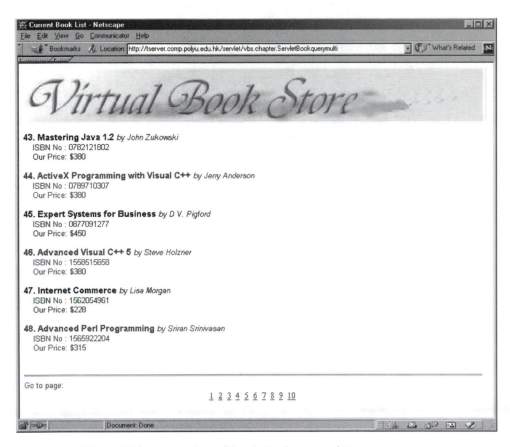

Figure 5.14   A snapshot of ServletBookquerymulti program output

5.6   ADVANCED JDBC SERVLET: VBS ADVANCE BOOK SEARCH ENGINE

5.6.1   VBS advance book search engine

One of the major components of the VBS is the advance book search engine. A book search servlet JDBC program (`SearchEngine.java`) is given in Chapter 15, which allows users to perform a book search according to the following categories:

- Author name
- Book title

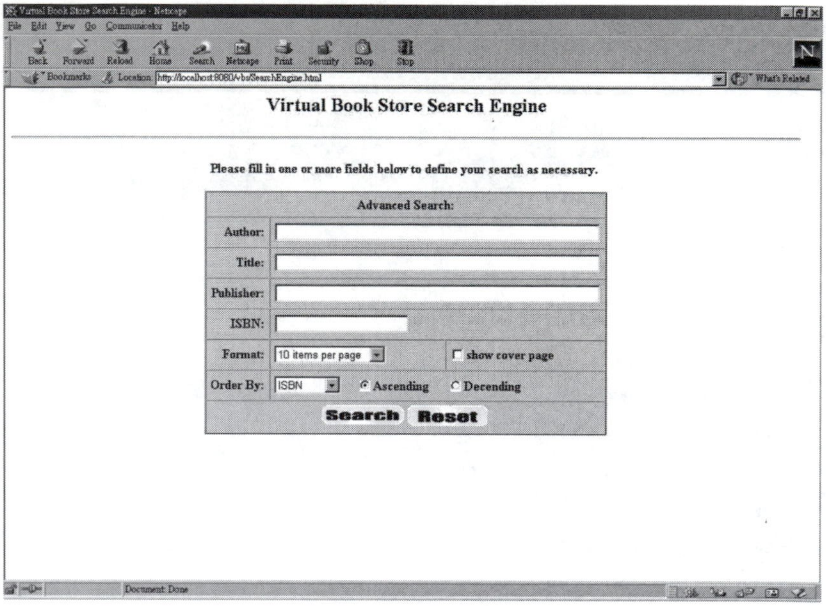

Figure 5.15   A snapshot of the Advance Book Search Engine

- Publisher name
- ISBN number

In addition to this function, the search engine provides the following additional facilities:

- Users can choose whether or not to see the book cover image in the search result.
- Users can choose the number of books being displayed on each page.
- Users can sort the search results under different categories and choose the order in which they are displayed (either ascending or descending order).

A snapshot of the Advance Book Search Engine HTML form is shown in Figure 5.15, and the corresponding HTML document is given in Figure 5.16.

5.6.2   How does the SearchEngine.java work?

The basic program logic for the `SearchEngine` servlet is similar to the `Servlet-Bookquerymulti.java` program, namely

```
<html>

<head>
<title>Virtual Book Store Search Engine</title>
</head>

<body bgcolor="#FFFFFF">
<!--- Title of this Page --->
<h2 align="center">Virtual Book Store Search Engine</h2>
<hr align="center">
<b>
<p align="center">Please fill in one or more fields below to
  define your search as necessary.</b> </p>

<form name="search" action="/servlet/vbs.mall.searchengine.
  SearchEngine" method="get">
 <div align="center"><center><table border="1"
   cellpadding="5" cellspacing="0"
 bgcolor="#FFCC99" bordercolor="black">
  <tr>
    <td align="center" colspan="3"><b>Advanced Search:<b></td>
  </tr>

<!--- Authors Field --->
  <tr>
    <td align="right" nowrap><b>Author:</b></td>
    <td colspan="2"><input type="text" size="50" maxlength="50"
      name="author"></td>
  </tr>
<!--- Title Field --->
  <tr>
    <td align="right" nowrap><b>Title:</b></td>
    <td colspan="2"><input type="text" size="50" maxlength="50"
      name="name"></td>
  </tr>

<!--- Publisher Field --->
  <tr>
    <td align="right" nowrap><b>Publisher:</b></td>
    <td colspan="2"><input type="text" size="50" maxlength="50"
      name="publisher"></td>
  </tr>
```

Figure 5.16   HTML document of the Advance Book Search Engine Form

```html
<!--- ISBN Field --->
  <tr>
    <td align="right" nowrap><b>ISBN:</b></td>
    <td colspan="2"><input type="text" size="20" maxlength="20"
      name="isbn"></td>
  </tr>

<! --- Format --->
  <tr>
    <td align="right" nowrap><b>Format:</b></td>
    <td align="left"><select name="itemsperpage" size="1">
     <option value="10" selected>10 items per page</option>
     <option value="20">20 items per page</option>
     <option value="50">50 items per page</option>
    </select></td>
    <td><input type="checkbox" name="textonlyflag" value="ON">
   <b>show cover page</b></td>
  </tr>

<! --- Order Field --->
  <tr>
    <td align="right" nowrap><b>Order By:</b></td>
    <td align="left" colspan="2"><select name="orderby" size="1">
     <option value="isbn" selected>ISBN   </option>
     <option value="price">Price   </option>
     <option value="year">Year   </option>
     </select>     <input type="radio"
       name="orderasc" value="true" checked><b>Ascending</b>
            
     <input type="radio" name="orderasc" value="false">
     <b>Decending</b></td>
  </tr>

<!--- Clear / Submit Buttons --->
  <tr>
   <td align="center" colspan="3"><a href="/servlet/vbs.mall.
     searchengine.searchengine"
   onClick="document.search.submit(); return false;"><img
   src="/vbs/mall/images/searchbutton.gif" alt="Search" border="0"
   width="105" height="25"></a><a href="/servlet/vbs.
     mall.searchengine.searchengine"
```

Figure 5.16 (*Continued*)

```
  onClick="document.search.reset(); return false;"><img
  src="/vbs/mall/images/resetbutton.gif" alt="Reset" border="0"
  width="100" height="25"></a> </td>
 </tr>
 </table>
 </center></div>
</form>
</body>
</html>
```

Figure 5.16   (*Continued*)

1. Perform program initialization (e.g. get the hidden form element(s)).

2. Create the SQL statement.

3. Call the `booksearch()` method.

4. Execute the SQL statement.

5. Display the query result using the `displayResult()` method.

The only difference is that the `SearchEngine` adds several search elements (i.e. criteria) via the HTML form, which are included in a SQL statement before it is submitted to the `booksearch()` method. If the search results are over one page long, one could use the Hidden Form Field technique to move these to the output result HTML page.

As an exercise, we are going to build a complete "search engine" in Chapter 15. Figure 5.17 shows a snapshot of the search results page.

5.7   SUMMARY

In this chapter, we have considered the basic concepts of relational database systems, the syntax of SQL statements, and the usage of some fundamental SQL commands.

We have also set out the basis of JDBC, discussed what it is, the basic infrastructure of JDBC, and different types of JDBC drivers that exist in the market. Using the book query program as an example, we have discussed how to build the following JDBC programs:

• a simple `Bookquery` Java program using JDBC;

• a simple servlet-based book query program – `ServletBookquery`; and

• a multipage servlet book query program – `ServletBookquerymulti`.

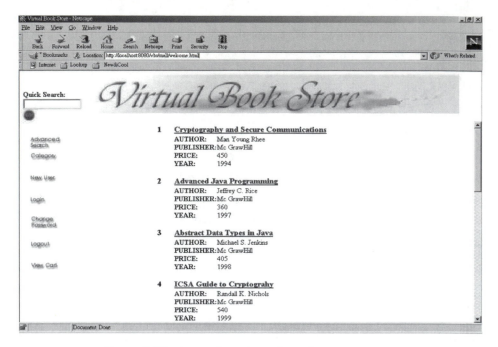

Figure 5.17   A snapshot of search results screen output

Finally, we have introduced the advanced book search engine, the `SearchEngine` program – one of the major components of the VBS project, and described how the program is developed based on what we have set out in this chapter.

REFERENCES

Callway, D. R., *Inside Servlets*, Addison-Wesley, Reading, MA, 1999.
Hunter, J. and Crawford, W., *Java Servlet Programming*, O'Reilly & Associates, Inc., 1998.
Moss, K., *Java Servlets*, McGraw-Hill, New York, 1998.
Williamson, A. R., *Java Servlets: By Example*, Manning Publications Co., 1999.

RECOMMENDED READING

Moss, K., *Java Servlets*, McGraw-Hill, New York, 1998.
Hunter, J. and Crawford, W., *Java Servlet Programming*, O'Reilly & Associates, Inc., 1998.

Williamson, A. R., *Java Servlets: By Example*, Manning Publications Co., 1999.

Callway, D. R., *Inside Servlets*, Addison-Wesley, Reading, MA, 1999.

These are some very valuable books on Java Database Connectivity (JDBC) using Java Servlet technology.

Hamilton, G., Catell, R. G. G., and Fisher, M., *JDBC Database Access with Java*, Addison-Wesley Longman, Reading, MA, 1997.

Taylor, A., *JDBC Developer's Resource: Database Programming on the Internet*, Prentice-Hall, Upper Saddle River, NJ, 1997.

These are good references for readers who want to have an in-depth knowledge of JDBC.

Groff, J. R. and Weinberg, P. N., *SQL: The Complete Reference*. McGraw-Hill, New York, 1999.

This is a worthwhile reference for a complete discussion of SQL.

Simovici, D. A., *Relational Database Systems*, Academic Press, New York, 1995.

Ozsu, M. T., *Principles of Distributed Database System*, Prentice-Hall, Upper Saddle River, NJ, 1996.

These books provide good starting points for readers who are interested in relational database (and more explicitly, distributed databases).

The SQL statements and the JDBC infrastructure presented in this chapter are generic in the sense that they are useful for the system developer who would like to integrate the web system with any types of database systems. However, if readers would like to know more about the database connectivity with their own database system in detail, they can refer to the following for the Oracle system, the SQL Server, the MS Access, and the Sybase system, respectively:

Koch, G., *Oracle 8: A Complete Reference*, Osborne/McGraw-Hill, Berkeley, CA, 1997.

Coffman, G., *SQL Server 7: The Complete Reference*, Osborne/McGraw-Hill, Berkeley, CA, 1999.

Hobuss, J. J., *Building Access Web Sites*, Prentice-Hall, Upper Saddle River, NJ, 1998a.

Hobuss, J. J., *Building Sybase Web Sites*, Prentice-Hall, Upper Saddle River, NJ, 1998b.

6

Server-Side Programming III: Session Tracking

6.1 Introduction

6.2 Traditional Session Tracking Techniques

6.3 The Servlet Session Tracking API

6.4 A Practical Case: VBS Shopping Cart

6.5 Summary

References

Recommended Reading

In the previous two chapters, we covered the key server-side programming techniques for supporting e-commerce applications, including basic server-side programming tools and database connectivity.

Maintaining user state (commonly referred to as "session tracking") is one of the fundamental requirements in e-commerce applications. For example, in B2C e-commerce systems such as a virtual shopping mall, one needs to keep track of the user's "shopping cart." In B2B e-commerce systems, it is important to handle and maintain login transactions.

In this chapter, we first discuss and compare the traditional session tracking techniques including cookies and hidden form fields. Then we present the Java Servlet session tracking API with some examples to illustrate its application.

6.1 *INTRODUCTION*

6.1.1   A realistic case in session tracking: Shopping in VBS

In previous chapters, we learned various programming techniques for building a virtual store, including

- Client-Side Programming: how to build web pages using HTML and JavaScript.
- Server-Side Programming I (Servlet Fundamentals): how to write simple server-side programs with Java Servlet.
- Server-Side Programming II (Database Connectivity): how to communicate with the backend database systems, using Java Servlet and JDBC technologies.

To implement a simple virtual store such as the e-pizza ordering store as shown in Figure 6.1, users are usually provided with an electronic form (e-form) to fill in the order. After submitting the form to the server, the order can then be processed accordingly.

This approach is fine for a simple "e-retail business," which carries a small number of products. For large e-retail businesses, it is impractical to display all the products on a single e-form.

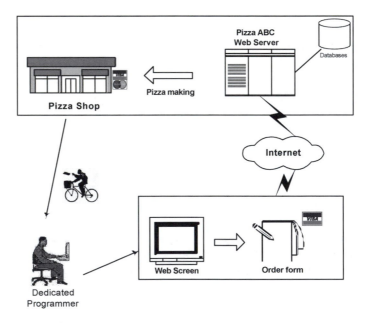

Figure 6.1   A pizza order scenario using the e-form mechanism

Let us look at a "physical" shopping scenario, for example, shopping in a super-market. The shopping process is as follows:

- enter the supermarket;
- get a shopping cart;
- walk around the store;
- choose the goods and put them into the shopping cart; and
- finally check out at the cashier's counter.

To emulate the above shopping process in the cyber world, we need to implement a shopping cart.

6.1.2 Issues involved in implementing the *shopping cart* object in the internet environment

Technically speaking, it is not difficult to build a shopping cart object. The main problem is how to manage it in a web-based e-commerce system because the HTTP is stateless.

Generally speaking, there are two issues to be resolved. The first one is how to assign and map a shopping cart to a user. Note that in most B2C e-commerce systems, a user does not need to log into the system before shopping. The second issue is how to keep track of the shopping cart and its contents. This means that by using only the stateless HTTP, a web server does not know whether the current request is from a previous client or from a new client. During an e-shopping situation, we may access the VBS, get a shopping cart, and then browse another web site for a while before returning to the VBS again. The challenge is how to "get back" the previous shopping cart, in order to continue shopping instead of restarting from the beginning. The solution is session tracking.

In this chapter, we will examine the traditional session tracking techniques including Hidden Form Field, URL rewriting, HTTP user authorization, and Cookies. In addition, we will discuss the servlet session tracking API for supporting user authentication and building the shopping cart.

6.2 *TRADITIONAL SESSION TRACKING TECHNIQUES*

To support session tracking for web-based applications, a number of techniques have been developed. The following are the most common ones [Hunter and Crawford, 1998; Callway, 1999]:

- Hidden form field
- URL rewriting
- HTTP user authentication
- Cookies

In this section, we give an overview of these techniques and compare their advantages and disadvantages.

6.2.1   Hidden form field

As part of the HTML standard, Hidden Form Field (HFF) provides a simple solution to session tracking. In fact, in Chapter 5 we talked about the use of HFF for implementing the "book search" program. For instance, in the "Advanced Book Search Engine" example, the whole workflow is as follows:

- First, the user browses the "Advanced Book Search" web page, which provides an HTML form for the user to fill in the search criteria for the book required, such as book name, publisher name, ISBN number, year of publication, etc.
- After submitting the form to the VBS web server, the corresponding servlet program `"SearchEngine"` is launched.
- In the VBS web server, the servlet engine processes the request, parses the search criterion, and executes the SQL statement.
- Once the search result is obtained, the program formats the information using HTML and returns it to the user browser for display.
- If the search result consists of multiple pages, some page pointers are presented to guide the user to the desired page.
- The program uses HFF to return the search criteria together with the previous ISBN of the book being displayed. Hence, the books can be displayed accordingly.

In fact, this already demonstrates a simple session.

Let us study how HFF can be used to implement a simple shopping cart. The general format of HFF is as follows:

```
<FORM ACTION="your_program" METHOD="POST">
<INPUT TYPE=HIDDEN NAME="username" VALUE="ray">
   ⋮
</FORM>
```

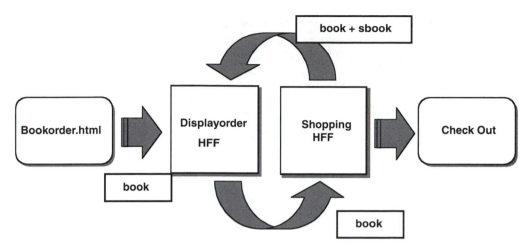

Figure 6.2 System flow diagram for the simple bookstore using HFF

To implement a shopping cart using HFF we can define a hidden field element called "username" in an HTML form. This can be used to keep track of the user session and hence the shopping cart.

A simple VBS*

In this section, we use a simple example to demonstrate how to implement a "simple bookstore" using HFF for session tracking. Essentially, a simple shopping cart is built. The system flow of this simple bookstore is shown in Figure 6.2.

The simple bookstore consists of four major modules as follows:

1. Bookorder.html – This is the homepage or "front-door" of the whole system.
2. DisplayorderHFF – This servlet program is used to display the selected book(s).
3. ShoppingHFF – This servlet program allows users to continue shopping by (1) consolidating the previous book selection and (2) displaying the book list again for selection.
4. Check out – This allows the user to "check out."

For illustrative purposes, the simple bookstore carries only six books. A snapshot of the Bookorder.html web page is displayed in Figure 6.3, and the corresponding HTML file is shown in Figure 6.4.

---

*This is inspired by the Hidden Form Field Shopping Cart program in Hunter and Crawford [1998].

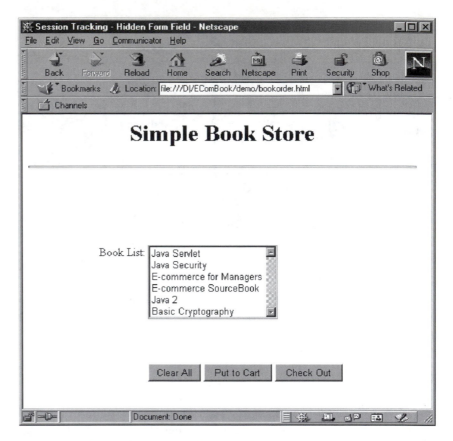

Figure 6.3 A snapshot of the Bookorder.html page

As shown in Figures 6.3 and 6.4, the `Bookorder.html` file provides the "main entry" for the whole system. The HTML page consists of a simple book list and three buttons. A user may

• click the `"Clear All"` button to reset the book selection;
• click the `"Put to Cart"` button to "put" the selected item(s) into the shopping cart; or
• click the `"Check Out"` button to exit.

Note that no matter which button is selected, the request is handled by the same server-side program, `"displayorderHFF."` The parameter value of the `"Submit"` button is used to identify the action required. The listing for the `"displayorderHFF"`

```html
<html>
<head>
<title>Session Tracking - Hidden Form Field</title>
</head>

<body>
<h1><center>Simple Book Store</center></h1>
<hr><br><br>

<form action="/servlet/csstlee.servlet3.displayorderHFF" method="POST">
<center><br><br>
<table border=0>

<!--- Book List --->
<tr valign=top>
<td align=right>Book List:</td><br>
<td align=left>
<select name=book size=6 multiple>
<option>Java Servlet
<option>Java Security
<option>E-commerce for Managers
<option>E-commerce SourceBook
<option>Java 2
<option>Basic Cryptography
</select>
</td>
</tr>

<!--- Submit Order --->
<tr>
<td></td>
<td>
<br><br><br>
<input type="reset" value="Clear All">
<input type="submit" name=action value="Put to Cart">
<input type="submit" name=action value="Check Out">
</td>
</tr>

</table>
</center>
</form>
</body>
</html>
```

Figure 6.4 The Bookorder.html source code

program is given in Figure 6.5. Its main functions are described as follows:

1. *To display the list of books selected by the user*: First of all, the program uses the `"getParmetervalues()"` method to retrieve the parameter values passed from the `Bookorder` page as follows:

```
books = req.getParameterValues("book");
sbooks = req.getParameterValues("sbook");
```

As shown in the program listing (Figure 6.5), `"DisplayorderHFF"` retrieves two parameters `"book"` and `"sbook"` from the request. The parameter `"book"` can come from either the `"Bookorder"` page or the `"ShoppingHFF"` program, while the parameter `"sbook"` is solely for handling the data passed from the `"ShoppingHFF."` Note that the `"book"` parameter contains the books currently in the shopping cart and the `"sbook"` parameter contains the books just selected by the user.

According to the book(s) "embedded" in both the `"sbook"` and `"book"` parameters, all the books are displayed in the same HTML table.

2. *To handle different actions selected by the user in the Bookorder page*: The action required is extracted by `getParameterValue("action")`. Having determined the action, the program will invoke one of the following servlets:

    • launch the `"checkout"` program if the user clicks `"Check Out"` button;
    • launch the `"shoppingHFF"` program if the user clicks `"Put to cart"` button.

3. *To create the HFF element(s) in the response*: In order to keep track of the books in the shopping cart, the program finally "embeds" all the books within the `"book"` and `"sbook"` parameters, into an HFF called `"book."` A sample screen of the HTML output from `displayorderHFF` is shown in Figure 6.6.

Next, we consider the `"shoppingHFF"` program.

If the user selects the `"Put to Cart"` option, `"displayorderHFF"` will launch the `"shoppingHFF"` in the `"next"` action (when the user clicks the `"Continue"` button, which is the only button that he can choose).

The main function of the `"shoppingHFF"` program is to allow the user to continue the shopping process, which involves the following actions:

1. *"Store-and-forward" the books in the shopping cart*: Firstly, the program uses the `"getParameter("book")"` command to retrieve all the books in the shopping cart and store them in a string array called `"books"` as follows:

```
books = req.getParameterValues("book");
```

```java
package csstlee.servlet3;

import java.io.*;
import java.util.*;
import javax.servlet.*;
import javax.servlet.http.*;

public class displayorderHFF extends HttpServlet
{
 //Use the Post method to invoke this servlet
   public void doPost(HttpServletRequest req,
   HttpServletResponse resp)
   throws ServletException, IOException
 {
  // Specify the content type
  resp.setContentType("text/html");

  // Get a PrintWriter object for writing the response
  PrintWriter out = resp.getWriter();

  // Write the response
  out.println("<html>");
  out.println("<head>");
  out.println("<title>Simple Book Shop</title>");
  out.println("</head>");
  out.println("<body>");
  out.println("<h1><center>Your selected items are");
  out.println("</h1><hr><br>");

  String books[];
  String sbooks[];

  // Get the action
  String[] action=req.getParameterValues("action");

  // Get the selected item
  books = req.getParameterValues("book");
  sbooks = req.getParameterValues("sbook");

  // Display the selected books
  if (books == null){
   out.println("<b>No book selected!!<b>");
  }
  else {
   out.println("<table border =1><tr><th>Selected Book List</tr>");
```

Figure 6.5 Program listing of displayorderHFF.java

```
 for (int j=0; j<books.length; j++){
  out.println("<tr><td>" + books[j]+"</tr>");
 }
 if (sbooks != null){
  for (int j=0; j<sbooks.length; j++){
   out.println("<tr><td>" + sbooks[j]+"</tr>");
   }
   }
   out.println("</table>");
}

 // Display buttons for the customer to check out or continue shopping
 if (action[0].equals("Check Out")){
 out.println("<form action=\"/servlet/csstlee.servlet3.
 checkout\" method=post>");
 }
 else {
  out.println("<form action=\"/servlet/csstlee.servlet3.
  shoppingHFF\" method=post>");
  }

 // Send the book list using hidden form fields
 if (books != null) {
  for (int i=0; i<books.length; i++) {
   out.println("<input type=hidden name=book value=\"" + books[i] + "\">");
  }
 }

 if (sbooks != null) {
  for (int i=0; i<sbooks.length; i++) {
   out.println("<input type=hidden name=book value=\"" + sbooks[i] + "\">");
  }
 }
 out.println("Please choose one ...<br>");
 out.println("<input type=submit name=action value=\"Continue... \">");
 out.println("</form>");
 out.println("</center></body></html>");
 out.flush();
 }
}
```

Figure 6.5 *(Continued)*

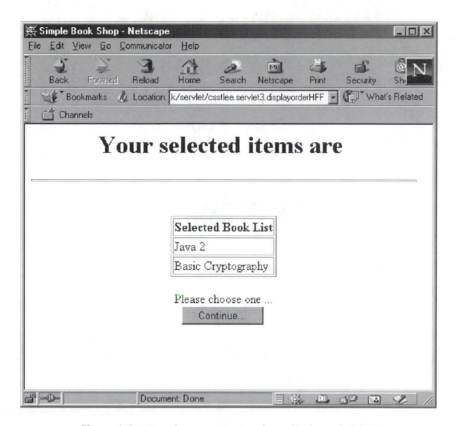

Figure 6.6 Sample output screen from displayorderHFF

It then forwards these items to the `"next"` program by using another HFF called `"book."`

2. *Display a book list for user selection*: The program shows a selection menu from which the user may continue the book selection. It is important to notice that `"sbook"` and `"book"` contain the currently selected books and the books inside the shopping cart, respectively. A snapshot of the screen output from the `"shoppingHFF"` program is shown in Figure 6.7, and the corresponding program is given in Figure 6.8. In this example, we select the last two books: `"Java 2"` and `"Basic Cryptography."` Then we press the `"Put to Cart"` button and finally the "Continue" button to return to the main program.

As shown in the program listing (Figure 6.8), whether the user clicks the `"Put to Cart"` or the `"Check Out"` button, the same program `"displayorderHFF"` is

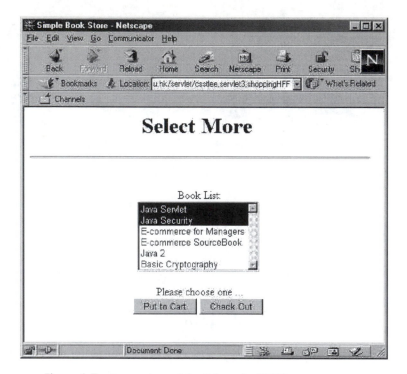

Figure 6.7 A snapshot of the "shoppingHFF" screen output

launched. A snapshot of the screen output for the `displayorderHFF` program is shown in Figure 6.9. In this case, we click the `"Check Out"` button to launch the `displayorderHFF` program (actually this screen is the same if we click the `"Put to Cart"` button).

The main function of the `"checkout"` program is to provide an `"exit"` for the system, so it just displays a simple `"check out"` message. To complete the discussion, Figures 6.10 and 6.11 show the screen output and the program listing of the `"checkout"` program, respectively.

6.2.2   URL rewriting

Recall that a URL consists of the following components:

• the domain name (e.g. `www.comp.polyu.edu.hk`)
• the URI (e.g. `/Servlet/welcome/hello`), which specifies the directory and the file (an HTML document or a program)

```java
package csstlee.servlet3;

import java.io.*;
import java.util.*;
import javax.servlet.*;
import javax.servlet.http.*;

public class shoppingHFF extends HttpServlet
 {
 // Use the "Post" method to invoke this servlet
    public void doPost(HttpServletRequest req,
    HttpServletResponse resp)
    throws ServletException, IOException
    {
     // Specify the content type
     resp.setContentType("text/html");

     // Get a PrintWriter object for writing the response
     PrintWriter out = resp.getWriter();

     // Write the response
     out.println("<html>");
     out.println("<head>");
     out.println("<title>Simple Book Store</title>");
     out.println("</head>");
     out.println("<body>");
     out.println("<h1><center>Select More");
     out.println("</h1><hr><br>");

     String books[];

     // Get the selected item(s)
     books = req.getParameterValues("book");

     // Display buttons for the customer to check out or
     // continue shopping
     out.println("<form action=\"/servlet/csstlee.servlet3.
     displayorderHFF\" method=post>");
     // Send the book list using hidden form fields
```

Figure 6.8   Program listing of shoppingHFF.java

```
if (books != null) {
 for (int j=0; j<books.length; j++) {
  out.println("<input type=hidden name=book value=\""
  + books[j] + "\">");
 }
}

out.println("</tr><!--- Book List --->");
out.println("<tr valign=top>");
out.println("<td align=right>Book List:</td><br>");
out.println("<td align=left>");
out.println("<select name=sbook size=6 multiple>");
out.println("<option>Java Servlet");
out.println("<option>Java Security");
out.println("<option>E-commerce for Managers");
out.println("<option>E-commerce SourceBook");
out.println("<option>Java 2 ");
out.println("<option>Basic Cryptography");
out.println("</select>");
out.println("</td>");
out.println("</tr><br><br>");

out.println("Please choose one ...<br>");
out.println("<input type=submit name=action
value=\"Put to Cart\">");
out.println("<input type=submit name=action
value=\"Check Out\">");
out.println("</form>");
out.println("</center></body></html>");
out.flush();

 }
}
```

Figure 6.8   *(Continued)*

The basic concept of "URL rewriting" is to modify, and more precisely rewrite the URL to a specific URL for each user. In other words, each user is given a specific URL for "talking" to the web server.

In terms of implementation, the following are two commonly used methods to identify a session:

Figure 6.9   Screen display of the next displayorderHFF program output

Figure 6.10   Screen display of the checkout program output

```java
package csstlee.servlet3;

import java.io.*;
import java.util.*;
import javax.servlet.*;
import javax.servlet.http.*;

public class checkout extends HttpServlet
{
  // Use the "Post" method to invoke this servlet
    public void doPost(HttpServletRequest req,
    HttpServletResponse resp)
    throws ServletException, IOException
    {
      // Specify the content type
      resp.setContentType("text/html");

      // Get a PrintWriter object for writing the response
      PrintWriter out = resp.getWriter();

      // Write the response
      out.println("<html>");
      out.println("<head>");
      out.println("<title>Simple Book Store</title>");
      out.println("</head>");
      out.println("<body>");
      out.println("<h1><center>Check Out ...");
      out.println("</h1><hr><br>");

      out.println("</center></body></html>");
      out.flush();

    }
 }
```

Figure 6.11 Program listing of the checkout program

1. To add an extra directory to the original URL
2. To add additional parameters at the end of the URL
   Let us explain them with a simple example. Suppose that the original URL is

```
http://www.comp.polyu.edu.hk/Servlet/welcome/hello
```

Using the first method, a user with session number 007 will access the URL as

```
http://www.comp.polyu.edu.hk/Servlet/welcome/007/hello
```

In other words, each user is assigned a different directory so that the web server can identify the client accordingly.

Alternatively, using the second method, the user state is appended to the URL as follows:

```
http://www.comp.polyu.edu.hk/Servlet/welcome/hello?session_no=007
```

In this case, the program knows that the request is from the session number 007.

6.2.3 HTTP user authentication

This method supports session tracking by means of the HTTP authentication scheme. Therefore, it can also be used to control user access. Authentication is done by asking the user to provide his username and password.

Let us look at the following example to see how it can be implemented.

- The web server is configured to use the HTTP authentication scheme.
- When a user accesses the web server for the first time, he needs to fill in the username and password for authentication as shown in Figure 6.12.
- The information is then passed to the web server for authentication. Subsequently, the web server can retrieve the user information (and hence the session information) from the HTTP headers. For example, with the servlet API, the username can be obtained from the "getRemoteUser()" method as follows:

```
String username = req.getRemoteUser( );
```

- Once the web server identifies the user, appropriate actions can be taken for that user.

6.2.4 Cookies

In Chapter 2, we discussed the use of cookies for passing information to the server. In summary, cookies are "small" pieces of information stored in the client browser.

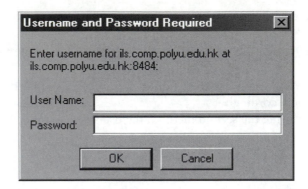

Figure 6.12   Sample page for a web site that needs user authorization

For instance, in an e-shopping scenario, one can use cookies for session tracking as follows:

- When a user accesses a B2C web site for the first time, the web server asks for the user information (e.g. username). Then the web server can ask the client browser to "store" a cookie by including this cookie in the HTTP response header. For example,

```
Set-Cookie: Username=ray
```

  The cookie with "Username=ray" is then stored in the client browser for later use.
- Each time the user returns to the web site, the client browser will send this cookie in the HTTP request message. Hence, the cookie can be used for session tracking purposes.

6.2.5   Comparison of the above session tracking methods

Let us compare the advantages and disadvantages of the above session tracking techniques [Hunter and Crawford, 1998; Callway, 1999]. In general, the cookies and HFF techniques are more commonly used in practice. This is because they are simple to implement, can be supported by most of the browsers, and can provide anonymous session tracking (i.e., does not require user's preregistration). However, each cookie can store only a limited amount of information, and there are security concerns in using cookies because it involves saving something on the client side. In fact, a browser may be disabled to accept cookies. For the HFF technique, its implementation can be quite clumsy if we want to keep track of a lot of information. Furthermore, it can be used only for dynamic web pages, otherwise the HFFs cannot be generated continuously throughout the whole session. In fact, most people think that to build a flexible system, the session tracking mechanism should be separated from the content creation. Obviously, this is not the case for HFFs. While URL rewriting is also easy to implement, the "Adding an Extra Path" method may not work well for complex applications and the "Adding an Extra Parameter" method can be used only with "hyperlinks" but not with form posting. As HTML forms are commonly used, its applicability is quite limited. The User authentication method is more suitable for an intranet environment because it depends on pre-registration. For many B2C e-commerce systems, it is difficult to implement this method. Furthermore, this technique cannot support multiple sessions at a web site.

6.3 THE SERVLET SESSION TRACKING API

6.3.1 Introduction

Java Servlet API provides a set of classes, namely the Session Tracking API, for session management purposes. The advantages of using this API are as follows:

- It can be used in any servlet program with little additional programming effort.
- It can be used in conjunction with other Java components such as CORBA, RMI, etc.
- It can be easily integrated with the Java Security API and Java Cryptography API to develop secure servlets.

In general, the Servlet Session Tracking API supports the following session tracking functions:

- setting up of a session object
- management of different sessions
- handling the life cycle of a session object

In fact, once a session is established, its management is handled *automatically* by the servlet engine.

6.3.2   How the servlet session tracking API works

The Session Tracking API for HTTP is called "`javax.Servlet.http. HttpSession,`" which includes classes and methods to manage sessions under the web environment. Imagine that the servlet engine within the web server contains a filing cabinet with each drawer containing the session object(s) for each session connecting to the web server. The main function of these "drawers" is for each client to store the session object(s). For instance, suppose that a servlet program is used to implement an e-shopping mall application. Every time a client sends a request to the server, a shopping cart object is generated with a unique session identity (ID). If the client puts an item into the shopping cart, the status of the shopping cart object will be updated in the corresponding "drawer" within the servlet engine. If the user "leaves" the shopping mall for a while and then "returns" later, the servlet program can retrieve the session object (e.g. a shopping cart) for that user based on the session ID. This allows the user to continue shopping with the previous shopping cart. To pass the session ID between the server and the client, the cookie method is usually used. Note, however, that the cookie is used to pass the session ID only. Alternatively, the URL rewriting method can be used. Let us look at how the Java Session Tracking API can be applied for our VBS as follows:

• When a user visits the VBS for the first time, the servlet engine will automatically assign a session ID to the user. The session ID is passed to the user using the "`Set-Cookie`" command such as

  `Set-cookie: Session id= 9786421343242`

• Once the client's browser gets this cookie, the cookie and hence the session ID will be stored.
• Whenever the user returns to the VBS, the client browser sends this cookie (i.e. the session ID) to the web server.
• By identifying the session ID, the corresponding shopping cart object can be retrieved for shopping.

A schematic diagram of the servlet session tracking mechanism is shown in Figure 6.13. As shown in the figure, each session can have many different objects, and each object is assigned a name for identification purpose.

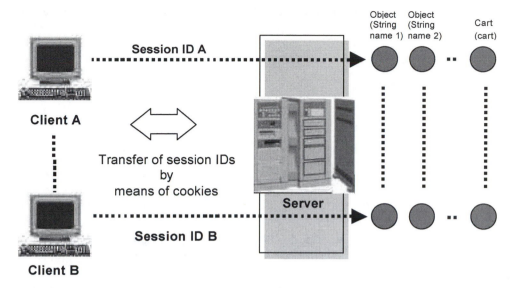

Figure 6.13 A schematic diagram of Servlet Session Tracking API

In the diagram, there is a shopping cart object (Cart) for both clients A and B. We will later discuss about how to implement this object. Essentially, this object is a Java class. The "Cart" object is identified by the name "cart." By using the session ID, which is passed between the server and the client by means of cookies, the corresponding shopping cart for a client can be identified. As shown later, we can implement many useful methods for this shopping cart object.

6.3.3   Some common methods for servlet session tracking

The most important method for servlet session tracking is "getSession()" with the following format

```
HttpSession.getSession(boolean new);
```

Its purpose is to provide the current session object for the client based on the given session ID. If the client is a new visitor, a new session will be created if parameter "new" is "true."

Although Session Tracking API uses cookies to keep track of the sessions, its operation is transparent to the user because session management is done automatically.

Besides the `"getSession"` method, other commonly used methods in the session tracking API include

- `getId()`
- `getValue(String name)`
- `getValuesNames()`
- `putValue(String name, Object value)`
- `removeValue(String name)`
- `invalidate()`

As mentioned, each session is assigned an ID. The corresponding ID for a session can be obtained by the `"getId()"` method. The `"getValue()"` method gets the value of the corresponding session object. As shown in Figure 6.13, each session object has a name and a value. The `"putValue()"` method is used to update the value of a session object or put a new session object into the servlet engine. The `"getValueNames()"` method is for retrieving the names of all the session objects of the current session. To remove a session object, the `"removeValue()"` method can be used. Finally, a session can be closed by using the `invalidate()` method. Further details on these methods can be found in the JSDK Hunter and Crawford [1999].

6.3.4   A simple session tracking example

For ease of illustration, we demonstrate the functionality of the Servlet Session Tracking API by using a simple example. In this example, a customer enters his name on an HTML form. After submitting the form to the SessionDemo servlet, a session is created for the customer.

A snapshot of the program output is shown in Figure 6.14 (after the second "visit"), and the corresponding program listing is shown in Figure 6.15.

This simple program illustrates the basic methods and procedures for manipulating session objects using the Servlet Session Tracking API. Figure 6.16 shows the system flow for the whole program. As shown in Figure 6.16, the program first "retrieves" the session with the `"getSession()"` method as follows:

```
HttpSession session = req.getSession(true);
```

If the session does not exist (either the client visits the web site for the first time or the previous session has been terminated due to "timeout"), the servlet engine will

Welcome

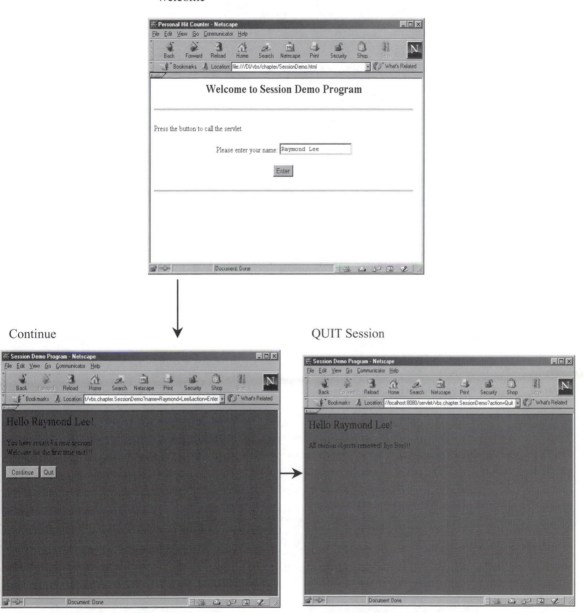

Figure 6.14   A snapshot of SessionDemo program output

```java
package vbs.chapter;
import java.io.*;
import javax.servlet.*;
import javax.servlet.http.*;

public class SessionDemo extends HttpServlet {

  public void doGet(HttpServletRequest req,
  HttpServletResponse resp)
  throws ServletException, IOException {

    String CUST = "CUST";
    String BKCOLOR = "BKCOLOR";
    String ACT_ENTER = "Enter";
    String ACT_QUIT = "Quit";
    String ACT_CONTINUE = "Continue";

    resp.setContentType("text/html");
    PrintWriter out = resp.getWriter();
    String custname = req.getParameter("name");
    String action = req.getParameter("action");

    //Get the session object and create one if there is none
    HttpSession session = req.getSession(true);

    String cust = (String)session.getValue(CUST);

    out.println("<html><head><title>Session Demo
    Program</title></head>");
    out.println("<font color=BLACK size=5>");

    // Check if the cust object exists
    if (cust == null){
      // Not exist,create one
      cust = new String(custname);

      // Set the background color
      String bkcolor = new String("RED");

      // Display a hello message for first time visitors
      out.println("<body bgcolor=" + bkcolor+ "<h1>Hello "
      + cust + "!</h1>");
```

Figure 6.15 Program listing of SessionDemo.java

```java
            out.println("You have created a new session!<br>");
            out.println("Welcome for the first time visit!!!<br>");

         // Store the two session objects
         session.putValue(CUST, cust);
         session.putValue(BKCOLOR, bkcolor);

         // Create the buttons
         out.println("<form method=GET action=\"vbs.chapter.SessionDemo\">");
         out.println("<input type=submit name=action value=\"Continue\">");
         out.println("<input type=submit name=action value=\"Quit\">");

      } else if (action.equals(ACT_CONTINUE)){
         // If the user continues, get the BKCOLOR object
         String bkcolor = (String)session.getValue(BKCOLOR);

         // Change background color and update the session object
         if (bkcolor == "RED"){
            bkcolor = "BLUE";
         } else { bkcolor = "RED"; }
         session.putValue(BKCOLOR, bkcolor);

         // Display the welcome message with the current
            background color
         out.println("<body bgcolor=" + bkcolor+ "<h1>Hello " + cust + "!</h1>");
         out.println("<form method=GET action=\"vbs.chapter.SessionDemo\">");
         out.println("<form method=POST action=\"vbs.chapter.SessionDemo\">");
         out.println("Welcome for the revisit!!!<br><br>");

         // Create the buttons
         out.println("<input type=submit name=action value=\"Continue\">");
         out.println("<input type=submit name=action value=\"Quit\">");

      } else if (action.equals(ACT_QUIT)){
         // If the user chooses "quit", remove the session objects
         session.removeValue(CUST);
         session.removeValue(BKCOLOR);
         out.println("<body bgcolor=RED <h1>Hello " + cust + "!</h1>");
         out.println("All session objects removed! Bye Bye!!!");
      }
      out.println("<p>");
      out.println("</font></body></html>");
   }
}
```

Figure 6.15 (*Continued*)

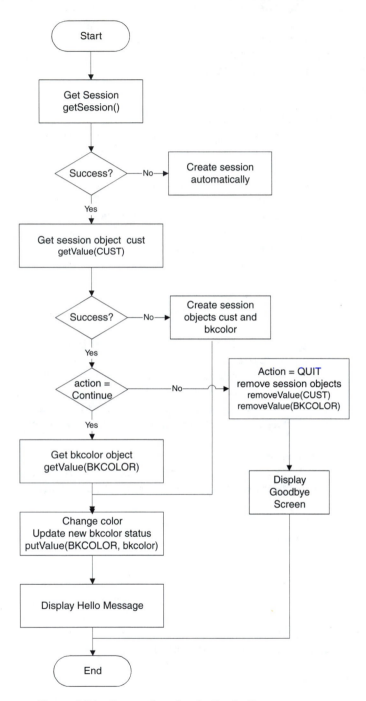

Figure 6.16   System flow for the SessionDemo program

create a new session for the user. The program then retrieves the customer's name using the `"getParameter()"` method, i.e.,

```
String custname = req.getParameter("name");
```

The program also creates a background color object for the session. The background color toggles between red and blue by updating the background color object continuously.

The program then puts the `"custname"` and `"bkcolor"` objects into the session for the customer, using the following statement:

```
session.putValue(CUST, cust);
session.putValue(BKCOLOR, bkcolor);
```

Both `"CUST"` and `"BKCOLOR"` are string objects whose values are defined by the parameters `"cust"` and `"bkcolor,"` respectively.

In the subsequent visits (i.e., after the session has been created), the program will retrieve the session objects and print the customer name with the background color accordingly. The program will also update the background color object for the next visit. Finally, the session objects are put back into the session.

As for the customer, he can press the `"Continue"` button to see a personalized welcome message with the background color alternating between red and blue. Finally, he can terminate the session by pressing the `"Quit"` button.

6.3.5   A simple shopping cart example

Introduction

Moss [1998] gives a very good example of the use of the Session Tracking API in a user login program. Using some of the ideas and methods of his program, but a different program logic, a servlet called SimpleCart is written to demonstrate how the Session Tracking API can be used to support user authentication and to build a simple shopping cart. We assume that after logging into the system, the user will be provided with an object called the simple shopping cart object (`SCart`). The corresponding source code is shown in Figure 6.17. It contains the following:

- `Customer name`: the full name of the customer
- `Bonus points`: the bonus points of the customer

Essentially, the simple shopping cart is used to store the user information for the current session. The information is obtained from the `"Customer"` table of

```
package vbs.chapter;

public class SCart
{
        String cust_name; // Customer name
        int nBonus = 0; // Bonus point
        int c_item_no; // Number of items
        double c_total; // Total price

        public void Cart() // Implementation
        {c_item_no = 0;
         c_total = 0.0;}

        public void setCustName(String name) // Set customer name
        {cust_name = name;}

        public String returnCustName() // Return customer name
        {return cust_name;}

        public void setBonus(int bonus) //  Set bonus points
        {nBonus = bonus}

        public int getBonus() // Return bonus points
        {return nBonus;}

        public void setItemNo(int value) // Set item no.
        {c_item_no = value;}

        public int returnItemNo() // Return item no.
        {return c_item_no;}

}
```

Figure 6.17   Program listing for SCart.java

the simple database called `"mall."` This table contains the following informa-tion:

- `CustID` – Text field contains the customer ID.
- `Password` – Text field contains customer password.
- `Fname` – Text field contains the first name of the customer.

- Lname – Text field contains the last name of the customer.
- Bonus – Number field contains the bonus points for the customer.

Note that the CustID may not be user-friendly because it has to be unique (there may be many "Raymond Lee" in the world). Once the username and password are verified. The server can then put the full name of the user into the shopping cart so that it can be displayed whenever required.

Main modules in SimpleCart

First, let us look at the major functional modules of the SimpleCart program as follows:

1. doPost: This is the main module that controls the program flow and also the "entry point" of the system. The required action is retrieved by using the "getParameter()" method, and different actions can be handled according to the value stored in the "ACTION" form field.
2. loginDialog: This method displays a user login dialog box for the user to fill in the username and password.
3. checkLogin: This method is used to check the username/password against the Customer table. It returns a boolean result, either True (if found) or False (if not found). If the login is successful, the full customer name as well as his bonus points will be written into the shopping cart, and the shopping cart will be put into his session.
4. HelloScreen: Once the customer passes the authentication procedure, a hello screen with his full name and the bonus points is displayed. The customer will also see this hello screen if he has successfully logged in previously (i.e., the user has logged in and there is a shopping cart already).

Program flow of SimpleCart.java

For ease of illustration, a schematic diagram of the SimpleCart.java program is shown in Figure 6.18, followed by the program listings in Figure 6.19.

The program makes use of the "doPost()" method as the main "control center" for the whole program, and the "ACTION" parameter to indicate the required action.

First of all, the program retrieves the session connection from the system by using the "getSession()" method. If no session is found, a new one will be created.

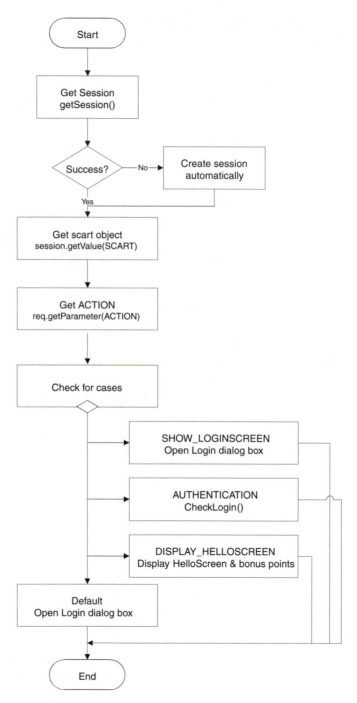

Figure 6.18 System flow of the SimpleCart program

```
package vbs.chapter;
import javax.servlet.*;
import javax.servlet.http.*;
import java.sql.*;
import java.io.*;

public class SimpleCart extends HttpServlet
{
  // Define the variables
  String DRIVER_NAME = "sun.jdbc.odbc.JdbcOdbcDriver";
  String CONNECTION_URL = "jdbc:odbc:mall";
  String SCART = "SCART";
  String ACTION = "action";
  final int LOGIN = 0;
  final int SHOW_LOGINSCREEN = 1;
  final int AUTHENTICATION = 2;
  final int DISPLAY_HELLOSCREEN = 3;
  String USERNAME = "username";
  String PASSWORD = "password";

    // This is the main program
    public void doPost(HttpServletRequest req, HttpServletResponse
     resp)
    throws ServletException, IOException
    {

      // Specify the content type
      resp.setContentType("text/html");

      // Get the PrintWriter object for writing the response
      PrintWriter out = resp.getWriter();

      // Set the default action
      int action = -1;

      // Get the session object
      HttpSession httpsession = req.getSession(true);

      // Get the simple cart object from the session
      SCart scart = (SCart) httpsession.getValue(SCART);
```

Figure 6.19 SimpleCart.java program listing

```
try{
 // Get the action
 action = Integer.parseInt(req.getParameter(ACTION));
}catch(NumberFormatException e){
 //The NumberFormatException occurs when no
   action is specified
 action = -1;
}


// Define the cases
if ((scart == null) && (action != LOGIN)){
    // Case 1 : Show login dialog box
    action = SHOW_LOGINSCREEN;
}else if ((scart == null) && (action == LOGIN)){
 // Case 2 : User authentication
 // Create a scart object
 scart = new SCart();
 action = AUTHENTICATION;
}else if (scart != null){
 // Case 3 : Dispaly Hello Screen
 action = DISPLAY_HELLOSCREEN;
}


try{
switch(action){
 case SHOW_LOGINSCREEN:
  // Open the login box
  loginDialog(out);
  break;

 case AUTHENTICATION:
  // Verify the username and password
  if (checkLogin(scart, req, out)==true) {

  // Upon successful login, put the scart
    object into the session
  httpsession.putValue(SCART, scart);

  // Display the hello screen
  HelloScreen(scart, out);
 }
```

Figure 6.19   (*Continued*)

```
     break;
    case DISPLAY_HELLOSCREEN:
     // Display the hello screen~directly as the user has
      logged in before
     HelloScreen(scart, out);
     break;

   default:
    // The default case is to prompt the user to login
    loginDialog(out);
  }
  }
  catch (Exception e) {
   // Print the exceptions
   e.printStackTrace(out);
  }

  out.flush();
  out.close();
}

public void doGet(HttpServletRequest req, HttpServletResponse
 resp)
throws ServletException, IOException
{
 // Handled by the doPost method above
 doPost(req, resp);
}

// Verify the username and password
 public boolean checkLogin(SCart scart, HttpServletRequest
  req, PrintWriter out)
{
 // Get Connection object
 Connection connection = null;

// Get Statement object
Statement statement = null;

// Get ResultSet object
ResultSet resultSet = null;

// Get the username and password
String username = req.getParameter(USERNAME);
```

Figure 6.19   (*Continued*)

```
String password = req.getParameter(PASSWORD);
// Set up the JDBC connection
 try {
 // Create a JDBC driver
 Class.forName(DRIVER_NAME).newInstance();
 connection = DriverManager.getConnection(CONNECTION_URL);

 // Create the SQL statement
 String sqlquery = "SELECT Fname, Lname, Bonus from Customer
  where CustID='"+username+"' and Password='"+password+"'";

 // Create the statement object
 statement = connection.createStatement();

 // Execute the SQL query
 resultSet = statement.executeQuery(sqlquery);

 if (resultSet.next()){
    // Upon successful login, update the scart object
     attributes
    scart.setCustName(resultSet.getString("Fname")+
     " "+resultSet.getString("Lname"));
    scart.setBonus(resultSet.getInt("Bonus"));
   }else{
    out.println("<html>");
    out.println("<head>");
    out.println("<title>Error</title>");
    out.println("</head>");
    out.println("<h1 align=center>*** Wrong
     username/password !! ***</h1>");
    out.println("</html>");
    return false;
   }
      }
  catch (Exception e) {
   // Catch and ignore the exceptions
  }
  finally {
  try {
  // Close resultSet, statement and connection objects
    if (resultSet != null) {
    resultSet.close();
```

Figure 6.19   (*Continued*)

```
      }
      if (statement != null) {
       statement.close();
      }
      if (connection != null) {
       connection.close();
      }
     }
     catch (Exception e) {
      // Catch and ignore the exceptions
     }
    }
    return true;
  }


// Display the Hello Screen
public void HelloScreen(SCart scart, PrintWriter out)
 {
  out.println("<html>");
  out.println("<head>");
  out.println("<title>Simple Cart Demo: Hello Screen</title>");
  out.println("</head>");
  out.println("<img src=\"/vbs/chapter/simple_cart.jpg\">");
  out.println("<h1 align=center>Hello " +scart.returnCustName()+ " !</h1>");
  out.println("<h2 align=center>Welcome to Simple Cart
   Hello Screen</h2>");
  out.println("<h3 align=center>Your current bonus
  points: "+scart.getBonus()+" .</h3>");
  out.println("</html>");
 }
// Open the login box
public void loginDialog(PrintWriter out)
 {
  out.println("<html>");
  out.println("<head>");
  out.println("<title>Simple Cart User Login</title>");
  out.println("</head>");
  out.println("<img src=\"/vbs/chapter/simple_cart.jpg\">");
  out.println("<h1 align=center>Simple Cart User Login</h1>");
  out.println("<h3 align=center>Please enter your username and
   password</h3>");
```

Figure 6.19   (*Continued*)

```
out.println("<form method=POST action=\"/servlet/vbs.chapter.
 SimpleCart\">");
out.println("<br>Username:");
out.println("<input type=text name="+
 USERNAME + " size=20>");
out.println("<br>Password:");
out.println("<input type=password name="+
 PASSWORD + " size=20>");
out.println("<br><br>");
out.println("<input type=hidden name=" +
 ACTION + " value=\"" + LOGIN + "\">");
out.println("<input type=submit name=submit value=Login>");
out.println("</form>");
out.println("</html>");
 }

}
```

Figure 6.19 (*Continued*)

Then the program will get the current user action by using the `req.`
`getParameter(ACTION)` method. Based on the user action, there are three cases
to consider as described below:

Case 1: SHOW_LOGINSCREEN – In the first case, no session object is retrieved
and no action is specified. This occurs when the user accesses the URL for the first
time. The program returns the login form to the user so that he can log on to the
system.

Case 2: AUTHENTICATION – In this case, there is no session object but the action indicates that login is required. This request actually comes from case 1 after
the user has submitted the login form to the server. After receiving the request, the
program calls the `"checklogin()"` method to check for user authentication. If
the verification is successful, the program will update the shopping cart using the
`"putValue(SCART, scart)"` method. Note that `"SCART"` is the session object name,
and `"scart"` is the actual session object, which is a SCART object as defined in
Figure 6.17.

Case 3: DISPLAY_HELLOSCREEN – In the last case, the `"scart"` session object
exists. It means that the user has already passed the authentication process before
(in case 2), and therefore, he does not need to login again but can go directly to the
hello screen by using the `"HelloScreen()"` method.

For illustrative purposes, a snapshot of the login screen and the hello screen are
shown in Figures 6.20 and 6.21, respectively. Note that, in general, a user will log
into the system by going through case 1, then case 2, and finally case 3.

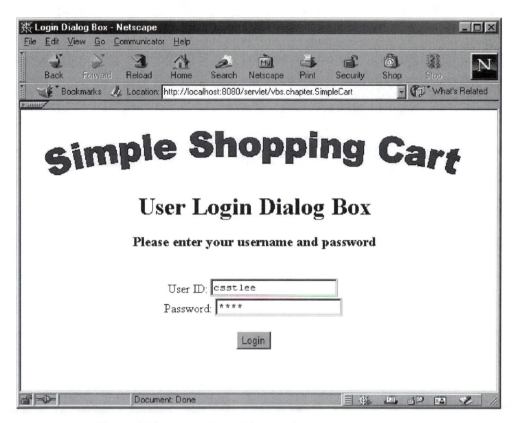

Figure 6.20   A snapshot of the SimpleCart User Login screen

The `SimpleCart` program provides simple account management only. All other functions such as "create user account" or "user account maintenance" are not included. These functions are included in the account management program of the VBS in Chapter 15.

6.4   A PRACTICAL CASE: VBS SHOPPING CART

6.4.1   What is a shopping cart?

In this chapter, a simple shopping cart is built. Later in Chapter 15, we will build a comprehensive shopping cart. In general, a shopping cart contains the following information:

Figure 6.21   A snapshot of SimpleCart welcome main page

- user ID
- number of items being selected
- total price of the goods being selected
- list of goods selected including product code, quantity purchased, item price, and item description

A complete listing of the shopping cart object (`ShoppingCart.java`) is given in Figure 6.22.

6.4.2 Basic functions of the shopping cart object

In our VBS, the main functions of the shopping cart object include the following:

```java
// ShoppingCart.java
package csstlee.mall.shoppingcart;
// Set your own package instead

public class ShoppingCart
{
     // Customer name
    String cust_name;

    // Bonus point
    int nBonus;

    // Number of items
    int c_item_no;

    // Item code
    String[] c_item_code= new String[50];

    // Item description
    String[] c_item_desc= new String[50];

    // Item quantity
    int[] c_item_qty = new int[50];

    // Item price
    double[] c_item_price = new double[50];

    // Total price
    double c_total;

    // Implementation
    public void Cart()
    {
        c_item_no = 0;
        c_total = 0.0;
    }

    // Set customer name
    public void setCustName(String value)
    {
        cust_name = value;
```

Figure 6.22   ShoppingCart object program listing

```
        }

        public String getCustName()
        {
                return cust_name;
        }

        // Set bonus points
        public void setBonus(int value)
        {
                nBonus = value;
        }

        // Get bonus points
        public int getBonus()
        {
                return nBonus;
        }

        // Set item no.
        public void setItemNo(int value)
        {
                c_item_no = value;
        }

        public int getItemNo()
        {
                return c_item_no;
        }

        // Add an item to the shopping cart
        public void addItemDetail(String cISBN, String cName, int cQty,
        double cPrice)
        {
                setItemDetail(cISBN, cName, cQty, cPrice, getItemNo());
                setItemNo(getItemNo() + 1);
        }
        // Delete the item from the shoping cart
        public void deleteItem(int no)
        {
```

Figure 6.22   (*Continued*)

```
            if ( no >= getItemNo() || no < 0 )
                    return;
            for ( int i = no ; i < getItemNo() -1 ; i++ ) {
                    c_item_code[i] = c_item_code[i+1];
                    c_item_desc[i] = c_item_desc[i+1];
                    c_item_qty[i] = c_item_qty[i+1];
                    c_item_price[i] = c_item_price[i+1];
            }
            setItemNo(getItemNo() - 1);
    }


    // Update the item in the shoping cart
    public void setItemDetail(String cISBN, String cName, int cQty,
    double cPrice, int cindex)
    {
            c_item_code[cindex] = cISBN;
            c_item_desc[cindex] = cName;
            c_item_qty[cindex] = cQty;
            c_item_price[cindex] = cPrice;
    }


    // Return the ISBN of an item
    public String getItemISBN(int cindex)
    {
            return c_item_code[cindex];
    }


    // Return the item description
    public String getItemName(int cindex)
    {
     return c_item_desc[cindex];
    }

// Return the quantity of an item
 public int getItemQty(int cindex)
 {
            return c_item_qty[cindex];
 }
 // Return the price of an item
 public double getItemPrice(int cindex)
 {
     return c_item_price[cindex];
```

Figure 6.22 *(Continued)*

```
    }
    // Calculate the total cost
    public double Cart_total()
    {
        double aux=0.0;

        for (int i=0; i<c_item_no; i++)
        {
                aux += ( getItemPrice(i) * getItemQty(i));
        }
        return aux;
    }
    // Calculate the total quantity
    public int Cart_totalQty()
    {
        int aux=0;

        for (int i=0; i<c_item_no; i++)
        {
                aux += getItemQty(i);
        }
        return aux;
    }
    // Reset the number of items and the total amount
    public void Empty_Cart()
    {
        c_item_no = 0;
        c_total = 0.0;
    }
}
```

Figure 6.22 *(Continued)*

1. Add items: This function is used to add a selected book into the shopping cart object. If the shopping cart does not exist (due to "timeout" or "first visit"), the program will create a new shopping cart object.
2. Update items: This allows the user to update the items in his shopping cart (e.g., change the book quantity, or even delete the whole entry).
3. Clear items: This function allows the user to remove all the items in the shopping cart so that he can start the purchase from scratch.

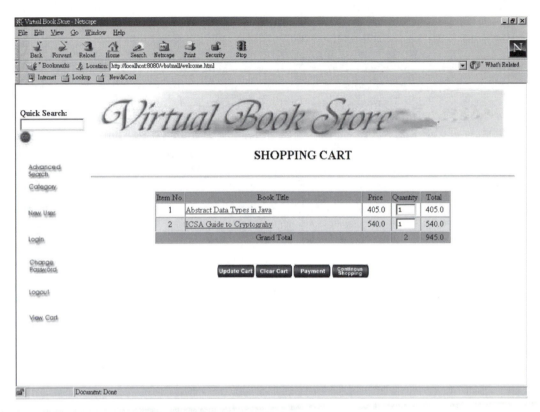

Figure 6.23 A sample shopping cart in VBS

Besides these basic operations, the VBS also provides other supporting functions such as "viewCart()" to display current status of the shopping cart. All these features are included in the program "CartServices.java." Please refer to Chapter 15 for details. A sample shopping cart screen is shown in Figure 6.23.

6.5 SUMMARY

In this chapter, we explored different techniques for maintaining user state or "Session Tracking." The traditional methods are Hidden form field, URL rewriting, HTTP user authorization, and Cookies.

We have discussed these technologies and how they can be used for session tracking and have also considered their main advantages and shortcomings. In the second part of this chapter, we introduced the Servlet Session Tracking API. In order to demonstrate its functions, we presented two programming examples.

Finally, it is worth mentioning that in many web-based e-commerce systems, multiple servers (commonly known as "Web Server Farm") are often used to handle user requests. The prime reason for using a Web Server Farm is for "load-balancing" [Loutonen, 1998; Kameda *et al.*, 1998]. The commonly used techniques include (1) round-robin DNS, (2) persistence cookies, (3) URL routing, and (4) load-balancing switches. Many web servers can now be configured to support the above load-balancing schemes in conjunction with various session tracking techniques. An example is the Network Load Balancing (NLB) package provided by MS Windows 2000 Advanced Server.

REFERENCES

Callway, D. R., *Inside Servlets*, Addison-Wesley, Reading, MA, 1999.

Hunter, J. and Crawford, W., *Java Servlet Programming*, O'Reilly & Associates, Inc., 1998.

Kameda, H., Li, J., Kim, C., and Zhang, Y., *Optimal Load Balancing in Distributed Computer Systems*, Springer-Verlag, Berlin, 1998.

Loutonen, A., *Web Proxy Server*, Prentice-Hall PTR, Upper Saddle River, NJ, 1998.

Moss, K., *Java Servlets*, McGraw-Hill, New York, 1998.

RECOMMENDED READING

Hunter, J. and Crawford, W., *Java Servlet Programming*, O'Reilly & Associates, Inc., 1998.

Callway, D. R., *Inside Servlets*, Addison-Wesley, Reading, MA, 1999.

These give a general overview of session tracking using different technologies.

Moss, K., *Java Servlets*, McGraw-Hill, New York, 1998.

This book provides a good description of basic servlet session tracking as well as advanced session tracking programming including connection pooling and HTTP tunnelling. It also contains a login program, which provides a good reference for building access control system using Java Servlet.

Loutonen, A., *Web Proxy Server*, Prentice-Hall PTR, Upper Saddle River, NJ, 1998.

This book provides an overview of web performance tuning using various techniques such as capacity planning and system load-balancing.

Kameda, H., Li, J., Kim, C., and Zhang, Y., *Optimal Load Balancing in Distributed Computer Systems*, Springer-Verlag, Berlin, 1998.

This gives an in-depth description of optimize network and system.

7

Basic Cryptography for Enabling E-commerce

7.1   Security Concerns

7.2   Security Requirements

7.3   Encryption

7.4   Two Basic Principles for Private Key Encryption

7.5   The Key Distribution Problem

7.6   Diffie–Hellman Key Exchange Protocol

7.7   Public Key Encryption

7.8   RSA Encryption Algorithm

7.9   Hybrid Encryption

7.10 Other Public Key Encryption Methods

7.11 Stream Cipher and Block Cipher

7.12 Message Digest

7.13 Message Authentication Code

7.14 Digital Signature

7.15 Digital Signature Standard

7.16 Authentication

7.17 Summary

References

Recommended Reading

In previous chapters, we discussed how to build a web-based e-commerce system without considering security. Needless to say, security is of primary importance in e-commerce. If an e-commerce system is not secure, people will not have the confidence to use it particularly to carry out high-value business transactions. Unfortunately, the internet is not a secure network. In order to build a secure e-commerce system, we need to employ cryptographic techniques. Cryptography is originally about keeping messages secret. Nowadays, it is more than a technique for scrambling information into a form that is only readable by authorized people, but is used to address different security requirements. In this chapter, we will give an overview of cryptography – an important enabling technology for e-commerce.

7.1   SECURITY CONCERNS

The internet is based on an open network architecture, so information can be transferred freely and efficiently. While this greatly facilitates the development of e-commerce applications, it also raises many security concerns. If you have bought something over the internet before, you may have had the following worries:

- *Worry 1*: I transmit my credit card information over the internet. Can people other than the intended recipient read it?
- *Worry 2*: I agree to pay $200 for the goods. Will this payment information be captured and changed by someone on the internet?
- *Worry 3*: This company claims itself to be Company X. Is this the real company X?

Fortunately, by using modern cryptographic techniques, we can make e-commerce transactions over the internet very secure. In fact, it may be even more secure than conducting commerce in the physical world.

7.2   SECURITY REQUIREMENTS

In general, the aforementioned worries can be summarized into three security requirements namely Confidentiality, Integrity, and Authentication* [Knudsen, 1998; Nichols, 1999]. Confidentiality makes sure that a message is kept confidential or secret such that only the intended recipient can read it. This eliminates the

---

* Some people may like to call them Confidentiality, Integrity, and Availability. In this case, the authentication requirement may be integrated with the integrity requirement.

first worry because even if an intruder captures your credit card information on the internet, he cannot read the information. To provide data confidentiality, encryption is used. Integrity makes sure that if the content of a message is altered, the receiver can detect it. This addresses the second worry because if the payment information is changed, the message is no longer valid. A digital signature is commonly used to ensure data integrity. Finally, authentication is about verifying identity. This eliminates the third worry as the identity of the company can be verified before carrying out a transaction. In an open e-commerce system, a digital certificate is employed to satisfy the authentication requirement. Furthermore, there is also the requirement of nonrepudiation. This ensures that the involved parties cannot deny the occurrence of a transaction. In general, if integrity and authentication can be ensured, the nonrepudiation requirement can also be satisfied.

In the remaining sections, we will give an overview of the cryptographic techniques used for addressing these security requirements.

7.3 ENCRYPTION

Encryption is for ensuring data confidentiality. For example, when a customer wants to send sensitive payment information to the VBS, encryption can be used to prevent other people from reading it. Figure 7.1 illustrates the basic concept of encryption.

Basically, the original message, known as plaintext is passed through an encryption process. The output message is called the ciphertext, which is a scrambled message. The encryption process is controlled by an encryption key. In many encryption algorithms, this is just a binary number. The encryption key governs how the plaintext is converted or transformed into ciphertext [Feghhi *et al.*, 1999]. In other words, different encryption keys will produce different output messages. The

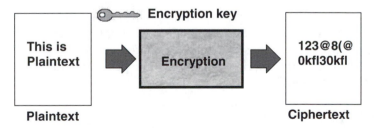

Figure 7.1 Encryption

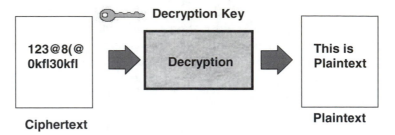

Figure 7.2   Decryption

reliability of an encryption algorithm is related to the key size or number of bits in the encryption key. To recover the plaintext, a reverse process known as decryption is used as shown in Figure 7.2. In this case, the ciphertext is passed through a decryption process as controlled by a decryption key. By using the correct decryption key, the plaintext can be obtained.

To facilitate the later discussion, we define the following encryption and decryption functions, respectively:

```
E[plaintext|encrypt_key]=ciphertext
D[ciphertext|decrypt_key]=D[E[plaintext|encrypt_key]|decrypt_key]
                        =plaintext
```

where `plaintext` is the original message before encryption, `ciphertext` is the secret message after encryption, `encrypt_key` is the encryption key, and `decrypt_key` is the decryption key.

In general, we will use the following notation for describing various cryptographic functions.

```
Output=Functionalgorithm[Input|Keytype,owner]
```

In this notation, "Function," "Input," and "Output" are mandatory. Other parameters are used to describe a function in more specific terms. Each "Function" has an "Input" and an "Output." The "Function" can be implemented using a particular "algorithm." Furthermore, most functions are controlled by a "key." A key may have a "type" and we may also specify its "owner." The possible parameters are given as follows:

- function: {E, D, H, S, . . . }
- algorithm: {RSA, DES, MD5, . . . }
- type: {public, private, session, . . . }

where E, D, H, and S represent encryption, decryption, hash, and digital signature, respectively. We will explain the last two functions and other parameters later. In the first example as discussed previously, the function, input, output, and key are E, plaintext, cipertext, and encrypt_key, respectively.

There are two types of encryption methods: symmetric key encryption and asymmetric key encryption. They are also called private key encryption and public key encryption, respectively. In symmetric (private) key encryption, the encryption key and the decryption key are the same. In asymmetric (public) key encryption, they are different.

7.4   TWO BASIC PRINCIPLES FOR PRIVATE KEY ENCRYPTION

Nearly all the early encryption methods were based on symmetric key encryption, and many of them were implemented by mechanical means. In general, symmetric key encryption follows two basic principles, namely substitution and transposition [Schneier, 1996; Stallings, 1999; Tanenbaum, 1996].

Caesar cipher is a good example of the substitution technique. In this encryption method, each letter of the alphabet is substituted with another letter nth place(s) further down the alphabet. The letters are arranged in a cyclic manner such that Z is followed by A. The number n can be regarded as the encryption key. For example, if we encrypt the plaintext "THIS IS A SECRET" with an encryption key $n = 3$, the ciphertext becomes "WKLV LV D VHFUHW." However, substitution is not a secure technique because the same input will always give the same output (e.g., the first "T" and the last "T" are both transformed to "W"). Hence, by counting how frequently a letter appears, one can guess what the letter is likely to be, especially if the message is long.

A better technique is transposition. It rearranges the positions of the letters as controlled by a key. For example, if the message "THIS IS A SECRET" is divided into a block of four letters and the letters of each block are transposed according to a key "4213" such that the letters in the first, second, third, and fourth positions are moved to the fourth, second, first, and third positions, respectively, the ciphertext becomes "IHSTSI S EAERTC." Note that the spaces are treated as a character as well. Unlike the substitution method, the same letter appearing in different positions in the plaintext may become a different letter for each position after the transformation (e.g., the first "T" becomes an "I" but the last "T" becomes a "C").

It is also possible to combine substitution and transposition to develop a more secure encryption algorithm. The Data Encryption Standard discussed in the next section adopts this approach.

7.4.1   Data Encryption Standard

Data Encryption Standard (DES) is the most popular private key encryption method based on research work by IBM. It was adopted by the government in the United States as an encryption standard in 1977. Basically, DES encrypts 64-bit data blocks through many stages of transposition and substitution, using a 56-bit encryption key. In this book, we use the following notation to represent DES encryption and decryption, respectively:

```
ciphertext=E_DES[plaintext|key]
```

```
D_DES[ciphertext|key]=D_DES[E_DES[plaintext|key]|key]=plaintext
```

where `plaintext` and `ciphertext` are defined as mentioned earlier and key is the encryption/decryption key. Note that in DES, the same key is used for encryption and decryption.

To make DES more secure, we can use more stages of encryption. In particular, there is a triple DES method. In a typical implementation, instead of using three stages of encryption, it uses two stages of encryption and one stage of decryption as shown by the following function:

```
E_DES[D_DES[E_DES[plain_text|key1]|key2]|key1]=cipher_text
```

Hence, it is also called DESede where "ede" stands for "encryption, decryption, and encryption." In this case, only two keys (`key1` and `key2`) are used. Note that if the two keys are the same, effectively it becomes the single-stage DES. Hence, it allows backward compatibility with the conventional DES.

7.4.2   Other symmetric key encryption algorithm

Besides DES, there are other symmetric key encryption algorithms. The International Data Encryption Algorithm (IDEA) was invented by Xuejia Lai and James Massey. It encrypts 64-bit data blocks with a 128-bit key. In fact, IDEA is often regarded as the major competitor of DES. CAST was invented by Carlisle Adams and Stafford Tavares in the United States. The key size is variable, ranging between 40 and 128 bits. The lower key size (e.g. 40 bits) is for exporting outside the United States. RC2 and RC5 were developed by Ron Rivest. RC2 encrypts data in 64-bit blocks, and a variable key size can be used. Unlike RC2, RC5 allows variable block size as well as variable key size.

7.5 THE KEY DISTRIBUTION PROBLEM

Unfortunately, it is difficult to employ private key encryption in an open e-commerce system because it uses the same key for the encryption and decryption keys. This implies that one needs to establish a different secret key with each receiver. Referring to our VBS, we must establish a different secret key with each customer in the world. Obviously, this is not effective at all. Furthermore, we need to find a secure way of passing the secret key between two parties. This is important because the private key encryption method relies on keeping the private key secret; otherwise the method becomes useless. In general, there are two ways to pass a private key between our VBS and a customer X. First, customer X can obtain the private key from VBS's physical office (i.e., the private key is handed out by physical means). Second, VBS and customer X can obtain the private key from a trusted party (key distribution centre) through a secure channel. After establishing the first secret key, the VBS and customer X can also change the secret key regularly by encrypting the new key with the old key [Stallings, 1999].

Obviously, these key distribution methods may not work well in an open e-commerce system because the VBS and customer X may not know each other previously and may be in different locations in the world.

7.6 DIFFIE–HELLMAN KEY EXCHANGE PROTOCOL

In 1976, Diffie and Hellman proposed an innovative protocol (now known as the Diffie–Hellman key agreement protocol) to establish a secret key between two parties even if they have never met before. This marked the beginning of a new type of encryption method called public key encryption as explained later. By using the Diffie–Hellman protocol, two unknown parties can set up a secret key securely over the internet. The basic operation of the protocol is explained here according to [Nichols, 1999]. First, two numbers n and g are selected where n is a large prime number and g is primitive mod n (i.e. the calculation of g^z mod n where $1 \leq z \leq n - 1$ will produce all the possible values of z). The notation "mod" will be described later. It is assumed that the parameters g and n are disclosed to everyone in the system. Suppose that the VBS and customer X wants to establish a shared secret key. This can be done as follows:

- *Step 1*: Customer X selects a random number x and sends $u = g^x$ mod n to the VBS.
- *Step 2*: The VBS also selects a random number y and sends $v = g^y$ mod n to customer X.

- *Step* 3: Customer X and the VBS compute the shared secret key as u^x mod n and v^y mod n, respectively. It can be shown that the computed values are both g^{xy} mod n, so it can be used as the shared secret key.

The foundation of the Diffie–Hellman protocol relies on the difficulty in computing discrete logarithms. Basically, given g^x mod n, g^y mod n, n, and g (i.e., even these parameters are disclosed), it is almost impossible to determine g^{xy} mod n provided that the prime number n is very large.

7.7   *PUBLIC KEY ENCRYPTION*

As private key encryption relies heavily on a secure key distribution method, it cannot be deployed easily in a public network like the internet and hence in an open e-commerce system. By using public key encryption, this difficulty can be resolved automatically. In public key encryption, everyone has a pair of keys called the public key and the private key. The private key is kept confidential but the public key can be disclosed to the public. If a public key encryption algorithm is effective, it is almost impossible to deduce the corresponding private key from the public key. If someone wants to encrypt a message for you, he will use your public key to encrypt the message. To decrypt the secret message, your private key must be used. Figure 7.3 illustrates the basic concept of public key encryption. It is also possible to use the private key for encrypting data. In this case, the corresponding public key must be used for decryption. As we will see later, this is used in generating a digital signature.

7.8   *RSA ENCRYPTION ALGORITHM*

Unlike private key encryption, which is usually based on transposition and substitution techniques, public key encryption is usually based on number theory. A popular public key encryption method is the RSA algorithm, named after its inventors Rivest, Shamir, and Adleman. Before discussing about this algorithm, we will review the mathematical operator "mod."

Basically $X = Y$ mod Z means "When Y is divided by Z, the remainder is X." For example, when 7 is divided by 3, the remainder is 1, so $1 = 7$ mod 3. Please try the following examples to make sure that you fully understand this notation.

- $2 = 2$ mod 4, is it right or wrong?
- $X = 18$ mod 7, what is X?
- $5 = Y$ mod 10, what is Y?

public key

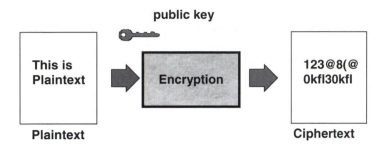

Plaintext   Ciphertext

private key

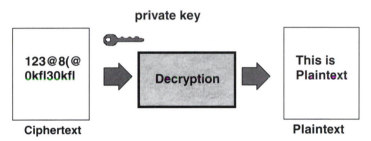

Ciphertext   Plaintext

Figure 7.3 Public key encryption/decryption

Here are the answers. Of course 2 = 2 mod 4 is right because when 2 is divided by 4, the remainder is 2. In the second example, $X = 4$ because when 18 is divided by 7, the remainder is 4. Y has many solutions such as 5, 15, 25, ... in the third example.

As e-commerce system relies heavily on the RSA encryption algorithm, it is of interest to learn this algorithm in detail as described here. First we need to generate a public key and a private key by following these steps [Stallings, 1999; Tanenbaum, 1996]:

- *Step 1*: Pick two large prime numbers p and q
- *Step 2*: Multiply p and q together to get n (i.e. $n = pq$)
- *Step 3*: Choose d, such that d and $w = (p - 1)(q - 1)$ are relatively prime (i.e., they have no common factor other than one). Note also that d must be smaller than w
- *Step 4*: Compute e such that $1 = (d \times e)$ mod w (i.e., when $(d \times e)/w$, the remainder is 1)
- *Step 5*: The public key is $<e, n>$
- *Step 6*: The private key is $<d, n>$

Suppose that there is a message with a message code m, then the secret code s is worked out by the following formula:

$s = m^e \bmod n$ (i.e., the remainder when m^e is divided by n)

Decryption is the reverse process. If the recipient receives the secret code s, the original message code m can be worked out by the following formula:

$m = s^d \bmod n$ (i.e., the remainder when s^d is divided by n)

Let us study a simple example by repeating the aforementioned steps. Firstly, we need to generate the public and private keys as follows.

- *Step 1*: Pick two large prime numbers: $p = 19$, $q = 7$ (here we simply use two small prime numbers to illustrate the basic operation)
- *Step 2*: Multiply p by q to get n, so $n = pq = 133$
- *Step 3*: $w = (p - 1)(q - 1) = 108$, we choose $d = 31$ because 31 and 108 have no common factor
- *Step 4*: $1 = 31e \bmod 108$, so $e = 7$

Therefore, the keys are $<e = 7, n = 133>$ (public key) and $<d = 31, n = 133>$ (private key). Next we perform encryption for a message code $m = 29$:

- *Step 5*: Since $s = m^e \bmod$ n, if $m = 29, s = 15$.

That means, the secret code is $s = 15$. Finally, let us check that the original message code can be recovered by means of decryption.

- *Step 6*: $m = s^d \bmod n$ (Note that $d = 31$ and $n = 133$).
- *Step 7*: $m = 15^{31} \bmod 133 = 29$

Hence, the original message code is recovered in Step 7. Other than testing all the possible $<d, n>$ (i.e., using an exhausive key search), another possible way to break RSA is to factorize n in order to obtain p and q and then d. If n is a very large number, this is almost impossible because it is computationally unfeasible to factorize large numbers.

Using the aforementioned notation, a `plaintext` is converted to a `ciphertext` using RSA encryption as follows:

`ciphertext=E`$_{RSA}$`[plaintext|key`$_{public}$`]`

Similarly, the ciphertext is recovered as follows:

```
plaintext=D_RSA[ciphertext|key_private]
```

Note that in the above notation, the "type" for public key and private key are "public" and "private," respectively.

7.9   HYBRID ENCRYPTION

Although public key encryption can be deployed more easily in a public network, it is generally slower than private key encryption. Hence, it is more effective to combine private and public key encryptions in order to improve processing efficiency while maintaining the advantages of public key encryption (i.e., no key distribution problem). A common method is to use the RSA encryption method to distribute a temporary DES key called a session key between the sender and receiver. The session key can then be used for DES encryption and decryption. For example, if a customer wants to establish a secure session with the VBS, a session key ($key_{session}$) is generated and encrypted by using the public key of the VBS ($key_{public,VBS}$), i.e., E_{RSA} [$key_{session}$ | $key_{public,VBS}$]. Recall that using this notation, "$key_{session}$" means that it is a session key and "$key_{public,VBS}$" means that it is a public key belonging to the VBS. The encrypted key is then sent to the VBS. By means of decryption with the corresponding private key, the VBS can obtain the session key. The VBS and the customer can then use this session key to perform DES encryption for each other. Another advantage of using the session key is that it can thwart replay attack since the session key is not the same for different sessions. The Secure Socket Layer (SSL) adopts a similar approach to ensure secure data transfer between a web client and a web server.

7.10   OTHER PUBLIC KEY ENCRYPTION METHODS

Currently, RSA is the most commonly used public key encryption method. Although the Diffie–Hellman key agreement algorithm is often related to public key encryption, it is used only for generating a secret key between two parties. Subsequently, private key encryption is used with the secret key. Another public key encryption method is called the ElGamal method, invented by Taher ElGamal. It is similar to the Diffie–Hellman key agreement protocol, but it can be used for encryption and digital signature like RSA. Interested readers may refer to the book by Knudsen [1998] for the algorithm and its implementation details using Java Cryptography. Currently, a new encryption technique called Elliptic Curve Cryptography (ECC) is being developed. Many researchers believe that ECC has the potential to replace RSA because it can achieve the same level of security with a lower key size. For details on ECC, please refer to more advanced text on cryptography.

7.11   STREAM CIPHER AND BLOCK CIPHER

In terms of implementation, there are two types of symmetric key encryption, namely stream cipher and block cipher. Stream cipher processes one bit or one byte of input data at a time. An example is RC4. On the other hand, block cipher handles a block of input data, typically 64 bits at a time. Most encryption algorithms are based on this approach. We will describe the block cipher approach only because it is more commonly used nowadays. For the block cipher, as a message may not be a multiple of 64 bits, padding bits are added. Basically, a message is broken into a block of 64 bits for processing. If the last block is not 64 bits long, "dummy bits" (called padding bits) are added to make it a 64-bit block.

The block cipher can operate in different modes that govern how the output ciphertext blocks are produced from the input plaintext blocks. The basic mode is known as Electronic Code Book (ECB). In this case, each plaintext block is processed independently to give a ciphertext block. While this is easy to implement, it is relatively less secure. There are other more secure modes of operation. For example, the cipher block chaining (CBC) mode processes each plaintext block by mixing it with the preceding block of ciphertext by means of the bit-wise XOR function before encryption. The resultant block at each stage is then encrypted to produce the next ciphertext block. To start off the process, the first plaintext block is mixed with an initialization block. Other modes of operation can be found in other advanced books on cryptography e.g., Schneier [1996] and Knudsen [1998].

7.12   MESSAGE DIGEST

Although encryption can ensure data confidentiality, it is time consuming especially if it is implemented by means of software and the input message is large. In many cases, users are concerned about data integrity rather than data confidentiality. For example, when a customer sends an inquiry to the VBS, he probably does not mind if other people can read the message as long as the content remains unchanged. Of course, with encryption, data confidentiality as well as data integrity can be ensured simultaneously. However, this is done at the expense of a longer processing time. Therefore, we need a more efficient technique to address the integrity requirement. A message digest forms the basis of this technique. Message digest is also called

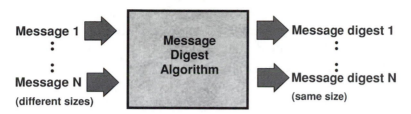

Figure 7.4 Message digest

a hash function. As shown in Figure 7.4, the purpose of the message digest is to compute a checksum, a hash value, or a "fingerprint" for a message. In most message digest algorithms, the size of the "checksum" is irrespective of the size of the input message. In this book, we denote the message digest of a message M as H[M].

An effective message digest algorithm should have the following properties based on [Tanenbaum, 1996]:

1. For any message M, we can compute the message digest H[M] easily.
2. It is infeasible to find the corresponding message of a message digest (i.e., it is infeasible to find M based on H[M]).
3. Each message digest is unique to the corresponding message. In other words, it is practically impossible to find two messages with the same message digest.
4. If the input message is changed slightly (i.e., even if one character is changed), the message digest will be changed significantly. This makes it extremely difficult to break the message digest algorithm.

7.12.1 MD5 message digest algorithm

The commonly used message digest algorithm is the MD5 algorithm invented by Rivest. The algorithm basically works as follows [See RFC1321]:

- *Step 1*: Padding bits and a 64-bit length field are added to the original message such that the resultant message becomes an integer multiple of 512 bits.
- *Step 2*: The resultant message from step 1 is broken into blocks of 512 bits: B_1, $B_2, \ldots, B_n$.
- *Step 3*: The message blocks are processed by a compression function C as follows:

$$V_k = C(V_{k-1}, B_k); \quad k = 1, 2, \ldots . n$$

where V_{k-1} and B_k are the input values to the compression function and V_k is the output value, which is 128 bits long. To start the process, the initial value V_0 is specified in the MD5 standard.

- *Step 4*: Eventually the message digest is given by V_n.

Note that for MD5, no matter how long the input message is, the resultant message digest is still 128 bits long.

7.12.2   Other message digest algorithms

Besides MD5, other well-known message digest algorithms include MD2, MD4, and Secure Hash Algorithm (SHA). MD2 and MD4 were also designed by Ron Rivest. They can be viewed as the early versions of MD5. Among MD2, MD4, and MD5, MD4 is the most efficient but it is less secure than MD5 [Naik, 1998]. SHA is essentially based on MD4 and it has been adopted by the US government. While SHA also handles messages in blocks of 512 bits as MD5, it results a longer message digest of 160 bits.

7.13   *MESSAGE AUTHENTICATION CODE*

Consider the following scenario.* Suppose that a VBS customer sends an order message as well as its message digest to the VBS. The VBS computes the message digest for the order message and finds that this is the same as the received message digest. Unfortunately, the message digest alone cannot guarantee message integrity. This is because of the possibility that if an intruder captures the message, he can change the message and generate another message digest for the modified message because message digest algorithms are usually open. One way to ensure message integrity is to generate a message authentication code (MAC). In general, this is done by finding the message digest of the message together with a secret key (i.e., a large random number) shared between the sender and receiver. In this case, after receiving the order message and the MAC, the VBS can compute the MAC by finding the message digest of the message together with the shared secret key. If it matches the received MAC, message integrity is verified. Unlike the previous case, even though an intruder can change the message, he cannot generate the corresponding MAC because he does not know the shared secret key. A more secure way to generate a MAC is by using the HMAC algorithm as specified in RFC2104. In this case, the MAC is generated as follows [Stallings, 1999; RFC2104]:

---

* This is inspired by another scenario in Knudsen [1998].

- *Step 1*: The secret key is padded to the correct length to produce a padded key K.
- *Step 2*: K is added to an initialization padding value PAD1 by using the bit-wise exclusive OR function (XOR).
- *Step 3*: The original message T is then concatenated with the resultant message digest from step 2.
- *Step 4*: The message digest for the resultant message from step 3 is found.
- *Step 5*: K is added to another initialization padding value PAD2 by using XOR.
- *Step 6*: The resultant message from step 4 is concatenated with the resultant message from step 5.
- *Step 7*: The HMAC is found by calculating the message digest of the resultant message from step 6.

Mathematically, this operation can be represented by the following formula:

$$HMAC = H[(K \oplus PAD2) \parallel H[(K \oplus PAD1) \parallel T]]$$

where $\parallel$ and $\oplus$ denote concatenation and XOR, respectively.

7.14 *DIGITAL SIGNATURE*

Besides MAC, a Digital Signature is another method used to provide data integrity. It can be viewed as a combination of message digest and public key encryption. A popular example is the RSA/MD5 digital signature algorithm. This algorithm employs RSA and MD5 for performing encryption and message digest, respectively. As shown in Figure 7.5, basically a sender signs a file by computing the message digest of the file first and then encrypting the message digest with the sender's private

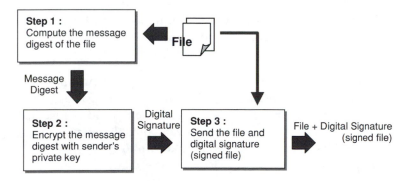

Figure 7.5 Steps in digital signature generation (extension of the work of Knudsen [1998] and Ford and Baum [1997])

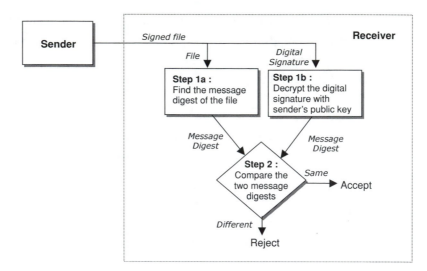

Figure 7.6 Steps in digital signature verification (extension of the work of Knudsen [1998] and Ford and Baum [1997])

key (key$_{\text{private,sender}}$) to produce the digital signature. By using the previous notation, the digital signature (digital_signature) for a file F is

```
digital_signature=E_RSA[H_MD5[F]|key_private,sender]
```

The message and the digital signature are then sent to the receiver. To verify the digital signature, the recipient performs the following steps as shown in Figure 7.6.

- *Step 1*: Decrypt the digital signature with the sender's public key (key$_{\text{public,sender}}$) to get the message digest, i.e., D_{RSA} [digital_signature | key$_{\text{public,sender}}$].

- *Step 2*: Find the message digest of the file, i.e., H_{MD5}[F].

- *Step 3*: Compare the two message digests as found in steps 1 and 2. If the content of the file has not been changed, H_{MD5}[F] should be equal to D_{RSA} [digital_signature | key$_{\text{public,sender}}$].

By doing so, data integrity can be ensured because if the two message digests are different, the file must have been changed, so it will no longer be valid. Note that although it is possible for an intruder to capture the file and change its content, it is impossible for the intruder to regenerate a valid digital signature for the modified message because the sender's private key is unknown to the intruder.

To simplify the notation, we can define a new digital signature function S as follows:

```
S_RSA/MD5[F]=E_RSA[H_MD5[F]|key_private,sender]
```

This digital signature function employs RSA and MD5 to produce the digital signature for an input file F.

7.15   DIGITAL SIGNATURE STANDARD

Besides the RSA signature algorithm, another commonly used digital signature method is the Digital Signature Standard (DSS). DSS employs SHA and is based on the ElGamal public key algorithm. It was endorsed by the US government in 1991. Subsequently, two revised versions were issued in 1993 and 1996 to address some weaknesses such as increasing the original key size. However, DSS is often criticized for two major disadvantages. First, the ElGamal algorithm has not been tested as rigorously as the RSA algorithm [Tanenbaum, 1996]. In other words, to determine whether it can achieve the same level of security requires more study. Second, in terms of signature verification, DSS is more time consuming [Naik, 1998]. As signature verification is usually performed more frequently than signature generation, this is obviously not desirable.

7.16   AUTHENTICATION

Finally, let us talk about the last security requirement, i.e. authentication. Its purpose is to verify identity. This is extremely important in e-commerce. Consider the situation where you visit the VBS; you would certainly like to verify that it is the real VBS before carrying out any transaction. In general, authentication can be performed by using one, or a combination of, the following principles*:

- What you know (e.g. password)
- What you possess (e.g. identity card)
- What you are (e.g. fingerprint)

One common authentication method is by means of "username and password." Suppose that the VBS has kept the username and password of its customers in a database. When a customer accesses the VBS, he will need to enter his username and password. By checking the username and password against the records in the database, the customer's identity can be verified. While this method is simple to use, it may not be secure. If an intruder can capture the username and password on the internet, he can simply resend it to the VBS. This is known as replay attack. There are a variety of methods to address this problem. For example, we can encrypt the username and password with a shared secret key between the VBS and the

---

* These were heard during a seminar some time ago.

customer. The Unix system uses a similar method to ensure access security. However, it is generally difficult to employ the username and password method in B2C e-commerce because the customer and the virtual store may not have a preestablished relationship.

7.16.1   Public key infrastructure

As it is more effective to deploy public key encryption in an open e-commerce system, we focus on discussing authentication in a public key system. To build a public key infrastructure for e-commerce, we need to address two issues:

- How can we obtain the public key of the other party?
- How can we verify that this is the real public key of the other party?

There are basically two solutions, namely a centralized approach and a distributed approach [Nichols, 1999; Stallings, 1999]. In the centralized approach, a key distribution center is established, which stores the public keys of all users. The key distribution center is trusted by all people, and all users are assumed to have the public key of the key distribution center. When someone wants to obtain the public key of a person, he can obtain it from the key distribution center. The key distribution center distributes the key by encrypting it with its private key. The recipient then obtains the key by means of decryption with the public key of the key distribution center.

The obvious drawback of this method is scalability. If there is a large number of people, the key distribution center will become a bottleneck. A better approach is to use a distributed method so that two people can exchange their public keys without involving a third party. This is exactly what the digital certificate does. Its concept and operation are explained in the next section.

7.16.2   Digital certificate

A digital certificate is an identification document. It functions like your passport or any other identity card [Feghhi *et al.*, 1998]. To illustrate the basic concept, we first consider a simplified digital certificate as shown in Figure 7.7 [Ford and Baum, 1997]. We discuss the digital certificate standard later in this section. Among other information, the content (C) of a digital certificate consists of the owner's information (I) and the owner's public key (K). The content is signed digitally by a trusted party called the certification authority (CA). Here we assume that the RSA/MD5 signature

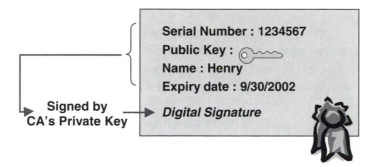

Figure 7.7   General format of a digital certificate

method is used. That means, the digital signature is given by

$$E_{RSA}[H_{MD5}[C]|key_{private,CA}]$$

where $key_{private,CA}$ is the private key of the CA.

The VBS can apply for a digital certificate from a CA. Before issuing the digital certificate, the CA will verify the identity of the VBS. Upon successful verification, a digital certificate will be issued and the public key of the VBS will be embedded in the digital certificate. If a customer wants to verify the identity of the VBS, a copy of the digital certificate will be passed to the customer. It is assumed that the customer trusts the CA and possesses the CA's public key and so the content of the digital certificate can be verified by checking the digital signature. Upon successful verification, the public key of the VBS can be extracted from the digital certificate so that it can be used to encrypt data for the VBS. In addition, the public key can also be used to verify the RSA digital signature generated by the VBS.

7.16.3   X.509: A digital certificate framework

Let us now look at how a digital certificate is implemented in practice. The International Telecommunication Union (ITU) X.509 standard specifies a framework for supporting digital certificates using a public-key infrastructure. Since its first version issued in 1988, the X.509v1 specification was revised in 1993 to produce X.509v2. X.509v2 was further updated in 1996 to produce the X.509v3 specification. A X.509v3 certificate contains the following fields [Feghhi, Feghhi, and Williams, 1998]:

Version	The version number
Serial number	A unique number for identifying the certificate
Signature algorithm identifier	Information on the signature algorithm
Issuer	The CA that issues the certificate
Validity period	The period of time during which the certificate is valid
Subject	The owner of the public key
Subject public key information	Information on subject's public key
Issuer unique identifier	Optional field for identifying the issuer uniquely
Subject unique identifier	Optional field for identifying the subject uniquely
Extension fields	This is for including additional data
Digital signature	The digital signature for the above fields

In terms of naming, a number of alternatives can be used in a X.509v3 certificate including, but not limited to, the X.500 naming system, internet domain name, and URL [Ford and Baum, 1997]. In the early version of X.509 certificates, only the X.500 naming system was allowed. For example, a valid X.500 name may have the following elements: country, organization, organization unit, and common name. Therefore, Henry Chan of the Department of Computing, the Hong Kong Polytechnic University may be represented as

```
{Country="China", Organization="Hong Kong Polytechnic University",
Organization Unit="Department of Computing" and Common Name="Henry
Chan"}
```

The format (i.e. data structure) of a X.509 certificate is defined using the Abstract Syntax One (ANS.1) notation. To encode data for communication purpose, either the Distinguished Encoding Rules (DER) or the Basic Encoding Rules (BER) can be used.

7.16.4 Certificate chain/verification path

The above approach works well if all the certificates are issued by a single CA. However, in reality there is more than one CA in the world and it is not feasible for a user to know all the CAs.

Consider the following problem posted in Stallings [1999]. Customer X and the VBS may obtain digital certificates from two different CAs say CA_1 and CA_2, respectively. We denote X's certificate as $CERT_{X|CA1}$ and VBS's certificate as $CERT_{VBS|CA2}$. If X does not know CA_2 and hence does not have the corresponding public key of CA_2, how can X verify VBS's certificate signed by CA_2, i.e. $CERT_{VBS|CA2}$? Here is a possible solution. Suppose that CA_2 has a certificate signed by CA_1, i.e. $CERT_{CA2|CA1}$. VBS can pass the following certificates to X: $CERT_{CA2|CA1}$ and $CERT_{VBS|CA2}$.

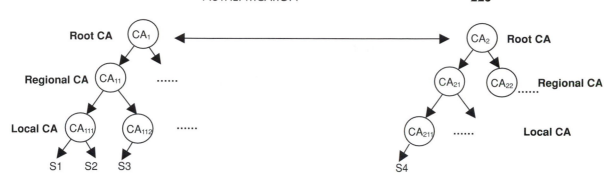

Figure 7.8 Hierarchical digital certificate system

Obviously, X can verify the CA2's certificate because X has the public key of CA_1. After verifying the certificate, X can then obtain the public key of CA_2 and verify VBS's certificate. Technically, X verifies VBS's certificate by going through a certificate chain or verification path as represented by*

$$CA_1 \Rightarrow CA_2 \Rightarrow VBS$$

where $\Rightarrow$ indicates issuing of certificates: CA_1 to CA_2, CA_2 to VBS, and so on. In some complex situations, the certificate chain or verification path can contain more elements (see the example in the next section). In the aforementioned example, we consider that the VBS passes a chain of certificates to X for verification. Alternatively, VBS may just pass its certificate to X. In this case, X needs to go through the verification path by obtaining the certificates from the respective directories or CAs.

7.16.5 An hierarchical trust system

In practice, an hierarchical trust system can be used to provide a scaleable solution. An example is shown in Figure 7.8 [Feghhi, Feghhi, and Williams, 1998] with three levels of hierarchy: root CA, regional CAs, and local CAs. Of course, this architecture can be expanded easily to include more levels. At the highest level, there is a root CA. It can be the government administration of a country or a city, e.g., the Post Office in Hong Kong. This root CA is trusted by everyone in the system and everyone has the public key of the root CA. To build a scaleable architecture, the root CA delegates its responsibility of issuing digital certificates to the lower level CAs. This is done by certifying the identity of the regional CAs by issuing each one with a digital certificate. Each regional CA can also delegate the responsibility further by issuing certificates

---

* Please refer to Stallings [1999] for the formal X.509 notation.

to the corresponding local CAs. Typically, subscribers obtain certificates from their local CAs. In an even larger system (e.g., the global internet), there may be many communities, each with its own root CA. To establish a global certification system, the notion of "islands of trust" [Feghhi, Feghhi, and Williams, 1998] is used. In this case, the root CA of each independent system needs to cross-certify other root CAs (i.e., by issuing to each other a digital certificate).

Figure 7.8 illustrates an hierarchical digital certificate system. We use it to explore some illustrative examples, say, a subscriber S1 can verify the certificates of three different subscribers S2, S3, and S4. It is assumed that each subscriber has the public keys of the root CA and issuer CA. Hence, S1 has the public keys of CA_1 and CA_{111}. Subscribers S1 and S2 belong to the same local CA, so S1 can verify the certificate of S2 easily by using the public key of the local CA (i.e. CA_{111}). S1 and S3 belong to two different local CAs attached to the same regional CA. To verify S3's certificate, S1 needs to go through the following verification path:

$$CA_1 \Rightarrow CA_{11} \Rightarrow CA_{112} \Rightarrow S3$$

As S4 belongs to another system, S1 needs to verify S4's certificate by going through the following path:

$$CA_1 \Rightarrow CA_2 \Rightarrow CA_{21} \Rightarrow CA_{211} \Rightarrow S4$$

7.16.6   Challenge and response authentication protocol

It is important to note that when someone sends a digital certificate to you over the internet, it does not guarantee that the sender must be the subject stated on the digital certificate. Digital certificates are exchangeable and so other people may also possess the subject's digital certificate. This is similar to the situation that when someone passes you a valid name card, you cannot conclude that he is the person stated on the name card. Of course, after obtaining the public key from the digital certificate, we can encrypt data for that sender using the public key. Unless that sender is the subject stated on the digital certificate, he does not have the required private key for decrypting the data.

Suppose that a customer X and the VBS have exchanged their digital certificates and hence the public keys. X can verify VBS's identity by using the following "challenge and response" protocol.

- *Step 1*: X generates a random number, encrypts it with VBS's public key, and sends the encrypted random number to VBS. Note that VBS's public key is obtained from VBS's certificate.

- *Step* 2: VBS receives the encrypted random number and decrypts it with the respective private key.
- *Step* 3: VBS then encrypts the random number with X's public key and sends it to X.
- *Step* 4: By means of decryption, X verifies that the random number is correct and hence confirms the identity of VBS. Note that only VBS has VBS's private key.

This "challenge and response" protocol forms the basis of many authentication protocols. In fact, the random number can be used as a session key for performing DES encryption.

7.16.7 Certificate revocation

Although a certificate is given a validity period, it may still become invalid before its expiry date. Such a situation may arise when the owner loses the private key. This is similar to the situation when you lose a credit card. In this case, you inform the credit card center to make the credit card invalid. In digital certificate terminology, this is called revocation, i.e., a digital certificate is assigned invalid by its CA for special reasons. A CA uses a certificate revocation list (CRL) to provide information on valid certificates that have been revoked.

Basically, a CRL contains the serial number of all revoked certificates, timing information, and other administrative information. The content of a CRL is digitally signed by the CA's private key so that if the content is changed, the digital signature will no longer be valid. By checking the CRL, a user can verify whether a certificate has been revoked. A user can access the CRL through a number of different mechanisms [Ford and Baum, 1997; Feghhi, Feghhi, and Williams, 1998]:

- *Pull* – For some CAs, the CRL is stored in a directory for public access.
- *Push* – Another mechanism is to distribute the CRL to all users once it is updated (i.e., when a certificate is revoked). However, this may overload the network.
- *Interactive* – Finally, a user can make an on-line inquiry with the CA to check the validity of a certificate (i.e., whether the specified certificate has been revoked).

7.17 SUMMARY

In this chapter, we have given an overview of cryptography techniques for enabling e-commerce on the insecure internet. In general, these techniques are used for addressing three security requirements, namely Confidentiality, Integrity, and Authentication. Encryption is used to ensure confidentiality whereby a message is transformed into a secret message. There are two types of encryption: symmetric (private) key encryption and asymmetric (public) key encryption. It is difficult to employ symmetric key encryption in an open e-commerce system because of the key distribution problem. Asymmetric key encryption solves this problem automatically because the encryption and the decryption keys are different. To enhance processing efficiency while maintaining the advantage of public key encryption, a hybrid encryption method using both the private key encryption and public key encryption is often used. A message digest provides a unique checksum ("fingerprint") for a message. By combining the message digest and encryption, the MAC method and the Digital Signature method can be used to provide message integrity. The digital certificate is used for authentication in an open e-commerce system. The ITU-T recommendation X.509 specifies a digital certificate framework.

REFERENCES

Feghhi, J., Feghhi, J., and Williams, P., *Digital Certificates*, Addison-Wesley, Reading, MA, 1998.

Ford, W. and Baum, M. S., *Secure Electronic Commerce*, Prentice-Hall, Upper Saddle River, NJ, 1997.

Knudsen, J., *Java Cryptography*, O'Reilly & Associates, Inc., 1998.

Naik, D. C., *Internet Standards and Protocols*, Microsoft Press, 1998.

Nichols, R. K., *ICSA Guide to Cryptography*, McGraw-Hill, New York, 1999.

Schneier, B., *Applied Cryptography*, Wiley, New York, 1996.

Stallings, W., *Cryptography and Network Security*, Prentice-Hall, Upper Saddle River, NJ, 1999.

Tanenbaum, A. S., *Computer Networks*, 3rd edn., Prentice-Hall, Upper Saddle River, NJ, 1996.

RECOMMENDED READING

The purpose of this chapter is to give an overview of the cryptographic techniques for enabling e-commerce. To keep the information as concise as possible, we address only the three Ws (WWW): Why they are required? What they are in general? How they basically work. We leave out most of the implementation details. Interested readers are encouraged to read the following references.

Tanenbaum, A. S., *Computer Networks*, 3rd edn., Prentice-Hall, Upper Saddle River, NJ, 1996.

Naik, D. C., *Internet Standards and Protocols*, Microsoft Press, 1998.

These books give a good introduction to cryptography in Chapter 7 and Chapter 5, respectively.

Stallings, W., *Cryptography and Network Security*, Prentice-Hall, Upper Saddle River, NJ, 1999.

This gives an excellent overview of cryptography and network security. It covers most of the popular algorithms and their implementation details.

Schneier, B., *Applied Cryptography*, Wiley, New York, 1996.

Nichols, R. K., *ICSA Guide to Cryptography*, McGraw-Hill, New York, 1999.

These are classical references on cryptography. In particular, the former contains nearly all the available algorithms and also source code in C for implementing these. The Wired Magazine said that this is *the book the National Security Agency wanted never to be published.*

Knudsen, J., *Java Cryptography*, O'Reilly & Associates, Inc., 1998.

This is a representative text on Java cryptography. It covers the cryptographic programming in Java in great detail and is highly recommended for those who want to explore Java cryptography.

Feghhi, J., Feghhi, J., and Williams, P., *Digital Certificates*, Addison-Wesley, Reading, MA, 1998.

This book is specially written on digital certificates.

Ford, W. and Baum, M. S., *Secure Electronic Commerce*, Prentice-Hall, Upper Saddle River, NJ, 1997.

This book also covers digital certificates and public key infrastructure in great detail.

There are also many good references on the internet. In particular, the RSA laboratory maintains an excellent Q&A on cryptography at http://www.rsasecurity.com/rsalabs/faq/. Readers are strongly encouraged to visit this informative web site. One of the well-known CAs for digital certificates is Verisign whose web site is http://www.verign.com.

8

Internet Security

8.1 IPSec Protocol

8.2 Setting up Security Associations

8.3 The Authentication Header (AH) Service

8.4 The Encapsulating Security Payload (ESP) Service

8.5 Preventing Replay Attack

8.6 Application of IPSec: Virtual Private Network

8.7 Firewalls

8.8 Different Types of Firewalls

8.9 Examples of Firewall Systems

8.10 Secure Socket Layer (SSL)

8.11 Putting Everything Together

8.12 Summary

      References

      Recommended Reading

In Chapter 7, we introduced various cryptographic techniques to address the Confidentiality, Integrity and Authentication security requirements. In this chapter, we will examine how to make use of the cryptographic techniques to build a secure e-commerce system. Basically, security can be addressed at either the network layer or the transport layer. Serving as the first line of defense, firewalls are commonly employed to protect an intranet (private network) against possible attacks from the internet (public network). They typically control the admission of packets entering an intranet. The original Internet Protocol (IP) does not address security issues. As an option, IPSec provides both authentication and encryption services to IP packets. By using IPSec, companies and their trading partners can build secure virtual private networks over the public internet. At the transport layer, the Secure Socket Layer (SSL) protocol is used to ensure secure data transfer between two host computers particularly for HTTP. Typically, SSL is used for transferring sensitive data (e.g. credit card information) between a web client and a web server. Therefore, SSL is extremely important in B2C e-commerce. By combining firewalls, IPSec, and SSL, we can build a very secure e-commerce system over the internet. The rest of this chapter will discuss these technologies.

8.1 *IPSec PROTOCOL*

As a security option for the current IP, IP Security Protocol (IPSec) [RFC 2401–2406] supports authentication and/or encryption service(s) at the network layer. As shown in Figure 8.1, this is done by adding a new IPSec header between the IP header and the IP payload. The header is inserted either by an end user's computer if the computer can support IPSec or by an IPSec-enabled gateway. As explained later in this chapter, this new IPSec header provides the necessary protection. There are two types of IPSec headers or IPSec services, namely the Authentication Header (AH) and the Encapsulating Security Payload (ESP). The AH verifies the identity of an IP packet and ensures the content integrity. In other words, if the content is altered, the receiver can detect it so that appropriate action can be taken (e.g., request the sender to retransmit the packet). However, the content of the packet is

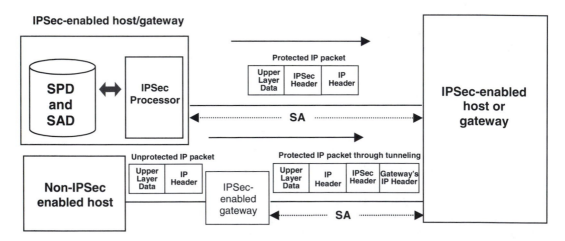

Figure 8.1   IPSec service (extension of the work of Oppliger [1998])

not kept confidential because the packet is not encrypted. At the expense of a longer processing time, ESP provides an encryption service and an optional authentication service. There are two modes of operation for both AH and ESP, namely the transport mode and the tunnel mode. For the transport mode, the upper-layer data (i.e., data above the network layer) is protected. It is usually used if the end users can support IPSec. For the tunnel mode, the protection covers the whole packet. In this case, the end users do not need to support IPSec because an IPSec-enabled gateway is employed to apply the required protection. It will be explained in detail later in this chapter.

8.2 *SETTING UP SECURITY ASSOCIATIONS*

Before employing IPSec between two devices, they need to setup a security association (SA) which defines a simplex security relationship between them. That means, if two hosts X and Y want to use IPSec in both the X-to-Y and Y-to-X directions, they need to set up two SAs. Note that the configuration for the two SAs can be different. Thus, for instance, they could use different cryptographic algorithms. Among other information, each SA basically defines [Smith, 1997]

- the required protection (AH or ESP)
- the encryption and/or authentication methods
- the corresponding key(s) for performing the cryptographic functions

An SA can be set up either manually or dynamically [Doraswamy and Harkins, 1999]. The set-up procedure involves the establishment of various cryptographic keys and security parameters. In the manual case, a network administrator can configure the SA during system setup. In the dynamic case, two computers negotiate an SA by using the Internet Key Exchange (IKE) protocol as defined in RFC2409. IKE is based on the internet Security Association and Key Management Protocol (ISAKMP) as defined in RFC2408 and the Oakley key management protocol. The latter protocol is an enhanced version of the Diffie–Hellman key exchange protocol that was described in the previous chapter. Generally speaking, the ISAKMP defines the generic protocol including the data structure for establishing the cryptographic key(s) and setting up the security parameters. Once an SA is established, a security parameter index (SPI) is assigned to the SA. The SPI is specified in the IPSec header of all IP packets belonging to the SA. Note that an SPI may not be globally unique. Therefore, the SA of an IP packet is identified by the SPI in the IPSec header together with the destination IP address in the IP header.

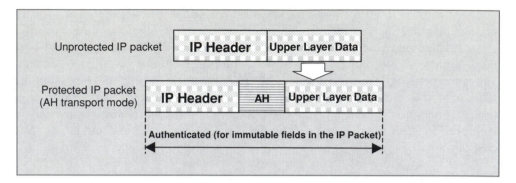

Figure 8.2 AH service (Transport mode) [see also RFC 2402; Murhammer *et al.*, 1999]

To implement IPSec, two databases are required, namely an SA Database (SAD) and a Security Policy Database (SPD). SAD stores the information on the SAs, and SPD defines the security policy and maintains the mapping between IP traffic and the SAs. Note that an IP packet may belong to more than one SA (i.e. a bundle of SAs). For example, as described later, it is possible to combine the transport mode and the tunnel mode to provide end-to-end security inside an IP tunnel. The SA(s) of an IP packet is/are identified by selected fields in the IP packet known as "selectors." For example, the source IP address can be used as a selector. In this case, the IPSec device identifies the SA by matching the source IP address in the IP packets with that of the SPD fields. After finding a match, the corresponding IPSec protection will be applied to the packet.

The basic operation of the IPSec service is as follows [RFC2401; Stallings, 1999]. After receiving an outgoing packet, the IPSec device identifies the SA of the packet from the SPD based on the selector fields in the IP packet. Then the required IPSec header with the corresponding SPI will be added and the required protection will be applied to the packet. The resultant packet is then transmitted to the destination. Having received the inbound packet, the receiving IPSec device identifies the SA by reading the SPI and other information in the packet. The packet is then processed with the required cryptographic algorithms before it is delivered to the receiver.

8.3 *THE AUTHENTICATION HEADER (AH) SERVICE*

Figure 8.2 shows how to apply an Authentication Header (AH) to an IP packet* by using the transport mode. Basically, the AH is inserted between the IP header and the

---

* In this book, we consider IPv4 packets only because they are currently the most commonly used IP. For IPv6, the IPSec header is actually an extension header.

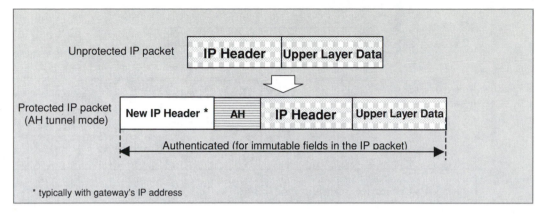

Figure 8.3   AH service (Tunnel mode) [see also RFC 2402; Murhammer *et al.*, 1999]

upper layer data. Inside the AH, a cryptographic check value is included to ensure content integrity. Essentially, it is generated by means of a Message Authentication Code (MAC) algorithm such as Keyed MD5 or HMAC as explained in Chapter 7 (see RFC1828). The computation only applies to fixed or predictable fields in the IP packet. Note that certain fields in the IP header (e.g. time-to-live field) may be altered during transit, so the protection does not cover these mutable fields. Figure 8.3 shows the AH service under the tunnel mode. In this case, the sending host may not support IPSec, so it needs to send the packet to an IPSec gateway for applying the IPSec service. After receiving the packet, the IPSec gateway inserts its own IP header into the original IP packet. Then the AH is included by treating the original IP packet as the new IP packet payload. In other words, the original packet is encapsulated inside a new packet. This is why it is called tunnelling.

8.4   THE ENCAPSULATING SECURITY PAYLOAD (ESP) SERVICE

Figure 8.4 shows how to apply the ESP service to an IP packet by using the transport mode. As shown in the figure, the ESP header is added between the IP header and the upper layer data. The ESP trailer is then attached to the IP packet. The upper layer data together with the ESP trailer is encrypted to ensure data confidentiality. The default encryption method is DES in the Cipher Block Chaining (CBC) mode. Should authentication be required, an ESP authentication trailer (ESP Auth) is appended to the end of the packet. This trailer contains a cryptographic check value to ensure data integrity. The computation applies to the ESP header, the IP packet payload (i.e. the upper layer data), and the ESP trailer.

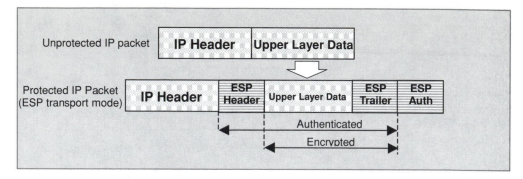

Figure 8.4 ESP service (transport mode) [see also RFC 2406; Murhammer *et al.*, 1999]

As with the AH service, some computers may not support IPSec. In this case, the tunnel mode can be used. The IP packet is first sent to an IPSec gateway. The gateway then appends its IP header to the original IP packet before adding the ESP header, ESP trailer, and ESP Auth and applying the required protection as shown in Figure 8.5.

8.5 PREVENTING REPLAY ATTACK

IPSec also defines a mechanism to prevent replay attack as shown later based on [Doraswamy and Harkins, 1999; Stallings, 1999]. In other words, it prevents an intruder from attacking the network by replaying a previous packet. This antireplay attack service applies to both AH and ESP services. In general, this is done by including a sequence number in the IPSec header (both the AH and ESP header) for each SA and by employing a sliding window in the receiver to determine whether a packe

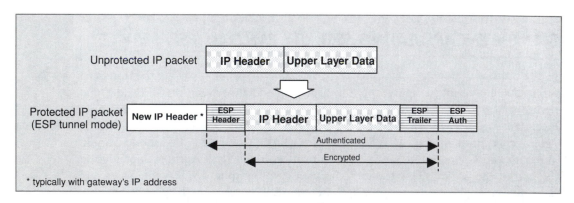

Figure 8.5 ESP service (tunnel mode) [see also RFC 2406; Murhammer *et al.*, 1999]

should be accepted. After setting up an SA, the sending side will keep track of the sequence number of the corresponding packets. Before transmitting a packet of the SA, the corresponding sequence number will be written into the IPSec header of the packet. Note that the nth packet of the SA has a sequence number of n. When n equals 2^{32}, the SA will be set up again. This ensures that all accepted packets of an SA have unique sequence numbers. On the receiving side, a sliding window is kept. Denote R as the largest sequence number of the packet that has been accepted and L as the lowest sequence number of the packet that can be accepted or has been accepted. Hence, R and L give the right and left bounds of the sliding window, respectively. The window size T is fixed where $32 < T$ (the recommended value is 64). Hence, we have $R = L + T - 1$. Having received a packet of a particular SA, it will be accepted only if it meets all of the following conditions:

a. It has not been received before. As described later, all accepted packets will be flagged in the sliding window.
b. It is validated according to the corresponding SA, e.g., the cryptographic check value is correct.
c. Its sequence number is greater than, or equal to, that of the left bound of the window, i.e., greater than, or equal to, L.

If a packet is accepted, the position in the sliding window will be flagged. This indicates that the packet has been received, so any future packet with the same sequence number will be rejected. If the accepted packet is outside the sliding window, i.e., its sequence number is greater than R, the sliding window will be moved accordingly (i.e. to the new R). Note that the left bound of the window will also be increased to keep the window size fixed at T. This may reject valid packets that have been delayed in the network because of the third condition mentioned previously. However, as the window size is large, this should occur infrequently.

8.6 APPLICATION OF IPSec: VIRTUAL PRIVATE NETWORK

Let us examine a typical application of IPSec. Suppose that our VBS wants to establish a secure connection with a business partner. If the sender and receiver can support IPSec, an SA can be established between them by using the AH or ESP service in transport mode. In this case, the required IPSec service is applied by the end user's computers. However, many existing computers may not support IPSec and it may not be cost-effective to upgrade all computers to support IPSec in the short term. Alternatively, virtual private networks or extranets can be formed between the VBS and the business partners. Figure 8.6 shows how a basic virtual private network can

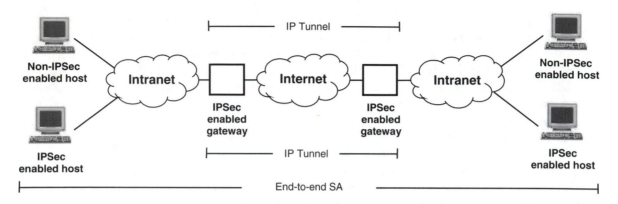

Figure 8.6 Virtual private network

be set up between two intranets (i.e. private networks) by using the IPSec protocol. In this case, the host computers do not necessarily support IPSec. As shown in the figure, IPSec gateways are employed to connect two Intranets over the Internet. Packets are forwarded to the gateways first so that the required protection can be applied by using the AH or ESP tunnel mode service. Essentially, the gateway adds its own IP packet header to the original IP packets and then inserts the required IPSec header and trailer, if any, before sending the packets to the internet. Essentially, a "tunnel" is formed between the two gateways and packets are delivered via the "internet tunnels" to the receiving gateway. The receiving gateway processes the packets accordingly (e.g., checking the cryptographic check value), strips off the outer IP packet header, and then forwards the original IP packets to the receiving host. Note that the inner packets may not necessarily be IP packets. In other words, the intranets can run other network protocols, e.g. IPX, and use the "internet tunnels" to deliver non-IP packets to the other end. As shown in Figure 8.6, the end user's computers can also implement an end-to-end SA inside a tunnel SA if they can support IPSec. This gives a better degree of security.

8.7 FIREWALLS

Next we discuss firewalls, which can exist in various forms ranging from a general computer to a special networking equipment. As shown in Figure 8.7, a firewall is installed between a secure intranet and the insecure internet [Murhammer, 1999]. All inbound traffic (i.e., traffic entering the intranet) and outbound traffic (i.e. traffic leaving the intranet) need to pass through the firewall so that a particular security policy can be carried out. Besides protecting against possible attacks from the internet,

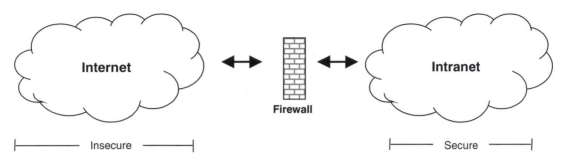

Figure 8.7   Firewall

a firewall is commonly used for performing network management and implementing the aforementioned IPSec protocol due to its strategic location [Stallings, 1999]. For some organizations, firewalls may be used to perform network address translation. An organization may use its own IP address scheme within the intranet. For outbound traffic, valid (i.e. globally unique) IP addresses must be used. The address translation is done at the firewalls [Lodin *et al.*, 1998]. This approach may provide a temporary solution to the shortage of IP addresses. Of course the long-term solution is to use IPv6.

8.8   *DIFFERENT TYPES OF FIREWALLS*

In general, there are three types of firewall: packet filtering router, application gateway, and circuit level gateway [Stallings, 1999; Semeria, 1996; Murhammer *et al.*, 1999]. As described later, they can be combined to build an even more secure firewall system.

8.8.1   Packet filtering router

The packet filtering router (see Figure 8.8*) operates at the network layer. It filters packets according to predefined filtering rules typically based on source/destination IP address and source/destination port number on the packets. For example, a packet filtering router may be configured to allow inbound packets to access the public web server only. In this case, the packet filtering router will examine the destination IP address of all incoming packets and admit only those packets that are destined for the web server to enter the intranet. This prevents inbound packets being able to access other computers in the intranet. In addition, a packet filtering router can be used to

---

* Figures 8.8–8.10 are modified from the work by Semeria [1996] with the aim of showing how different types of application traffic pass through the three types of firewalls.

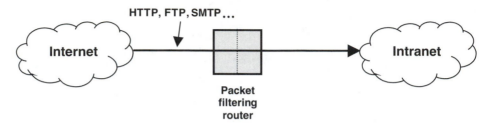

Figure 8.8 Basic operation of a packet filtering router

filter packets based on the service used [Semeria, 1996]. In this case, users are limited to access certain internet applications only typically based on the port number on the packet. Recall that some port numbers indicate the types of services being used such as 23 for TELNET. For example, the firewall of our VBS may disallow external users to use the TELNET service by denying packets destined for port 23. A packet filtering router can also be configured to disallow certain hosts to access a particular service [Smith, 1997]. For example, the firewall of our VBS may be configured such that a particular user (based on the source IP address) cannot access the TELNET service.

While the packet filtering router is simple to use, it is often difficult to set filtering rules for a large network. Furthermore, as it only operates on the network layer, it cannot cater for all security requirements. For example, it cannot restrict the use of application level commands (e.g. allow copying data only). In some cases, it might even be possible to go through a packet filtering router by means of tunnelling (i.e., a packet which should be discarded by a packet filtering router might gain access to the intranet by encapsulating it inside another packet) [Naik, 1998].

8.8.2 Application gateway/proxy server

In contrast to packet filtering routers, application gateways (see Figure 8.9) operate at the application layer. Acting as a proxy server, access control is performed at the application layer rather than the network layer. In order to use a particular application, the corresponding proxy service must be installed in the application gateway. A user

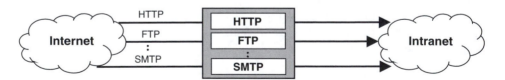

Figure 8.9 Basic operation of an application gateway/proxy server

first connects to the application gateway. The application gateway then accesses the required service on behalf of the user. For example, a user first accesses the application gateway through the corresponding proxy service. After successful authentication, the application gateway connects to the remote computer and transfers the application data accordingly. Hence, the connection between the sender and the receiver is broken into two connections: the connection between the host and the application gateway and the connection between the application gateway and the destined host. Compared to packet filtering routers, it is more powerful. In particular, it can be used to control the users' behavior (i.e., control how users can use a particular application) [Smith, 1997]. For instance, the firewall of our VBS may disallow users to download executable files due to concern over viruses. Application gateways are more secure not only because they can control application level commands but they can also make the internal hosts hiding from the outside world. This is because whenever a packet is sent out to the internet, only the source IP address of the application gateway is included in the IP packet. Hence, the IP address of the originated host can be kept confidential. However, application gateways introduce more processing delay. In other words, they may become the bottleneck of the intranet.

8.8.3 Circuit level gateway

In a similar manner to application gateways, circuit level gateways also serve as an "agent" between the sender and the receiver as shown in Figure 8.10. Conceptually, it works like a "telephone connection." A user needs to make a connection before data can be transferred. Hence, special client software may be required. After establishing a connection, packets are transferred between the internet and the intranet over the connection. A well-known example is the SOCKS protocol version 5 (see RFC1928). In this case, a client makes a TCP connection to port 1080 of the SOCKS server. After successful authentication, the requested connection is available for transferring

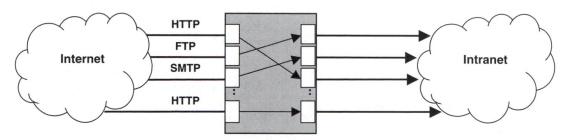

Figure 8.10   Basic operation of a circuit level gateway

data. SOCKS version 5 supports a wide range of authentication mechanisms (e.g. IPSec), key management protocols (e.g. SKIP), and encryption methods (e.g. DES) [Murhammer, 1999].

8.9 EXAMPLES OF FIREWALL SYSTEMS

Based on the examples given by Semeria [1996] and similar examples found in other books on firewalls such as Murhammer *et al.* [1999] and Cheswick *et al.* [1994], let us look at some commonly used firewall systems. In general, an organization like the VBS has two types of servers: public servers such as the web server and private servers. The former allows public access while the latter is restricted to internal access only. Internal hosts are typically connected in a LAN. In a large organization, there may be many LANs interconnected by internal routers as well. The objective of a firewall system is to protect the internal network(s) (called intranet) while allowing external people to access a limited set of resources such as the web server and other public servers.

In the simplest firewall system, a packet filtering router can be installed between the intranet and the internet. To maximize the protection, the default filtering rule is to discard all packets (i.e., a packet is discarded unless it is explicitly allowed). For example, the packet filtering router can be configured to admit traffic destined for the web server only. This can be done by setting the filtering rule based on the IP address or port number of the web server (e.g., port 80, the default port for HTTP). By doing so, all inbound packets not destined for the web server will be discarded by the packet filtering router. This prevents inbound traffic accessing computers other than the web server within the intranet.

In the second example, as shown in Figure 8.11, a packet filtering router and an application gateway are combined to achieve a greater degree of security. It is often known as a screened host firewall system [Semeria, 1996]. The packet filtering router serves as the first line of defense by filtering inbound packets. In particular, it can restrict inbound packets to reach the public server (e.g. web server) and the bastion host only. The bastion host is a very secure station in which the application gateway is installed. It controls information access at the application level and acts on behalf of an internal user to access other external servers. By doing so, it can restrict a user to use a particular set of application level commands. To eliminate a single point of contact between the internal and the external connections, two network interfaces are installed in the bastion host. Hence, it is called a dual home bastion host. As shown in the filtering table, the packet filtering router is configured such that it denies all packets except those originating from, and destined to, the bastion host and the public server(s).

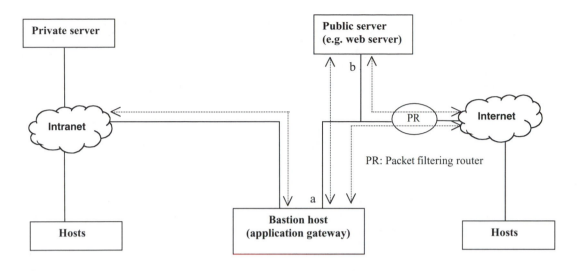

Illustrative filtering rules for the packet filtering router

Source IP Address	Source Port	Destination IP address	Destination Port	Action (allow/ deny)	Remarks
*	*	b	*	Allow (inbound only)	Allow internet hosts to communicate with the public server.
b	*	*	*	Allow (outbound only)	Allow the public server to communicate with internet hosts.
*	*	a	*	Allow (inbound only)	Allow internet hosts to communicate with the intranet through the bastion host.
a	*	*	*	Allow (outbound only)	Allow intranet hosts to communicate with the Internet through the bastion host.
*	*	*	*	Deny	Deny all other packets.

*(Note : Each small letter represents an IP address. * means any value. A specific port may also be set)*

Figure 8.11 Basic operation of a screened host firewall system with a dual home bastion host (extension of the work of Semeria [1996])

In the third example, we can build a very secure system by using the so-called screened-subnet firewall system with a demilitarized zone (DMZ) [Semeria, 1996]. As shown in Figure 8.12, this involves setting up a bastion host with two packet filtering routers. A network called DMZ is created to separate the internet from the intranet. The public servers, modems, and bastion host are installed within the DMZ. The security features include the following:

- Acting as the "security guard", the outside packet filtering router eliminates malicious packets from the internet by filtering packets according to a predefined filtering rule.
- The outside packet filtering router is configured such that inbound packets can only reach the bastion host and the public server(s). Furthermore, it admits only outbound packets from the bastion host and the public server(s).
- The inside packet filtering router is configured to admit packets from the bastion host only. In other words, only the bastion host can send packets into the intranet.
- The inside packet filtering router is configured such that intranet hosts can only use the internet applications through the bastion host.

8.10 *SECURE SOCKET LAYER (SSL)*

In general, firewalls and IPSec protocol provide security at the network layer. Alternatively, we can also address security at the transport layer. Currently, the most popular security protocol for the transport layer is the Secure Socket Layer (SSL) protocol proposed by Netscape in 1994. Working above the TCP layer, SSL provides a secure data transport service for the application layer protocols. In many secure e-commerce systems (e.g. banking applications), SSL works in conjunction with HTTP to support secure data transfer between a web client and a web server. In the context of our VBS, the customers can make use of SSL to send sensitive data, such as credit card information, to the web server over the insecure internet. Recall that the default port number for HTTP is 80. If SSL is used, the TCP connection is set up to port 443 instead of port 80 of the web server. In the URL, the protocol part is specified as "https" rather than "http." Although SSL is commonly used for transferring credit card information, it is not a specific payment protocol but only a generic security protocol. In fact, other application layer protocols such as the file transfer protocol can also make use of SSL. We will discuss payment protocols in the next chapter. At the time of writing, the latest version is SSL version 3, which can be available at http://home.netscape.com/eng/ssl3/draft302.txt. Furthermore, the

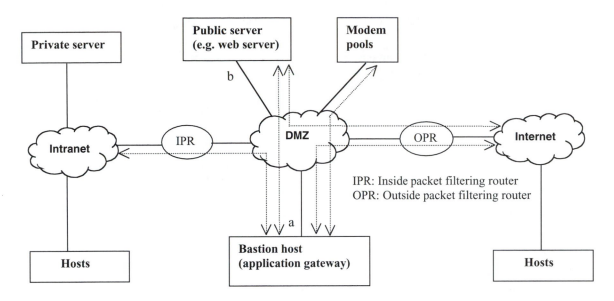

Illustrative filtering rules for the outside packet filtering router

Source IP Address	Source Port	Destination IP address	Destination Port	Action (allow/ deny)	Remarks
*	*	a	*	Allow (inbound only)	Allow internet hosts to communicate with the bastion host.
*	*	b	*	Allow (inbound only)	Allow internet hosts to communicate with the public server directly.
a	*	*	*	Allow (outbound only)	Allow intranet hosts to communicate with the internet through the bastion host.
b	*	*	*	Allow (outbound only)	Allow the public server to communicate with internet hosts.
*	*	*	*	Deny	Deny all other packets.

*(Note : Each small letter represents an IP address. * means any value. A specific port may also be set.)*

Figure 8.12 Basic operation of a screened subnet firewall system with a DMZ (extension of the work of Semeria [1996])

Illustrative filtering rules for the inside packet filtering router

Source IP Address	Source Port	Destination IP address	Destination Port	Action	Remarks
a	*	*	*	Allow	Allow internet hosts to communicate with the intranet through the bastion host. (from the DMZ to the intranet only)
*	*	a	*	Allow	Allow intranet hosts to communicate with the internet through the bastion host. (from the intranet to the DMZ only)
*	*	*	*	Deny	Deny all other packets.

*(Note : Each small letter represents an IP address. * means any value. A specific port may also be set.)*

Figure 8.12 (*Continued*)

Internet Engineering Task Force (IETF) has established a special group to develop a transport layer security standard based on SSL.

SSL operates over TCP/IP. It has four subprotocols as follows:

- *SSL handshake protocol*: It is used for a web server and a web client to create a session (i.e., a logical relationship). Through the handshake protocol, the two sides can authenticate ("handshake") with each other and set up the security parameters for the subsequent data transfer.
- *SSL alert protocol*: It is for passing alert messages between the web client and the web server if an abnormal event occurs.
- *SSL change cipher spec protocol*: It simply changes the cipher spec for the current connection. It is used towards the end of the handshaking phase as described in the next subsection.
- *SSL record protocol*: It provides encryption and data integrity services for transporting the application layer data.

8.10.1 SSL handshake protocol

Before transferring data between a web client and a web server securely, a session should be set up between them by using the SSL handshake protocol. Among other information, each session state contains a session identifier, the corresponding cipher spec, and a shared master secret. For each session, multiple connections can be set up between the client and the server. Each connection typically uses the same

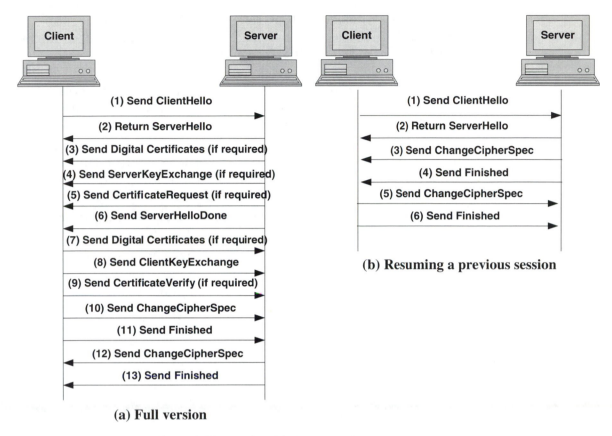

(a) Full version

Figure 8.13 SSL handshake protocol

session parameters but may employ different keys for carrying out the cryptographic algorithms. For example, a specific encryption algorithm is defined for a session, but each connection may use a different key for encrypting the data.

As shown in Figure 8.13a, a normal session is established by going through the following handshaking procedures [see http://home.netscape.com/eng/ssl3/draft302. txt.; Stallings, 1999; Thomas, 2000; Garfinkel, 1997]:

1. The client sends a ClientHello message to the server. The message includes the SSL version supported by the client, the client's random, a session identity (ID) (if any) for identifying the session, the possible cipher suites (i.e., cryptographic capabilities supported by the client), and the compression methods supported by the client. The client may specify a previous session ID to resume a previous session (see Figure 8.13b). For a new session, the client leaves the session ID blank.

2. The server returns a ServerHello message to the client including the SSL version, compression method, and cipher suite it has chosen, together with the server's random and session ID.

3. In most cases, the client needs to verify the identity of the server. If authentication is required, the server sends its digital certificate(s) to the client. In some cases, a list of digital certificates may be forwarded to the client for authentication purposes (see Chapter 7).

4. If required, the server may also send a ServerKeyExchange message to the client. This is for exchanging key parameters in order to establish the necessary cryptographic key(s). For example, the server and the client may use the Diffie–Hellman protocol to establish a shared secret key.

5. Optionally, the server may send a CertificateRequest message to the client requesting the client to send its digital certificate(s) to the server.

6. The server sends a ServerHelloDone message to terminate the "hello" phase and then listens for the client's response.

7. After successful verification of the information provided by the server, the client forwards its digital certificate(s) to the server if requested. Currently, this step is not used very often, but it will be used more commonly in the future when digital certificates are widely deployed.

8. The client sends the ClientKeyExchange message to the server. This is a compulsory step in order to establish a shared secret key between the client and the server. For example, if RSA is used for the key exchange, the client will encrypt a 48-byte premaster secret with the server's public key as obtained from its digital certificate(s) and then send it to the server. By using the premaster secret, a master secret key will be generated by both the server and the client based on a predefined formula in the SSL standard. The master secret key is used to generate other necessary cryptographic keys for the subsequent data transfer, e.g., keys for creating the MAC.

9. If required, the client needs to send a CertificateVerify message to the server to verify its certificate explicitly. This step is required if the client's digital certificate has signing capability. The verification message is generated based on the message digest of the previous handshake messages. This makes it impossible for other people to regenerate this verification message.

10. The client forwards a ChangeCipherSpec message to the server and updates the new cipher spec to be used.

11. Then the client sends the Finished message to the server according to the new cipher spec.

12. Upon receiving the client's message, the server returns a ChangeCipherSpec message to the client accordingly.

13. Finally, the server sends the Finished message to the client to complete the handshaking phase.

This shows the full version of the handshaking procedures. If a web client wants to resume a previous SSL session, the simplified handshaking procedures as shown in Figure 8.13b can be used to speed up the processing time [Apostolopoulos *et al.*, 2000].

8.10.2   SSL record protocol

After setting up a session by using the SSL handshake protocol, the application level message (e.g. HTTP messages) is then transported securely by using the SSL record protocol. The basic operation is as follows [Thomas, 2000; http://home.netscape.com/eng/ssl3/draft302.txt.]:

1. *Fragmentation*: The application information is divided into messages known as records.
2. *Compression*: Each record is usually compressed by a lossless compression method.
3. *Protection to ensure confidentiality and integrity*: A MAC is appended to the compressed record from step 2 to ensure message integrity. The resultant record is then encrypted by using the agreed encryption method (the one agreed during the handshake phase).

After this processing, a header is attached to each record before transmitting it over the internet using the TCP/IP protocol.

8.10.3   The SSL change cipher spec protocol and the alert protocol

There are also two SSL subprotocols called the SSL change cipher spec protocol and the SSL alert protocol. The former protocol is simply used to change the cipher spec for the respective session. As described earlier, it is used towards the end of the SSL handshake protocol.

The purpose of the SSL alert protocol is to send an alert message to the other side, should an abnormal event occur. An alert message has two fields, which are used to indicate the alert level ("warning" or "fatal") and the corresponding alert code, respectively. A variety of alert codes are defined in the SSL standard. For example, if the client receives a revoked certificate, it will send an alert message to the server with an alert code of 44.

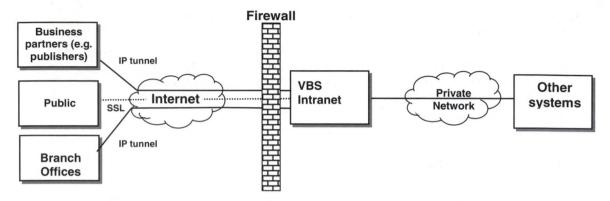

Figure 8.14 Secure system for the VBS

8.11 *BUILDING A SECURE VBS*

Finally, let us combine the aforementioned technologies in order to build a secure e-commerce system for our VBS. Figure 8.14 shows the schematic overview of this secure system. The center of the system is the intranet of the VBS. It is a private network consisting of the web server, e-mail server and other servers, and computers. Traffic leaving for the internet must go through the application proxy inside the bastion host. The application proxy relays application level traffic and controls users' access to the internet. VBS is connected to its business partners (e.g. publisher), branch offices, and mobile employees by using extranets or virtual private networks. Essentially, IP tunnels are established for providing secure data transfer over the internet. The general public can access the VBS through the internet. Typically, customers need to access the web server and the e-mail server. Firewalls are employed to restrict customer access to these two servers only. To achieve a greater degree of security, the DMZ configuration can be used. When customers send sensitive information to the VBS such as credit card information, an SSL service is used to ensure secure data transfer. In this case, the payment server is SSL enabled and carries a digital certificate signed by an established CA. With all these in place, a very secure VBS can be built.

8.12 *SUMMARY*

In this chapter, we have given an overview of Internet security for building a secure e-commerce system. IPSec provides an option for the current IP to implement security at the network layer. There are two types of services, namely, the AH service for authentication to IP packets and ESP service for encryption and authentication. A typical application of IPSec is to build a virtual private network (or extranet) between two or more intranets. Firewalls are usually installed between an intranet and the internet in order to prevent attacks from the internet. As previously mentioned, there are three types of firewalls, namely, packet filtering router, application gateway, and circuit gateway. Typically, the packet filtering router and the application gateway can be combined to build a secure firewall system. At the transport layer, SSL can be used to provide secure data transfer (e.g., transfer of credit card information) between a web client and a web server. It consists of four subprotocols, namely, the handshake protocol, record protocol, change cipher spec protocol, and alert protocol.

REFERENCES

Apostolopoulos, G., Peris, V., Pradhan, P. and Saha, D., Securing Electronic Commerce: Reducing the SSL Overhead, *IEEE Network*, Jul./Aug. 2000, 8–16.

Cheswick, W. R. and Bellovin, S. M., *Firewalls and Internet security: repelling the wily hacker*, Addison-Wesley, 1994.

Doraswamy, N. and Harkins, D., *IPSec*, Prentice-Hall, Upper Saddle River, NJ, 1999.

Garfinkel, S., *Web Security and Commerce*, O'Reilly & Associates, Inc., 1997.

Lodin, S. W. and Schuba, C. L., Firewalls fend off invasions from the net, *IEEE Spectrum*, Feb. 1998, 26–34.

Murhammer, M. W. *et al.*, *TCP/IP Tutorial and Technical Overview*, Prentice-Hall, Upper Saddle River, NJ, 1999.

Naik, D. C., *Internet Standards and Protocols*, Microsoft Press, 1998.

Oppliger R., Security at the Internet Layer, *IEEE Computer*, Sep. 1998, 43–47.

Semeria, C., *Internet Firewalls and Security*, http://www.3com.com/technology/tech_net/white_ papers/500619s.html, 1996.

Smith, R. E., *Internet Cryptography*, Addison-Wesley, Reading, MA, 1997.

Stallings, W., *Cryptography and Network Security*, Prentice-Hall, Upper Saddle River, NJ, 1999.

Thomas, S., *SSL and TLS Essentials*, Wiley, New York, NY, 2000.

RECOMMENDED READING

Smith, R. E., *Internet Cryptography*, Addison-Wesley, Reading, MA, 1997.
    This book gives a general overview of internet security.

Stallings, W., *Cryptography and Network Security*, Prentice-Hall, Upper Saddle River, NJ, 1999.

This gives an excellent technical overview of network security including IPSec, firewalls, and SSL.

Doraswamy, N. and Harkins, D., *IPSec*, Prentice-Hall, Upper Saddle River, NJ, 1999.
This book is specially written for IPSec protocols.

Semeria, C., *Internet Firewalls and Security*, http://www.3com.com/technology/tech_ net/white_ papers/500619s.html, 1996.

Bellovin, S. M. and Cheswick, W. R., Network firewalls, *IEEE Commun. Mag.* Sept. 1994, 50–57.
These are two excellent papers on firewalls.

Murhammer, M. W. *et al.*, *TCP/IP Tutorial and Technical Overview*, Prentice-Hall, Upper Saddle River, NJ, 1999.
This book also gives a good overview on firewalls, in particular the SOCKS package.

Cheswick, W. R. and Bellovin, S. M., *Firewalls and Internet Security: Repelling the Wily Hacker*, Addison-Wesley, Reading, MA, 1994.
This is a classic reference on firewalls.

Goncalves, M., *Firewalls Complete*, McGraw-Hill, New York, 1998.
This book is considered to be a practical guide on firewalls.

Garfinkel, S., *Web Security and Commerce*, O'Reilly & Associates, Inc., 1997.

Stein, L. D., *Web Security*, Addison-Wesley, Reading, MA, 1998.
These books give a good overview of web security.

The fundamental RFCs for IPSec are RFC2401–2406.

9

Advanced Technologies for E-commerce

9.1 Introduction to Mobile Agents

9.2 WAP: the Enabling Technology for Mobile Commerce

9.3 XML (eXtensible Markup Language)

9.4 Data Mining

References

Recommended XML Web Sites

In previous chapters, we discussed about the underlying technologies for building a web-based e-commerce system. Currently, a number of advanced technologies are also emerging to complement the existing technologies in providing more sophisticated e-commerce services. Current e-commerce systems are based on a client–server architecture. While this architecture is simple to use, it may not be effective in certain situations. Mobile agents are mobile software programs that can move across the internet for performing specific tasks autonomously. Due to their flexibility and mobile function, they can complement the existing client/server-based system to provide more advanced e-commerce services (e.g. product searching). Currently, most e-commerce applications can be accessed only via a fixed terminal. It is expected that the current WEB (Web-based Electronic Business) will evolve to become the MEB* (Mobile Electronic Business) (i.e., by turning the W upside down to become the M). At the moment, the enabling technology for realizing the MEB is the Wireless Application

---

* This is based on a similar idea from Nokia.

Protocol (WAP). It allows users to access internet services in general, and mobile commerce services in particular, through portable terminals. In the current e-commerce system, nearly all web pages are created using HTML. A more general and powerful markup language called eXtensible Markup Language (XML) has been developed in recent years. In general, HTML uses "tags" for formatting data (i.e., it tells the web browser how the data should be formatted or displayed). In contrast, XML allows users to define different tags in order to convey the meaning of the data. Hence, XML has significant advantages over HTML, in particular to facilitate B2B transactions such as to support internet-based EDI. In Chapter 1, we mentioned that one of the key driving forces of e-commerce is the "Information Age." In the digital economy, information is a valuable asset. To explore the full potential of e-commerce, data mining techniques can be used to turn data into information and information into knowledge. In this chapter, we will give an overview of these advanced technologies.

9.1 *INTRODUCTION TO MOBILE AGENTS*

The current e-commerce system is primarily based on a client and server architecture. Basically, commercial transactions are handled by many request–response interactions over the internet. As the internet is a best-effort network, sometimes a user may experience a long waiting time. For some applications such as comparing product prices in the market, the mobile agent approach provides a better solution. This involves sending a mobile software program called a mobile agent to a remote system. The agent can then interact with other agents on the remote system. This releases the resources of the original system for doing other tasks. The results of the interactions are finally returned to the user. Let us use the following example to illustrate the benefits of mobile agents. Suppose you want to buy a book. In order to search for the seller who can offer you the best price, you need to visit a number of bookstores and compare the prices yourself. By using a mobile-agent-based system, you can delegate the work to one or more mobile agent(s). The following table shows the advantages of this compared with the client/server approach.

Client/server approach	Mobile-agent-based approach
1. The searching process may be boring because you need to repeat it at many different sites.	You need to specify only the requirements and the mobile agent can do the searching for you.
2. The search process ties down your resources while you visit each site in turn	The search process, if conducted by a mobile agent, frees up your resources.

3. If the network goes down during the searching process, you may need to start it from the beginning.	It is less dependent on the network condition as the searching is done at the remote sites by mobile agents.
4. This is time consuming because you visit the sites only one by one.	This is more efficient as the search can be proceeded in parallel by sending out multiple agents.

In summary, the mobile-agent-based system can reduce unnecessary network traffic, provide better reliability, support more advanced services, and utilize the resources more effectively. Point 2 of the table is particularly critical for an electronic broker, where the server side will be receiving many requests per minute, each of which would require a search of several sites. By using a mobile agent for each request, the broker can continue to use its resources to service other requests. A mobile agent can also interact with other mobile agents on the internet before returning to the originating host. In addition, it can complement the existing client/server-based system. Currently, there are some mobile-agent-based e-commerce systems being developed such as

- *Tabican* [Lange and Oshima, 1998] – An electronic marketplace for air tickets and package tours using Aglets.
- *Nomad* [Sandholm and Huai, 2000] – An electronic auction system using Concordia.
- *MAGNET* [Dasgupta *et al.*, 1999] – A networked electronic trading system using Aglets.

9.1.1 Overview of mobile agents

Agents are commonly defined as software programs that can help users to perform tasks autonomously. In particular, they are useful for handling routine tasks, searching for information, and facilitating decision making. Mobile agents are agents that can move across different systems to perform specific tasks. Due to their mobile function, it is expected that mobile agents will play an increasingly important role in the future e-commerce system. In particular, they can be used to complement existing client/server-based e-commerce systems.

To implement mobile agents, a number of development kits are currently available as described below [Dasgupta *et al.*, 1999]. All of them are based on Java.

- *IBM's Aglet* (http://www.trl.ibm.co.jp/aglets): Aglet is created from the words *Agent* and App*let*. It can be viewed as a mobile Applet. Its development tool Aglet Software Development Kit (ASDK) provides the environment for creating Aglets.

- *Objectspace's Voyager* (http://www.objectspace.com/voyager/whitepaper/ VoyagerTechOverview.pdf): It makes use of Java Remote Method Invocation (RMI) and Java Object Request Broker for developing mobile agents to support distributed computing.

- *General Magic's Odyssey* (http://www.genmagic.com/technologyodyssey.html): This is another mobile agent development tool based on Java RMI.

- *Mitsubishi's Concordia* (http://www.meitca.com/HSL/Projects/Concordia/ MobileAgentConf_for_web.htm): It is component-based and makes use of Java RMI for building various distributed applications.

Currently, IBM's Aglet is widely used for developing mobile-agent-based e-commerce applications because it is lightweight and simple to use. In this chapter, we will use Aglet as an example to explain how a mobile agent basically works (see Lange and Oshima [1998] for details). Conceptually, other mobile-agent-based systems work in a similar manner.

As mentioned earlier, `Aglet` can be viewed as a mobile applet. In the ASDK, there are three main Java interfaces/classes, namely `Aglet`, `AgletProxy`, and `AgletContext` [Lange and Oshima, 1998; Dasgupta et al., 1999]. The `Aglet` class is for developing Aglets and controlling their activities by means of an event-driven model as explained later. For security reasons, other objects can interact with an Aglet only via its proxy. The `AgletProxy` interface is available for this purpose. The `AgletContext` interface provides the required operational platform for Aglets. Furthermore, the ASDK includes an Aglet server called Tahiti for system management. This server provides a graphical user interface for monitoring the activities of the Aglets. Aglets are transferred by means of a protocol called the Agent Transfer Protocol (ATP). Some people like to call it ATTP because it looks like HTTP.

9.1.2 Typical life cycle of an Aglet*

The typical life cycle of an Aglet is described as follows. First of all, the Aglet is created. Then it is transferred to a remote host across the network. After performing the required tasks, it will be returned to the originating host to present the results. For some applications, the Aglet may visit other hosts before returning to the originating host. Furthermore, the Aglet may be deactivated for a while and then re-activated.

---

* Part of this section is based on information in Mr. Benjamin Lam's MSc Thesis, Department of Computing, Hong Kong Polytechnic University.

Finally, the Aglet will be disposed of to release the system resources. Let us explain this life cycle in the context of the ASDK based on the work of Lange and Oshima [1998].

Creation and cloning

An Aglet can be created by using the `getAgletContext().createAglet` method as follows:

```
getAgletContext().createAglet(codebaseURL, "agletcode",  object);
```

The first argument specifies the code base URL or where to find the required class file(s). We can use the `getCodeBase` method to get the current code base. Alternatively, it can be defined by setting up a URL object as follows

```
URL codebaseURL = new URL("http://www.vbs.com/aglets");
```

In this case, the code base is at the "aglets" directory of the web server "www.vbs.com."

The second argument specifies the name of the Aglet class file, and the third argument specifies any object that is passed for initializing the Aglet.

After creating an Aglet, we can also make an identical copy by using the clone method.

Event driven model

Basically, the activities of Aglets are event-driven. That means that when a certain event occurs as detected by some "listeners," the specific actions for that event will be executed. For monitoring the events, there are three major Aglet listeners, namely `CloneListener`, `MobilityListener`, and `PersistentListener`. In particular, the `MobilityListener` is frequently used because it is for monitoring mobility events, so we discuss it in more detail. Other "listeners" follow a similar approach. The `MobilityListener` consists of three main methods:

- `onArrival ( )`: It is invoked when the Aglet arrives at a Tahiti server.
- `onDispatching ( )`: It is invoked when the Aglet is dispatching.
- `onReverting ( )`: It is invoked when the Aglet is reverting.

Here is an example showing the syntax for monitoring the mobility events of an Aglet. By including these statements, the system will print out the messages

"Dispatching" and "Arrival" when the Aglet is being dispatched to a server and when it arrives at a server, respectively (See [Lange and Oshima, 1998]).

```
public void onCreation (Object args) {
    addMobilityListener (new MobilityAdapter( ) {
        public void onArrival (MobilityEvent evt) {
                    System.out.println ("Arrived");
        }
        public void onDispatching(MobilityEvent evt) {
                    System.out.println ("Dispatching");
        }
    });
}
```

Dispatch

To dispatch an Aglet to a remote host, the dispatch method is used. For example, the following command dispatches an Aglet to the remote host magics.vbs.com by using the ATP.

```
dispatch(new URL("atp://magics.vbs.com"))
```

As discussed later, MAGICS stands for Mobile-Agent-based Internet Commerce System, which is being developed at the Hong Kong Polytechnic University.

Disposal

Finally, when an Aglet has completed its tasks, it should be disposed to release the system resources. This is done by calling the `dispose` method, i.e. `dispose( )`.

9.1.3 A simple programming example

Let us explain the basic operation of an Aglet with a simple programming example (see Lange and Oshima [1998] for details on Aglet programming). In Chapter 6, we discuss how to search for books from the VBS database by using a client/server-based approach. In this example, we present an approach which will do the same search by using a mobile agent (Aglet). The program listing is given in Figure 9.1. The ISBN to be searched, the server's name, and the destined port number are specified

```
//** The following program is written by Mr. Benjamin Lam of the
//** MAGICS research group of the Department of Computing,
//** Hong Kong Polytechnic University.
//** The program listing is used with his permission.

package magics;
import com.ibm.aglet.*;
import com.ibm.aglet.event.*;
import java.net.*;
import java.io.*;
import java.sql.*;

// Set the "atp" of SecurityPerference as follows:
// Source:
// Runtime accessClassInPackage.examples.update
// Target:
// FileSystem "JdbcOdbcSecurityCheck","read, write"
// Property "jdbc.*","read"


public class JDBCAglet extends Aglet
{
    final static int SENDER = 1 ;
    final static int VBS = 2 ;
    private int whereamI = VBS;
    private String[] m_strResult = null;
    private String m_strSQL = null;
    private URL m_urlOrigin = null;
    private long m_lRoundTrip = 0;

    private String m_strISBN = "0071125027";
    private String m_strHost = "VBS";
    private int m_nPort = 5534;

    public void run()
    {
        System.out.println("--- Run ---");
    public void onDisposing()
    {
```

Figure 9.1   Programming listing for JDBCAglet.java

```
        System.out.println("--- OnDispose ---");
   }
public void onCreation(Object args)
{
   m_urlOrigin = getAgletContext().getHostingURL();

   addMobilityListener(new MobilityAdapter()
      {
         public void onDispatching(MobilityEvent evt)
         {
            System.out.println("Dispatching");
         }

         public void onArrival(MobilityEvent evt)
         {
            System.out.println("Arrival");

            switch (whereamI)
            {
            case SENDER:
               m_lRoundTrip = System.currentTimeMillis() -
                m_lRoundTrip;
               System.out.println("SQL: " + m_strSQL);
               if (m_strResult != null)
               {
                  for (int i = 0; i < m_strResult.length; i++)
                     System.out.println("" + (i + 1) + ":
                      " + m_strResult[i]);
               }
               if (m_lRoundTrip < 1000)
                  System.out.println("Round Trip Time =
                   " + m_lRoundTrip + "ms");
               else
               dispose();
                  System.out.println("Round Trip Time =
                   " + (m_lRoundTrip/ 1000) + "s");
               break;

            case VBS:
```

Figure 9.1 (*Continued*)

```
            try
            {
                processQuery();
                whereamI = SENDER;
                dispatch(m_urlOrigin);
            }
            catch (Exception e)
            {
                dispose();
            }
            break;
        }
    }
}
);
System.out.println("--- Create ---");
dispatchAglet();
}

public boolean dispatchAglet()
{
    // Set m_strHost and m_nPort
    if (m_strHost == null || m_strHost.length() == 0)
        m_strHost = m_urlOrigin.getHost();
    if (m_nPort == 0)
        m_nPort = 4434;

    try
    {
        m_strSQL = "SELECT * FROM bookstore where ISBN=\'" +
         m_strISBN + "\'";
        m_lRoundTrip = System.currentTimeMillis();

        System.out.println("Dispatch to " + m_strHost + ":" +
         m_nPort + " SQL=" +
        m_strSQL);

        dispatch(new URL(m_urlOrigin.getProtocol(), m_strHost,
         m_nPort,
        m_urlOrigin.getFile())));
    }
```

Figure 9.1 (*Continued*)

```
    catch (Exception exp)
    {
        System.out.println("Fail to dispatch");
        dispose();
        return false;
    }
    return true;
}

// Process the query
private void processQuery()
{
    if (m_strSQL == null || m_strSQL.length() == 0)
        return;

    Connection connection = null;
    Statement statement = null;
    ResultSet resultset = null;
    String strMsg = null;

    try
    {
        strMsg = "Database connection";
        // Create the JDBC driver
        Class.forName("sun.jdbc.odbc.JdbcOdbcDriver").newInstance();
        // Create the database connection.
        connection = DriverManager.getConnection("jdbc:odbc:mall");
        System.out.println("Database connected: " + connection);

        strMsg = "Statement creation";
        // Create the statement object
        statement = connection.createStatement();
        strMsg = "Execute query";
        // Execute the query
        resultset = statement.executeQuery(m_strSQL);

        int nRows = 0;
        while (resultset.next())
            nRows++;
```

Figure 9.1   (*Continued*)

```
      resultset = statement.executeQuery(m_strSQL);
      if (nRows > 0)
      {
         m_strResult = new String[nRows];
         int i = 0;
         while (resultset.next() && i < nRows)
            m_strResult[i++] = resultset.getString(1) + " " +
            resultset.getString(2);
      }
   }
   catch (Exception e)
   {
      System.out.println("Exception: " + strMsg + ": " + e);
   }
   finally
   {
      // Close the following objects:
      try
      {
         strMsg = "Statement closed";
         if (resultset != null)
            resultset.close();
         if (statement != null)
            statement.close();

         strMsg = "Connection closed";
         if (connection != null)
            connection.close();
      }
      catch (Exception e)
      {
         // Catch and print any exception
         System.out.println("Exception: " + strMsg + ":
          " + e.getMessage());
      }
   }
  }
 }
}
```

Figure 9.1   (*Continued*)

by the variables `m_strISBN`, `m_strHost`, and `m_nPort`, respectively. After executing the program, an Aglet will be created and then dispatched accordingly by using the ATP. At the destination, the Aglet will perform the search by using the SQL command. The result will be stored in the Aglet. After searching, the Aglet will be dispatched back to the originating host, and the search result will be displayed to the user.

In general, the program is self-explanatory. Let us go through the main points. The JDBCAglet class is for creating the Aglet. There is a `Mobilitylistener` object. For the `Onarrival` method there are two conditions as determined by the `whereamI` variable. If the `whereamI` variable is "VBS" (i.e. with a value of 2), it means that the Aglet is at the VBS. In this case, the Aglet will perform the search by calling the `processquery` method. As we can see, this method uses standard JDBC programming techniques for retrieving data from the database. The results are stored in an array called `m_strResult`. Furthermore, at the VBS, the `whereamI` variable is set to "SENDER" (i.e. with a value of 1). Once the search is completed, the Aglet will be dispatched back to the originating host or sender. Again, the `onarrival` method will be executed when the Aglet arrives at the originating host. This time, as `whereamI` is "SENDER" (i.e. with a value of 1), the first condition will be executed in which the search result will be displayed to the user. In addition, the round-trip time will also be displayed.

9.1.4 Overview of MAGICS

At the Department of Computing of the Hong Kong Polytechnic University, we are developing a *Mobile-Agent-based Internet Commerce System* (MAGICS). It is based on a four-layer model as shown in Figure 9.2. The foundation layer is the *Java-based Agent Development Environment* (JADE) or the "raw materials." It consists

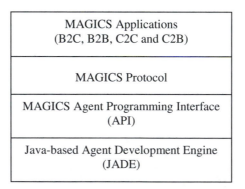

Figure 9.2 The MAGICS framework

of development tools and special Java classes for building mobile agents in general. We are employing IBM Java Aglet as well as developing special Java classes. The second layer is the MAGICS Agent Programming Interface (API) layer. Making use of JADE, we are developing a specific API for supporting internet commerce in particular. Some examples are seller agents, buyer agents, and auction agents. Our aim is to build generic agents so that they can be reused, or adapted to many different scenarios. Having developed the agents, we need different protocols for them to interact with each other effectively, efficiently, and securely. The third layer or the MAGICS protocol layer is devoted to this purpose. Some of the protocols include a buying protocol, a selling protocol, and a negotiation protocol. Finally, making use of the previous layers, we can build various MAGICS applications at the fourth layer. In general, these applications can be divided into four categories: B2C, B2B, C2C, and C2B e-commerce.

9.2 *WAP: THE ENABLING TECHNOLOGY FOR MOBILE COMMERCE*

Fuelled by the explosive growth of cellular phones and the growing demand for mobile internet services (e.g. online information retrieval), there is a compelling need for accessing the internet through mobile devices, particularly cellular phones. As mentioned earlier, it is expected that the current WEB will evolve to become MEB. Currently, the key enabling technology for MEB is the Wireless Application Protocol (WAP). Hence, we will focus on discussing WAP in this chapter.

As the current web technologies are primarily designed for desktop computers working under a wired network environment, they cannot be applied directly to mobile devices such as cellular phones and palm computers. In fact, these devices are relatively less powerful in terms of CPU speed, screen size, memory, input device capability, and battery life. Moreover, there are other operational constraints in wireless networks such as limited bandwidth and unstable operating conditions. Hence, new solutions are required for providing internet access to these devices [Unwired Planet, 1999; Mann, 2000].

Mid 1997 marked a major milestone of WAP when Ericsson, Motorola, and Nokia found the WAP Forum with Unwired Planet. With the aim of developing standards for providing internet access to handheld mobile devices, the main goals of the WAP Forum are [Wireless Application Protocol, 1998]:

- to provide internet-based services to wireless phones and other wireless terminals;
- to provide a global wireless protocol specification for developing wireless applications; and

- to provide a framework for creating contents and applications that can be applied to different wireless networks.

In order to accomplish these goals, the WAP Forum has developed the WAP specification for mobile devices.

At the time of writing, the latest version of the WAP specification is 1.2. It is largely based on the existing internet technologies such as HTTP, HTML, and JavaScript. An overview of the WAP specifications is as follows (see Mann [2000] for details). In terms of programming, the WAP model is largely based on the existing web programming techniques, to facilitate integration with the existing web system. To format data on the user interface effectively, a simple markup language called Wireless Markup Language (WML) is developed based on XML (see Section 9.3). To enhance the functionality of WML (e.g., for generating a dynamic page), a scripting language called WMLScript is developed. In principle, it provides functions similar to those of JavaScript. Finally, a microbrowser specification is provided to support WML and WMLScript, and a Wireless Telephony Applications (WTA) framework is defined for integrating the microbrowser and telephone functions.

9.2.1 The WAP model

In Chapter 2, we explored the web model – a client-server interaction model based on the request/response computing model. The WAP model works in a similar fashion. To enable a WAP device to "talk" to a web server, a "middleman" called the WAP gateway is needed. Technically, it functions as a proxy server situated between the user agent and the web server. Figure 9.3 illustrates the basic WAP model for ordering books from our VBS via a WAP device (e.g. WAP-enabled mobile phone).

As shown in Figure 9.3, a user places an order to the VBS through a WAP device (e.g. WAP phone). On the WAP device, the order information is entered. Upon submitting the order request, the WAP phone will convert the user request into a GET request statement (similar to the HTTP request) as follows:

```
GET www.vbs.com/servlet/bookorder HTTP/1.1
```

where bookorder is the servlet program being triggered for book ordering.

Before sending the request message to the WAP gateway, the message is converted into a compact binary format so that the data size can be reduced for transmission over the bandwidth-limited wireless link. Upon receiving the request, the WAP gateway converts the binary message back into the text-based format. The request message is then forwarded to the web server (in this case the VBS web server). Once the web server receives the request, it will process it (in our case, a servlet program

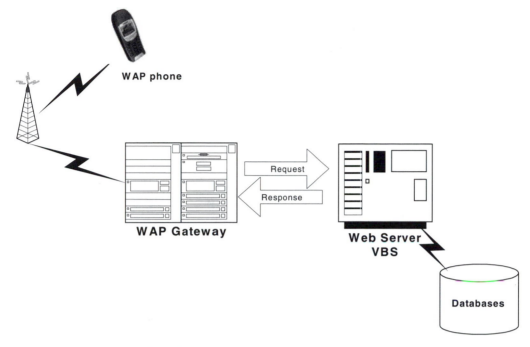

Figure 9.3   The WAP programming model

"bookorder" will be invoked), update the backend database (if necessary), and return the response accordingly.

Upon receiving the response from the web server (typically a WML document), the WAP gateway converts it into the compact binary format and forwards it to the WAP device over the wireless link. Finally, the WAP device converts the binary message to the text format and displays the content accordingly.

9.2.2   WAP architecture

Having given an overview of the WAP model, let us examine the WAP architecture. Basically, it consists of six layers as shown in Figure 9.4 [Wapa, 1998; Mann, 2000].

Application layer – Wireless Application Environment (WAE)

The WAE provides an environment for developers to create interoperable WAP applications. Generally speaking, it provides the following development components:

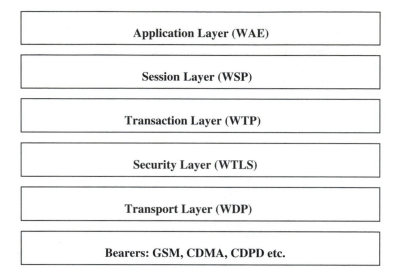

Figure 9.4 WAP architecture

WML, WMLScript, and WTA as explained earlier. In addition, special components such as images, calendar information, etc. are also provided for facilitating the development work.

Session layer – Wireless Session Protocol (WSP)

It provides a connection-oriented session service and a connectionless session service to the WAE. The former and the latter operate over the Wireless Transaction Protocol (WTP) and the Wireless Datagram Protocol (WDP), respectively, which are described as follows.

Transaction layer – Wireless Transaction Protocol (WTP)

It is a lightweight transaction protocol mainly for supporting reliable/unreliable one-way request messages and reliable two-way request–response messages.

Security layer – Wireless Transport Layer Security (WTLS)

Based on the Transport Layer Security standard, the WTLS is a security protocol for addressing the security requirements (confidentiality, integrity, and authentication) as discussed in Chapter 7. In principle, it functions like the SSL protocol.

Transport layer – Wireless Datagram Protocol (WDP)

It enables the upper layers to operate over different bearer services [e.g. GSM (Global System for Mobile Communication), CDMA (Code Division Multiple Access), CDPD (Cellular Digital Packet Data)] in a uniform manner.

9.2.3 Benefits of WAP to e-commerce

The WAP technology provides an effective solution for accessing WEB in the short term and realizing MEB in the long term. Through the use of WAP devices, such as WAP phones, people can keep in touch with the internet world anywhere and at any time. It is expected that this will lead to the development of many innovative e-commerce services.

9.3 XML (EXTENSIBLE MARKUP LANGUAGE)

In this section, we examine another of the extended topics, namely XML (or the eXtensible Markup Language). Both XML and HTML, which we introduced in Chapter 3, are derivatives of SGML, another more general markup language.

Work on XML started initially in 1996, and by 1998 XML 1.0 achieved the status of a world wide web (W3C) recommendation and drafts for Xlink (XML Linking Language) and Xpointer (XML Pointer Language) were proposed.

Firstly, we compare HTML and XML. Then we look briefly at the syntax of XML documents, followed by display methods, programming interfaces, and categories of applications of XML, and lastly its architecture.

9.3.1 HTML and XML

At the outset it is useful to compare XML and HTML in order to understand their different strengths. A brief summary of the differences is given in Table 9.1.

A careful examination of the points raised in Table 9.1 should make one realize that XML is not intended to simply be a more powerful replacement for HTML. This is because HTML's primary purpose is to specify the display of data while XML's primary purpose is to describe the logical structure of data.

9.3.2 Syntax of XML documents

The full syntax of XML is described in several voluminous standards. Here, we will only briefly review a simple XML document to get a sense of what XML documents

Table 9.1 Comparison between HTML and XML

HTML	XML
1. HTML only provides predefined tags, such as header, paragraph, heading, etc. In other words, users cannot add to this predefined list of tags.	XML does not have predefined tags, and tags can be defined using a Document Type Definition (DTD). It is possible to define tags for a particular domain or application.
2. HTML is mainly designed to represent a *presentation* structure of a document. It enables a browser to interpret and display the document to humans. This makes HTML more suitable for machine–human interaction rather than machine–machine interaction.	XML is basically designed to represent the *logical* structure of documents. The tag names give abstract semantics to the associated data. Hence, XML can be used more effectively for machine–machine interaction.
3. In traditional HTML, the content and presentation format/style are mixed (i.e. not separated).	In XML, the content and presentation format/style are separated. The former is written into an XML document, while the latter is specified in style sheets using XSL or CSS.
4. Searching for and retrieval of specific information based on semantic content is difficult and is sensitive to minor alterations in the document, such as adding blank lines, etc.	Searching and retrieval of information is greatly simplified and not particularly sensitive to document layout and minor changes to it.
5. In general, HTML searches return large amounts of data because of its poorly defined logical structure.	XML searches return data more precisely associated with the query because of its well-defined logical structure.
6. In HTML, links are unidirectional, i.e., it connects only two resources and a link has no semantics.	In XML, with Xlink, one can use bidirectional links, link up more than two resources and, specify a "role" to the link by associating semantics with it.
7. Compared with XML, HTML has a relatively loose syntax. For example, some syntactical errors may be acceptable (i.e., the document may still be processed even if a syntactical error occurs).	The syntax for XML is strictly defined.

```
< ? XML version = "1.0"?>
< ! DOCTYPE VBS SYSTEM "book.dtd">
<book>
<title> XML for beginners </title>
<author> Elizabeth Chang </author>
<abstract>  This is an introductory book on XML, for use by people
 who have no previous acquaintance with it </abstract>
<subject>      < keyword = "internet programming">
               < keyword = "internet database">
               < keyword = "messaging">
</subject>
<price> 25 US Dollars</ price>
<availability> 2 days </availability>
< / book>
```

Figure 9.5   A simple XML document

look like. Consider the example of a simple XML document given in Figure 9.5, which describes a book in the VBS.

The first line gives the XML Declaration and is always included as it defines the version of XML that the document conforms to. The second line indicates the Document Type Definition (DTD) the document conforms to and also the file in which the DTD definition can be found, e.g. "book.dtd." A copy of the contents of this file is shown in Figure 9.6. The DTD describes the structure, syntax, and vocabulary of XML documents that conform to it.

Note that this DTD suffices for all authored book elements in the VBS.

Each document has a root element. In this document, the root element is <book>. The remaining lines define the child elements of the root book (title, author, abstract,

```
<? XML version "1.0" >
<! Element book (title, author, abstract, subject, price,
   availability)>
<! title (#PCDATA)>
<! author (#PCDATA)>
<! abstract (#PCDATA)>
<! ATTLIST subject ID CDATA # Required>

<!price <#PCDATA)>
<!availability <#PCDATA)>
```

Figure 9.6   File book.dtd containing DTD

subject, price, availability). The last line defines the end of the root element </book>. Here are some notes on the XML documents:

- Elements begin with a <start tag> and end with an <end tag>, and the data is placed between them. For example,

  <title> XML for beginners </ title>

  ‿   ‿   ‿

  Start tag   Data   End tag

- An element with attributes does not need an end tag, but could be of the form <element name attribute name = "a">.
- The tag names are case-sensitive.
- The tags must be properly nested.
- XML element names start with a letter or underscore and the rest of the name can contain letters, digits, dots, underscores, or hyphens, but no spaces are allowed.
- Elements can have subelements, but these must be properly nested.
- Attributes consist of a name and a value separated by "=" and the value is within quotation marks. There can be more than one attribute in an element.
  For example,
  <keyword = "internet programming">
- One can also add comments, which are enclosed within comment tags
  <!--comments-->

An XML document is said to be *Well Formed* if it meets the well-formed constraints specified in the XML 1.0 Recommendation, some of which are mentioned in the previous list (i.e., starts with XML Declaration, must have a root element, each element has an end tag or autotag tag, and elements must be properly nested).

An XML document is *Valid* if it meets the validity constraints (VCs) specified in the XML 1.0 Recommendation. This document must include a <!DOCTYPE> definition (2nd line of the example XML document), which specifies the DTD against which the document can be validated (i.e., a valid document must conform to the DTD).

We note that the XML document as created here does not do the following:

1. Formatting and styling for display – this is done using style sheets, which are discussed in Section 9.3.3.
2. Transformation of information – this can be done using XSLT.

3. Processing of XML documents – this can be done using APIs , such as DOM, SAX, and Event Handler in conjunction with languages such as JAVA, C++, Perl, etc.

4. Linking – this can be achieved using Xlink and Xpointer.

The main role of the XML document is to logically structure information within documents.

9.3.3   Displaying XML documents – Style sheets

As XML documents do not present any information related to formatting and styling for display of information to humans, style sheets are provided for doing this. Among the different approaches to styling, one could use:

1. Extensible Style Language (XSL)
2. Document Style and Semantics Language (DSSSL)
3. Cascading Style Sheets (CSS), both Level 1 and Level 2

CSS were originally designed for displaying HTML; however, XML browsers can also use this. These were discussed in detail in Chapter 3, and hence we do not discuss them further here. We should note that currently CSS is more widely supported, but this may change in future.

We will now concentrate our discussion on XSL. Unlike CSS, which utilizes the formatting and style instructions to directly display the XML document, XSL normally first transforms the XML document into a suitable format for display, such as HTML or RTF (Rich Text Format). It then sends this to an XSL processor (such as a browser or application), which then generates the required HTML output or RTF output. Thus, the XSL style sheet has two parts: (1) transforming and (2) formatting and styling.

An example of an XSL style sheet for displaying book titles and their prices is shown in Figure 9.7.

9.3.4   Processing XML documents and programming interfaces

In order to process an XML document, it may be necessary to access its internal structure. Three widely used application program interfaces (APIs) have been defined for this purpose, namely

```
<? XML version = "1.0"?>
< XSL Style Sheet xmins:xsl = http://www.w3.org/TR/WD-xsl>
< XSL template match = "/" >
<XSL apply-templates/>
</XSL : template>
<XSL : template match = "book price list">
<html>
<head>
<title> Price list for books </title>
</head>
</html>
</XSL:template>
<XSL template match = "book">
<font face = "Times New Roman", size = 5>
<p>
<em> book title: </em>
<XSL: value of select = "title"/>
</p>
<p>
<em> price: </em>
<XSL: value of select = "price"/>
</p>
</font>
</XSL: template>
</XSL: Style Sheet>
```

Figure 9.7   Example of an XSL style sheet

1. Document Object Model (DOM)
2. Simple API for XML (SAX)
3. Element Handler

We will briefly discuss the first two and include some of the features of the third. DOM was released by W3C recommendation in late 1998.

The DOM essentially stores the structure of the XML document as a tree structure whose nodes can be Elements, Attributes, Data, Document fragments, etc. Thus, the DOM tree corresponding to the example XML document of Figure 9.5 is shown in Figure 9.8.

DOM has a number of interfaces, which can be interpreted as classes. These classes can be implemented in Java. Amongst these classes are Node, Document, Element, Attribute, Processing instruction, CDATASection, Document fragment, Entity, etc.

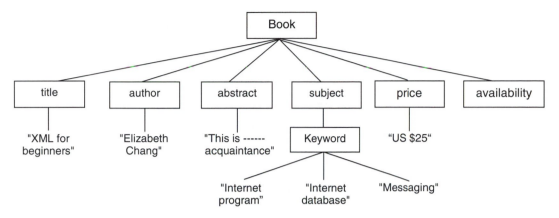

Figure 9.8   DOM for example program

When using the DOM API, essentially one first parses the XML document to develop an in-memory DOM tree and then accesses the internal structure of the document using the DOM tree.

In contrast, SAX provides serial access to an XML document by scanning the document and generating events. These events can be used by applications to obtain the required elements or attributes. The applications utilise event handlers, which are essentially callback functions. These must be registered with parser objects. When the XML processor encounters a start element tag, it calls the event handler.

The third API Element Handler utilises both event handlers that are notified when a particular element is encountered, much like SAX, and also a DOM tree.

9.3.5   Applications of XML

It is anticipated that XML will provide a basis for a variety of applications that would be built on top of XML, and these include the following:

- Channel Definition Format (CDF)
- Database applications
- Document mark up (with HTML)
- Mathematical Markup Language (MATHML)
- Messaging between different business platforms
- Metacontent definition

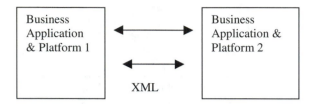

Figure 9.9   Application of XML for B2B e-commerce

- Platform for Internet Context Selection (PICS)
- Platform for Privacy References Syntax Specification (P3P)
- Resource Description Framework (RDF)
- Scaleable Vector Graphics (SVG)
- Synchronized Multimedia Integration Language (SMIL)

Of these, messaging is by far the most important from an e-commerce point of view. To conduct B2B e-commerce effectively, it is essential that the computing platforms and systems in one business be able to exchange information electronically with anothers (see Figure 9.9).

Previously, this used to be achieved using traditional EDI. However, as explained in Chapter 12, this has a number of disadvantages including cost, limited presence of the technology only with some large organizations, etc. This is where XML comes in, provided that

1. the two corporations that wish to use XML for data interchange utilize the same DTD; they can directly interchange information in XML.
2. if they use different DTDs, one can use LMX technology as explained in Chapter 12.

However, using the same DTD is much more preferable, and it requires standardization work on XML. Some corporations such as ARIBA have already produced a version of XML suitable for e-commerce, e.g. c-XML. However, if several corporations do this independently, we are likely to see a plethora of DTDs for the area leading to an "Electronic Tower of Babel" situation. A recognition of this has led to standardization efforts proceeding to a definition of ebXML. This leads to the following layered structure for ebXML (see Figure 9.10).

- XML documents are written according to an industry-specific standardized scheme.

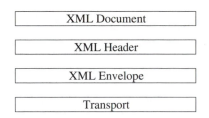

Figure 9.10   Layered structure for ebXML

- XML header provides session startup and shutdown, request/response, publish/subscribe facilities.
- XML envelope provides security feature, routing, information, message identification.
- Transport layer provides the protocol support, e.g. HTTP, HTTPS, etc.

With industry-specific standardization of vocabularies, schemas, and DTDs, one will create a powerful infrastructure for message interchange in B2B e-commerce. This is expected to be one of the most significant applications of XML in e-commerce.

9.3.6   Architecture for XML and some features

XML employs a layered architecture consisting of the following:

- Layer 1 – Underlying technology layer
- Layer 2 – Supporting layer
- Layer 3 – Application layer

Layers 1 and 3 have been discussed in previous sections, so here we briefly describe the supporting layer, which is illustrated in Figure 9.11.

Note that most of the items in Figure 9.11 have been discussed in previous sections. We will briefly consider three items here, namely Hyperlinks, Schemas, and Name spaces.

In Section 9.3.2, we described the use of DTDs to specify the structure, vocabulary, and set of rules for defining legal elements, which the XML documents have to satisfy in order to be valid. This facilitates the sharing of XML documents that conform to the same DTD even if they have been produced by different people on different systems. However, DTDs have a number of disadvantages including the fact that DTDs themselves are not written using an XML syntax; the atomic data types (#PCDATA) are only "strings." In order to overcome some of these disadvantages,

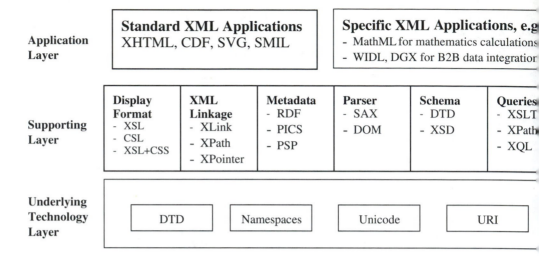

Figure 9.11   XML architecture

the notion of an XML Schema Language has been developed. This uses XML syntax to describe the structure of and relationships for XML documents. This permits the use of all the same techniques as for the XML documents (e.g. DOM trees, parsers, etc.) for this XML schema. The XML Schema Language allows definition of complex data types as well as user-defined data types. One can think of these XML schemas as essentially describing constraints on Well Formed XML documents. In future this could take over the role of DTDs.

The RDF is a data model for associative metadata. It tells us about resources that can be accessed by the Universal Resource Identifier (URI). It forms the underlying basis for defining platforms, taxonomies, site maps, etc. (see Figure 9.11).

To understand the notion of namespaces, we note that XML allows one to specify one's own tags, but these tags could have different semantics in different applications. Consider the tag 'name.' This could be used to specify a product 'name' in one e-commerce application and a customer 'name' in another. In order to address this issue, one needs to pick global naming conversions and use a URI address to specify where this "universally agreed to collection of names" can be found. This URI is then used in all XML documents that use this namespace.

As noted at the beginning of this section, XML allows more complex linking than just unidirectional links, which are used to link one resource to another. XML Linking (Xlink) provides this hyperlinking facility.

Xlink has two kinds of links:

- Simple links, which are similar to HTML links (i.e., simple unidirectional inline links)
- Extended links

In order to use Xlink, one uses the Xlink:attribute to specify a link, e.g.,

```
<Example    xlink:type="simple"
xlink:href = "book.xml">
```

An extended link can connect several resources, can be bidirectional, and can have roles.

XML is certain to play a major role in e-commerce in the future. In this section, we have provided only a brief introduction. More detailed information can be found at the web addresses and in the references given at the end of this chapter.

9.4 DATA MINING

One of the features of e-commerce systems is that one starts to collect large amounts of data arising from the following:

1. previous customer orders;
2. web accesses recorded in a web log;
3. if the e-commerce system is a broker that uses agents to visit other web site information on the structure and contents of these web sites.

Currently in most systems, only very limited use is made of these large volumes of data. Consider the information stored in a database on previous purchases made by customers. The main kind of information obtained from such a database is a set of records that satisfies a particular condition, e.g., obtain all purchasers of Toyota for the month of July 2000 in Hong Kong Island. This query would be made in SQL as explained in Chapter 6. It would return the set of records that fulfilled these conditions. Instead of just obtaining a set of records, one could look for different types of patterns or knowledge in the data. An example of such a pattern would be

If one purchased a Toyota Camry in the last three years and earns more than US$80,000, the person is very likely to purchase a BMW.

Such a rule does not retrieve a particular set of records but provides knowledge or patterns that are embedded in the data. Such knowledge or patterns are very useful for targeted marketing. They can help to identify the likely future purchase a customer will make given the customer's previous purchases.

The value of data mining to determine patterns or knowledge in data has not been confined to e-commerce systems, but the ability to utilize this knowledge once it is uncovered is considerably greater in the e-commerce system as each customer identifies himself when he next visits the web site, allowing the system to trigger appropriate patterns and hence present him with a list of targeted products that he is likely to be interested in immediately. Or alternatively, if he chooses to purchase an item, an associative rule will be triggered to display other likely items he might purchase. An example of this is illustrated in the discussion of Amazon.com in Chapter 11 where a list of books that the purchaser is likely to be interested in, based on his particular previous purchasing patterns, is presented to the purchaser on his subsequent visits to the web site. This greatly increases cross-selling, with visitors buying other books in addition to the one they actually came to purchase. There are several different techniques for discovering such patterns or knowledge. We will briefly discuss two techniques, namely (l) association rules and (2) inductive learning using decision trees.

9.4.1 Association rules

Association rules represent relationships between items in very large databases [Agrawal, Imilienski, and Swami, 1993; Agrawal and Srikant, 1994]. Specifically, they address market basket databases. An example would be "given a market database, it was found that 80% of customers who bought the book 'XML for beginners' and 'internet programming' also bought a book on 'Java programming' ." If X and Y are two sets of disjoint items, then an association rule can be expressed as conditional implication

$$X \Rightarrow Y$$

i.e. the occurrence of the set of items X in the market basket implies that the set of items Y will occur in this market basket. Two important aspects of an association rule are confidence and support and these are defined as [Agrawal and Srikant, 1994].

The confidence of an association rule r: $X \Rightarrow Y$ is the conditional probability that a transaction contains Y given that it contains X, i.e. confidence $(X \Rightarrow Y) = P(X, Y)/P(X)$.

The support of an association rule is the percentage of transactions in the database that contain both X and Y, i.e. Support $(X \Rightarrow Y) = P(X, Y)$.

The problem of mining association rules can be stated simply as follows: Given predefined values for minimum support and minimum confidence, find all association rules which hold with more than minimum support and minimum confidence.

This problem is normally broken down into two subproblems [Agrawal and Srikant, 1994]:

1. find all *frequent* item sets in the database with support greater than or equal to minimum support
2. for each *frequent* set X, generate all association rules $Y \Rightarrow X - Y \mid Y \subset X$ with confidence greater than or equal to minimum confidence.

A major computational effort goes into finding frequent item sets and a number of algorithms such as the a priori algorithm have been developed to obtain this.

9.4.2 Decision trees

Decision trees can be represented as a directed graph consisting of nodes and directed arcs.

The decision tree consists of

- a root node from which the decision tree is expanded;
- intermediate nodes that can be further expanded; and
- leaves that cannot be further expanded and correspond to a specific output class.

Both the root node and intermediate nodes correspond to a test, which determines the directed arc to be traversed at this point, as shown in Figure 9.12 [Sestito and Dillon, 1993]. Any intermediate node can be considered a root for the subtree starting from that point leading to a recursive definition. Choosing the test to apply at a particular node can be reduced to selecting an attribute for testing. The choice of the order in which the attributes are selected greatly affects the quality, shape, and number of nodes in the tree. When constructing a tree, one needs to have a means of determining

- the important attributes needed for classification
- the ordering of the important attributes

A feature selection criterion is used to determine the ranking of the input attributes. Each criterion test using the feature selection criterion is normally restricted to being a function of one of the attributes at a time. There are several feature selection criteria and these include

1. the information gain criteria [Quinlan, 1993];
2. the symmetric Goodman Kruskall Tau developed by Zhou and Dillon [1991].

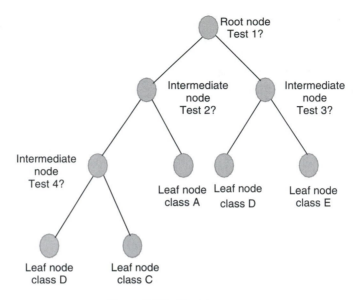

Figure 9.12   Decision trees

Since the data is likely to be noisy, with missing attributes, it is important that the feature selection criterion be able to cope with this. The second criterion is robust with respect to these.

Essentially, when using the decision tree method, one defines a set of output classes a customer might belong to and also a set of input variables, which will help classify this customer. The data is analyzed using an appropriate feature selection criterion, and a decision tree is developed. This decision tree is then used to categorize any customer by noting his individual purchasing behavior. The output classes could, for instance, be individual purchasing circles.

9.4.3   Web mining

In addition to mining patterns from data on purchases and orders in databases, there is also a related area of web mining. This can address the problem of determining patterns in

1. datalogs of web accesses to determine the pattern of accesses to a web site; this is called web usage mining and provides important information on the usability of the web site architecture [Chang and Dillon, 1999].

2. the structure of a web site to determine the site architecture of a web site and related links. The focus here is on link information. This is called web structure mining and could be of use to agents used by brokers to visit other web sites.

3. the content of web sites to determine any pattern in the content of web sites. This is referred to as web content mining and again could be useful to visitor agents.

A full discussion of web mining as defined above is beyond the scope of this book, and the reader is referred to references at the end of this chapter for further information [Cooley, Mobasher, and Srivsation, 1997; Spertus, 1999].

REFERENCES

Mobile agents

Dasgupta, P., Narasimhan, N., Moser, L. E., and Melliar-Smith, P. M., "MAGNET: Mobile agents for networked electronic trading," *IEEE Transactions on Knowledge and Data Engineering* **11** (4) (1999), 509–525.

Lange, D. B. and Oshima, M., *Programming and deploying Java mobile agents with Aglets*, Addison-Wesley, Reading, MA, 1998.

Sandholm, T. and Huai, Q., "Nomad: Mobile agent system for an Internet-based auction house," *IEEE Internet Computing* 4 (2) Mar./Apr. (2000), 80–86.

WAP

Mann, S., *Programming Applications with the Wireless Application Protocol*, Wiley, New York, 2000.

Unwired Planet, Inc., The Wireless Application Protocol: Wireless Internet Today, 1999. http://www.phone.com/pub/feb99WAPWP.pdf.

Wireless Application Protocol Forum, Wireless Application Protocol Architecture Specification, 1998.

Data mining

Agrawal, R., Imilienski, T., and Swami, A., "Mining association rules between sets of items in large databases," in *Proc. of the ACM SIGMOD Int'l Conf. on Management of Data*, May 1993.

Agrawal, R. and Srikant, R., "Fast algorithms for mining association rules," in *Proc. of the 20th VLDB Conference*, Santiago, Chile, 1994.

Chang, E. and Dillon, T., Audience centred web based design, in *Proc. IEEE Conf. in Systems, Men & Cybernetics*, Tokyo, vol 2, pp. 99–104, Oct. 1999.

Cooley, R., Mobasher, B., and Srivastava, J., Web mining: Information and pattern discovery on the world wide web, in *Proc. of the IEEE Conf. on Tools with AI*, 1997.

Quinlan, J. R., *C4.5: Programs for Machine Learning*, Morgan Kaufmann Publishers, San Mateo, CA, 1993.

Sestito, S. and Dillon, T. S., *Automated Knowledge Acquisition*, Prentice-Hall, 1994.

Spertus, E., Mining structural information on the web, in *Proc. of the Int. Conf. on WWW*, 1999.

Zhou, X. and Dillon, T. S., A statistical-heuristic feature selection criterion for decision tree induction, *IEEE Transactions on Pattern Analysis and Machine Intelligence* **13** (1991), 834–841.

RECOMMENDED XML WEB SITES

http://www.w3.org/XML/
http://www.w3.org/TR/REC-xml
XSL: eXtensible Stylesheet Language http://www.w3.org/TR/xsl/
Xpointer (XML Pointer Language) http://www.w3.org/TR/xptr
Xlink (XML Linking Language): http://www.w3.org/TR/xlink/
DOM (Document Object Model): http://www.w3.org/TR/DOM-Level-2-core/
SAX (Simple API for XML): http://www.megginson.com/SAX
Primer: http://www.w3.org/TR/xmlschema-0/
Structures:http://www/w3.org/TR/xmlschema-1/
Datatypes: http://www.w3.org/TR/xmlschema-2/
RDF (Resource Description Framework):http://www/w3.org/TR/REC-rdf-syntax/
Requirements:http://www.w3.org/TR/xmlquery-req
OASIS: http://www.oasis-open.org/
EbXML: http://www.ebxml.org/
Biztalk: http://www.biztalk.org/

Part 2

Applications

10

Internet Payment Systems

10.1   Characteristics of Payment Systems

10.2   4C Payment Methods

10.3   SET Protocol for Credit Card Payment

10.4   E-cash

10.5   E-check

10.6   Micropayment System

10.7   Overview of Smart Card

10.8   Overview of Mondex

10.9   Putting It All Together for Payments in the VBS

10.10 Summary

      References

      Recommended Reading

In previous chapters, we discussed the basic technologies for building a web-based e-commerce system. To make an e-commerce system functional, we also need to incorporate payment functions into the system. In the physical world, we have four main types of payment methods: cash, credit card, check, and credit/debit (funds transfer). Each of these payment methods has its own unique characteristics. To build a complete e-commerce system, we also need to implement these payment methods in cyberspace. In this chapter, we give an overview of the major internet payment methods, namely the Secure Electronic Transaction (SET) protocol, for implementing credit card payment, an electronic check system for supporting check payment, and an electronic funds transfer system and an electronic cash system for emulating physical cash payment. We will also present two micropayment methods and smart card payment methods.

10.1 *FEATURES OF PAYMENT METHODS*

In general, when we evaluate a payment method, there are several features as follows [Furche and Wrightson, 1996; Lynch and Lundquist, 1996; Schneier, 1996]:

- *Anonymity*: This refers to whether the payment method is anonymous. In other words, this is concerned with whether a third party can trace back who was involved in the payment transaction.
- *Security*: This is concerned with whether the payment method is secure, in particular whether it is easy to perpetrate different kinds of fraud such as a forged payment.
- *Overhead cost*: This refers to the overhead cost of processing a payment.
- *Transferability*: This refers to whether a payment can be carried out without the involvement of a third party such as a bank.
- *Divisibility*: This refers to whether a payment can be divided into arbitrary small payments whose sum is equal to the original payment.
- *Acceptability*: This refers to whether the payment method is supported globally, i.e., not by a closed user group only.

These characteristics provide a basis for the evaluation of payment methods.

10.2 *4C PAYMENT METHODS*

In the physical commerce system as mentioned earlier, we have four main methods of payment, namely Cash, Credit card, Check, and Credit/debit (i.e. direct fund transfer). We call these the 4C payment methods. Table 10.1 compares the 4C payment methods in terms of the aforementioned characteristics. Ideally, we need a payment method that is very secure, has a low overhead cost, is transferable, is acceptable anywhere, and is divisible. In many cases, we prefer it to be anonymous as well. As you can see from the table, no payment method can satisfy all the desired characteristics. This is one of the reasons why we need four different payment methods so as to cater for different payment requirements. To build a complete e-commerce system, we also need to implement these four payment methods in cyber space.

Table 10.1 Comparison of the 4C payment methods

	Cash	Credit card	Check	Credit/debit
Anonymity	Yes, in general	No	No	No
Security	Good	Good	Good	Good
Overhead cost	Lowest, in general	Higher than cash and credit/debit because of the paperwork involved	Highest, in general	Low
Transferability	Yes	No	No	No
Divisibility	Not completely divisible	Yes	Yes	Yes
Acceptability	Yes, in general	Yes, in general	No, in general it can only be used locally	No, in general it can only be used locally

In the rest of this chapter, we discuss how to implement the 4C payment methods on the internet, for e-commerce.

10.3 SET *PROTOCOL FOR CREDIT CARD PAYMENT*

Let us begin with credit card payment. At present, the credit card is one of the most commonly used payment methods in e-commerce, in particular B2C e-commerce. Before the introduction of the Secure Electronic Transaction (SET) protocol, secure credit card payment was usually carried out over an SSL connection. While SSL can ensure the secure transmission of credit card information over the internet, it is not a complete credit card payment method. For example, it cannot support on-line credit card authorization. SET is specially developed to provide secure credit card payment over the internet. It is now widely supported by major credit card companies including Visa and MasterCard. The current SET specification is divided into three books. Book 1 gives the general overview. Book 2 is a programmer's guide for developing SET applications. Book 3 gives the formal protocol definition. One can download these specifications from http://www.setco.org/download.html/#spec.

In general, SET aims at satisfying the following security requirements in the context of credit card payment:

- *Confidentiality* – Sensitive messages are encrypted so that they are kept confidential.
- *Integrity* – Nearly all messages are digitally signed to ensure content integrity.
- *Authentication* – Authentication is performed through a public key infrastructure.

10.3.1 SET network architecture

Figure 10.1 gives a schematic representation of the network architecture for SET. Basically, it has the following components [SET Book 1; Stallings, 1999]:

- *Merchant*: This refers to a seller, which is connected to an acquirer.
- *Cardholder*: This refers to a registered holder of the credit card who is a buyer.
- *Issuer*: This refers to the bank that issues the credit card to a cardholder.
- *Acquirer*: This refers to the bank that serves as an "agent" to link a merchant to multiple issuers. By doing so, a merchant can process various credit cards through a single acquirer. Each acquirer has a payment gateway* through which it can process authorization and other necessary transactions for the merchants.

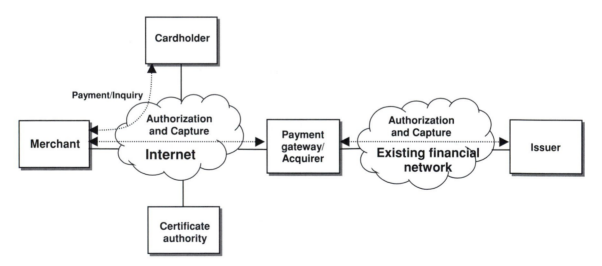

Figure 10.1   Network architecture of SET system

---

* In some implementations, the payment gateway can be provided by a third party.

- *Payment gateway*: This is typically connected to the acquirer. The payment gateway is situated between the SET system and the financial network of the current credit card system for processing the credit card payment.

In addition, it is assumed that there are certification authorities in the SET system, which issue digital certificates to concerned parties.

In general, the SET protocol addresses interactions among these network components. More specifically, the SET protocol addresses communications between a cardholder and a merchant and between a merchant and a payment gateway. Communications between an acquirer and an issuer are handled by reusing the financial network in the current credit card system.

10.3.2   SET digital certificate system

The authentication system of SET is based on the X.509 digital certificate framework as discussed in Chapter 7. This allows merchants, cardholders, and acquirers to verify the identities of each other by exchanging digital certificates. Figure 10.2 shows the basic framework of the SET digital certificate system. In the hierarchy, there is a common root CA, and all parties in the SET system should have the public key of this root CA. This root CA is responsible for issuing digital certificates to the brand CAs such as Visa, MasterCard, etc. Each brand CA then issues digital certificates to its regional CAs. For example, a brand CA may set up a CA in each country. Under each regional CA, there are three types of CAs, namely cardholder CA, merchant CA, and payment gateway CA, which issue digital certificates to the respective parties. As everyone has got the public key of the root CA, any digital certificate in the SET system can be verified even if the two parties involved are in different parts of the world. In the most complex case, the verification path needs to start from the root CA.

10.3.3   Dual signature generation and verification

In the physical credit card system, the Payment Instructions (PI) including the cardholder's credit card number and signature are not kept confidential in general. While data integrity can basically be ensured by using printed receipts, cardholder's authentication relies on simple signature checking only. In an electronic credit card system, the Order Information (OI) and PI can be digitally signed to ensure data integrity. However, the sensitive credit card information may still be disclosed to other people. SET introduces a novel method called the dual signature (DS) to ensure data integrity while protecting the sensitive information. In this section, we describe the DS method.

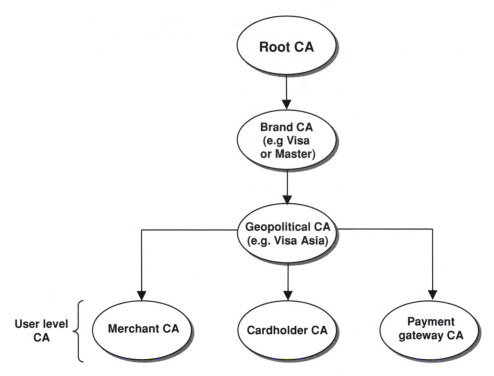

Figure 10.2   The digital certificate system for SET [SET Book 1]

Then we talk about the digital envelope method to ensure data confidentiality in SET.

To facilitate the discussion, we will use the cryptographic notations as defined in Chapter 7. Given OI and PI, the DS is generated by the following steps [SET Book 1; Stallings, 1999] as shown in Figure 10.3:

- *Step 1*: The message digests of PI (H[PI]) and of OI (H[OI]) are computed.
- *Step 2*: The two message digests from step 1 are then combined and the resultant message digest HPIOI is found as follows:

```
HPIOI = H[H[PI] || H[OI]]
```

where || is the concatenation operator.

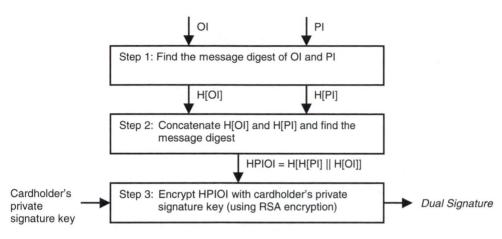

Figure 10.3 Steps in generation of a dual signature

- *Step 3*: The dual signature is produced by encrypting the message digest from step 2 using the cardholder's private signature key* ($key_{private\_sign, cardholder}$). Mathematically, it can be expressed as

```
DS = E_RSA[HPIOI | key_private_sign,cardholder]
```

Let us next look at how the merchant and the payment gateway can verify the dual signature.

The merchant is provided with OI, H[PI], and DS. The dual signature can be verified as follows:

- *Step 1*: The merchant first finds H[H[PI] || H[OI]].
- *Step 2*: He then decrypts the digital signature with the cardholder's public signature key as follows:

```
D_RSA[DS | key_public_sign, cardholder]
```

where the $key_{public\_sign, cardholder}$ denotes the public signature key of the cardholder. This can be obtained from the cardholder's digital certificate.

---

* Each participant (e.g. cardholder) in the SET system possesses two pairs of RSA keys: one for generating digital signatures and the other one for exchanging secret keys as shown later. The private key for generating digital signatures is called the private signature key and the corresponding public key is called the public signature key. The private key for exchanging secret keys is called the private key-exchange key and the corresponding public key is called the public key-exchange key.

- *Step 3*: Finally, he compares the two terms H[H[PI] || H[OI]] and D_{RSA}[DS | key$_{public\_sign, \ cardholder}$]. They should be the same if the transmitted DS has not been changed; otherwise the order is not valid.

Similar to above, the payment gateway is provided with PI, H[OI], and DS. The dual signature can also be verified as follows:

- *Step 1*: Find H[H[PI] || H[OI]].
- *Step 2*: Compare the result of step 1 with D_{RSA}[DS | key$_{public\_sign, \ cardholder}$].
- *Step 3*: If the two terms in step 2 are the same, the order is valid.

By using the dual signature method, each cardholder can link OI and PI while releasing only the necessary information to the relevant party. That means, the merchant knows only the OI but not the PI (the merchant only knows H[PI]). Similarly, the acquirer only knows the PI but not the OI. Nevertheless, if either the OI or PI is changed, the dual signature will no longer be valid. In other words, OI and PI are dependent on each other through the dual signature method.

10.3.4 Digital envelope

In the SET protocol, a digital envelope is used to transfer sensitive information between two parties securely. Suppose that a customer X wants to send a sensitive message M to the VBS. The basic operation is as follows:

1. A random DES key (key$_{random}$) is first generated to encrypt the message, i.e. E_{DES}[M | key$_{random}$].
2. key$_{random}$ is then encrypted by the VBS's public key-exchange key, say key$_{public\_exchange, \ VBS}$, i.e. E_{RSA}[key$_{random}$ | key$_{public\_exchange, \ VBS}$].
3. E_{DES}[M | key$_{random}$] and E_{RSA}[key$_{random}$ | key$_{public\_exchange, VBS}$] are sent to the VBS.
4. To obtain the message M, VBS first obtains key$_{random}$ by decrypting E_{RSA}[key$_{random}$ | key$_{public\_exchange, VBS}$], i.e. D_{RSA}[E_{RSA}[key$_{random}$ | key$_{public\_exchange, VBS}$] | key$_{private\_exchange, VBS}$] = key$_{random}$, where key$_{private\_exchange, VBS}$ denotes the private key-exchange key of the VBS.
5. After obtaining key$_{random}$, the VBS can obtain M by decrypting E_{DES}[M | key$_{random}$], i.e., to find D_{DES}[E_{DES}[M | key$_{random}$] | key$_{random}$] = M.

The aforementioned process is illustrated in Figure 10.4.

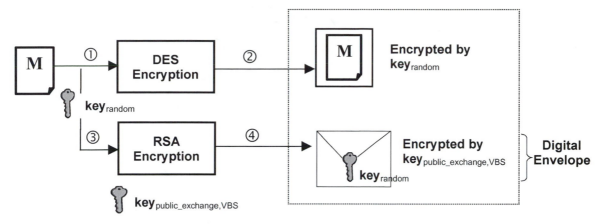

Figure 10.4   Generation of a digital envelope

As only the VBS knows the $key_{private\_exchange,\,VBS}$, no one can obtain the key_{random} to decrypt $E_{DES}[M \mid key_{random}]$. Effectively, $E_{RSA}[key_{random} \mid key_{public\_exchange,\,VBS}]$ is a digital envelope. Only by "opening" the digital envelope can one get the required key to decrypt the message M.

10.3.5   SET protocol

In general, the SET protocol has four phases: initiation, purchase, authorization, and capture as shown in Figure 10.5. First the cardholder sends a purchase initiation request to the merchant for initializing the payment. Then the merchant returns a response message to the cardholder. In the second phase, the cardholder sends the purchase order together with the payment instruction to the merchant. In the third phase, the merchant obtains the authorization from the issuer via the payment gateway. Finally, the merchant requests a money transfer to its account. Optionally, the cardholder may make an inquiry about the status of the payment by issuing an inquiry request to the merchant after the second phase. Upon receiving the inquiry, the merchant will send a response to the cardholder. We will discuss the key protocols as follows [SET Book 1; O'Mahony, Peirce, and Tewari, 1997].

10.3.6   Purchase initiation

Having decided to buy something, the cardholder sends a purchase initiation request to the merchant. Among other information, the message contains a local transaction

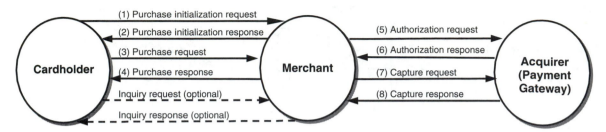

Figure 10.5 General SET information flow [see also SET Book 1; O'Mahony, Peirce, and Tewari, 1997]

identity (ID) and a nonce N1 for thwarting "replay" attack. Furthermore, the cardholder may send a list of cached certificate(s) so as to inform the merchant that there is no need to include the certificate(s) in the subsequent messages.

After receiving the request, the merchant sends a response to the cardholder. The response includes a unique transaction ID, the nonce N1 sent by the cardholder for verification purpose, and a nonce N2 generated by the merchant. The unique transaction ID, which is generated based on the local transaction ID, is for identifying the transaction throughout the whole session.

The response is signed digitally by using the merchant's private signature key. The merchant also sends its certificate(s) and the payment gateway's certificate(s) to the cardholder if required.

After receiving the response, the cardholder verifies the certificates and obtains the corresponding public keys for later use. The cardholder also verifies the merchant's response by checking the digital signature of the response with the merchant's public signature key. Recall that this is done by decrypting the digital signature to get the message digest followed by comparing it with the message digest of the response. Furthermore, by checking the previous nonce N1, the cardholder can confirm that the response is sent from the intended merchant for the current session.

10.3.7 Purchase request

Having completed the purchase initiation phase, the cardholder prepares the OI and the PI. Besides other order details, the OI contains the unique transaction ID, nonce N1, and nonce N2 from the initialization phase. The PI includes the transaction ID, the payment amount, and the message digest of the order description.

A dual signature is generated for OI and PI. PI is encrypted with a random symmetric key A. Key A and the cardholder information is then encrypted with the public key-exchange key of the payment gateway to form a digital envelope.

After the aforementioned processing, the following information is transmitted to the merchant:

1. OI + DS + H[PI]
2. PI + DS + H[OI] (all encrypted by using key A)
3. key A + cardholder information (all encrypted by using payment gateway's public key-exchange key)
4. cardholder's certificate(s)

Note that the information in points 2 and 3 will be sent later to the payment gateway via the merchant. The merchant cannot read the contents of these.

After receiving the purchase request, the merchant verifies the cardholder's certificate(s) and the dual signature. Recall that as the merchant is provided with OI and H[PI], the DS can be verified by comparing $D_{RSA}[DS \mid key_{public\_sign, \; cardholder}]$ with $H[H[OI] \parallel H[PI]]$. The public signature key of the cardholder ($key_{public\_sign, \; cardholder}$) can be extracted from the respective digital certificate.

After successful verification, the merchant processes the request and forwards the PI and the associated information to the payment gateway. The merchant also creates a purchase response and forwards it to the cardholder together with its certificate(s). The purchase response is digitally signed with the merchant's private signature key. After receiving the purchase response, the cardholder verifies the certificate(s) and the purchase response.

10.3.8 Payment authorization

In the payment authorization phase, the merchant needs to obtain payment authorization from the acquirer. This is done by generating an authorization request, which includes the transaction ID, amount requested for authorization, message digest of the order description, and other transaction information.

The authorization request is encrypted with a random symmetric key B. Key B is then encrypted by using the public key-exchange key of the payment gateway to form a digital envelope. Note that only the payment gateway can get key B and use it to decrypt the authorization request. The merchant sends the following to the payment gateway:

• The encrypted authorization request and the encrypted key B
• The following information as received from the cardholder:
  – PI + DS + H[OI] (all encrypted by using key A)
  – Key A + cardholder information (all encrypted by using the payment gateway's public key-exchange key)

- Cardholder's and merchant's certificates

After receiving the authorization request, the payment gateway processes it as follows:

- Obtains key B by means of decryption and uses it to decrypt the authorization request.
- Verifies the merchant's certificate(s) and the digital signature on the authorization request.
- Obtains key A and the cardholder information by means of decryption.
- Uses key A to obtain the PI, DS, and H[OI].
- Verifies the DS accordingly.

The payment gateway also verifies that the received transaction ID is the same as the one in the PI [SET Book 1]. Recall that the PI also contains the message digest of the order description. By checking this with the message digest of the order description in the authorization request message, it can be verified that the order has been accepted by the cardholder and the merchant.

Upon all successful verifications, the payment gateway forwards an authorization request to the issuer via the current payment system. After receiving the authorization from the issuer through the current system, the payment gateway sends an authorization response to the merchant. The response message includes the transaction ID, authorization code, amount that has been authorized, and other information about the transaction.

The authorization response is first signed by using the payment gateway's private signature key and then encrypted with a random symmetric key C. Subsequently, key C is encrypted by using the merchant's public key-exchange key to form a digital envelope. A capture token is also generated, signed, and encrypted by using a random symmetric key D. Key D and the cardholder information are then encrypted by using the payment gateway's public key-exchange key to form another digital envelope. The capture token is for the merchant to initiate payment to the bank account at a later stage. The payment gateway sends the following to the merchant:

1. Signed authorization response (encrypted by key C)
2. Key C (encrypted by merchant's public key-exchange key)
3. Signed capture token (encrypted by key D)
4. Key D + cardholder information (encrypted by payment gateway's public key-exchange key)

After receiving the authorization response from the payment gateway, the merchant obtains key C by decryption and uses it to decrypt the authorization response.

The merchant verifies the payment gateway's certificate and the digital signature on the authorization response. It then stores the response message and the capture token for later use. Having obtained the authorization, the merchant then complete the order accordingly (e.g. by providing the service).

10.3.9 Payment capture

Eventually, the merchant will credit the bank account using the capture tokens. This is done through the payment capture process. Note that batch processing can be used in which a batch of capture tokens is sent to the acquirer. To start the payment capture process, the merchant generates a capture request, which includes the transaction ID, capture amount, and other information about the capture request.

The capture request is first signed by using the private signature key of the merchant and then encrypted with a random symmetric key E. Key E is then encrypted by using the public key-exchange key of the payment gateway to form a digital envelope. Then the merchant sends the following to the payment gateway:

1. Signed capture request (encrypted by using key E)
2. Key E (encrypted by using payment gateway's public key-exchange key)
3. Signed capture token (encrypted by using key D)
4. Key D + cardholder information (encrypted by using payment gateway's public key-exchange key)
5. Merchant's digital certificates

Recall that the information in points 3 and 4 are obtained from the previous authorization response. After receiving the capture request, the payment gateway obtains key E by decryption and uses it to decrypt the capture request. The payment gateway also verifies the digital signature of the capture request by using the merchant's public signature key. The payment gateway obtains key D by decryption, uses the key to decrypt the capture token, and verifies the capture token. After successful verification, the payment gateway sends a payment transfer request to the issuer via the current system. Furthermore, the payment gateway creates a capture response, which includes the transaction ID, capture amount, capture code, and other information about the transaction.

The capture response is signed by using the payment gateway's private signature key and is then encrypted with a random symmetric key F. Key F is then encrypted by using the merchant's public key-exchange key to form a digital envelope. The payment gateway forwards the following information to the merchant:

1. Signed capture response (encrypted by key F)
2. Key F (encrypted by merchant's public key-exchange key)
3. Payment gateway's digital certificate(s).

After receiving the capture response, the merchant decrypts it accordingly and verifies its digital signature. Finally, the capture response can be saved for record-keeping purpose.

10.4 E-CASH

Let us next discuss electronic cash (e-cash). Its aim is to emulate physical cash payment. As mentioned earlier, physical cash has two special characteristics: anonymity and transferability. In other words, payment is anonymous and no third party is involved in the payment process. Till now, no software-based payment method can fulfill the transferability requirement. The main problem is that people can duplicate data in a computer easily, so it is almost impossible to prevent double spending unless a third party is involved to verify the transaction during the payment process. Hence, the current aim of e-cash is to achieve only anonymity. A representative example is e-cash (DigiCash) invented by David Chaum [Chaum, Fiat, and Naor, 1988; Chaum and Brands, 1997; O'Mahony, Peirce, and Tewari, 1997]. At the time of writing, e-cash is provided by a company called ecashtechnologies (http://www.ecashtechnologies.com). There is a good demo to illustrate the basic operation of e-cash at that web site. Based on an innovative method called Blind Signature, e-cash enables anonymous payment over the internet. In other words, there is no way for a third party to trace back to identify the payer (unless the payee reveals the payer's identity of course). The Mark Twain bank in the United States has been offering e-cash service since 1995.

10.4.1 Blind signature

Before discussing the e-cash protocol in detail, it is important to understand the blind signature method [Schneier, 1996; O'Mahony et al., 1997]. In the blind signature method, RSA encryption is commonly used. Consider that a bank has a pair of RSA keys (see Chapter 7): public key $<e, n>$, private key $<d, n>$, and a coin of serial number s is created by the user. The problem is that we want the bank to sign the serial number s by encrypting it with $<d, n>$* but we do not want the bank to

---

* In this case, signing a coin means encrypting the serial number of the coin with the bank's private key.

know s. Mathematically, we want the bank to provide s^d **mod** n without knowing s. The basic operation for this is given below [O'Mahony, Peirce and Tewari, 1997; Schneier, 1996].

- Each e-cash user has a special wallet for generating e-cash coins. To create a coin, a random serial number s and a random blinding factor $r(0 < r < n)$ are selected for the coin.
- The user blinds the coin as $t = sr^e$ **mod** n and passes it to the bank.
- After signing the coin as $t' = t^d$ **mod** n, the bank passes it back to the user.
- The user unblinds the coin as $(r^{-1}t')$ **mod** n where r^{-1} is defined as the inverse of r. That means, $(r^{-1}r)$ **mod** $n = 1$. It can be proved that $(r^{-1}t')$ **mod** $n = s^d$ **mod** n (i.e., this is equivalent to encrypting the serial number with the bank's private key).

Hence, the bank has signed the coin with its private key $<d, n>$ without knowing the serial number!

Let us look at the following example*. Suppose that the bank has a pair of RSA keys: public key $<e, n> = <3, 33>$; private key $<d, n> = <7, 33>$. The user's wallet creates a coin with a randomly chosen serial number $s = 10$ and selects a random blinding factor $r = 2$ $(0 < r < n)$. The coin is blinded as $t = s(r)^e$ **mod** $n = 10(2)^3$ **mod** $33 = 14$ and passed to the bank. After signing the coin as $t' = t^d$ **mod** $n = 20$ the bank passes it back to the user. The user unblinds the coin as $(r^{-1}t')$ **mod** $n = (17)(20)$ **mod** $33 = 10$. Note that a possible value of r^{-1} is 17 because $(17)(2)$ **mod** $33 = 1$. Note also that s^d **mod** $n = 10^7$ **mod** $33 = 10$. That means, the coin is signed correctly with the bank's private key. However, the bank does not know the serial number of the coin.

To certify the value of each coin, the bank uses a specific private key for signing coins of different values. For example, if a user generates a \$1 coin, it will ask the bank to sign it with the \$1 key and debit the account accordingly. Note that it is useless for a user to cheat by asking the bank to sign a coin with a higher value key (e.g., sign a \$1 coin with a \$10 key). This is because the coin cannot be verified successfully later and hence it will be useless.

10.4.2 Payment by e-cash over the internet

The basic operation of the e-cash system is as shown in Figure 10.6 [O'Mahony et al., 1997; Sherif, 2000]. To use e-cash, a user needs to install a special electronic

---

* This example is based on So Hon Lam's MSc thesis, Department of Computing, Hong Kong Polytechnic University, 2000.

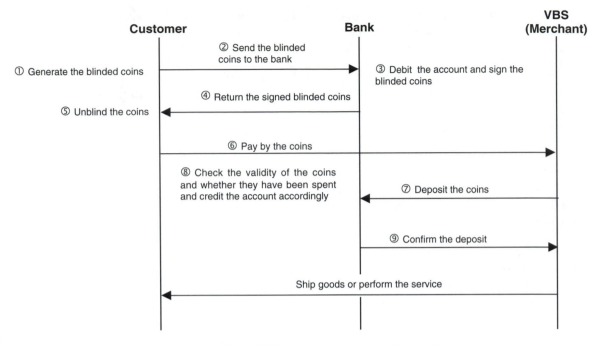

Figure 10.6   Basic operation of the e-cash system

wallet in his computer. Firstly, the user creates a coin of the appropriate value by the wallet software. By using the blind signature method, the coin is signed by the bank without knowing its serial number. Furthermore, the corresponding bank account is debited accordingly. When the user decides to purchase something on the internet with e-cash, the signed e-cash coin(s) is/are passed to the merchant wallet software. The merchant then deposits the coins. As it is possible that an e-cash coin may be further duplicated, the bank needs a mechanism to make sure that multiple spending cannot occur. To do this, the bank uses a database to store the serial numbers of all deposited coins. When a coin is deposited in the bank, the bank checks whether its serial number is already in the database. If not, the deposit is approved and the appropriate bank account is credited accordingly, otherwise the deposit is rejected. To keep the database at a reasonable size, each coin has a validity period. Outdated coins are deleted from the database. Therefore, each user has to deposit an e-cash coin to the bank within its validity period, otherwise the coin will become useless. After verifying that the coin is not outdated, is valid, and has not been deposited before, the merchant will be notified and its account will be credited accordingly. Finally the merchant can ship the goods or provide the service accordingly. Note that e-cash ensures that the bank does not know the original owner of the coin, i.e. it supports anonymous payment. Of course, the bank knows the payee because he needs to make deposits in his account.

10.5 *E-CHECK*

In general, credit card payment and E-cash are very suitable for B2C e-commerce because the payer and the payee may not have a preestablished relationship, and the payment amount is relatively small. For B2B e-commerce, check and credit/debit payment methods are more suitable because the transaction amount is usually much higher.

The basic concept of an electronic check (e-check) is as follows. Suppose that the content of an e-check is C including the payment amount and other information. The e-check can be signed by computing the message digest of C and then encrypting it with the payer's private key. Mathematically, it is

$$E_{RSA}[H[C] | key_{private, payer}]$$

where $key_{private, payer}$ denotes the private key of the payer. The e-check together with the digital signature is then forwarded to the payee. The payee can send the e-check to the bank for clearing through the existing check clearing system. To perform check clearing, the bank can verify the digital signature on the e-check by using the payer's public key. This public key can be sent to the bank through the payer's digital certificate.

A well-known e-check project is being conducted by the Financial Services Technology Consortium (FSTC) founded by some financial institutions and other related organizations in the United States. (Further information can be found at www.echeck.org.) Currently, a good overview is given at www.echeck.org/library/wp/architectualoverview.pdf. To set up the e-check system, a secure device is installed in each computer for generating e-checks using the public key infrastructure. The FSTC framework defines four different cases. Suppose that the VBS (payer) buys some books from a publisher (payee) and uses the FSTC e-check system to settle the payment. The four possible cases are described below and illustrated in Figure 10.7 [www.echeck.org/library/wp/ArchitectualOverview.pdf; O'Mahony, Peirce, and Tewari, 1997; Turban *et al.*, 2000].

10.5.1 Deposit-and-clear

This is similar to the traditional check system. First the VBS signs an e-check digitally and sends it to the publisher. The publisher deposits the e-check in its bank. The VBS's bank and the publisher's bank perform check clearance so that the funds are transferred. Statements/reports are sent to the VBS and the publisher.

10.5.2 Cash-and-transfer

This is used when the publisher's bank cannot support e-check. Upon receiving the signed e-check from the VBS, the publisher forwards the check to the VBS's bank

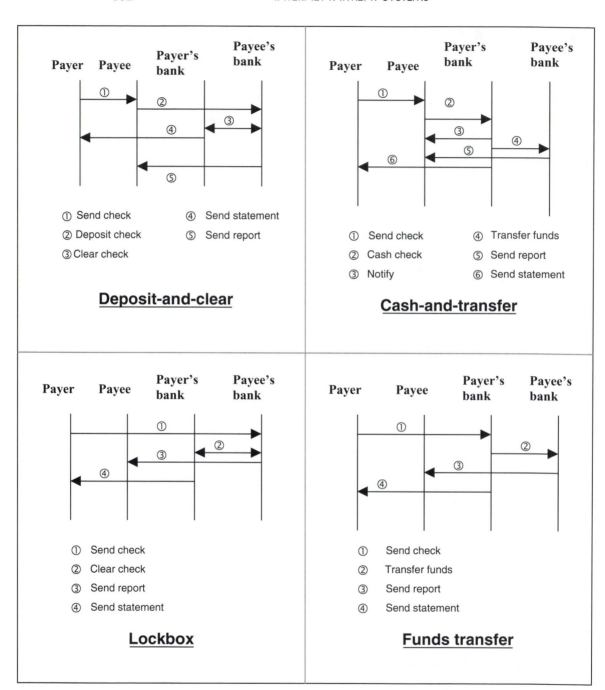

Figure 10.7 The four different scenarios of the FSTC e-check system

directly. The VBS's bank verifies the e-check and transfers the funds via the existing financial system.

10.5.3 Lockbox

The publisher needs to open a special account known as a lockbox with its bank. With this special account, the publisher's bank can accept e-checks for the publisher. This is particularly useful for large organizations that need to handle a large number of checks. Having received an e-check by the publisher's bank, all other steps follow those of a deposit-and-clear scenario.

10.5.4 Direct fund transfer

Essentially, this is the credit/debit payment method (the last among the 4C payment methods). The VBS sends the e-check to its bank for initiating the fund transfer. Then the VBS's bank credits the publisher's account accordingly via the existing electronic funds transfer system.

10.6 *MICROPAYMENT SYSTEM*

The aforementioned payment methods are often referred to as macropayment methods. In these payment methods, the amount involved is reasonably high to justify the overhead cost. In e-commerce, there are also situations in which the macropayment method may not be justified because the payment amount is too small. For example, a customer may only be charged a few cents to download a video clip or to view a page in an e-book. In these circumstances, we need a micropayment system. The challenge of the micropayment system is that it must be cost-effective while maintaining a reasonable degree of security mainly to prevent forged payment. There are two representative examples, namely Millicent and Paywords. The former and the latter are prepayment-based and postpayment based, respectively. We will give an overview of these two protocols in the next two sections [http://www.millicent.com/works/details/papers/millicent-w3c4/millicent.html; Rivest and Shamir, 1997; O'Mahony, Peirce, and Tewari, 1997; Sherif, 2000].

10.6.1 Millicent

With the aim of providing a lightweight and secure payment method, Millicent introduces a digital currency known as *scrip*, which is accepted only by its respective vendor.

Each scrip has a unique ID, which is associated with a scrip secret. Scrips can now be used in conjunction with HTTP as well. The Millicent system involves three parties namely, customers, brokers and vendors. Vendors sell their scrips through brokers (e.g. Bank of Ireland in Europe [Sherif, 2000]) to customers in an aggregate fashion. For example, customer X can purchase VBS's scrip, company1's scrip, company2's scrip, company3's scrip, etc. all from the same broker. The vendor scrips are sent to the customer and the purchase is settled by a macropayment method such as a credit card. To ensure that the content of a scrip cannot be modified, each scrip comes with a certificate produced by hashing the content of the scrip with a scrip-specific secret. According to the scrip ID, the vendor can identify the secret from a database and hence reproduce the certificate. By comparing the reproduced certificate with the one sent by the customer, the validity of the scrip can be verified. When a customer wants to purchase something from a vendor, he sends the scrips summing up the total payment amount to the vendor. Before accepting a scrip, the vendor verifies that the scrip is valid by checking the associated certificate and that it has not been spent before. To satisfy the latter requirement (i.e. to prevent a scrip from spending more than once), each vendor uses a database to record all the used scrips. This is similar to the mechanism used in the e-cash system to prevent multiple spending. Figure 10.8 illustrates the basic operation of the Millicent protocol.

Besides sending the scrips "in the clear," the Millicent protocol also provides the "private and secure" and "secure without encryption" methods for enhancing the security of the protocol. In the former method, each scrip is protected by a shared secret key between the customer and the vendor. In the "secure without encryption" method, a "request signature" is generated for each scrip based on the content of

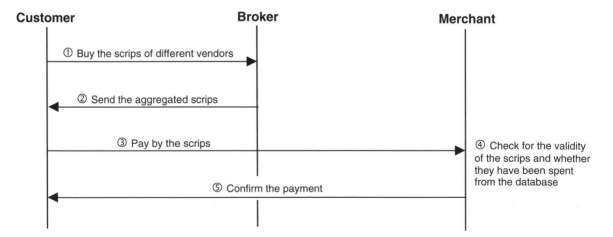

Figure 10.8 Basic operation of the Millicent protocol

the scrip, the customer request message, and the customer secret. According to the customer ID on the scrip, the vendor can identify the customer secret and regenerate the "request signature." Hence, the owner of the scrip can be verified by checking the "request signature." Detailed operations are available at http://www.millicent. com/works/details/papers/millicent-w3c4/millicent.html.

10.6.2 Payword

Payword was proposed by Ron Rivest and Adi Shamir [1997] for supporting cost-effective micropayment. Payment is made by sending a chain of message digests called paywords to the payee. Let us explain the basic operation with an example as shown in Figure 10.9. Suppose that a customer X wants to pay the VBS by using the payword method. To generate the paywords, he needs to obtain a payword certificate from a broker. Among other information, the certificate contains X's identity, the broker's identity, and X's public key. The content of the certificate is digitally signed by the broker's private key. Essentially, the broker serves as a CA. Suppose that customer X wants to generate m paywords each with a value of 1 cent. The aggregate value of the paywords is m cents. By using this chain of paywords, he can pay a maximum of m cents to the VBS. The paywords are generated as follows. First he creates a

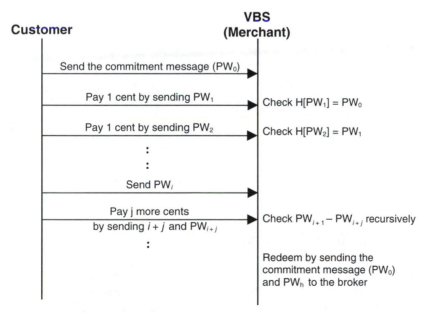

Figure 10.9 Basic operation of the Payword protocol

random number PW_m. Then he generates the kth payword $(0 \le k \le m - 1)$ by using the following formula:

$$PW_k = H[PW_{k+1}]$$

Here PW_{m-1} is the message digest of PW_m, PW_{m-2} is the message digest of PW_{m-1}, etc. To initiate the payment, customer X sends a "commitment message" to the VBS. Among other information, this message includes customer X's payword certificate and PW_0. The message content is digitally signed by customer X's private key. After sending this commitment message, customer X can then pay 1 cent to the VBS by sending PW_1. The VBS can validate PW_1 by checking whether the message digest of PW_1 is equal to PW_0. Recall that this is how PW_0 is generated, i.e. $PW_0 = H[PW_1]$. Subsequent payments can be made in increment of 1 cent as shown in Figure 10.9 and the paywords are verified accordingly by the VBS. According to [Sherif, 2000], payword is transferable and can be made anonymous. Furthermore, vendors can be protected from replay attack by storing unexpired paywords.

In most cases, a payment is more than 1 cent. Suppose that customer X wants to pay j more cents and the last payword sent to the VBS is PW_i. Of course, customer X can pay by sending PW_{i+1}, PW_{i+2}, ..., PW_{i+j} to the VBS. To improve efficiency, customer X can just send the highest index $i+j$ and the highest index payword PW_{i+j} to the VBS. The paywords are validated by finding the message digests recursively, i.e., check whether

$$PW_{i+r} = H[PW_{i+r+1}], \quad 0 \le r \le j - 1$$

starting from PW_{i+1}. Note that $i+j$ must be less than m because PW_m is the highest index payword in the chain. To make a payment beyond m cents, a new chain must be used.

To credit its account the VBS needs to send the "commitment message" to the broker together with the latest payword received, say $PW_h(1 \le h \le m)$. Note that if PW_h is received, h cents have been paid. Upon successful verification, the broker transfers h cents from the customer X's account to the VBS's account.

10.7 OVERVIEW OF SMART CARD

Another internet payment method is by using smart cards. Conventional credit cards and bank cards can be regarded as the first generation smart cards. However, they can store only a limited amount of data typically on a magnetic stripe. Later, more advanced memory cards were introduced to store data on a memory chip. Nowadays, smart cards are embedded with a microprocessor chip. They are more "intelligent" because data on a smart card can be manipulated through programs or commands. Furthermore, data is better protected by means of cryptographic techniques. Hence, it cannot be copied easily. In other words, this makes smart cards more tamper-proof. Smart cards have numerous applications such as electronic payments, authentication, and health care. In particular, smart cards are playing an important role in e-commerce [Elliot and Loebbecke, 1998]. By carrying a smart card, people can conduct different types of electronic transactions anywhere in a secure and efficient manner over the internet. It is expected that future smart cards will be even more "*i*ntelligent" (they are multifunctional), "*i*nteractive" (they can interact with other devices on the internet), and "*i*nteroperable" (different smart cards can communicate with each other). We call these the 3*i* requirements.

Figure 10.10 shows the basic structure of a smart card. Typically, a smart card has the dimensions 8.56 cm × 5.4 cm × 0.08 cm. Technically, this form of smart card is called ID-1. There is another form of a smaller size called ID-000, which is used in small terminals such as cellular phones. As mentioned before, an integrated circuit chip with a microprocessor is embedded in the smart card. The chip also provides mechanical contacts to connect to external devices, for providing power supply, supporting data transfer, etc. In general, the chip of a smart card contains the following components [Hansmann *et al.*, 2000; Rankl and Effing, 1997]:

- *Central processing unit (CPU)*: It controls the operation of the smart card. Typically, an 8-bit microprocessor is used. In some smart cards, an additional cryptographic processor may be incorporated to perform cryptographic functions.

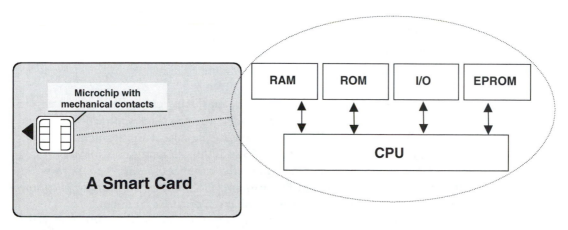

Figure 10.10 Schematic overview of a smart card (modified from [Furche *et al.*, 1996])

- *Random-access memory (RAM)*: It is used for storing temporary data. That means, data is retained only when the power is on.
- *Erasable programmable read-only memory (EPROM)*: It is for storing long-term data such as cryptographic keys and software applications. Data is maintained irrespective of the power status but it can be erased by electrical means.
- *Read-only memory (ROM)*: It stores permanent data such as the operating system. Data is loaded into the card at the production stage and it can only be read.
- *Input/output interface (I/O)*: It provides data input/output functions.

Generally speaking, a smart card is manufactured by going through the following steps [Hansmann *et al.*, 2000]:

- *Step 1*: The chip is fabricated.
- *Step 2*: A module is produced by using the fabricated chip from step 1.
- *Step 3*: The plastic card is manufactured.
- *Step 4*: The module from step 2 is added to the plastic card.
- *Step 5*: Data and programs are loaded into the chip.
- *Step 6*: Personalized data is loaded into the chip.

Most smart cards are governed by the ISO 7816 standards. The key issues are defined in the following documents [Husemann, 1999; Rankl and Effing, 1997]:

- ISO 7816-1: Defines the physical characteristics.
- ISO 7816-2: Defines the dimensions and location of the physical contact.
- ISO 7816-3: Defines the electrical signals.
- ISO 7816-4: Defines the file system and communication protocol.
- ISO 7816-5: Defines mainly the numbering system.

In particular, ISO-7816-4 specifies how a smart card can communicate with a smart card application (e.g. a smart card reader) by means of Application Protocol Data Units (APDUs). In general, a command APDU is sent by the smart card application to the smart card [Hansmann *et al.*, 2000]. Among other information, a command APDU contains the command and the command parameters. In response to a command APDU, the smart card returns an APDU to the smart card application. This APDU provides the status after processing the previous command.

ISO 7816-4 also specifies a simple file system for smart cards with three types of files, namely master file (MF), elementary file (EF), and dedicated file (DF)

[Hansmann, 2000]. A smart card has only one MF, so it functions like a root directory. EFs and DFs can be attached to the MF. The MF is also commonly used to keep cryptographic keys. A DF can function like a directory, holding EFs and its child DFs. EFs are data files. ISO 7816-4 also specifies how files can be read, written, etc.

10.8 *OVERVIEW OF MONDEX*

At present, there are a number of smart card payment systems in use. In particular, three of them are used internationally, namely [Turban and McElroy, 1998]

• Mondex (http://www.mondex.com)
• Visa Cash (http://www.visa.com)
• Proton (http://www.protonworld.com)

Mondex is of particular interest because currently it is the only transferable and anonymous smart card payment system [Rankl and Effing, 1997]. Hence, we use it as an example to describe the typical operation and functions of a smart card payment system. Mondex provides different devices for supporting payments. For example, the Mondex wallet is used for transferring "electronic money" between two smart cards. This device resembles a small calculator with a little LCD display and a numbered keypad. To transfer money, the payer's Mondex card is inserted into the wallet. The payer then types in the transfer amount on the keypad and the card is removed. Finally, the payee's Mondex card is inserted into the wallet and the money will be transferred to the payee's smart card accordingly. Besides the Mondex wallet, special devices are provided to transfer Mondex money over telephone networks and also the internet. Furthermore, users can check the balance of a Mondex card using a portable balance finder. A Mondex card can support multiple currencies. To keep track of the transactions, a certain number of transaction records are maintained inside a Mondex card.

As far as we know, the details of the protocol have not been disclosed in particular how "money" can be transferred between two cards in a secure manner. Basically the protocol relies on public-key cryptography. In general, the basic operation of the Mondex protocol is as follows [Rankl and Effing, 1997]. Suppose that smart card A wants to obtain some money from smart card B. Before transferring the "money," preliminary data is exchanged through a "handshaking phase." Then smart card A informs smart card B of the required amount to be transferred. The message is signed digitally to ensure message integrity. Having receiving the message, smart card B will validate the message as well as the identity of smart card A. This can be done by exchanging digital certificates. Upon successful verification, the appropriate amount is debited from smart card B and a credit message is sent to smart card A. Again the message is digitally signed. Having received the credit message, smart card A credits the amount accordingly.

10.9 *BUILDING A SECURE PAYMENT SYSTEM FOR VBS*

Let us put together all the payment methods in the context of our VBS. The VBS needs to provide payment solutions for both the B2C part and the B2B part. For the B2C part, many different payment solutions are typically provided. Most consumers are likely to pay by credit cards using either SSL or SET. In the SSL approach, the payment request is directed to an SSL-enabled server so that the credit card information can be transferred to the server securely. In the case of SET, we need to set up a special payment server to implement the SET payment protocol as a merchant. This server is linked to a payment gateway through the Internet. It is worth mentioning that some companies provide services to handle credit card payments. Two examples are Internetsecure (http://www.internetsecure.com/) and Tellan (http://www.tellan.com/) [Schneider and Perry, 2000]. By using these services, our VBS can subcontract the payment part. Credit cards are most widely used by a number of e-retailers as their means of accepting payments. Besides credit card payments, in our VBS we would also like to support e-cash and e-check by installing the appropriate payment servers. In particular, e-cash is used to provide anonymous payment. While it is not common at present, some consumers may like to pay by using smart card money (e.g. Mondex) through the Internet in the future. Nearly all e-retailers at the moment only support macropayment methods. It is possible to conceive of the use of micropayment methods particularly when providing a service. Therefore, besides the macropayment methods, our VBS should also provide micropayment services (e.g. Millicent) to handle low-value transactions. For example, this allows the VBS customers to read a certain chapter of an electronic book. Besides Millicent, there are also other commercial micropayment services available such as Internet dollar (http://internetdollar.com/) and Clickshare (http://www.clickshare.com/home/). In particular, Clickshare is specially designed for the publication industry. In general, they work on the same principle as the Millicent and Paywords protocols as described in this chapter. Currently, there is a Micropayment Working Group within W3C to work on various micropayment standards for the web. There are also other micropayment-like services such as Beenz. While Beenz can be used for micropayment, it has a marketing purpose. Basically, consumers can earn and spend "bonus points" among the web sites that can support Beenz. To a certain extent, it functions like "coupons" in the physical commerce system. It is also worth mentioning that a consumer can install an electronic wallet in his computer to facilitate the payment process on the client side. These electronic wallets not only store the customer's information but also fill in the payment form for the customer. Two examples are E-wallet and Agile wallet [Schneider and Perry, 2000]. The W3C Micropayment Working Group is standardizing a special markup language for supporting electronic wallets.

For the B2B part, the solution is relatively simple because usually there is a preestablished relationship. Our VBS can set up a Virtual Private Network with the business partners through which payment transactions can be carried out using XML according to a predefined agreement. Furthermore, e-check provides another viable solution for B2B e-commerce. For example, we can pay the book suppliers by sending digitally signed e-checks to them through e-mails.

10.10 SUMMARY

In this chapter, we discussed the 4C payment methods for e-commerce. Currently, the most commonly used payment method is the credit card. The SET protocol is specifically designed to support secure credit card transactions over the internet. It consists of four phases: initiation, payment, authorization, and capture. By using an innovative dual signature method, it can link the OI and the PI without releasing the credit card information to the merchant. The FSTC e-check project is a comprehensive electronic check system. It addresses four different scenarios: deposit-and-clear, cash-and-transfer, lockbox, and direct fund transfer. The direct fund transfer method is in fact a credit/debit payment method. E-cash is an electronic cash system for supporting anonymous payment on the internet. It is based on an innovative blind signature method so that a bank can sign a coin without knowing the serial number. Millicent and Paywords are two micropayment methods. The former and the latter are noncredit based and credit based, respectively. Smart card is another attractive payment method for e-commerce. Three representative examples are Mondex, Visa Cash, and Proton. Currently, Mondex is the only transferable and anonymous smart card payment method.

REFERENCES

Chaum, D. and Brands, S., "'Minting' electronic cash," *IEEE Spectrum*, **34** (1997), 30–34.

Chaum, D., Fiat, A., and Naor, M., "Untraceable electronic cash," *Advances in Cryptology (CRYPTO '88)* S. Goldwasser, (ed.), Springer-Verlag, Berlin, 1988, 319–327.

Elliot, S. and Loebbecke, C., "Smart-card based electronic commerce: Characteristics and roles," in *Proc. 31st Hawaii International Conference on System Sciences*, 1998, 242–250, vol. 4.

Furche, A., and Wrightson, G. *Computer Money: A Systematic Overview of Electronic Payment Systems*, Morgan Kaufmann, San Mateo, CA, 1996.

Hansmann, U., Nicklous, M. S., Schack, T., and Seliger, F., *Smart card: Application Development using Java*, Springer-Verlag, Berlin, 2000.

Husemann, D., "The smart card: Don't leave home without it," *IEEE* Concurrency, **April–June** (1999), 24–27.

Lynch, D. and Lundquist, L. H., *Digital Money*, John Wiley and Sons, New York, 1996.

O'Mahony, D., Peirce, M., and Tewari, H., *Electronic Payment Systems*, Artech House, 1997.

Rankl, W. and Effing, W., *Smart Card Handbook*, John Wiley & Sons, Chichester, UK, 1997.

Rivest R. L. and Shamir A., PayWord and MicroMint: Two Simple Micropayment Schemes, *Lecture Notes in Computer Science 1189*, Springer-Verlag, Berlin, 1997, 69–87.

Schneier, B., *Applied Cryptography*, John Wiley & Sons, New York, 1996.

Schneider, G. P. and Perry, J. T., *Electronic Commerce*, Course Technology, 2000.

SET Book 1: Business Description, May, 1997.

Sherif M. H., *Protocols for Secure Electronic Commerce*, CRC Press, 2000.

Stallings, W., Cryptography and Network Security, Prentice-Hall, Upper Saddle River, NJ, 1999.

Turban, E., Lee, J., King, D., Chung, H. M., and Lee, J. K., *Electronic Commerce – A Managerial Perspective*, Prentice-Hall, Upper Saddle River, NJ, 2000.

Turban, E. and McElroy, D., "Using smart cards in electronic commerce," in *Proc. 31st Hawaii International Conference on System Sciences*, 1998, 62–69, vol. 4.

RECOMMENDED READING

Lynch, D. and Lundquist, L. H., *Digital Money*, John Wiley and Sons, New York, 1996.

Furche, A., and Wrightson, G. *Computer Money: A Systematic Overview of Electronic Payment Systems*, Morgan Kaufmann, San Mateo, CA, 1996.

These books provide a general overview of digital money/electronic payment systems.

O'Mahony, D., Peirce, M., and Tewari, H., *Electronic Payment Systems*, Artech House, 1997.

This is an excellent book, covering nearly all the available electronic payment systems. Readers are recommended to read this book for further details on internet payment systems.

Besides e-cash and FSTC e-check, the Information Sciences Institute of the University of Southern California has also developed a Netcash system and a Netcheck system for cash and check payment over the internet, respectively. More information can be found at http://www.isi.edu/gost/info/netcheque/ and from the following:

Medvinsky, G. and Neuman, B. C., "NetCash: A design for practical electronic currency on the Internet," in *Proceedings of the 1st ACM Conference on Computer and Communication Security*, November 1993.

Neuman, B. C. and Medvinsky, G., "Requirements for network payment: The NetCheque perspectives," in *Proceedings of IEEE COMPCON'95*, March 1995, 32–36.

Elliot, S. and Loebbecke, C., "Smart-card based electronic commerce: Characteristics and roles," in *Proc. 31st Hawaii International Conference on System Sciences*, 1998, 242–250, vol. 4.

Turban, E. and McElroy, D., "Using smart cards in electronic commerce," in *Proc. 31st Annual Hawaii International Conference on System Sciences*, 1998, 62–69, vol. 4.

These give a general overview of the application of smarts card in e-commerce.

Rankl, W. and Effing, W., *Smart Card Handbook*, John Wiley & Sons, Chichester, UK, 1997.

Guthery, S. and Jurgensen, T. M., Smart card developer's kit, Macmillian Technical Publishing, 1998.

These are two good reference books on smart cards.

Hansmann, U., Nicklous, M., S., Schack, T., and Seliger, F., *Smart card: Application Development using Java*, Springer-Verlag, Berlin, 2000.

Readers are recommended to read this book for further information on Java cards.

Stallings, W., Cryptography and Network Security, Prentice-Hall, Upper Saddle River, NJ, 1999.

This book gives a good overview of the SET protocol.

The full specification of the SET protocol can be downloaded from http://www.setco.org/download.html/#spec. In particular, readers are encouraged to read Book 1 of the specification (i.e. [SET Book 1]). There is much information on internet payment systems at the W3C web site (http://www.w3.org/ecommerce/micropayments/). Information about the e-check project can be found at www.echek.org/library/wp/index.html.

11

Consumer-Oriented E-commerce

11.1 Introduction

11.2 Traditional Retailing and E-retailing

11.3 Benefits of E-retailing

11.4 Key Success Factors

11.5 Models of E-retailing

11.6 Features of E-retailing

11.7 Developing a Consumer-oriented E-commerce System

11.8 The PASS Model

11.9 Summary

References

Recommended Reading

Consumer-oriented e-commerce or e-retailing involves selling directly to consumers who are the end users on the internet. It frequently involves a temporary relationship. The buyers visit the selling site either casually or very infrequently, perhaps only once. It has a relatively low volume of transactions and involves relatively small payments. In marked contrast, business-oriented (B2B) e-commerce involves transactions between two business organizations. These transactions may frequently be specified within a formal contract. It usually involves much more documentation and record-keeping, which is necessary for a business. The volume of transactions in B2B e-commerce is likely to be high and certainly much higher than in customer-oriented transactions. The amounts of payments involved are also quite large. As the transaction volumes and the payment levels are high, the buyer normally has much more buying leverage in B2B e-commerce.

The objectives of the chapter include a description of the differences between traditional retailing and e-retailing. We describe some of the features and concepts of traditional retailing and show how these map to some new concepts in retailing on the internet. Next, we describe the benefits and disadvantages associated with e-retailing. We look at different models for e-retailing and describe some of the features of e-retailing, which give it a unique character. We also describe the impact of e-commerce on retailing in general. Lastly, we look at the technical issues related to creating an e-retailing site.

11.1   *INTRODUCTION*

E-retailing essentially consists of the sale of goods and services. Sometimes we refer to this as the sale of tangible and intangible goods, as shown in Figure 11.1. We can divide tangible goods into two categories: physical goods and digital goods. Examples of physical goods would be a book, a television set, a video recorder, a washing machine, etc. Examples of digital goods are software and music, which may be downloaded from the internet. The sale of intangible goods is sometimes called e-servicing. Examples of services that may be sold are information such as the most recent stock prices, the most recent foreign exchange rate, or education. Entertainment such as games that would be played on the internet are also examples of e-services. So are the sales of services such as telecommunication services or banking services. The sale of tangible and intangible goods are all referred to as customer-oriented e-commerce or e-retailing, if they are sold directly to the consumer who is the end user. E-services are discussed in Chapter 13. Here we discuss the sale of tangible goods.

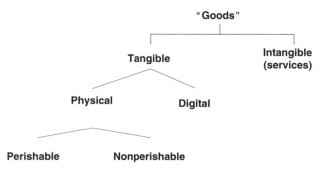

Figure 11.1   Selling of different types of goods

11.2   *TRADITIONAL RETAILING AND E-RETAILING*

11.2.1   Traditional retailing

Before we begin a discussion of e-retailing, it would be useful to look at some aspects of traditional retailing. This helps to identify some essential characteristics of retailing.

Traditional retailing essentially involves selling to a final customer through a physical outlet or through direct physical communication. This normally involves a fairly extensive chain starting from a manufacturer to a wholesaler and then to the retailer who through a physical outlet has direct contact with the final customer.

Examples of physical outlets that retailers currently use are [Lusch and Lusch, 1987]

* malls
* generalized stores (e.g. department store)
* specialized stores
* franchise stores

Malls consist of a collection of individual stores, each of which are under their own separate management. The mall management only provides the physical location where the retailer can create his outlet.

In contrast to that, generalized stores are stores that essentially have one unified management but carry several different product lines. So a generalized store may carry everything from shoes to books, to beds, to television sets. It does not specialize in a specific area of merchandise that it actually retails.

Specialized stores, on the other hand, sell a specific product line. They may choose to be in clothes and may be in a particular segment of the clothing market. Thus, a specialized store may position itself at the high end of the clothing market and sell only brand names like Peirre Cardin, Gucci, Lacoste, etc. Alternatively, it may be one that does discount selling and sells inexpensive brands, which go directly to customers. These two positions in the market would be aimed at different classes of customers.

Franchise stores, on the other hand, are stores where there is a single marketing chain and brand name for the store, but the individual store may be run by a different management with a royalty arrangement back to the franchisee. The franchisee would normally be responsible for the marketing, advertising, and sometimes supply of merchandise.

We will later see that each of these classes of stores have an equivalent counterpart in e-retailing. It is useful to reflect that even in traditional retailing we have moved away from just using a static physical outlet within which a customer can have direct contact with the retailer. Thus, more recent forms of traditional retailing include

- direct mailing
- telemarketing
- door-to-door sales
- vending machines

Direct mailing to a customer normally involves sending a brochure or catalog to a customer. The customer browses through this catalog and then carries out mail ordering. In some respects, this notion of browsing through a catalog is a forerunner of e-retailing. Direct mailing, telemarketing, door-to-door sales, or the use of vending machines includes other forms that have actually moved away from a physical fixed outlet and in a way are an intermediate form of the movement away from traditional physical retailing outlet to the virtual retailing we see on the internet.

11.2.2   E-retailing

In this section we look at how some of these traditional outlets for retailing map to the new medium of e-retailing. Let us first take specialized stores. They specialize in a particular product line. Thus, we get specialized e-stores, such as 1-800-Flowers, which specializes in selling flowers, and Amazon.com®, which started by specializing in selling books.

The internet has allowed a new kind of specialization to emerge. Instead of specializing just in a special product line, they allow specialization in particular classes of customers and sellers. Thus, we see lastminute.com, which allows last minute purchases of travel tickets, gift, and entertainment to be matched against last minute sellers of the same items. Here, we see specialization not in a product line but in a class of purchasers and a class of sellers. This kind of specialization would not have been possible before we had the internet.

In addition to these specialized stores, we also get generalized e-stores where a store sells several product lines under a single management. Examples of these generalized stores include JC penny and Walmart.

We also have the electronic counterpart of malls or e-malls. E-malls essentially provide a web-hosting service for your individual store much in the way that malls provide a hosting service in the sense of a physical location for your store. Examples of these e-malls are Yahoo!Store, GEOShops, and CNET stores.

In the future we may see the equivalent of franchise stores developing.

One new class of business that is developing very quickly on the internet is the e-broker. The e-broker does not sell directly to a customer but brings the customer in touch with a particular supplier, so that a given set of criteria specified by the customer is satisfied. For example, the customer may want to buy goods at the cheapest price and so the e-broker would then do a search to find the supplier that would provide the cheapest goods. Or, a customer may want to find a particular kind of goods and the e-broker sets about determining which supplier would provide those goods. This area of e-broking is likely to grow very greatly in the near future. It takes several forms, some of which, such as comparison shopping, we will discuss in detail later.

In summary, we can, therefore, map traditional forms to e-retailing as follows:

- Specialized stores → specialized e-stores
- Generalized stores → Generalized e-stores
- Malls → E-malls
- Franchise stores → ?
- New form of business: e-broker

11.3   BENEFITS OF E-RETAILING

11.3.1   To the customer

Customers enjoy a number of benefits from e-retailing. The first of these is convenience. It is convenient for the customer as he does not have to move from shop to shop physically in order to examine goods. He is able to sit in front of a terminal and search the net and examine the information on goods. The second aspect of convenience he gets is in terms of time. Normally, the traditional shop has an opening time and a closing time and the customer can only visit the shop within these periods. On the net, the customer can choose at any time to visit a site to examine the goods that are available and actually carry out his purchasing at one's own convenient time. The third type of convenience that the customer gets is that he has access to a search engine, which will actually locate the products that he describes and also the site where they may be available, or perhaps even locate the sites where they may be available at the best price.

The second type of benefit to customers is better information. The Internet and the World Wide web are essentially communication media that allow retailers to put on quite extensive information related to their products, which is available to the customers. Furthermore, since the customer can look at several sites, he will be able to obtain different pieces of information from each site to build a far better picture for himself about the products that he is interested in. In some sites, there are customer reviews of different products as well as reviews by the business itself. An example of this can be found on Amazon.com. This allows the customer to finesse his requirements before actually making the purchase. It also gives different sources of information.

The third type of benefit that the customer gets is competitive pricing. This is due to two factors. The first is lowered costs to the retailer because he does not have to maintain a physical showroom, he does not have to hire several shop assistants, and these savings can be passed on to customers in the form of reduced prices. Secondly, competitive pricing pressure that arises from the fact that the customer is now able to look at prices at several sites. Therefore, the pressure is always there on the retailer to maintain a competitive price for his products.

The fourth benefit is customization. The customer can actually specify the features of the products that he would like and thus in some cases it is possible that the retailer may allow a customized product to be delivered. An example of this is on the Dell site. The computer site allows shoppers to custom specify their own computer software and hardware configurations. Thus, the customer is able to select exactly what he wants. This ability to get the business to deliver a product that the customer specifies he wants is the essence of C2B e-commerce.

In summary, the benefits of e-retailing to the customer include

- convenience
- better information
- competitive price
- customization
- shopping anywhere, anytime

So with e-retailing, the customer can shop anywhere around the globe without being restricted to his local vicinity. He could, for example, purchase goods overseas and have them delivered to a domestic address. He can also shop, as mentioned earlier, at any time. These are very considerable benefits of e-retailing to the customer. These benefits could see larger and larger numbers of customers move more and more of their shopping on to e-retailing sites in the future.

11.3.2   To the business

There are a number of benefits of e-retailing to the business itself. The first of these is global reach. The retailer now is no longer restricted to customers who are able to reach the store physically. They can be from anywhere around the globe. The retailer must, of course, deliver the goods of a purchase to the customer. We see later that this has an impact on the types of goods that are most easily handled through e-retailing.

The second benefit is better customer service. The use of e-mail and the use of electronic interchange of messages between the customer and the retailer allows better communication between the customer and the retailer. These allow one to easily field inquiries and deal with complaints. These also allow a much more rapid response time than was possible in the days of faxes and postal mail.

The third benefit is the lowered capital cost to the retailer. The retailer does not have to maintain showrooms, he can probably have lower inventories. Thus, while Amazon.com lists over a few million titles, it keeps an inventory of a few thousand best selling titles only. Therefore, the retailer has lower warehousing costs. He does not have to have many shop assistants who are physically answering questions and showing the customer goods.

The fourth benefit to the retailer is mass customization. Based on requests by the customers, the retailer is now able to carry out mass customization with reduced time to market for the customized products.

The next advantage is targeted marketing. The retailer is now able to pick on a specific targeted group of customers and direct marketing towards these customers.

The retailer is also able to provide more value-added services in the way of better information, add-on services to basic services, or add-on options to products that he is selling.

The last advantage to the retailer consists of different new forms of specialized stores that he is now able to utilize. As we have mentioned previously, now he does not have to specialize his store based just on a product line but could choose to specialize his store based on a specialized targeted group of customers. It also creates new opportunities for niche marketing.

A summary of the benefits to the e-retailer are

- global reach
- better customer service
- low capital cost
- mass customization
- targeted marketing
- more value-added services
- new forms of specialized stores and niche marketing

11.4   *KEY SUCCESS FACTORS*

11.4.1   For traditional retailing

There are a number of key success factors which have been identified for traditional retailing [Lusch and Lusch, 1987]. Two of these are the size and the number of outlets. The larger the retailer, the greater the buying muscle and therefore the lower the price for procurement. The number of outlets also allows the retailer to spread the purchase costs over a larger inventory.

In addition, the number of outlets provides for better visibility. The retailer is now visible to the customer at many geographical locations rather than just one. Location is, of course, an extremely important success factor in traditional retailing. The retailer may choose to be sited in the central business district, in a regional area, in a shopping complex, or in a street of shops. This may relate to the category of customers and the costs associated with the site.

Other factors that are very important in traditional retailing are store atmosphere and store layout [Lusch and Lusch, 1987]. Store atmosphere evokes a particular look and feel about the retailer and is therefore important to the positioning in the market. Store layout is important in creating an atmosphere but is also important in ensuring that one groups different sets of products together, so that the purchase of one product will frequently lead to the purchase of another, thus allowing for cross selling.

Price is important and here it is not necessarily the cheapest price, but the price which is consonant with what the customer expects to pay for the goods.

The variety of goods in the case of a large store, particularly of a department store, is also important because a customer would come in looking for one set of goods and then choose to purchase others.

Profit margins are important in traditional retailing, and last but not least is the level of turnover.

To summarize, the key success factors for traditional retailing are

- size
- number of outlets
- visibility
- location
- store atmosphere
- store layout
- price
- variety of goods
- profit margins
- turnover

11.4.2   For e-retailing

In this section, we explore how these success factors of traditional retailing translate to e-retailing. The first one considered is size. The important point to realize here is that no matter how large the company is your e-store presentation is still limited to the size of the computer screen, which may be, say, 15 in. It is not necessary to look at the number of outlets in cyberspace because you probably need only one web site set up. However, this web site is linked to other similar web sites and portals. Therefore, it is not the number of outlets that is important but the number of links from other important sites to your web site which is far more important.

When one thinks of visibility, it is all the more important in cyberspace. It is not just enough to create a web site; you have to let the world know the existence of your web site and that people can purchase from your e-store. When looking at visibility, the important point to realize here is that most people find information on the internet through the use of search engines. Therefore, it is very important to register the web site or e-store with the most common or the most widely used search engines, such as Lycos, Alta Vista, and Yahoo. It is also important to link your web site with other well-known web sites that have similar interests, or major portals such as Yahoo, which link back to your e-store. This can greatly increase the visibility of the web site.

When considering location, we note that the geographic boundaries no longer exist. A local e-store and a foreign e-store are both just "one click" away.

Store atmosphere is particularly important on the web. The "look and feel" of the web site should match with the company's image as well as the market position that it seeks to address. Thus, if you are selling very up-market clothes such as Gucci and Armani, your web site for these stores should have a sophisticated look and feel about it. On the other hand, if you are selling other kinds of goods, you could choose to have a slightly more jazzy image on your web site. The front page or the homepage of your e-store is particularly important. It may be the only chance that you get of luring a potential customer into your e-store. In some ways it plays a similar role for the e-store that the window display plays for the traditional store. What is also important is in going through this store. The layout of the store has to be such that it facilitates the customer's interests. The advantage of using store layouts in the e-store is that the layout can actually be made dynamic and be determined by the customer's interests. The customer's interests could be obtained from data mining his previous purchases at the e-store. This is the major difference between a traditional store and an e-store.

Price is very important in cyberspace because the customer can easily carry out comparison pricing between your e-store and other e-stores not just in your immediate neighborhood but all around the world. Also some e-brokers provide agents or services that carry out comparison pricing; therefore, the customer can easily find the cheapest price. For this reason, it is important that in e-retailing one sets up a competitive pricing structure. Next, when one looks at the variety of goods, one here needs to consider very carefully whether you are setting up a specialized e-store or an e-department store. If you are setting up a specialized e-store, then you need to gain access to the specific target group of customers you are interested in because they can travel so easily in cyberspace to reach you. When one looks at profit margin and turnover, generally profit margins per item tend to be lower with e-retailing, and so turnover must be higher. Lastly, if one examines profitability one finds that this is still important with the e-stores, but in recent times the share price of the e-store appears to have assumed more importance in the eyes of investors. However, in the long run, profitability will assume more importance.

11.5   MODELS OF E-RETAILING

There are several models for e-retailing and these include

• Specialized e-store
• Generalized e-store
• E-mall
• Direct selling by the manufacturer
• Supplementary distribution channel
• E-broker
• E-services

We discuss these in turn here, except for the last two, e-broker and e-services, which are discussed in Chapter 13 on e-services.

11.5.1   Specialized e-stores

The first class of model what we mention in e-retailing was the specialized e-store and here you can distinguish between two different kinds of specialization. The more traditional specialization along product lines and specialization by function (which we discuss later). When you have specialization by product line, essentially you have a store that decides to pick one particular product line, say books, flowers, CDs, clothes, and sells only this particular product line. It may also choose to position itself in a particular part of the product line, e.g. clothes; it could choose to position itself at the very expensive end of the market selling brand names like Gucci and Armani. Alternatively, it could do more mass marketing by selling non-brand names at a much lower price, or it could go into discount selling. So, you can have a specialization by product line, and then you could have specialization of positioning within that product line to cater for a particular part of the market. In contrast to this, a new kind of specialization is emerging on the internet, as mentioned earlier, namely specialization by function. A good example of this is lastminute.com.

In lastminute.com they sell gifts, travel tickets, and other items for last minute shoppers who want to purchase these items at a very short notice. Generally, when one purchases an item at a very short notice (e.g. travel), he often pays a premium, which is an extra amount for the convenience of booking the travel at the last minute. Now, this means that the air ticket is likely to cost much more than if he had purchased it some time before travelling and made use of different discounts or promotions. The producers of the web site lastminute.com realized that there are groups of customers who make these purchases at the last minute and feel some degree of angst at having to pay the premium for doing this shopping at the last minute. On the other hand, you will find that you may have sellers, e.g. airline companies, that have empty seats at the last minute which they are unable to fill. So, what lastminute.com does is bring together travellers who want to book at the last minute and an airline which has got spare capacity at the last minute, and allow the former to buy from the latter at the last minute. In this situation, the purchaser may get his airline ticket at a reduced price.

So, there is a win–win situation for both the purchaser and the seller. This is a unique kind of specialization. It is very difficult to do this unless one utilizes the internet to carry out this kind of specialization. Now, let us go on to discuss individual case studies under these two categories, namely specialization by product line and specialization by function. Let us start by considering specialization by product lines.

Case study 1: Amazon.com

The first example that I want to discuss is perhaps one of the best known among the internet e-retailers, and this is the Amazon.com. The homepage for this is given in Figure 11.2. We intend to discuss this in some detail to understand some of the features of an e-retailing site.

Amazon.com in the first quarter of 2000 had 4.7 million titles and a customer base of nearly 10.7 million customers.

Amazon.com started off as a company in July 1995 and the growth you have seen has all occurred only in the last five years. Now, when you compare this to the growth of a traditional retailer, you can see that the difference is quite staggering. Amazon.com emphasizes three things, which are very important to the customer. The first is ease of selection, the second is ease of use, and the third is price. Typically, its books cost almost 40–50% less than those sold through traditional bookshops.

Looking at the actual ordering process when using a web site, (Figure 11.3), we note the typical ordering structure, namely the order creation and order submission process. It begins with a welcome and then proceeds to allow you to select the method of payment, and then the company wants to know if you want this order to be treated

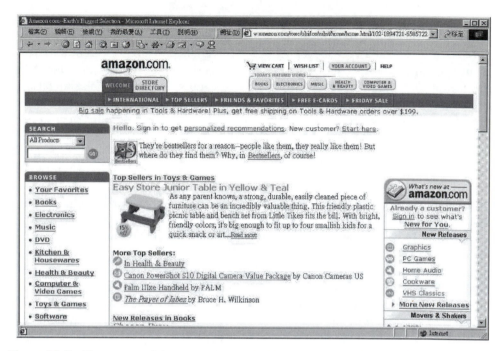

Figure 11.2 Homepage of Amazon.com (©2001 Amazon.com, Inc. All Rights Reserved. Reproduced with permission of Amazon.com)

as a gift. After that, it provides you a place to enter your shipping address for the order, and next it asks you to verify and check the order you have put in. Then it presents you with credit card information you have previously entered and allows you to select the particular card you intend to use. Lastly, it allows you to select a shipping option.

When you visit Amazon.com's web site you should look carefully at this order creation and order submission process. This site has some very important features that need to be utilized by e-retailers. Certainly, all facets in the order creation and order submission process, whether they are carried out in that sequence or a slightly different sequence, have to be matched by any order creation and order submission process by an e-retailer on the web.

But the strength of Amazon.com is not only in the order creation and order submission process. It greatly assists you to select the items you want. It provides two important means of selecting an item. The first relates to selection by subject or category. It lists its books under different categories and you can then select and browse the category or subject you are interested in and determine if the book you are looking for is there. An alternative means, which is not available in the traditional bookshop,

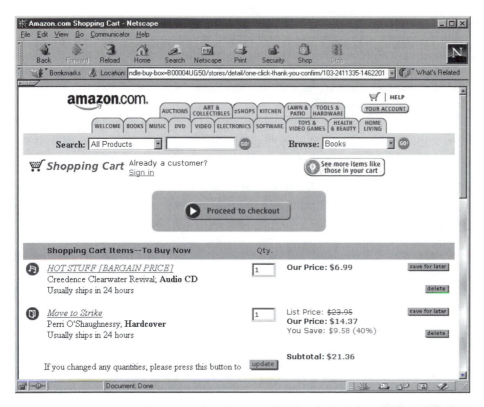

Figure 11.3 Ordering screens of Amazon.com (©2001 Amazon.com, Inc. All Rights Reserved. Reproduced with permission of Amazon.com)

is that it allows a key word search facility, which picks out the books of interest using a search engine.

The other feature that is added to the selection process and supports the customer is a purchasing circle. Here, information is analyzed by zip codes and by domain names for specific books and specific classes of users, and then a purchasing circle is created utilizing a technique called collaborative filtering. Therefore, one gets a group of customers who have a specific set of interests that can actually access a given purchasing circle. This allows one to display titles which may be of interest to purchasers within the purchasing circle and target special offers and reviews.

It also does the usual thing that the traditional bookstore does, i.e., it displays all the best-sellers at the outset. In order to aid the selection process it utilizes a shopping cart where one actually selects items by just using "one click" on the item, and this is automatically added to the shopping cart. When one has finally completed the selection of items, one can proceed to order creation and order submission. Of course, like any other web site, it has to ensure that it has got a secure e-payment system and that it goes into a secure mode allowing you to enter your information on your credit card directly through the internet. Alternatively, if you are hesitant to do that, it provides a means by which you can phone in the required information to Amazon.com after you have actually submitted the purchase order.

Other facts about Amazon.com that are very interesting are the very rapid growth rate in sales and revenue. As mentioned earlier, it was created in 1995, and by 1996 it had sales worth $15.7 million. In the first quarter of 2000, it had a revenue of $573 million. Now, this is a phenomenal growth in revenue over a very short period.

Later, we compare what Amazon.com is doing with an alternative book seller – Barnes and Noble – which utilizes a more traditional mode including a physical store as well an internet web site. We note that Amazon.com, even though it started by specializing in books, did not pick out a special segment of the book market unlike other stores that might just specialize in, say, only technical books. These stores are specialized in a specific segment within the book market. The other thing we notice about Amazon.com is that while it started as a specialized store concentrating totally on books, it has moved into several other areas and now includes a wide variety of items such as CDs, electronic goods, DVDs, computer games, and videos; but we also note that it has still restricted itself to a category of goods where the distribution costs are not likely to be high because the item involved is either relatively small or a high-value item. This is an important fact that has to be taken into account whenever you are doing e-retailing. Note what Jeff Bezos (who started Amazon.com) did when contemplating internet commerce; the first most interesting thing he did was to write down a list of products that he thought could be sold on the internet, and he finally settled on books. He thought very carefully about choosing the specific product before actually setting up the e-store. These are important factors to take into account if you are going into the business of setting up an e-store as they impact your business model significantly.

Perhaps at this stage you should go to the Amazon.com's site and look at some of the features we discussed so as to understand them more clearly. The web site is http://www.amazon.com.

Case study 2: 1-800-Flowers

1-800-Flowers (see Figure 11.4) is a leader in selling flowers and other gift products. While it provides a typical B2C e-commerce service like Amazon.com, flowers are perishable goods and so even better logistic arrangements have to be made. To tackle

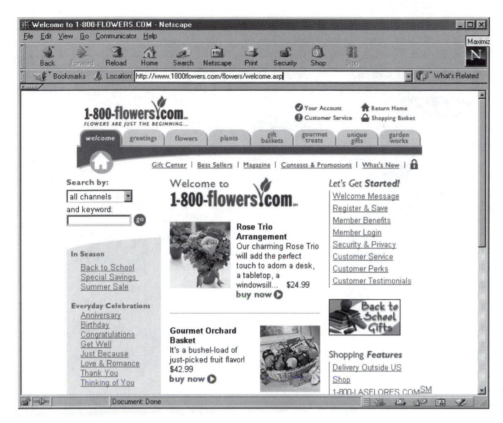

Figure 11.4 Homepage of 1-800-Flower.com (with permission of 1-800-FLOWERS.com)

this problem, 1-800-Flowers delivers flowers through many international affiliations. Besides ordering through the company's web site, customers can also place orders through a toll-free telephone number, some portal web sites, and the company-owned or franchised retail outlets.

Case study 3: CDNow

The third example of an e-retailer we consider is also one that specializes in a product line and is known as CDNow (see Figure 11.5). CDNow was created by Jason and Medolon in August 1994 and is essentially an on-line seller of music CDs. There are some important differences between CDNow and Amazon.com and 1-800-Flowers.

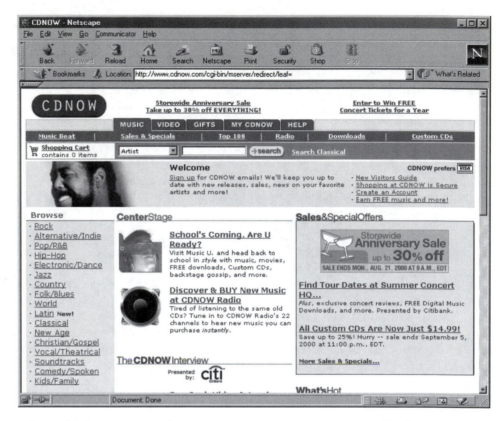

Figure 11.5   Homepage of CDNow.com [© 2000 CDNOW, Inc. (all rights reserved)]

The first is that one can actually access samples of the product because CDNow allows you to download and hear samples of the music that you might be thinking of purchasing. In addition, because it is a digital product, it can actually be downloaded, if necessary, to your machine directly after you have completed the purchase.

Unlike the other two products, which were books and flowers, while they can be ordered via the internet, nevertheless have to be delivered physically. So a somewhat different distribution mechanism can be utilized here, even though one can also deliver CDs by mail or through associated physical stores. When compared with Amazon.com and 1-800-Flowers, we note that CDNow provides search by the author, by the singer, by the song-title, or by the music. So again we note that this e-retailer has a browsing facility and a search facility.

As with the other two stores, there is an order creation, an order submission process, and you have to have an effective selection process.

11.5.2   Basic features of an e-retailing system

Now that we have examined three different case studies, you should visit their web sites. We are now in a position to provide a summary of some of the features of these e-retailing web sites. These web sites must provide

- a method for selecting your purchases (e.g., Amazon.com provides a shopping cart facility).
- a mechanism for creating and submitting an order.
- a secure e-payment facility for your purchases.
- an appropriate distribution mechanism, which has to be carefully thought out for the particular category of goods that are being sold.
- a browsing facility, normally by subject or by category.
- a searching facility, which will search for a particular good that you need.
- a mechanism for customer service and feedback.

The more sophisticated of these e-retailing systems also include some additional features, and these features provide analysis through data mining and through the creation of collaborative mechanisms on the web. The first of these will allow cross selling and targeted marketing by presenting to you preferences of products which have been purchased by other buyers who have made purchases similar to yours in the past. They might try to create purchasing circles through collaborative filtering as mentioned earlier in the case of Amazon.com. They might create new product combinations and product lines. These could be as a result of continuously evolving product lines based on the advice or the feedback from customers as to what they are seeking. Thus, we note that CDNow provides a facility for the consumer to suggest the type of CD he would like to have. They also frequently provide chat-room and community features trying to emulate some long-lost features that people in a village experienced when they went along to a store that had a community around it. They sometimes also provide "question and answer" facilities. Amazon.com also provides a facility for customer reviews of products.

In the long term, most of these e-retailing sites, as they become more sophisticated, will provide some of the more advanced features that are referred to here.

11.5.3   Specialization by function

Lastminute.com (see Figure 11.6) is an example of a web site that carries out e-retailing where we have specialization by function, which is specialized to a particular class of consumers and a specific class of sellers. Essentially, what the e-retailer

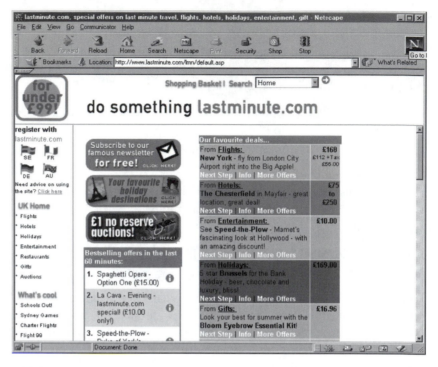

Figure 11.6   Homepage of Lastminute.com (Reproduced with permission of Lastminute)

provides is that it facilitates in bringing together last minute sellers of services or products and last minute buyers of that service or product. This ability to match last minute sellers with last minute buyers has essentially been made possible by the internet. It would have been difficult for a traditional store to provide this specialization by function because of the necessity to communicate information between specific large but dispersed groups. In order to understand this e-retailer, imagine that you have a plane taking off in two days' time from Hong Kong to London, and 30% of its seats are empty. On the other side, imagine that you have a whole lot of people who might like a holiday in London, but either have never been able to afford it or have been very busy and have not been able to make their plane bookings in time, and have to rush to make plane bookings and hotel bookings at the very last minute.

Generally when you make these plane bookings and hotel bookings at the last minute, you end up paying much more than you would if you had actually made the booking much earlier. However, by tapping into unused spare capacity which is available to the sellers, Lastminute.com is able to provide these services at a much reduced cost. It is almost as if they are utilizing and generalizing the idea of standby, which used to exist for flights where at the very last minute you could get on to a plane at a much cheaper price if the seat was not taken, except here the period is extended out a little beyond just the few minutes to may be a few days before the plane takes off. They do this last minute matching for a variety of things, including the last minute matching for flights, hotels, holidays, entertainment, restaurants, gifts, and even options. They sell packages and highlight special deals they have been able to get, which have to be fulfilled by the sellers and which have been created because the sellers have so much spare capacity at the very last minute. You might like to visit their web site and actually go through the process of selecting a hotel or a flight. Notice here that you will actually be specifying very clearly the type of thing you want. For example, in the case of selecting a flight, you have to indicate your starting point as well as your final destination, and this reduces the whole process of selecting considerably. This is unlike the situation that you have with books where you might get a book if you know its exact name, but if you don't, then you may just want to browse and look at a subject category, or just let the search engine help you by using some keywords. The facility here has been made possible by two factors that are related to the internet. The first allows the seller or the buyer to notify lastminute.com at the last minute through the use of the internet. This informs the e-retailer that he has either something to buy or something to sell at the last minute. The second facility which is utilized here is the search facility that looks at the notifications made by the buyers as well as by the sellers, and looks through all the sellers to see if it can find the sellers that match the services required by the buyers. So, utilizing these two facilities, one has created this special kind of specialization by function.

11.5.4 Generalized e-stores

The next category of e-retailing models that we intend to look at is generalized e-stores. Generalized e-stores sell a large number of product lines rather than confining themselves to just one or a very few product lines. First we examine Value America as an example of a generalized e-store that markets only through the internet and does not have physical stores to support it. In contrast, we see Walmart which started as a physical store and then moved on to utilize the internet as an alternative mechanism or channel for selling. We discuss each of these in turn.

Case study 4: Value America

Value America sells more than 2000 brands of products representing over 40 industries and covers everything from computers to CDs, perfumes, coffee, etc. An interesting aspect is that it concentrates on selling well-known brand names only as people cannot actually touch and feel the products and have direct acquaintance of the products. Value America, as in other cases, was started by someone who had a strong background in the particular business, that is, of running a general store as well as of the internet.

Value America General Store offers a consumer the convenience of shopping directly from his computer and sells the products at a lower price. Value America takes orders from the consumers and then passes them on to a manufacturer who supplies the goods. Value America only actually owns the goods once the manufacturer takes the order and the goods are in transit from the manufacturer to the consumer.

As with other internet stores, Value America sets up strategic alliances. In this case, Value America and Fedex have strategic alliances to assist with the process of distribution. Again, note that the distribution aspects have to be very carefully worked out, particularly where the range of products can vary widely. Here, one does not have the convenience of sticking to a specific kind of distribution structure. In order to make the whole thing work properly, Value America has also created a good return mechanism for the goods which is as easy for the consumers to use as in actual purchasing. At the time of writing, we note that it was facing financial difficulties.

Case study 5: Walmart

In constrast to Value America which is purely a cyber superstore, Walmart has created a generalized e-store to support its existing physical chain of superstores. Walmart has actually been around for many years. It started way back in 1962 and has grown to a huge company, which does traditional retailing concentrating on discounting and works on creating a local touch and a strong personal feel in its relationship with the customers. In order to extend this, it has added an internet shopping generalized e-store, which sells a wide variety of goods ranging from home appliances to cameras to hobbies and crafts and home electronics and a wide variety of other things which are normally available in their traditional stores. The advantage of Walmart in creating a generalized e-store is that it has existing physical stores to act as distribution points for products sold on the internet.

11.5.5   E-malls

The next e-retailing model we consider is the e-mall. In an e-mall, cyberspace is rented out to cyber e-stores that wish to sell their goods. This store could be a specialized or generalized e-store. So, several product lines can be present in a single e-mall. However, unlike the generalized e-store which is under a single unified management, in an e-mall, each store is under its own management. E-mall management is responsible only for creating the cyber sites that can be rented and can support services and marketing of the mall. It, thus, provides a web hosting service. Several e-malls also provide software tools, which can be utilized by a prospective e-store to create and maintain its e-store. The advantage for an e-store is that it is grouped together with other stores in a well-known e-mall site and, therefore, is likely to pick up visitors to the mall. Well-known examples of e-malls are Yahoo!Store and CNET stores.

Case study 6: Yahoo!Store

Yahoo!Store is an e-mall or portal that charges a fee based on the number of items the hosted e-store sells. Thus, for 50 items, the e-store only pays $100 and this can rise to several hundreds. It hosts small e-stores and big well-known stores. The e-retailers can customize their own store fronts. Note, however, that the individual e-store URL is a subdomain of the Yahoo! URL. Thus, if you opened an e-store called myestore, your customers would use the following URL to access your e-store, namely http://store.yahoo.com/myestore.

You can create, edit, and manage your e-store using a web-browser through a different URL. Yahoo also provides a directory and processes payment transactions for the e-store securely. Yahoo has a navigational guide and directory where the category for the e-store is manually designated by a Yahoo staff member. Yahoo also provides software tools such as Manager to assist you to manage the store, e.g. selection of payment methods. These also include communication tools, on-line forums, chat rooms, etc. Yahoo itself also generates revenue from on-line advertising, sponsorships, licensing, etc.

11.5.6   Direct selling by the manufacturer

A number of manufacturers with well-known brand name products have chosen to use the internet to carry out direct selling via the internet. One of the best known here is Ford (see Figure 11.7), which utilizes the internet to achieve direct selling but uses its dealer network to facilitate distribution and delivery. The other well-known examples are Cisco systems and Dell computers. Note that this approach permits mass customization to meet customer preferences. This direct selling by the manufacturer has an important disintermediation effect leading to reduced costs to the end customer and increased profitability to the manufacturer. A note of caution is important here. By and large, this approach can be used by manufacturers of well-known brands of products because the customer already knows the product. Secondly, the manufacturer must have a thorough understanding of customer preferences, otherwise he has to rely on the customer knowledge of a retailer.

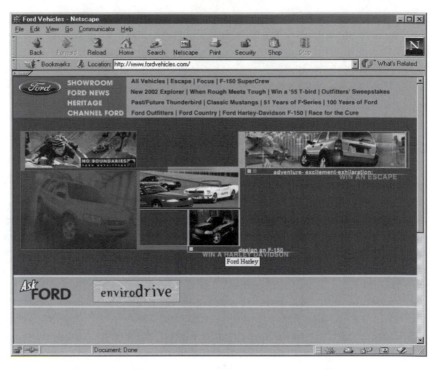

Figure 11.7   Homepage of Ford (Courtesy of Ford Motor Company)

11.5.7   Supplementary distribution channel

Several retailers that already have a highly successful "bricks and mortar" operation have turned to the internet and created an e-store. They have several motivations for doing this and these include

1. Fending off a challenge by an aggressive e-store in their line of product. An example of this is Barnes and Noble's response to Amazon.com's success in grabbing market share or Toysrus.com as a response to eToys.com.
2. Providing an additional sales-ordering mechanism.
3. Enhancing their service, such as customer service operation, through the internet.
4. Providing a mechanism of drawing people into their physical store as these could often be used for delivery and distribution for products sold on the internet.

Here, there are several different ways in which a bricks and mortar company could enter the e-retailing world. It could

1. integrate e-retailing into its business, e.g. Dell, Cisco, or Ford.
2. create an e-retailing subsidiary, e.g. Toysrus.com and Barnesandnoble.com (bn.com).
3. develop an alliance with an existing e-retailing company, e.g. Petsmart.com.

Case study 7: Barnes and Noble

Barnes and Noble (see Figure 11.8) is the largest physical retailer of books in the United States. In response to the challenge of internet retailers of books, it launched its own online subsidiary in March 1999 and is now among the top five e-retailers

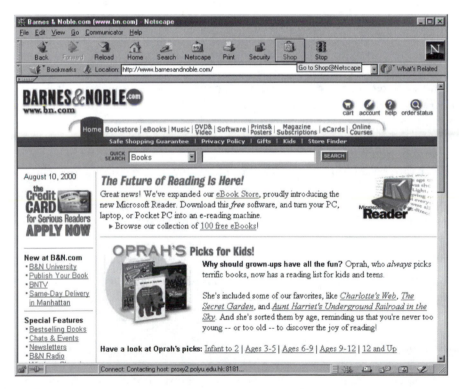

Figure 11.8 Homepage of barnesandnoble.com (bn.com) (Reproduced with permission of Barnes & Noble)

CONSUMER-ORIENTED E-COMMERCE

on the internet. Its web site is barnesandnoble.com (or bn.com). It retails books, music, cards, print and posters, software, and magazines. Unlike Amazon.com, it sells books through both the physical and electronic channels, but like Amazon.com it retails millions of titles. As with Amazon.com, it offers discounted books, reviews, excerpts from books, and recommendations from editors. It also has a community of readers and provides author chats and monthly readings. So, it creates new marketing mechanisms through the use of the internet.

11.5.8   Brokers or intermediaries

This class of e-retailers is essentially an extension of the notion of a broker from the physical to the cyber world. A broker is an intermediary who

- may take an order from a customer and pass it on to a supplier
- may put a customer with specific requirements in touch with a supplier who can meet those requirements
- may provide a service to a customer, such as a comparison between goods, with respect to particular criteria such as price, quality, etc.

Thus, brokers provide comparison shopping, order taking and fulfillment, and services to a customer. That is the reason why they are sometimes referred to as electronic intermediaries.

Examples of electronic brokers or intermediaries include priceline.com, mySimon. com, and bestbooksbuy.com.

There are several different models for electronic brokers and these include

- Brokers that provide a registration service with directory, search facilities, e-payment facilities, and security-related facilities. Any business can register with such an e-broker (e.g. anewshop.com).
- Brokers that meet a certain requirement such as a fixed price (e.g. Priceline.com).
- Brokers that provide comparison shopping between products (e.g. mySimon.com or bestbooksbuy.com).

Case study 8: anewShop.com

anewShop.com does not sell goods to customers; instead it provides an online shopping guide. Thus, it includes a list of retailers and an online catalog of goods which consists of books, flowers, computer hardware, etc. For each catalog item, a detailed description is given. anewShop.com provides a comparison of prices and provides its own opinion to help consumers make a choice.

Its revenue comes from advertisements by retailers on its site.

Case study 9: Priceline.com

Priceline.com (see Figure 11.9) is an electronic intermediary that asks customers to provide their pricing requirements for a number of items such as airfares, hotel rooms, cars, mortgages, loans, new cars, etc. The broker then puts a suggested price, say to a number of hotels in the case of a customer needing a hotel. The customer holds his bid price open for a given period, during which priceline.com tries to fulfill the request.

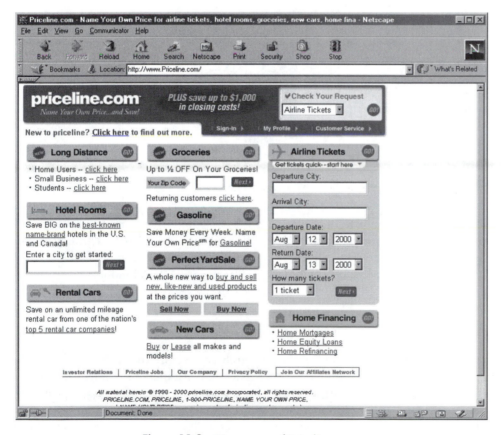

Figure 11.9   Homepage of Priceline.com

Figure 11.10　Homepage of mySimon.com (Reproduced with permission of mySimon)

He cannot refuse an offer that meets his bid price and, therefore, has to be flexible with respect to the airline or hotel he is willing to use. The revenue is generated from the difference the buyer is willing to pay and the price offered to the hotel.

Revenues in the half year to June 30, 1999 exceeded $160 million.

Case study 10: mySimon.com

mySimon.com (see Figure 11.10) does a search on several product categories such as apparel, books, music, computers and software, consumer electronics, flowers and gifts, office supplies, and toys. It does the search over several web merchants and returns the best deal with respect to price. It also incorporates buyer guides on new products such as digital cameras, a newsletter, a "great deals" section, and a chat facility suggesting products or merchants, etc.

DEVELOPING A CONSUMER-ORIENTED E-COMMERCE SYSTEM　　**341**

11.6　*FEATURES OF E-RETAILING*

Now that we have reviewed different models for e-retailing and examined several e-retailing web sites, we are in a position to distill some of the most important features, and these include

1. The provision of an on-line catalog, which allows one to browse through different categories of goods. Thus, it is dynamic and linked with order process.
2. The provision of a search engine, which is a very important feature that does not exist in traditional retailing.
3. The provision of a shopping cart, which allows convenient goods selection. An ability to provide an automatic price update.
4. Personalization of store layouts, promotions, deals, and marketing.
5. The ability to distribute digital goods directly. Thus, these goods can be downloaded instantly.
6. An on-line customer salesperson, "who" can help customers to navigate through the site.
7. An order status checking facility, which is a useful feature before submission.
8. The use of Forums (collaborative purchasing circles) to create a customer community and thus increase "stickiness."

11.6.1　The future of e-retailing

When one examines e-retailing, one can distinguish between two trends, namely

- Technologies that help you see and experience the product better, e.g. virtual reality, Java 3D, etc.
- Technologies that help you not to see at all but use an intelligent agent (or mobile agent) that does all the shopping tasks for you.

11.7　*DEVELOPING A CONSUMER-ORIENTED E-COMMERCE SYSTEM*

Software engineering is the discipline associated with building software systems. Software engineering has been progressively maturing as a discipline. It has moved through description techniques, which characterize aspects of control, through data

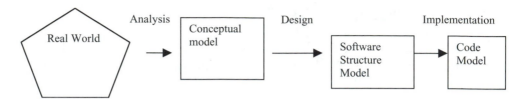

Figure 11.11   Three-stage modelling of software engineering process

flows, and eventually through methods that capture both structure and behavior. The emergence of object-oriented, component-based paradigms have allowed one to characterize a wide range of real world systems as the first step in constructing a software system. Dillon and Tan [1993] have characterized the software engineering process as a three-stage modelling process, as shown in Figure 11.11.

The following are the three models of interest:

1. Conceptual model
2. Software structure model
3. Code model

The conceptual model, which is the output of the analysis phase, is essentially a description of the relevant features of the real world using an expressive set of constructs. Here, no attention is payed to the implementation media or tool to be used to build the system. In contrast, the software structure model, which is the output of the design phase, must pay careful attention to the constructs available in the implementation medium as it essentially forms the blueprint for implementation. As noted by Dillon and Tan [1993], different categories of systems such as traditional procedurally oriented systems, database systems, and knowledge-based systems can be described by object-oriented and components-based models, during conceptual modelling and software structure modelling.

One important feature that should, however, be noted is that the real world is taken as given and fixed during this modelling process.

11.7.1   The emergent business model as the basis of e-commerce system development

This last factor represents an important point of departure between e-commerce system development and other more traditional system development whether they are procedurally oriented, database, or knowledge-based systems. The creation of an

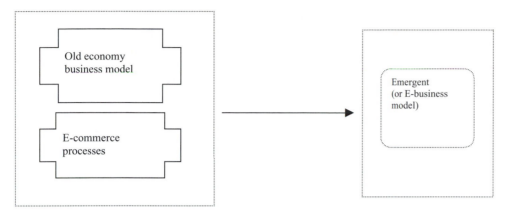

Figure 11.12   Emergent business model for e-commerce business development

e-commerce system presupposes a new way of doing business through the internet. This factor implies the following:

1. In the case of an existing "old economy" business, one would need a fusion of the "old economy" business with the new business leading to a metamorphosis of the business model. We call this new business model "An Emergent Business Model" or "E-business Model" (see Figure 11.12)

2. In case of a start up without any previous business operations, one would go through a nascent process to create an emergent business model or e-business model

This building of an emergent business model requires a description of the associated business processes. A business process can be defined as "a set of logically related tasks performed to achieve a defined business outcome" [Davenport and Short, 1990].

On examining the first case, we note that it has some similarities and some very important differences from Business Process Reengineering (BPR). BPR is essentially aimed at a "radical redesign of business processes to achieve dramatic improvements in critical, contemporary measures of performance such as cost, quality, service, and speed" [Hammer and Champy, 1993]. The metamorphosis process leading to an emergent business model involves a transformation of the business processes to effectively incorporate a new way of doing business through the internet. It frequently involves

1. the addition of new products and services, such as the sale of information

2. introduction of new sales and marketing modes

3. automation and streamlining of the backend processes to mesh with these

4. movement from mass production to mass customization

5. linking of the marketing process to ordering

6. targeted marketing

7. an electronic payment system

8. customization and personalization

Thus, one not only moves to reduce costs and improve efficiency but also adds new products and introduces new sales and marketing modes with a completely different reach from those that existed before. This is why it is important to distinguish the emergent business model from a purely reengineering business model.

11.7.2   Process-oriented e-commerce development approach

As the discussion in Section 11.2, an important first step in developing e-commerce systems is the definition of an emergent business model. This requires

1. A clear choice at the outset of the type of e-commerce system that is going to be utilized from the aforementioned four categories.

2. A definition of the goods and services that will be traded or some combination thereof.

3. A clear definition of the market mechanisms that will be adopted. For example, will the e-commerce system

   • carry out direct selling
   • act as intermediary or agent passing the orders onto someone else for order fulfillment
   • provide a virtual market where sellers and buyers could trade
   • act as a partial outlet for a bricks and mortar company
   • provide a fixed pricing structure or permit a request for quotation structure
   • carry out cross selling
   • provide an auction or reverse auction facility
   • define an e-payment mechanism

   These and a number of other issues have to be clarified.

4. One next needs to determine the type of goods and services that are to be traded. A careful decision of goods to be traded has to be made as not all goods are appropriate for trading on the internet. Again, a decision has to be made of whether one wants to specialize in the line of products traded and how they fit in

with the business imperatives. It is also important to characterize the key profit drivers and steer business towards them.

In a recent consulting job carried out by the authors, the company's business drivers required a strong link between sale of goods and sale of logistics services provided by the company, allowing strong cross-selling of logistics services.

5. the mechanism for order fulfillment and distribution has to be carefully worked out and this has to be appropriate for the goods being traded.

The next step in the overall scheme is to define the business processes involved. This requires a very clear delineation of

1. the set of logically related tasks
2. the intended functionality of each task
3. the sequencing in time of these tasks
4. the preconditions that apply before a task can be carried out and the post conditions that apply after it has been carried out
5. the information or data required by each task
6. the exception conditions that could arise

11.7.3   Steps in the development methodology

The steps in the analysis, design, and development of an e-commerce system can be summarized as follows:

1. Develop description of existing business model
2. Develop e-business model
3. Develop requirements statement through analysis; this leads to the conceptual model of the system
4. Choose system architecture and implementation platform(s)
5. Carry out design to develop software structure model including software architecture
6. Develop detailed design, including web UI interfaces, databases, system integration aspects with legacy systems
7. Programming and customizing the system
8. Testing and piloting the e-commerce system

In Step 3, besides the normal conceptual model with object property diagrams, sequence diagrams, or other dynamic representation, it is also important to

- develop a category hierarchy and structure for the goods and services being sold.
- define the search and browsing capability, e.g. browse by category and search by keyword.
- define a goods selection mechanism such as a 1-click, shopping cart, etc.
- define a careful purchase requisition and purchase order submission process.

In the aforementioned steps, unlike more traditional systems, in e-commerce systems, it is very important to model workflows. However, unlike normal workflow modelling, these require techniques that can handle exceptions, changes in the structure and nature of workflow, and capture attendant data.

11.8   THE PASS* MODEL

Before the end of this chapter, it is of interest to look at how a B2C e-commerce web site can really "make cents." We call the revenue model: PASS (i.e., *P*ublicity, *A*dvertisement, *S*ale of goods/services, and *S*ubscription). In the early days, electronic payment methods were not mature enough to support B2C e-commerce. At that time, companies usually set up web sites for publicity reason. This is an indirect way of generating revenue because the web sites may lead to sales possibly through physical commerce. For web sites with significant number of visitors such as Yahoo, advertisements provide a good source of income. Again for most companies, these are indirect income. Now with the advent of SET and other electronic payment methods, companies can carry out secure transactions particularly payments directly on the internet. This is a more direct way of generating revenue. Finally, subscription is a means of generating constant revenue. However, this may be difficult to implement unless you have very attractive products/services. For example, some well-known newspapers and magazines do offer subscription services. While the web sites are open to the public, certain parts are restricted for subscribers only.

11.9   SUMMARY

In this chapter, we considered various aspects of customer-oriented e-commerce, or e-retailing. In particular, we examined the features and success factors of traditional retailing and determined how they translated to retailing on the internet. We also

---

* The PASS model is proposed by Dr. Henry Chan.

looked at several different models of e-retailing and considered several case studies corresponding to these models. Lastly, we considered the process and a methodology for developing a consumer-oriented e-commerce system.

REFERENCES

Davenport, T. and Short, J., "The new industrial engineering: Information technology and business process redesign," *Sloan Management Review* **31** (4) (1990), 11–27.

Dillon, T. S. and Tan, P. L., *Object Oriented Conceptual Modelling*, Prentice-Hall, NJ, 1993.

Hammer, M. and Champy, J., *Re-engineering the Corporation: A Manifesto for Business Revolution*, Harper Business, New York, NY, 1993.

Luschs, R. F. and Lusch, V. N., *Principles of Marketing*, Kent Publishing Company, 1987.

RECOMMENDED READING

Schneider, G. P. and Perry, J. T., *Electronic Commerce*, Course Technology, 2000.

Anders, G., "Click and buy: Why and where internet commerce is succeeding," *The Wall Street Journal* December 7, 1998.

Lohse, G. L. and Spiller, P., "Electronic shopping," *Communication of ACM* **41** (7) (1998), 81–87.

Sandoval, G., "Net firm move from "clicks to bricks"," *CNET News. Com*, 26 October 1999.

Kane, M., "Bricks to clicks: Retail giants get the Net," *ZDNet News*, 15 December 1999.

Maruca, R. F., "Retailing: Confronting the challenges that faces bricks and mortar stores," *HBR* **July/Aug.**, 1999.

Turban, E., Lee, J., King, D., Chung, H. M., and Lee, J. K., *Electronic Commerce – A Managerial Perspective*, Prentice-Hall, Upper Saddle River, NJ, 2000.

12

Business-Oriented E-commerce

12.1 Features of B2B E-commerce

12.2 Business Models

12.3 Integration

12.4 Summary

References

Recommended Reading

In Chapter 1, we distinguished between four basic categories of e-commerce. In Chapter 11, we dealt with two of these, namely B2C and C2B. In this chapter, we intend to deal with the third category, namely Business-to-Business (or B2B) e-commerce. The important differentiating factor of this kind of e-commerce is that the vendor and the buyer of the goods or services involved in a transaction are both business organizations rather than individual customers who are end users of the goods purchased. The business that is the purchaser could either utilize the goods or services itself in conducting its business or, alternatively, transform the goods purchased (in the case of raw materials or components) into a manufactured product which it then sells. Generally speaking, the size of commerce carried out between businesses dwarfs the commerce between businesses and consumers. The potential for B2B e-commerce is now projected to be much larger than that for consumer-oriented e-commerce.

From Figure 12.1, one can see that we are only at the very beginning of exploiting B2B e-commerce, and its projected potential size is quite staggering.

In order to understand where this potential for B2B e-commerce arises from, we need to briefly examine some of the goods and services needed by businesses as well

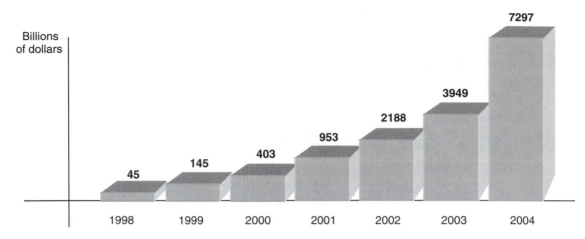

Figure 12.1   Projection growth of B2B e-commerce drawn from a report by Gartner Group

as some of those that are currently provided by one business to another in the bricks and mortar world of commerce.

Businesses currently need to

1. sell and distribute their goods to other businesses;
2. carry out procurement of goods and services;
3. have logistics to move goods to the appropriate place at the defined time and in the correct quantities, i.e. the Just-in-Time (JIT) management;
4. have storage or warehousing facilities at the right places in the presence of uncertain demand to store required components and materials as well as finished products, i.e. warehouse logistics;
5. carry out marketing and advertising of their goods and services;
6. have appropriate support services for different business support functions such as human resources, accounting, inventory control, order processing, and payment processing. It would be preferable if these could be integrated so that a change entered in one part of such a support service will be automatically reflected in other appropriate parts;
7. obtain appropriate information, forecasts, and market intelligence so as to best tune their activities to meet these.

Any of these activities are potential candidates for B2B e-commerce, as we shall see in this chapter. Thus, one could basically conduct one of the activities that falls into the aforementioned categories on the internet and the web, and thus carry out

B2B e-commerce. The advantages that would accrue to the business would be similar to those mentioned in the last chapter, namely

- global rather than local sales
- global purchasing
- ability to buy and sell 24 hr. (or hours) a day
- savings on staffing
- savings on premises and showrooms
- better customer service

However, in the case of B2B e-commerce, these only represent a small portion of the advantages. Far more significant advantages arise from

1. integration between the business processes of different business enterprises resulting in collaborative and fully-automatic Supply Chain Management (SCM) and Demand Chain Management (DCM) systems;
2. automation of the business processes within a business enterprise;
3. integration of the different back-office business functions resulting in an Enterprise Resource Planning (ERP) system;
4. integration between the front end and internet, and web server systems and backend systems;
5. JIT manufacture and delivery;
6. mass customization; and
7. Electronic Data Interchange (EDI)
8. Data warehousing

These factors will lead to sizable savings in business enterprises, and thus provide much of the current impetus for introducing B2B e-commerce in a number of existing bricks and mortar businesses. These will impact the type of e-commerce model that is ultimately adopted.

12.1 *FEATURES OF B2B E-COMMERCE*

In contrast to B2C e-commerce, B2B e-commerce is characterized by a number of features and these include [Turban *et al.*, 2000; Schneider *et al.*, 2000]

1. high volumes of goods traded;
2. high net value of goods traded;

3. multiple forms of electronic payment and other payment methods permitted. In B2C e-commerce, credit cards (or perhaps smart cards) are the main forms of payment, whereas in B2B e-commerce, several other banking instruments and internet payment schemes are also permitted;

4. prior agreements or contracts between the partners involved in the e-commerce business cycle, requiring a much higher level of documentation;

5. a much higher level of information exchange between the different trading partners involved in the e-commerce business cycle and a number of places where this information must be entered into the information systems of the businesses;

6. multiple levels of authorization of purchases, each level having its own limits on expenditure or even types of goods;

7. different types of taxation regimes depending on where the two parties are from and what goods are the subject of a transaction.

These features make the whole process of B2B e-commerce much more complex than B2C and require greater sophistication of the underlying software system.

12.2 BUSINESS MODELS

When looking at the issue of business models for B2B e-commerce, it is important to distinguish the business activities that the e-commerce system is meant to address, as these play a significant role in defining the form of the business model.

The first distinction we need to draw here is whether the e-commerce system deals in tangible goods or services.

If it deals in tangible goods, we can distinguish between three basic types of models, namely [Turban *et al.*, 2000]

1. A buyer-oriented e-commerce system

2. A seller-oriented e-commerce system

3. A virtual marketplace with multiple buyers and multiple sellers

In the case of services, the e-commerce system has a number of other characteristics, besides purchase requisition and purchase order submission. These include the actual delivery of the service, monitoring of the stages of the service and its status at any time, and finally, invoicing and payment on completion of the service.

12.2.1 E-procurement and buyer-oriented e-commerce systems

Buyer-oriented e-commerce business models are most suitable for big corporations that purchase large volumes of a large number of different items. These items could be of several different types. The first group is sometimes referred to as maintenance, repair, and operating (MRO) goods. The second group includes products needed to service a given project, excluding capital items. The third category involves components or raw materials used in manufacture. A fourth category refers to goods that are traded, say by a wholesaler, who purchases from a manufacturer and sells to a retailer. The fifth category includes large, less frequently ordered capital items. A large proportion of the effort of corporations goes into the first four categories. These frequently involve large volumes and a considerable number of business activities within the organization. They also normally have a complex interface associated with authorization of purchases within the company. The purchase could involve one or more suppliers outside the company. The whole process of starting with the generation of a purchase requisition followed by different levels of authorization, selection of possible suppliers, generating requests for quotations, negotiation, order placement, monitoring the order fulfillment process to ensure that the right quantities with the right quality are delivered to the right place at the right time, and finally, ensuring that the payments are made is referred to as procurement, to distinguish it from the narrower purchasing function [Kalakota and Robinson, 1999]. An examination of procurement reveals that there are two distinct classes of activities involved, and these are

1. Intracompany activities
2. Intercompany activities

12.2.2 Buy-side e-commerce – Intercompany activities of procurement

Of the aforementioned five categories of purchaseable goods, if we exclude the last three categories (i.e., raw materials/components, traded goods, and capital items), the remaining goods are referred to as operating resources. The management of these goods and services is sometimes referred to as Operating Resource Management (ORM) or Operating Resource Procurement. These are frequently high volume, low cost products. The US market alone, for this class of purchase by corporations, is estimated at $400 billion [Kalakota and Robinson, 1999].

Effective ORM will result in considerable savings, both in intercompany purchases and intracompany processes.

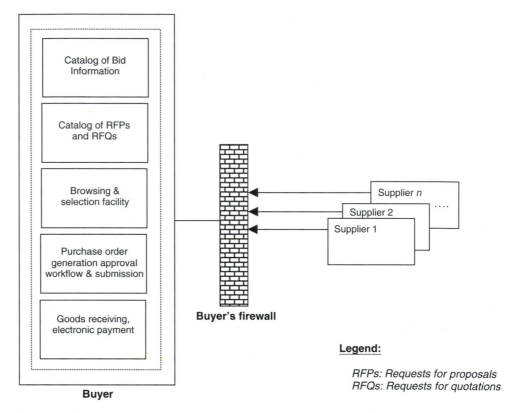

Figure 12.2 Schematic of buy-side e-commerce system [adapted from Kalakota and Robinson, 1999]

An effective approach to ORM is to set up a buy-side e-commerce system. The basic elements of the buy-side e-commerce system are shown in Figure 12.2.

The steps involved in the procurement cycle are shown in Figure 12.3.

In order to understand the manner in which this buy-side e-commerce system works, we note that the procurement department puts out Requests for Quotations (RFQs), which include a description of the goods and services.

Suppliers access these RFQs and put in bids, which include prices and specifications of the goods. These bids are stored in the catalog of bids, to be used by an actual buyer in the company after being vetted by the procurement department. This vetting can be manual or automated. This allows the procurement department to set up preferred suppliers for particular goods in the goods catalog. There may also be formal agreements in place with respect to these bids on the RFQs, after a process of negotiation. Once a preferred supplier has been designated and within the terms of any agreements between the supplier and the corporation, the supplier can electronically update bids.

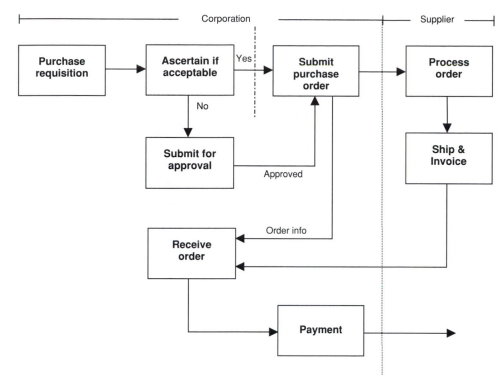

Figure 12.3 Purchasing using a buy-side e-commerce system

This catalog maintenance by suppliers and related RFQs is illustrated in Figure 12.4.

When a purchaser anywhere in the company, not necessarily in the procurement department, wishes to purchase an item, he uses a web browser to browse through the catalog, selects the required items, and creates a purchase requisition. This is then processed by the business rules which would determine if the buyer is authorized to carry out the purchase of such items and whether the value of them are within his authorized spending limits. If necessary the requisition would be electronically routed to an approver. Once approved, a purchase order can be submitted directly by the

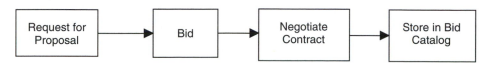

Figure 12.4 Catalog maintenance in buy-side e-commerce system

buyer to the supplier. If the goods are available with the supplier, then he fulfills the order, organizes logistics for delivery, and generates an electronic invoice.

When the goods are received and checked for quantity and quality, an electronic payment is generated by the receiving corporation to the supplier.

One of the important elements in the buy-side e-commerce system is that the corporation does not have to physically go out searching for suppliers. The suppliers come to the corporation once it has signaled its potential needs. All transactions between the supplier and the corporation are electronically handled. More importantly, the internal processing of the corporation is also streamlined electronically. In order to understand this, let us look at a schematic diagram illustrating some of the intracompany activities involved in the procurement process, shown below in Figure 12.5.

In order for the business to gain proper leverage from an e-commerce solution, these activities have to be automated electronically to reduce the flow and handling of

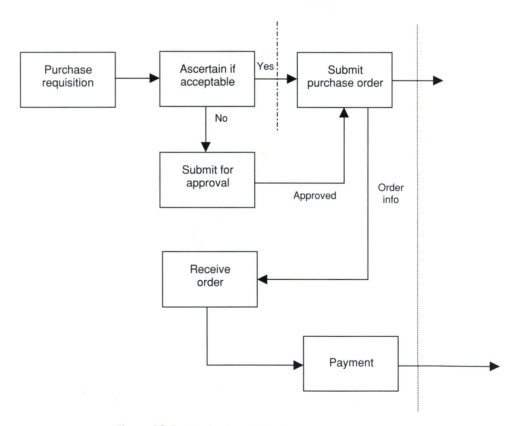

Figure 12.5 Internal activities in procurement process

paper within a company. This would normally be achieved using an intranet within the company.

General Electric developed one of the first e-procurement systems, namely GE's TPN (www.tpn.genis.com) system.

Software

One of the most widely used software environments for the buy-side or e-procurement system is Ariba's ORMS. Among the companies that use it are large corporations such as IBM and Cisco.

The buy-side e-commerce system also normally involves some degree of monitoring of the individual supplier performance, as well as provides better financial information to the corporation about expenditure patterns. It reduces random "invoiceable" purchasing, makes the administration and approval process electronic, reduces cycle times and transcription errors, with a reduced inventory. It also automates other features such as total monthly shopping calculations, etc. and allows for electronic payments.

12.2.3 Sell-side e-commerce

Sell-side e-commerce systems are most suitable for corporations that are producing or marketing products to a large number of small and large corporations. A sell-side e-commerce system is a one-to-many (supplier to buyers) system. The best of the sell-side e-commerce applications such as Dell and Cisco permit customization by the configuration which the buyer wishes to purchase. Dell provides computers while Cisco provides network solutions.

This facility for mass customization and on-line ordering has a major role in improving gross profit margins. Cisco's gross margin in 1999 was 64.8%, with 90% of orders over the internet.

The sell-side system also provides better demand forecasting as it is directly coupled to actual sales data. This leads to better product inventory control and reduced lead times.

The sell-side e-commerce system should provide the following information, namely

- product catalog
- product configuration (if applicable)
- business roles to allow automation of approval and ordering
- customer service

- fulfillment and shipping
- accounts receivable/invoicing and electronic payment
- monitoring of order status and account history

A schematic diagram showing a typical sell-side e-commerce system is shown in Figure 12.6.

The sell-side system will have business rules to ascertain if a purchase requisition is to be authorized for the particular purchaser from a given corporation with appropriate purchasing limits, etc. If approved, the purchaser is able to directly submit a purchase order. Several different types of connections between the sell-side e-commerce system and the buying corporation are possible as illustrated in

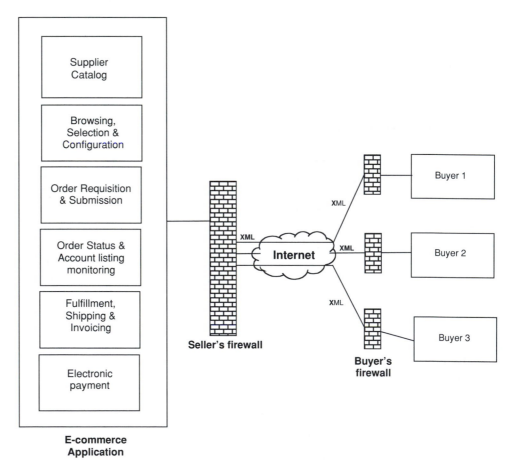

Figure 12.6   Sell-side e-commerce system

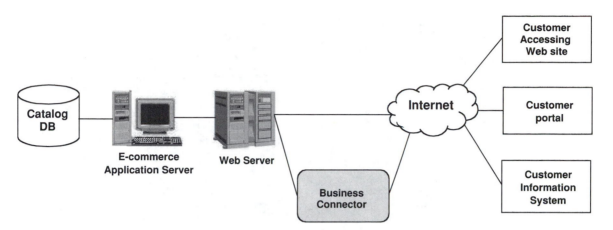

Figure 12.7 Connections in sell-side e-commerce systems

Figure 12.7. In addition, the seller's server will often provide a stored shopping cart of previous orders for frequent buyers so that order information from previous orders can easily be retrieved.

In the case of the web interface, the customer enters the information directly into the sell-side customers web site by downloading the web pages and returning the information to the web server of the sell-side e-commerce system.

In the case of the customer portal, the customer downloads a web module (perhaps even with a small database), does all the ordering, configuration, checking and data validation at the client site, and then sends the validated information to the sell-side web server. This is particularly useful either in the case of an unreliable internet connection between the client and the server or in one where considerable interaction between client and server is required.

In the last case, a direct connection between the client-server-and-information system and the sell-side e-commerce system is provided. Dell provides links with Ariba, mySAP.com, etc., using XML. Another business connection is BizTalk provided by Microsoft. A large number of systems and databases are now becoming XML-enabled such as the Oracle and Informix database systems, and this allows the use of XML as a business connector.

Software platforms

1. sell.com (see Figure 12.8) is a software platform that allows one to build a sell-side system.

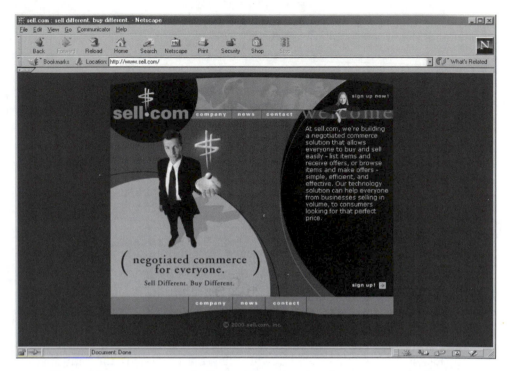

Figure 12.8   Homepage of sell.com (Reproduced with permission of sell.com)

2. WebDB is a software frontend to the Oracle DBMS, which allows one to build a portal that communicates directly with the Oracle DB. This is an integrated software platform for building a sell-side system.

12.2.4   Virtual markets

These are software applications that provide a meeting place for many vendors and buyers. They are referred to by many names including digital marketplaces, infomediaries, vertical portals, intermediary-oriented marketplaces, and digital exchanges. The most successful of these virtual markets are highly focused and address a specific sector of industry. Examples of these include

1. Boeing's PART system that allows airlines to purchase spare parts from different suppliers that are listed on the PART system.
2. Chemdex.com (see Figure 12.9) which is a marketplace for biological and chemical requests, which enables laboratory staff to find and order what they need.

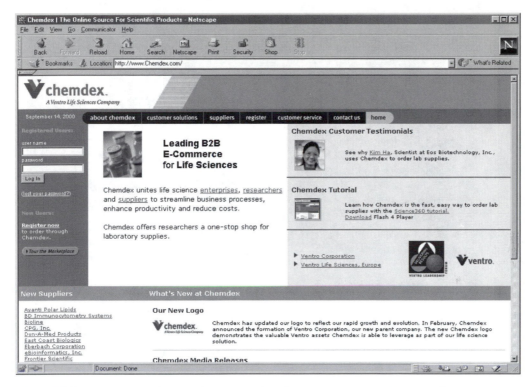

Figure 12.9 Homepage of Chemdex.com (Chemdex Corporation, a Ventro Life Sciences Company)

3. IPowerB2B.com (see Figure 12.10) which is a virtual marketplace for goods that need temperature-controlled and atmosphere-controlled storage, such as wines, perishable foods, silicon products, and silicon chips.
4. W.W. Grainger which is a marketplace for MRO supplies and services.

This area of virtual markets which addresses specific industry sectors is expected to be one of the growth areas in e-commerce. However, it is important that they are focused and that the industry sector addressed is carefully chosen. Some characteristics of industry sectors for which virtual markets are suitable include [Minder Chen, 2000]

1. products that are nonstandardized and require considerable customization;
2. a marketplace that is regionally widespread with buyers and sellers at myriad locations;
3. goods that are perishable require special logistics, warehousing or have limited lives;

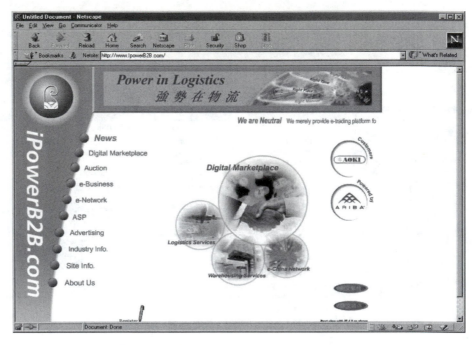

Figure 12.10   Homepage of IPowerB2B.com

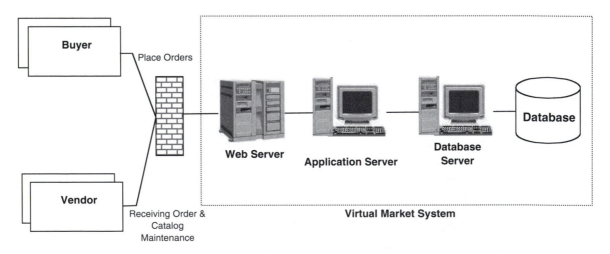

Figure 12.11   Architecture of a typical virtual market system

4. goods where temporary supply shortages can develop which in turn leads to price volatility.

These marketplaces also provide for the possibility of aggregation. Thus, an intermediary can collect a large number of buyers' requests for an item and make a single purchase much in the manner of a wholesaler in the traditional supply chain. This is sometimes known as reverse aggregation. An example of an aggregator of this type is FOBchemicals.com [Minder Chen, 2000].

The architecture of these virtual markets may vary somewhat. A typical schematic diagram is shown in Figure 12.11.

The buyers access the virtual market through a web server to place orders. If the prices are fixed, then the vendor is notified of the order. The vendor then notifies the purchaser regarding availability, delivery details, and invoices. On receipt of the goods, the buyer checks quality and quantity and makes an electronic payment.

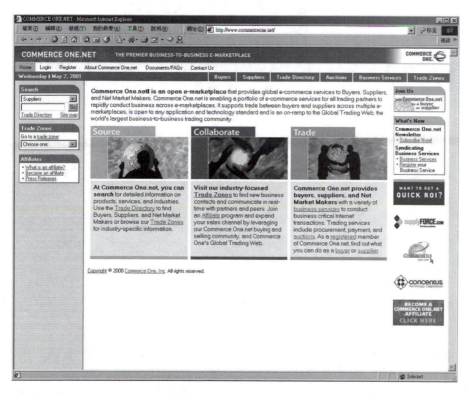

Figure 12.12 Homepage of Commerceone.com (Copyright © 2000 Commerce. One, Inc. All rights reserved.)

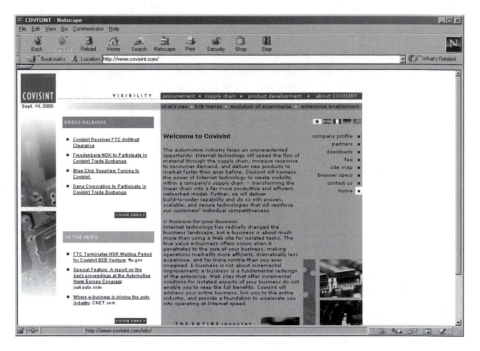

Figure 12.13   Homepage of Covisint.com (Courtesy of Covisint L.L.C)

The seller also needs to access the virtual marketplace to carry out catalog maintenance and updating from time to time. These virtual markets also allow RFQs, followed by negotiation of price. In this case, a purchase requisition to a particular supplier (an RFQ) is sent to the supplier who responds leading to the negotiation.

In addition to this, some virtual markets also provide facilities for forward and reverse auctions.

Two of the most widely used virtual market environments are Commerce One (see Figure 12.12) and Ariba's digital marketplace.

A recent trend in the development of these virtual markets is for a consortium of companies (strategic alliance) in a particular sector to get together and form a virtual market. Examples of such consortiums include

1. Covisint.com (see Figure 12.13) which markets automobiles with three major vendors – GM, Ford, and Daimler-Chrysler.
2. Ehitax.com where twelve computer manufacturers have joined to produce a single virtual marketplace for computers, including major players such as Hewlett-Packard and Compaq.

Figure 12.14 Sell-side vs buy-side e-commerce systems

What is interesting about this trend is that market players who are strong competitors of each other have joined to forge a consortium in a vertical market segment.

It is useful to consider the position of these virtual marketplaces vis-à-vis the sell-side and buy-side e-commerce systems as they have some of the features of both, as shown in Figure 12.14.

Procurement portals could be considered to be between buy-side and virtual marketplaces while distribution portals between sell-side and virtual marketplaces.

12.2.5 Collaborative supply chain management

In all the models we have considered till now, the only information that is exchanged is between two partners to allow a purchase to take place. For corporations that intend to fully exploit the opportunity for mass customization that e-commerce offers, it is important to optimize not only a single purchase segment between two parties but also the interaction between parties upstream of the purchase. In order to understand these ideas, consider a typical manufacturing process shown in Figure 12.15.

Downstream activities from the manufacturer as they were without e-commerce and the internet are shown in Figure 12.16; the same with internet and e-commerce would be as shown in Figure 12.17.

A comparison of Figures 12.16 and 12.17 shows that with e-commerce and the internet, the manufacturer is able to more accurately estimate near future demand as he can now base it on actual customer sales. However, the manufacturer can only effectively exploit these better estimates if he can be assured of supplies to enable the right kind of goods to be produced at the right time without holding too much inventory either upstream in raw materials, components, or modules or downstream in finished goods. To achieve these, his immediate suppliers and their suppliers must have the same access to his better estimates.

This leads to a new model of e-commerce where information is shared between the manufacturer and all suppliers up the chain to enable the whole process of production to be optimized. Dell, while it is widely known for exploiting downstream e-commerce activities, has also effectively moved upstream supply-side activities onto the internet in order to use the model of supply chain optimization. It permits its key suppliers access to its sales forecasts through the internet and also to what their

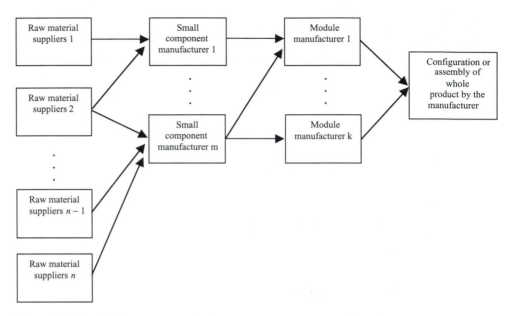

Figure 12.15   Collaborative supply chain management in manufacturing upstream processes

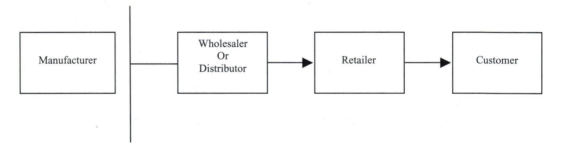

Figure 12.16   Downstream activities (without e-commerce and internet)

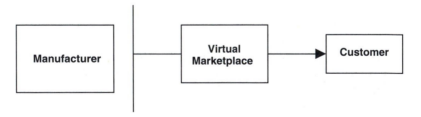

Figure 12.17   Downstream activities (with e-commerce and internet)

different customers are buying [Schneider *et al.*, 2000]. In return, Dell's suppliers have to provide Dell with information on production schedules, problems experienced by suppliers, and likely delays in supply. This optimization of the supply chain has allowed Dell to reduce inventories by a factor of 3–4. This process is only possible if there is a long-term link between the manufacturer and the preferred suppliers. This optimization of the supply chain process is also being used in different forms by other players who carry out mass customization, such as CISCO, Micro, Boeing and Ingram.

12.3 INTEGRATION

The discussion in the last section on different B2B models should have made it clear of the necessity for integration between corporations and their different systems as well as the necessity for transmission of information electronically. This integration needs to address the following:

1. Integration of systems between two or more corporations carrying out commerce or intercompany integration
2. Integration of systems within an organization, specifically frontend systems carrying out internet functions and commerce with backend systems
3. Integration of systems that address different functions within a company

12.3.1 Intercompany integration

Electronic interchange of information between companies is not new and dates back to the late 1970s with traditional EDI networks operating over dedicated telephone lines or value-added networks (VANs).

Standard bodies have also put in a great deal of effort in deriving common standards for EDI systems. Notable efforts are

1. Accredited Standards Committee 12 that developed the ASC X 12 standard under the ANSI (American National Standards Institution) umbrella.
2. The UN sponsored EDI for Administration, Commerce, and Transport (EDIFACT).

These traditional EDI systems essentially translate information or documents from the internal format of a corporation into a common format for transmission, and then retranslate into the internal format of the receiving organization. VANs are provided by VAN companies such as IBM and AT&T that store and forward messages through a VAN, rather than using point-to-point connections directly between the companies. Although traditional EDI achieves electronic interchange of information, it has several disadvantages including [Turban *et al.*, 2000]

1. a reasonably high entry cost for use of the EDI system and high operation cost.
2. being able to communicate only with firms that have traditional EDI facilities.
3. frequently long time delays to install EDI networks.
4. difficulties with firms or different VAN networks.

These factors have created a move towards EDI on the internet, which has an open architecture. Several new players such as IPNET, VTREE, Dynamic Web Enterprises, amongst others, have started to provide EDI facilities using the internet. Open EDI, as EDI on the internet is called, simplifies EDI implementation, facilitates integration between the information systems of business partners, reduces costs, and employs tools that are far more user-friendly. New standards such as a new ASC 12 taskforce has been set up, which seeks to incorporate XML into these standards. However, it is possible that XML itself may emerge as the de facto standard for providing interchange of information as a business connector between different systems.

12.3.2 B2B e-commerce communication using XML

In a real B2B e-commerce situation such as SCM, integration between different companies is important. Suppose a merchandizer in a department store (Company A) decides to place a purchase order (PO) to one of his suppliers (Company B) automatically via the internet using XML format. However, the databases involved for the applications being used in both companies ("purchasing system" for Company A and "sale system" for Company B) might not be the same (in reality, most of the time they are different) in terms of database structure and type of database systems (e.g., Oracle, IBM DB2, MS SQL Server, etc.). Each company may also have its own documents defined by its own specific DTD [Bradley, 2000], as shown in Figure 12.18.

In order to provide B2B trading utilizing automatic data transfer, one can use XML technology. The main problem is making different systems in each company capable of interoperation with each other. Also, one needs to address how automation of the updating of databases can be achieved in both companies even when their underlying database structures are totally different. In the earlier example of the purchase order processing system, one of the critical problems is how to make the inventory systems of both the companies (databases INV_A.db and INV_B.db) interoperate. Since both deal with the same subject, say "inventory", their DTDs logically should be quite similar. In other words, with the provision of the DTDs of all the related databases together with the XML document (electronic PO document

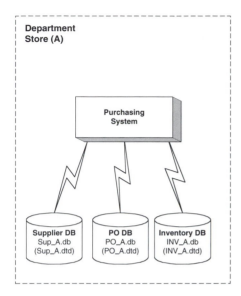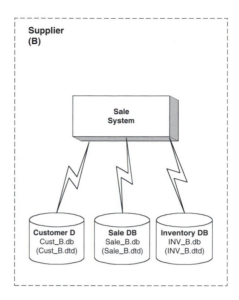

Figure 12.18 B2B e-commerce components in SCM system

in our case) during B2B internet trading, the system in the other company can make use of an XML converter (namely business connector) to convert a document in one DTD into another document in another DTD and vice-versa.

As shown in Figure 12.19, with the implementation of XML-based business connector technology, applications in both companies (purchasing system in Company A and sale system in Company B) can "talk" to all the underlying databases in both companies successfully via XML, although they have different DTDs. One of the main features is that the automatic data conversion and communication via XML are totally "transparent" to any application that involves access of the different databases. It should seem that they belong to the same database infrastructure and conform to the same DTD structure.

In fact, there are several options to implement the XML-based business connectors. One can use the "plug-ins" package such as MS BizTalk (www.biztalk.org) [Amor, 1999] as the XML portal, or integrate one's existing system with a tailor-made XML converter using Java interface such as IBM LMX converter (alphaworks.ibm.com/) [Maruyama *et al.*, 1999]. Another solution which is being vigorously pursued is to define an XML version for a particular domain. This ensures that the same DTD is used by all players in that domain. Thus, considerable effort is going into defining ebXML for use with e-commerce systems.

The importance of this type of intercompany integration is paramount for collaborative supply chains but also plays a significant role in all types of B2B e-commerce.

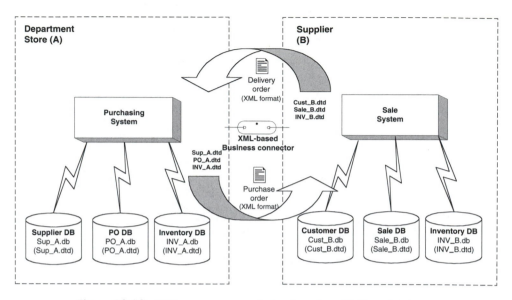

Figure 12.19   B2B e-commerce solution based on XML technology

12.3.3 Intracompany integration

Intracompany integration has two parts as mentioned at the start of Section 12.3. The first of them is to make sure that orders received by the e-commerce systems and consequences that flow from them are seamlessly communicated to backend systems such as databases, as well as application systems that carry out automated processing and fulfillment of the orders including arranging logistics and tracking the status of the order.

In addition to this, a larger corporation with several offices around the world would like to standardize information processes. Among the systems that may have to be integrated within an enterprise are

1. order entry
2. order fulfillment
3. logistics
4. Inventory
5. production planning and monitoring
6. accounting entry and financials systems
7. human resources including payrolls

Systems that provide integration across a multiplicity of functions across multi-sites are referred to as Enterprise Resource Planning (ERP) systems. These ERP systems provide a core of administrative and financial suites of applications. Furthermore, an update of one of these application programs results in consequential updates of the remaining applications.

One of the most widely used ERP applications is the SAP R/3 system. A number of the largest companies around the world started using ERP systems even before the e-commerce revolution. The important issue now, however, is that e-commerce application software has to be integrated with these ERP systems.

12.4 SUMMARY

In this chapter, we discussed B2B e-commerce systems. Three basic business models were considered, namely buyer side, seller side, and virtual markets.

In order to gain maximum leverage, it is important to integrate and optimize more than a single purchasing segment. This means upstream and downstream activities of a corporation should be integrated and the whole supply chain optimized. This also requires both intercompany and intracompany integration.

REFERENCES

Bradley, N., *The XML Companion*, Addison-Wesley, Reading, MA, 2000.

Maruyama, H., Tamura, K., and Uramoto, N., *XML and Java: Developing Web Applications*, Addison-Wesley, Reading, MA, 1999.

Amor, D., *The E-business (R)Evolution*, Prentice-Hall, Upper Saddle River, NJ, 1999.

Kalakota, R. and Whinston, A. B., *Electronic Commerce – A Manager's Guide*, Addison-Wesley, Reading, MA, 1997a.

Kalakota, R. and Whinston, A. B., eds., *Readings in Electronic Commerce*, Addison-Wesley, Reading, MA, 1997b.

Kalakota, R. and Robinson, M., *e-Business Roadmap for Success*. Addison-Wesley. MA, 1999.

Schneider, G. and James T. Perry, *Electronic Commerce*, Tomson Learning, Canada, 2000.

Minder Chen, *Business to Business Electronic Commerce*, Seminar for e-Executives Course Notes, Hong Kong Polytechnic University. August 2000.

Turban, E., Lee, J. K., King, D., Chung, H. M., and Lee, J. K., *Electronic Commerce: A Managerial Perspective*, Prentice-Hall, Upper Saddle River, NJ, 2000.

Karpinski, R., "Web links supply chain to storefront," *Internetweek* **21** (1999), 8, 9.

Stein, T. and Sweat, J., "Killer supply chains," *Information Week* **Nov** (1998), 36–42.

13

E-services

13.1 Categories of E-Services

13.2 Web-Enabled Services

13.3 Matchmaking Services

13.4 Information-Selling on the Web

13.5 E-Entertainment

13.6 Auctions and Other Specialized Services

13.7 Summary

References

In Chapter 11, we noted that intangible goods are also sold on the internet to end users in B2C e-commerce. These intangible goods can also be termed services.

In Chapter 12, we noted that amongst the purchases made by one business from another business are purchases of services. These services can be delivered via the internet.

This delivery of services via the internet to consumers or other businesses can be referred to by the generic term of e-services. There is a wide range of e-services currently offered through the internet and these include banking, loans, stock trading, jobs and career sites, travel, education, consultancy advice, insurance, real estate, broker services, on-line publishing, and on-line delivery of media content such as videos, computer games, etc.

This list is by no means exhaustive and it is growing all the time. In this chapter, we will give an overview of e-services.

13.1 *CATEGORIES OF E-SERVICES*

In order to bring some order to the discussion of these wide variety of e-services, we organize them into the following categories, namely

1. *Web-enabling services*, which were previously provided by humans in office agencies and/or their branches. The primary purpose here is that these services help to save time and effort for the user, bring convenience, and improve the quality of life. In many cases, it can result in a reduced cost for the consumer. E-services that fall into this category include
   - Banking
   - Stock trading
   - Education

   In some cases, this may bring a new dimension to the original service, enhancing and altering it. E-education is an example of this. It may also bring into the catchment new groups of consumers of the service to whom it might not have been previously accessible.

2. *Matchmaking services*. These take a need from an individual or business customer and provide mechanisms (from providers) for matching that need. E-services that fall into this category include
   - Jobs and employment sites
   - Travel
   - Insurance
   - Loans including mortgage loans
   - Real estate sales
   - Brokers

   The advantage of this kind of matchmaking through the internet is that the ability to search electronically over a wider area to satisfy the customer need and to more precisely meet the customer need is greatly facilitated by both computerization and communication over the internet.

3. *Information-selling on the web*. This group essentially sells information content of one sort or another and includes e-commerce sites that provide
   - on-line publishing such as web-based newspapers
   - consultancy advice
   - specialized financial or other information

4. *Entertainment services*. These provide internet-based access to videos, movies, electronic games, or theme sites. This e-entertainment sector is expected to grow rapidly in the next few years, with a convergence of TV and internet-based technologies.

5. *Specialized services such as auctions*. Many different auction sites have appeared and these are discussed in Section 13.13.

It is not possible to discuss all the different e-services in this chapter and so we will briefly sample only a few examples for each category.

13.2 WEB-ENABLED SERVICES

As mentioned in the last section, web-enabled services include personal banking, stock trading, and education. We discuss each of these in turn briefly in the next few subsections.

13.2.1 E-banking

Security First Network Bank (SFNB; www.sfnb.com/) was the first internet bank. It provides most of the banking services on the web (see Figure 13.1).

Therefore, you can do your banking with your fingers instead of your feet. Looking at e-banking, we can distinguish between two distinct models:

1. Pure cyberbanks
2. Traditional banks that provide e-banking to complement their retail banking

SFNB is a pure cyberbank, while the homepage of Bank of America (www.bankofamerica.com) illustrates the second model.

While not all banks offer the full range of services on the internet, banks in both the aforementioned groups offer a varied range of services including

1. personal banking
2. commercial banking for both small businesses and large corporations
3. financial services
4. loan application services
5. international trade including settlement instruments, foreign exchange transactions, etc.

There are significant advantages for both the individual or corporation as well as the bank in using e-banking. An individual doing personal banking on the internet can, amongst other things, pay bills, do account transfers, make queries on account

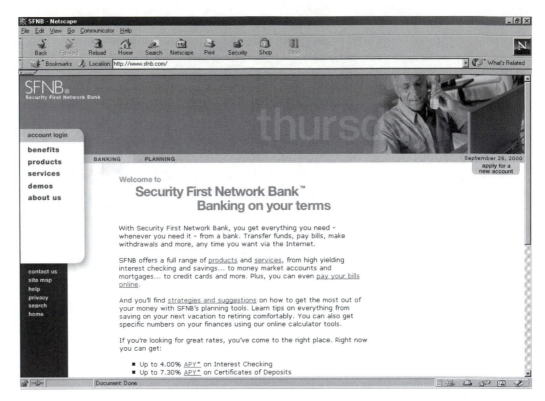

Figure 13.1 Homepage of SFNB

balances, obtain statements, in some cases view images of checks, etc., and import transactions directly into home account management software. Furthermore, one can make such transactions 24 hours a day from any place with internet access around the world.

In addition to these, a number of banks offer personal financial services including making personal loan applications on the internet. All these represent a large increase in convenience and time saving for the bank customer, saving him trips to the bank branch, queuing, etc.

The advantages to the banking institutions themselves include

1. reduction in the number of retail banking branches, saving rentals or ownership of the related properties.
2. reduction in staffing because of the reduction in paper processing as well as face-to-face bank teller contact.

3. bringing about increase in the time the bank hangs on to the money before making the required transfers, leading to increase in interest received by the banks.

These advantages are so significant that some banks offer customers a number of incentives to switch to internet banking, such as free checks, reduced fees, increased deposit rates, etc.

13.2.2 E-stocktrading and e-investing

Several companies such as E-Trade (www.etrade.com), Datek.on-line, American Express Financial Services, etc. allow you to trade stocks, bonds, mutual funds, etc. on the internet.

These companies offer you to trade at a very small cost compared to discount brokers or full-service brokers. This has resulted in these on-line trading companies grabbing an increasing market share. In response to this, discount brokers including Charles Schwab and full-service brokers have also moved to introduce internet trading of stocks. The steps involved essentially are the following [Turban *et al.*, 2000]:

1. place a request to trade, say buy a stock
2. the system responds with current "on the web site" prices
3. the internet trader has to confirm this trade or cancel it

Several companies allow one to create a simulated portfolio, which one watches over time without actually buying or selling the stocks in reality. An example of this can be found on the Smart Money site (www.smartmoney.com).

The major advantages to the person doing the trading are

1. the reduced cost;
2. the convenience of being able to trade anywhere in the world with internet access, e.g. while travelling; and
3. access to a wide variety of information on a number of sites (see Section 13.3).

In addition to actually allowing you to trade, these sites provide a considerable amount of information. The reduction in margins available to stockbrokers as a result of internet trading is beginning to have an effect on other more traditional forms of brokers. This has led to some traditional brokers also providing internet trading of stocks.

13.2.3 E-education

A number of e-universities are being spawned around the world. Again, three models can be seen:

1. Pure cyber universities, such as Jones International University (http://www. jonesinternational.edu).

2. Traditional universities setting up new cyber vehicles for providing university education perhaps with other business partners. An example of this is the Hong Kong CyberU (www.hkcyberu.com.hk; see Figure 13.2) which was set by the Hong Kong Polytechnic University and Pacific Century CyberWorks.

3. Traditional universities offering courses themselves on the internet. There are a number of web-based technology tools for this purpose. An example is WebCT.

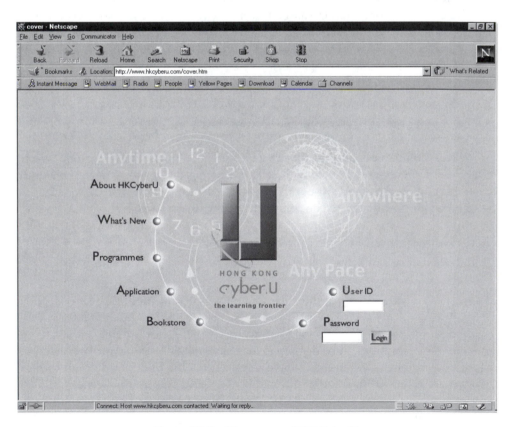

Figure 13.2   Homepage of HKCyberU

A number of so called "open universities" that previously provided distance learning have moved into providing an internet-based version of their courses. These traditional universities have a number of advantages. They can now reach a client base that is outside their catchment. They also expect to be able to deliver these courses at a reduced cost; however, the jury is still out on this. Another advantage a traditional university has on the internet over a new pure cyber university is that it has an established brand name.

There are a variety of issues that need to be explored carefully when preparing to deliver educational material on the internet and these include the following:

1. Does one use a distance learning model where the student uses a PULL model to acquire the material?

2. Does one use a traditional lecture model using video streaming? This is a PUSH model whereby a teacher "pushes" the materials to the students.

The use of the internet for education opens up many possibilities, namely use of quizzes, tests to provide the student with instant feedback on his/her mastery of the materials, use of graphics and animation to explain concepts, particularly those that have a dynamic character to them. It is anticipated that the internet will not only lead to cyber universities of one kind or another but will also have a marked effect on teaching and learning in traditional universities. One among some of the innovations that are being explored is the joint teaching by two universities on different continents in order to enhance the learning experience.

13.3 *MATCHMAKING SERVICES*

This has perhaps been the area in which there has been the greatest growth in e-services. Essentially, in most of these applications, the customer who could be an individual or business specifies his requirements in relation to the service. The e-commerce site then does a search over its own databases or over the internet using mobile agents (see Chapter 9), or over other databases or web sites to look for one or more matches to these requirements. The information is then returned to the e-service provider site to give the customer the required service. As explained in Section 13.1, there are number of services that fall into this category. We will discuss two of these and briefly explain the rest in Section 13.3.3.

13.3.1 Travel services

Before the internet, one might have gone along to a travel agent in order to book one's travel requirements such as air tickets, train tickets, car hire, hotel, tours, etc. The

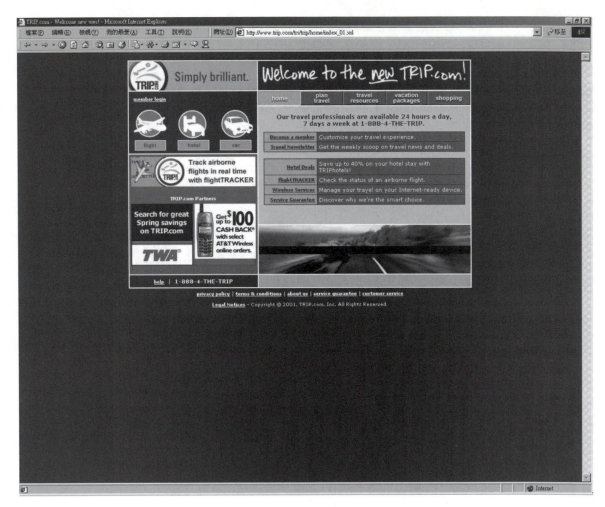

Figure 13.3   Homepage of Trip

travel agent would try his best to meet these requirements by providing information regarding schedules, pricing, promotions, as well as suggestions on changes to the itinerary. These bookings could be for individuals or corporations involving corporate rates, etc. A large number of e-commerce sites have appeared, which address this precise market segment. These include trip.com (www.trip.com; see Figure 13.3), travelweb.com, and priceline.com.

These web sites work in exactly the same way. When a customer provides his requirements, these sites do a search of their own databases or send agents out to explore other web sites and respond to the consumer. Amongst the requirements that the customer could specify is an acceptable price. A number of sites, such as priceline.com, require that provided the price specified is met, the customer cannot refuse the offer found.

These e-commerce sites are beginning to grab an increasing part of the travel market. They are attractive to consumers because of the convenience, the ability to meet requirements such as specified prices, and in some cases like lastminute.com, a special customer need (i.e., booking at the last minute). These travel sites often also have a lot of information on promotions, suggestions, etc., which are useful for customers. These e-commerce sites are having a strong "disintermediation" effect. Disintermediation refers to the removal of intermediaries such as travel agents from the process involved in the purchase of the service. A recent increasing trend has also seen the primary provider of a service such as an airline introducing internet-based booking at reduced prices, further emphasizing the disintermediation effect.

13.3.2   E-employment and e-jobs

There are several different kinds of services provided here, namely [Deitel *et al.*, 2001]

1. sites where you can get advice on developing your resumes and can post your resumes on the web
2. recruiters who use the web site to post available jobs, such as Hotjobs ((www.hotjobs.com); see Figure 13.4) or Jobdirect
3. employers who list available jobs on the web sites
4. matchmaking facilities that search the internet for jobs for jobseekers based on a specification, such as www.monster.com
5. matchmaking facilities to search the internet for resumes that best fit a job description given by a prospective employer
6. use of agents to do the search in the manner described in Section 13.3.

These approaches of using the internet for e-employment or e-jobs avoid many of the costs and difficulties associated with traditional approaches to advertising, such as high cost, limited duration, and minimal information.

13.3.3   Others

There are several other matchmaking functions, which were referred to in Section 13.1. These only represent a small sample of the matchmaking services on

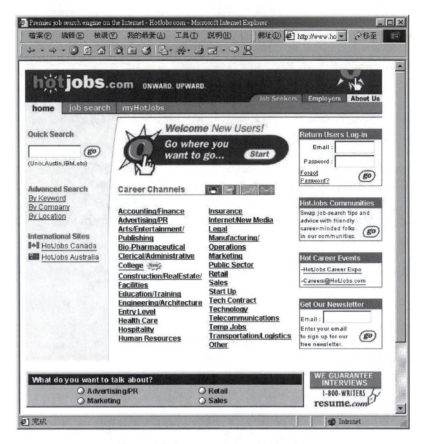

Figure 13.4 Homepage of Hotjobs

the internet. However, each of them is able to exploit the search, match facilities provided by the internet, and post the information, which has a global reach. In some areas, such as real estates e.g., (www.realestate.com), the visualization (3D) facilities provided on the web allow one to either

- show visualizations of buildings at the drawing board stage, or
- allow people distant from the physical site of building to actually visualize it.

This area of matchmaking and brokering services is expected to grow greatly in the near future with e-commerce sites exploiting new market niches. This is also an area with the greatest likelihood of disintermediation, and traditional agents or brokers will have to build new dimensions to their services in order to survive.

13.4 *INFORMATION-SELLING ON THE WEB*

These e-commerce sites sell information of one kind or another.

There are a number of distinct business models [Schneider *et al.*, 1999] varying from subscription only, mixed subscription/advertising, and fee-for-service for each access. They also often provide some information free. Sites in the other categories explained in Section 13.1 also frequently provide free information to attract customers to their web site, and then make their money on the transactions the customer carries out on their web site.

On-line publishing sites such as newspapers are discussed in Chapter 14.

The kind of information that is provided on the web varies greatly with sites specializing in different areas such as

1. investment information like [Deitel *et al.*, 2001]

   - stock evaluation (www.marketguide.com; see Figure 13.5)
   - investor information (www.investorguide.com)
   - mutual funds (www.morningstar.net)
   - general information (www.money.com)

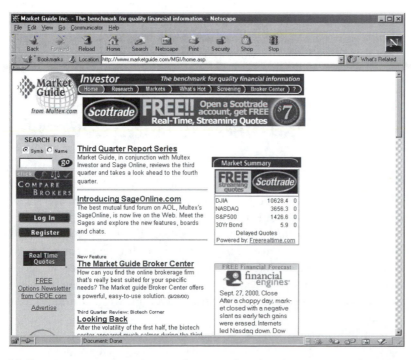

Figure 13.5 Homepage of Market Guide (Reproduced with permission of Market Guide)

2. resume-writing for jobs (www.resumelink.com)

3. contracts for jobs (www.ba.jobs.contract)

4. financial advice, planning, and counselling

5. mortgage information (www.mortgagenet.com)

The categories of information sold and the number of sites selling it are too numerous to enumerate here.

In order to view such sites, go to a search engine and type in the category of advice you are interested in and a number of sites will be listed, some of which offer free information and some of which will charge.

13.5 *E-ENTERTAINMENT*

This is expected to be a growing area of e-commerce in the future. A number of companies are gaining access to or have purchased large inventories of movies or other entertainment material with the view of allowing people to download this on the web. Sites here vary from theme sites that use a small amount of interactive entertainment to promote their products, such as Disney, to others that provide games either for a fee or are free coupled together with advertising that pays for the site. An important issue here is that the payments involved are relatively small for each transaction, and hence the use of micropayment techniques (see Chapter 10) is likely to be of considerable importance here.

13.6 *AUCTIONS AND OTHER SPECIALIZED SERVICES*

The use of auctions in the real world is used by sellers to achieve the best possible price for items that they wish to sell. The essential idea is that the seller puts up the items for sale but does not give a fixed price for it. The item is then subject to a series of bids until a bid is established that is acceptable or the time duration for the auction expires [Reiley, 2000], and the item is sold. The whole process is conducted by somebody called an auctioneer. There are several different types of auctions, the most common ones being an increasing bid auction (English auction), a decreasing bid auction (Dutch auction), and a price quantity pair auction. Auctions found their way onto the internet as early as 1995. In this section, we will briefly discuss these web-based electronic auctions.

Increasing bid auctions on the internet are sometimes referred to as forward auctions (Figure 13.6). Essentially, here the seller puts up an item for sale and specifies

Seller   Item for Sale   Potential buyers

Figure 13.6   Forward auction

an acceptable minimum price or reserve price that he is willing to accept. The item is then posted on the auction site together with the minimum price and the bidding is kept open for a specified period. During this period, potential buyers bid for the item and the latest high bid is displayed (but not the identity of the bidder). When the specified period lapses, the highest bidder is required to purchase the item at the bid price. There are clearly defined rules for the auction site that the bidder and the seller of the item are required to adhere to.

In the decreasing price option, or reverse auction (Figure 13.7), the seller puts up an item for sale at a high price. The price of this item is progressively reduced until a potential buyer accepts the bid and the items are then deemed to have been sold to the buyer.

The third option has potential buyers making a bid for a certain quantity of an item at a certain price and sellers offering to sell a given quantity at a specified price. The buyer's bids are progressively increased and seller's "asking" price progressively decreased until matching bids are obtained and the requisite quantity is then deemed to have been sold to the buyer at the right bid price.

Seller   Item for Sale   Potential buyers

Figure 13.7   Reverse auction

We will divide this brief discussion of auctions into two types [Schneider *et al.*, 1999]

1. C2C auction sites
2. B2B auction sites

13.6.1 C2C auction sites

C2C auction sites essentially involve a customer selling an item to another customer through an auction site. These auction sites can be

1. Generalized auction sites
2. Specialized auction sites
3. Agent-based auction supporting sites

Generalized auction sites like eBay (www.ebay.com), Auction Universe, etc. will allow a customer to put up many different kinds of items for sale on the auction site. eBay has a forward auction facility.

An example of a decreasing bid auction site is Klik klok, which auctions gold and jewellery. In contrast to the general auction sites, one can have some sites specializing in the auction of a particular class of items. Thus, Bid.com only deals with refurbished computers while Coin Universe (www.coinuniverse.com; see Figure 13.8) only deals with coin auctions.

The third class of auction related services are agent-based services or search engines that will allow a buyer to specify an item, and the mobile agent or search engine would then visit relevant new sites returning information on where the item can be found. An example of this is www.usaweb.com.

13.6.2 B2B auctions

There are basically three models for these B2B auction sites.

1. Use of a liquidation broker to sell excess items. In this case, the liquidation broker is essentially a third party auction site that does the auctioning for you.
2. Use of your own web site to auction items.
3. Use of the auction facility on a virtual market site that one is a participant in to auction excess inventory.

These approaches will be increasingly used by businesses, particularly if they are dealing with perishable commodities.

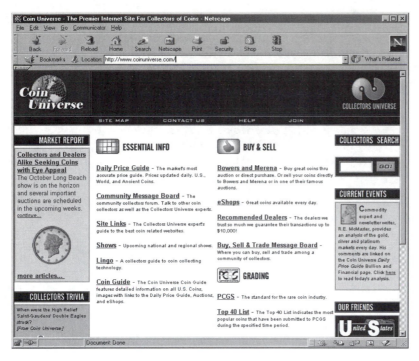

Figure 13.8   Homepage of Coin Universe (Reproduced with permission of Coin Universe)

13.7 *SUMMARY*

In this chapter we briefly reviewed e-services or the delivery of intangible goods on the internet. These can be basically divided into five categories, namely web enabling, matchmaking, information provision, delivery of entertainment content, and auctions.

Auctions on the internet provide several sources of revenue on the auction site including

1. a fee from the buyer and the seller
2. advertising revenue from businesses that wish to promote to buyers of particular categories of items

This area of provision of services is growing rapidly because of the ability of the internet to not only take the order for the service but also in many cases to actually directly deliver the service on the internet.

REFERENCES

Deitel, H. M., Deitel, P. J., and Steinbuhler, K., *e-Business and e-Commerce for Managers*, Prentice Hall, Upper Saddle River, NJ, 2001.

Machlis, S., "On-line auction services thriving," *Computerworld* **32** (24) (1998), 1, 2.

Reiley, D. L., "Auctions on the Internet: What's being auctioned, and how?", *The Journal of Industrial Economics*, Vol. 48, Sep. 2000, 227–252.

Schneider, G. P. and Perry, J. T., *Electronic Commerce*, Course Technology, 1999.

Sliwa, C., "Ebay tops in auction niche," *Computerworld* **33** (19) (1999), 38.

Turban, E., Lee, J., King, D., Chung, H. M., and Lee, J. K., *Electronic Commerce – A Managerial Perspective*, Prentice-Hall, Upper Saddle River, NJ, 2000.

14

Web Advertising and Web Publishing

14.1 Traditional Versus Internet Advertising

14.2 Internet Advertising Techniques and Strategies

14.3 Business Models for Advertising and Their Revenue Streams

14.4 Pricing Models and Measurement of the Effectiveness of Advertisements

14.5 Web Publishing – Goals and Criteria

14.6 Web Site Development Methodologies

14.7 Logical Design of the User Interface I – Abstract User Interface Object

14.8 Logical Design of the User Interface II – Flow of Interaction

14.9 Usability Testing and Quality Assurance

14.10 Web Presence and Visibility

14.11 Summary

References

Recommended Reading

In this chapter, we initially discuss Web Advertising and next Web Publishing. When considering web advertising we will examine the following topics, namely

- Traditional vs. internet-based advertising
- Web advertising techniques

- Business models for web advertising purveyors, including pricing models
- Measuring the effectiveness of web advertising

In the section on web publishing we will address the following subjects, namely

- Key criteria for good web publishing
- Design methodologies for web publishing
- Usability testing and quality assurance
- Authoring tools
- Web site maintenance
- Presence and visibility of the web site

The topics are extremely complex and an entire book could be devoted just to the subject matter of this chapter. For reasons of space, the discussion of some topics will have to be necessarily curtailed, but references and web sites referenced at the end of the chapter provide additional information through which the interested reader can further pursue the topics.

14.1 *TRADITIONAL VERSUS INTERNET ADVERTISING*

Currently, there are many traditional advertising channels including

- newspapers and magazines that utilize text and image
- radio that utilizes audio
- television that uses video
- direct mail that utilizes text and image
- telemarketing that utilizes audio

The internet provides a new media that can mix text, audio, images, graphics, animation, and video. This ability of the new media to exploit multimedia for e-advertising opens up new opportunities for commerce on the internet.

It is useful to briefly compare the features of traditional vs. internet advertising. Traditional advertising relies on two main marketing strategies, namely

1. A *one-to-many* or *mass marketing* strategy. A newspaper, television channel, or a radio broadcast is an example of such a mass marketing strategy. A feature of

mass marketing is that the content and sequencing of material in the advertisement are fixed at the outset for all viewers of the advertisement.

2. A *one-to-one* or *direct marketing* strategy using a salesperson to directly sell to a customer.

Internet advertising allows one to carry out the following:

1. A *many-to-one* or *targeted marketing* strategy. This allows one to tailor the content presented to a particular viewer of the web site based on an understanding of the viewers' preferences. These preferences could be determined from an understanding of the previous visits to the site or the user's choices on the current visit to the site. The nonlinear nature of publishing on the web also allows the user to choose to view particular things in an advertisement that might best suit his interests.

2. A *many-to-many* or *group marketing* model through the use of purchasing circles, user opinion forums, and chat rooms. This allows one to develop a self-segmenting approach to marketing.

In addition to these features, there are several other factors which make internet advertising very attractive. These include the following [Turban *et al.*, 2000]:

1. The rapidly growing number of internet users and web visitors around the world in almost all countries.

2. The global reach of internet advertising.

3. The fact that the advertising can be linked with the ordering process. Thus, when one views an advertisement, a link can be provided to an order form allowing one to immediately purchase the product advertised. Conversely, if one is selecting particular items for purchase, the e-store can advertise related products to allow cross-selling.

4. Web advertising is relatively easier to update and/or link with supplementary material.

5. Multimedia and interactivity provide additional dimensions.

6. The advertisements can be viewed 24 hours a day.

7. In many circumstances, they could be cost effective.

8. It allows for personalization.

Currently, the disadvantages are the relative immaturity of the medium with inadequate work being done on the issue of measurement of the effectiveness of advertisements. This is discussed further in Section 14.4.

14.2 *INTERNET ADVERTISING TECHNIQUES AND STRATEGIES*

On the internet, advertising techniques and strategies are often interwoven and so it is appropriate to deal with them together. It is useful to separate the techniques into mass marketing and targeted marketing strategies. Mass marketing techniques include the following:

1. E-mail
2. Banners

Apart from providing marketing services, some companies specialize in measuring and analyzing performance of internet marketing campaigns such as Jupiter Media Metrix (see Figure 14.1).

14.2.1 E-mail

E-mail is becoming increasingly widely used as a means of distributing advertising messages to people on the internet. Here, the marketing strategies, to be reasonably successful, require appropriate market segmentation and the development or purchase of suitable e-mail lists. E-mail advertising is increasingly being tied to the use of promotions and gimmicks. The advantages of e-mail advertising are that it is cheap to implement, can include the facility for feedback and return messages, and will allow one to progressively tailor the e-mail advertisements based on this. The downsides of this include the fact that internet users frequently read only messages from people they know and treat the rest as junk mail. In addition, the sending of unsolicited mail indiscriminately leads to spamming. Currently, legislation is progressively being put into place to provide better control of this. Some advertisers put in an interaction allowing one to deregister from receiving any mail containing advertising in the e-mail message itself, probably to convey the fact that they are making an effort to avoid a charge of spamming. However, progressively the effectiveness of e-mail in the future may be affected by the number of messages received by an internet user, and as this is growing very rapidly, it is likely to reduce its effectiveness if indiscriminately used.

14.2.2 Banners

Banners represent another widely used technique for advertising. A banner is a small display on the web consisting of text, graphics, and animations, which either appear

Figure 14.1   Homepage of Jupiter Media Metrix (www.jmm.com)

randomly when you surf the internet (random banners) or when a particular keyword is typed in during a search using a search engine (keyword banners) [Turban *et al.*, 2000]. These banners are normally linked to the web site of the advertiser, where further information can be obtained. If the user clicks on the banner, he is transferred to that web site. This leads to the concept of click through rates (the proportion of times that the banners are clicked when viewed), which is sometimes used as a (somewhat limited) measure of effectiveness (see Section 14.4). There is conflicting evidence on the effectiveness of banners. In 1998, AOL suggested that 50% of users recall them immediately after viewing them, and 9 out of 10 people react positively to them (www.adage.com). On the other hand, Nielson/Netratings has figures on their web site (www.nielson-netratings.com; see Figure 14.2) that show that click through rates are around 0.6%.

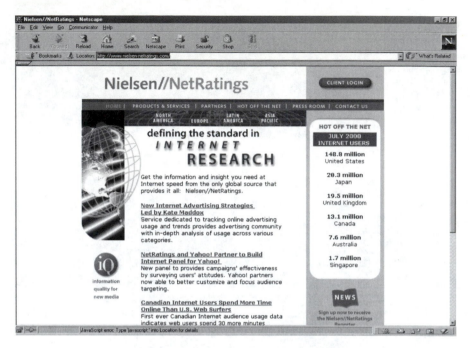

Figure 14.2 Homepage of Nielson Ratings

Therefore, the following two things are quite important:

1. to ensure that the banners are initially viewed by as many of the right groups of users as possible.
2. to achieve high click through rates.

In order to achieve the first criterion, several strategies are utilized:

1. banner swapping involving a direct exchange of displays of banners between two companies
2. use of banner exchanges, i.e. companies such as Eurobanner (www.Eurobanner.com/; see Figure 14.3), Linkexchange, etc.

These banner exchange companies essentially put together a group of members and there are agreements between the members and the banner exchange, such that one company A will display a banner for a member of the group, provided another company of the group is willing to display the first company's banner. The banner exchange company itself monitors agreements, provides software to all members to monitor their own click through rates, and also provides useful information on web

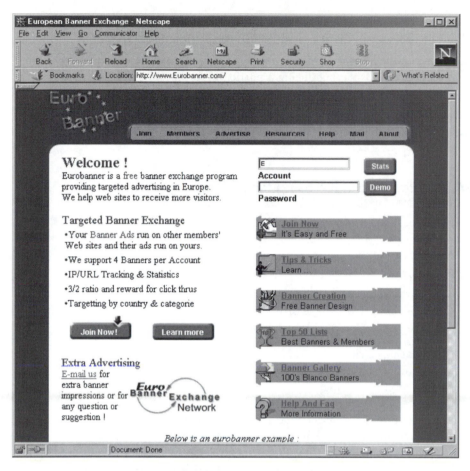

Figure 14.3 Homepage of Eurobanner

site advertising and visibility. Euro banner, for instance will display your banner twice on other sites for every three you display. Visit the Eurobanner site to understand and take their tour to understand the rules governing and the services provided by a typical Banner Exchange.

In addition to these, the design of the banner has to be such that downloading time is less so that the viewer does not lose patience and leave the site.

Purchasing of banner space for the leasing of space for a fixed period is also used to place the banner in the homepage of a search engine or a portal with high traffic, such as Yahoo!.

To achieve high click through rates, several different strategies such as the following are used:

1. use of discounts or free "somethings"
2. use of promotions involving entry into prize-winning competitions
3. display of the banner advertisement within a framework which has the right audience, e.g. displaying during a particular keyword search
4. use of a highly appealing and effective design. Some studies indicate that positioning a banner on the bottom right hand of a page achieves a better click through rate than one at the top of the page, as this is the "idle" position of the mouse.

14.2.3 Targeted advertising techniques

Targeted marketing techniques include

1. Broad targeted marketing
   - chat rooms
   - thematic web sites
   - portals that provide keyword-linked banner advertisements
2. Personalized targeted marketing
   - purchasing circles
   - data-mining-based associative advertising
   - permission marketing

Chat rooms provide an electronic means of exchanging messages. They allow for other participants of the chat room to read messages almost as soon as they are posted by one participant. They, therefore, provide an ideal gathering spot for people with a particular community of interest whether it be a hobby or a social cause of one kind or another. As the chat room attracts a particular clientele, an advertiser can pick or sponsor a specific chat room, the audience of which he believes to be an appropriate target for his advertising.

Hosting of chat sessions on their sites is provided by portals such as Yahoo! and MSN. The portals frequently host these chat rooms for free. One can link a chat room to your own site by creating a chat room using the provider's facilities and providing a hyperlink to the chat room. Advertising messages can then be targeted at the chat room participants. This allows one to progressively develop a theme within the advertising messages intended by the advertiser. Chat rooms are now used by a number of companies.

Thematic sites such as Disney and Calvin Klein use their web sites to advertise their products. They link the advertising to several interactive activities a user can engage in, e.g., Disney allows interactions with different characters. These thematic

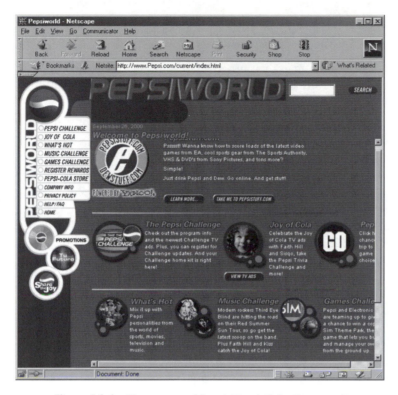

Figure 14.4 Homepage of Pepsi (Pepsi Cola Company)

web sites also frequently have promotions such as entering you into prize-winning competitions, sometimes often performing a simple quiz or test. An example of this is the Pepsi web site (www.Pepsi.com; see Figure 14.4).

Portals such as Yahoo! (www.Yahoo.com) provide keyword-related display of advertisements. Thus, if you do a search for a particular item, say digital cameras, when the page pops up, advertising in the form of a banner can be placed on the page. This allows very targeted marketing as it picks up users who are currently interested in knowing about or purchasing a particular product.

Purchasing circles are established by some businesses such as Amazon.com, using techniques called collaborative filtering or data mining to assign customers who are interested, say, in a particular class or category of books to a given purchasing circle. This allows the placement of targeted advertisements directed at members of this purchasing circle. These essentially analyze the previous behavior or purchases of a customer and then allocate him to the specific purchasing circle appropriate for him.

As explained in Chapter 9, association rules allow one to associate items in a transaction in a market-based database. An example of this is that *if one purchases sugar, milk, and bread, one is 80% likely to purchase cereal.* Thus, if a customer on a web site purchases the first three items, one could pop up a display advertisement for cereals.

Permission marketing is an approach that is finding increasing application on the web. Essentially, it consists of the following approach [Hanson, 2000]:

1. When a visitor is visiting a site, making a purchase, or having any other interaction with a web site, he is asked if he would like to receive additional or further information from the company or on that topic, i.e., permission is sought from him to send him further marketing information, product information, special offers, etc.

2. Marketing information normally in the form of carefully selected e-mails that match the target's interests are sent to him. As the target of these e-mails has chosen to include himself in the marketing loop, he is more likely to read and respond to the e-mails.

14.3 BUSINESS MODELS FOR ADVERTISING AND THEIR REVENUE STREAMS

Traditional media that provide outlets for advertising use a variety of different business models. Thus, one can get [Schneider *et al.*, 2000]

1. a purely advertising-supported business model such as that used by free-to-air television.

2. a purely subscription model as used by cable TV.

3. a mixed advertising- and subscription-supported business model such as that utilised by daily newspapers or sporting events.

Internet providers of advertising space or advertising facilities utilize these different models.

Thus, the purely advertising-supported web sites include

1. employment advertising sites such as careersite.com. They allow businesses to place employment advertisements which are distributed around the world by the web site (www.washingtonpost.com).

2. most chat rooms referred to in the last section.

3. sites that provide free games (Sony), or thematic sites supported by advertising (Disney).

4. the most widely used search engines or portals such as Netscape.

5. some newspaper sites such as of the Washington Post.

Mixed advertising and subscription sites include ESPN, which offers both free information and specialized information on a subscription basis. The site itself also sells advertising space. Newspapers such as the Wall Street Journal charge for viewing most of the information content but allow free access to classifieds, etc.

14.4 *PRICING MODELS AND MEASUREMENT OF THE EFFECTIVENESS OF ADVERTISEMENTS*

The two issues of pricing models and measurement of the effectiveness of advertisements are inextricably linked.

In a traditional advertising framework, the most commonly used pricing model and measurement of effectiveness is the CPM model, which is an exposure-based model. It is based on the number of times someone sees or views an advertisement, each view being referred to as an impression. CPM is the cost per thousand impressions. Thus, it is related to the size of the overall audience based on circulation, ratings, etc.

In order to develop a similar measure, internet providers of advertising space used *hit rate* as a measure of the traffic through the web site and developed pricing based on this. A hit corresponds to an access request to the web site. Thus, if one wanted to put an advertisement on a site, the hit rate was used to characterize the audience. It soon became clear that this was an inadequate measure for audience size for two reasons:

1. A single visit by a user could involve several hits. This led to the notion of *visits*. Each visit corresponds to one occasion a user visits a site, and this may consist of a sequence of requests each of which generates a hit. A second visit would be counted only if the user stopped making requests for some period of time and subsequently made a new visit corresponding to a new sequence of requests [Turban *et al.*, 2000].

2. The problem with just using visits is that there is no way of distinguishing whether a subsequent visit is made by the same user or another user. A measure of audience should really measure the number of *unique visitors* to the site. Thus, one could employ unique visitors as a measure of the number of unique views or impressions of an advertisement, and base a CPM measure on this. Such an approach would be approximately equivalent to the measure used by traditional media advertising. While one might be tempted to think that this

should satisfy anyone interested in pricing, it is not the end of the story. The problem arises from the fact that on the internet one is able to measure many other things. For instance, instead of working on the audience at a portal, Procter & Gamble proposed a pricing measure that does not utilize the number of views of a banner but rather the click through rate. As mentioned earlier, the click through rate is the proportion of the viewers of a particular banner who click on the banner to go to the web site of the company being advertised in the banner. This is a measure of interest in the product generated by the advertisement. Given the fact that click through rates are only a small fraction of views, this completely changes the pricing structure. Ultimately though, the advertiser is really interested in the number of sales made because of a particular advertisement. On the internet it is possible to measure this, while on traditional media this would be very difficult. However, this ability to measure many other things have added to a deal of nonstandardization and noise in the area of measuring effectiveness and pricing.

14.5   WEB PUBLISHING – GOALS AND CRITERIA

A web site could be developed by a business to serve one or more purposes in an e-commerce setting. Thus, a web site could be used for

1. conveying information,
2. carrying a marketing message,
3. allowing interactivity, say to place an order or customer service, and
4. exchanging information and opinions as in a chat room.

If the web site only conveys information it is sometimes referred to as a kiosk web site. This information could be made available free (say, in a library) or on a subscription basis. Such information could be fixed or updated periodically, say, for a web site providing stock prices. The marketing message could be used for brand development and projection as on the Calvin Klein site, or it could contain advertisements marketing specific products or a particular product or service.

Interactivity in a web site could include searching for products from a catalog, selecting products for purchase, order submission, and electronic payment. Alternatively, it could involve playing a computer game at a games web site, with the full range of interactivity that it requires.

Chat rooms allow interchange of information between group members in real time; hence, the set of facilities this provides are somewhat different from those of a company that conveys fixed information or information that updates the values of certain fixed fields periodically or in real time.

A web site could combine one or more of these purposes. Thus, a chat room may have advertising from sponsors. An e-commerce site might have a web site that serves all four purposes. The purpose(s) of the web site will influence the architecture, the web page layouts, content, use of multimedia effects, etc. Hence, when building a web site, it is important to understand its purpose at the outset. Thus, the first step in web site development is definition of the goals.

There are several features, however, which are common to all web sites and these include the following:

1. Navigational efficiency and ease of use. Navigation through the web site should correspond to the manner in which someone visiting the site accesses information rather than be dictated by other factors such as corporate structure.

2. Less downloading time. Users are unlikely to tolerate anything over 15 s and one should work towards much less than this. This has major implications for the amount of multimedia, or graphics used.

3. Browser compatibility with the main browsers. The look and feel on all the main browsers should be visually acceptable and meaningful.

4. An assurance of security and privacy must be maintained as well as communicated to the user.

5. Business content must be clear and audience- or customer-focused. This should include careful titling, clarity of text, and communication of contractual terms and conditions involved in any business transaction.

6. The presentation should be visually appealing, consonant with the market position, image, and branding and coherent with the overall marketing strategy.

7. Creation of web presence, which will ensure that the visibility of the site on the internet is high.

14.6 *WEB SITE DEVELOPMENT METHODOLOGIES*

The development of a web site or client side of an e-commerce system like any other software system requires a clear understanding of

1. the purposes of the web site.
2. the functions of the e-commerce system that the client side must provide. This would be identified during the systems analysis and conceptual modelling stage (see Chapter 11).
3. the audiences that the web site is meant to address.

Points 1 and 2 have been previously dealt with and point 3 is discussed in the next section.

14.6.1 Definition of an audience

We distinguish between several groups of users who utilize a web site. Each group consists of loosely knit group of users who wish to obtain particular categories of information from a web site or carry out particular actions at the web site. We call such a group of users that wish to access a web site an *audience*. An audience in general is a more diffused and fuzzy concept than users. Generally, when software is produced in a particular application domain, it is possible to understand (to a lesser or greater extent) the profiles of the likely users. The narrower the domain of application, the more likely that one can do this. This may not be the case with web-based users.

We define an audience as a group of users who access a web site to obtain the same type of information and have similar navigation patterns through the web site.

Here it is useful to distinguish between three different categories of audiences.

(I) *Crisp and accessible audience*: This is one where it is more likely to be able to identify the members of the audience, for example, enrolled students in an e-education site or registered customers. Here, we not only know the members of the audience but could also have the opportunity of interviewing them during the analysis phase. Existing customers of a B2B site would fall into this category.

(II) *Fuzzy and nonaccessible audience*: An example of this would be prospective customers in a B2C site.

(III) *Undefined or unknown audience*: This may consist of a group that web developers are unaware of, but who access the web site and their accesses would be roughly similar in both content and mode of access.

Each of these different audiences will have a considerable impact on the analysis phase, leading to a conceptual model of audience needs.

14.6.2 Categories of systems

In the development of web-based systems, one can encounter several different categories of systems. Here we distinguish between three categories:

(A) No web site exists and the system is developed completely from scratch.

(B) An organizational web site already exists and it may or may not be structured. Here one would essentially be developing a mediator between the existing web site and the audience category.

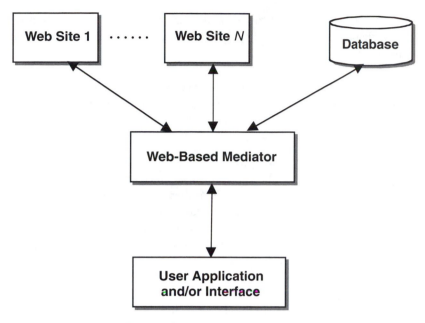

Figure 14.5 Web-based mediator

(C) We may wish to build a mediator between the audience category and several web sites or data sources.

The notion of a mediator for data resources was put forward by Wielderhold [1995]. Essentially, one can consider a mediator as a piece of software that sits between one or more data resources and user applications.

The mediator locates the required data or web information and integrates, abstracts, and presents it to the user application in the form it requires. The architecture of a web-based mediator is shown in Figure 14.5.

The category of system to be developed has an impact on the development methodology.

14.6.3 Overview of design methodology

We propose a design methodology that

1. determines audience categories.
2. carries out an analysis phase related to the requirements of each audience category.

3. develops a conceptual model for the audience category using objects and classes for the static part and a Flow of Interaction Net (FIN) diagrams to determine the dynamic navigational aspects.

In looking at the design methodology we need to examine the particular audience category and the specific system type. Hence, we will consider these in turn.

Audience category I – System type A

Here we are examining a crisp, accessible audience and building the web site from scratch. It is important to note that here we may have one web site accessed by several audiences. For instance, in a university web site we could have several audiences, say enrolled undergraduate students, postgraduate students, academic staff, and general staff who might wish to access the web site. Note that each of these audiences would belong to audience category I, as the users in each of these categories are clearly defined and accessible. In determining the audience requirements for a particular audience, say enrolled students, one would interview

1. enrolled students
2. departmental student advisors
3. faculty student advisors
4. student services staff

The last three groups would be interviewed to find out the sort of information students often ask them for. This interview would be used to construct an object-oriented conceptual model (OOCM) associated with the audience category. Note that other audience categories may require different information from the same object that is defined in this OOCM. Hence, it may be necessary to enhance the attributes and methods to allow for such an eventuality. The object that is defined on the web site can be called the Organization Object or Business Object [De Troyer, 1998].

One could consider the different OOCMs for each audience as perspectives of the organization object model in the sense defined by Chang and Dillon [1993] and Chang [1996] and as explained later.

In addition, in the logical design of the audience object conceptual model, one also needs to specify and represent the navigational structure of the interface. We use extended Flow of Interaction Net (FIN) [Chang, 1996; Chang and Dillon, 1998] for carrying out this as explained in Section 14.7.

Audience category I – System type B

In such a case, since the audience is accessible, the process of analysis is similar to that adopted in Section 3.1. An OOCM for the audience category can, therefore, be developed. However, two cases pertain here:

Case 1: The existing system is properly structured and an object model representing its structure is available.

Case 2: The existing system does not have a representation of the structure readily available.

In case 1, one treats the existing system as the organizational model and develops a mapping between the audience model and the organizational model utilizing perspectives as explained in Section 14.8.

In case 2, one has two choices. Firstly, one can begin by building an organizational model that is used as a wrapper for the existing system much in the manner carried out for database systems. The objects in this organizational model would then be linked to appropriate information in the existing web site. The links between this object wrapper and the web site would have to be maintained, whenever the structure of the existing web site evolves. Audience classes for any audience would use the objects in this wrapper to form perspectives. In this way the audience classes would not need to be maintained each time the existing web site evolves. An alternate but less desirable approach would be to link the audience classes directly to the information in the web site. This would require maintenance on these audience classes every time the existing web site was modified.

As a large number of web sites already exist and audience classes are being progressively identified, this will probably be the most likely situation encountered in future web-based development.

Audience category I – System type C

Here, one seeks to access several web sites, which could be on different servers and maintained by different web masters. Here since the audience category is available, the interview and analysis process is somewhat similar to I/A leading to an audience conceptual model for the specific audience. Next, one has to work out a mapping between this audience conceptual model and the different web sites from which information is obtained. An example of such a system would be an e-commerce site for a logistics provider, which provides information on train, air, truck, and shipping links and timetables. They provide information on the specific routes or lines, as well as time tabling information. This time tabling information currently exists at the web site of the relevant transport company. Hence, one has to map the information between the audience classes developed and the web sites at the different transport providers. If the timetables or pricing changed, the information at the logistics e-commerce site would automatically reflect this. A mediator architecture is appropriate here and the mapping between the audience classes and the information at the web sites is handled by this. This mediator could then be used by other organizations to build a similar system.

Audience category II – System types A, B, C

The major difference here is that members of the audience category II may not be readily accessible for direct interviewing during the analysis stage. An example of such an audience would be potential new customers at a B2C e-commerce site. However, domain experts will be available and are interviewed. Here, a twofold strategy has to be used and this essentially consists of surveying the potential user group for information they are likely to require, obtaining a small sample group of possible users and utilizing them as a focus group to ascertain requirements and to evaluate prototyped screens and navigational patterns. This is somewhat similar to the use of focus groups in the advertising industry. These interactions are utilized in creating a preliminary model. However, this model is likely to be inadequate in many places. Next, a prototype system based on this model is developed and deployed. Field testing of this web site is conducted with potential customers. An important addition to the web site has to be a questions/comments section where prospective users can advise the difficulties they have experienced and if possible their contact information.

This is next used to modify the prototype system leading to an enhanced prototype. If prospective users have left information, they are contacted to reuse the system providing a form of usability test for the system. The system is then progressively evolved until a relatively stable version of the system is developed. This, therefore, involves a spiral life cycle model.

Audience category III – System type B or C

When one has an existing system in place, it is possible that a fairly large group of users have accessed the information in a somewhat similar fashion but have not at the outset been identified as an audience category. In order to identify such an audience category, it is necessary to collect information on navigational pathways used by the users, within a certain web site and to carry out data mining on these (using the site access log) to determine if there are recurring patterns of navigation through that web site. If so, one should try to identify the group doing this and determine if they are of audience category type I or II and use the appropriate development strategy. If one is unable to put a coherent grouping of users to these navigational patterns, it may still be worthwhile treating them as an audience class and structuring an approach to development based on that used with system type B or C.

14.7 *LOGICAL DESIGN OF THE USER INTERFACE I – ABSTRACT USER INTERFACE OBJECT*

As explained in Chapter 3, the logical design of the UI involves (1) navigation-related aspects of the UI design and (2) data-related aspects of the UI design. The UI can be considered to be an external representation of the system. There should, therefore, be a relationship between the representations used to model and develop the aspects internal to the system and application and those external to the system. From the viewpoint of the UI design, we can regard portions of the UI as corresponding to different *perspectives* of the conceptual models [Chang and Dillon, 1993].

It is well known in relational databases that one can consider a conceptual schema and a logical schema, which define the semantics of the data as well as an external schema, which is related to the presentation of the data to the users and their inter-action with the data. This external schema consists of views. These views are defined by queries. In a relational database system, these views are virtual relations.

It has been recognized that the use of an object is important in defining the attributes, actions, and related events that characterize a concept as well as any associated relationship. In the conceptual modelling area [Dillon and Tan, 1993; Sterling, Dillon, and Chang, 1999], the notion of a *perspective* is used to capture the many different roles or aspects that the given concept might be used for in the given system. A perspective gives one access to the appropriate portion of both the static and dynamic structures of the conceptual model for a particular purpose. Unlike views of data models, *perspectives* as defined above capture both the dynamic and static aspects.

In addition, we need a representation of the interobject dynamic aspects of the UI or the flow of interaction. To accomplish this we will define and use a new category of Petri nets known as Flow of Interaction Net (FIN). The whole process of logical design is summarized in Figure 14.6.

Next, we give an informal introduction to perspectives, abstract UI objects, and concrete UI objects.

Consider a *Web-Based Hotel Guest Registration* system in an e-commerce site for a hotel. One of the domain objects from the conceptual model is the Hotel Guest. The object property diagram for it in a simplified system is shown in Figure 14.7.

From a user's perspective, we examine the domain object Hotel Guest to find certain information, and actions are needed for representing the Hotel Guest object externally on the screen. The abstract UI object named "Customer" is drawn as shown in Figure 14.8 and a screen layout is shown in Figure 14.9.

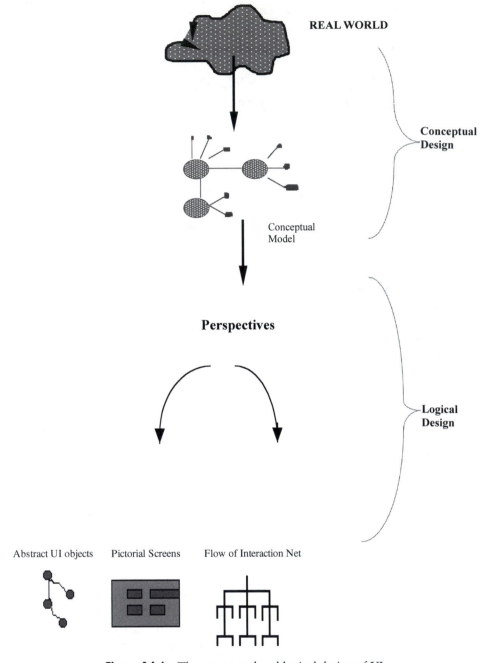

Figure 14.6 The conceptual and logical design of UI

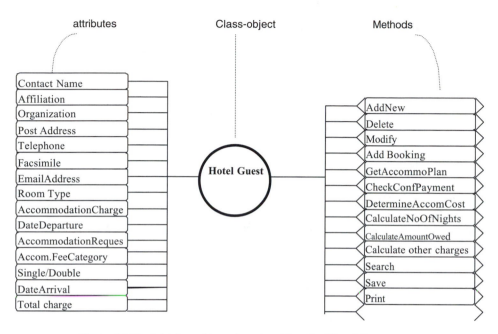

Figure 14.7 Initial problem domain object for Hotel Guest

Note that the attributes associated with this abstract UI object can be obtained by a projection of the object property diagram (OPD) of the attendee domain object and are a subset of the attributes of the attendee domain object. Note that several additional methods have been added to the participant UI object. Also note that the participant registration window itself is a composite object with each of the actions within it being associated with a UI command object and UI information object.

The corresponding concrete UI object for the aforementioned abstract UI object could be as shown in Figure 14.10.

Later, we will also see that the actual positioning of a particular window in the total web site structure will be described by FIN.

In this section, we have given an informal introduction to abstract UI objects and concrete UI objects. An abstract UI object may be a portion of a domain object, or portions of several domain objects. It is dependent on the perspective used. Abstract UI objects, in other words, describe what a screen should contain or what the interface should be. The use of guidelines helps to define how the UI object carries out what it is required to do.

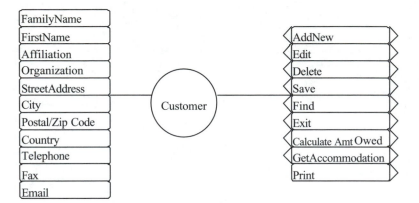

Figure 14.8 Abstract UI object for "Customer"

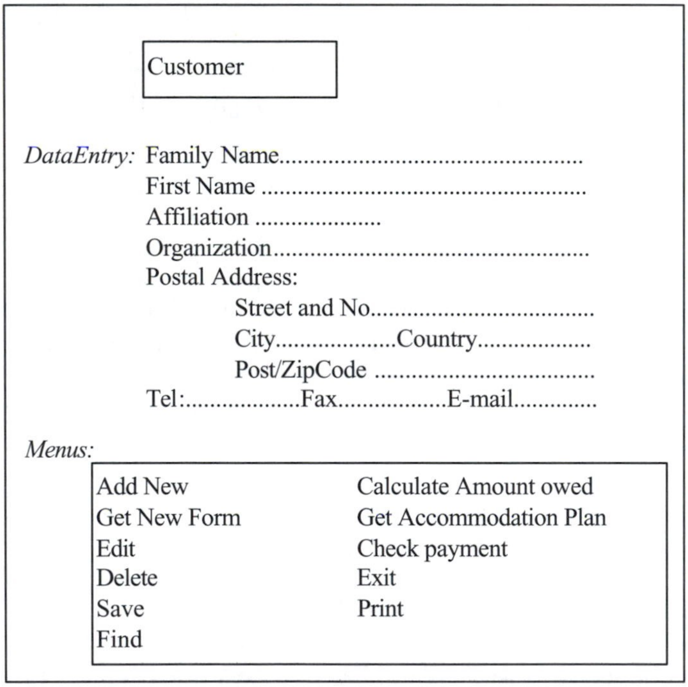

Customer

DataEntry: Family Name..
First Name ....
Affiliation ....
Organization...
Postal Address:
  Street and No.....................................
  City....................Country...................
  Post/ZipCode ....
Tel:...................Fax..................E-mail.............

Menus:

Add New	Calculate Amount owed
Get New Form	Get Accommodation Plan
Edit	Check payment
Delete	Exit
Save	Print
Find	

Figure 14.9 Pictorial presentation of screen for "Customer"

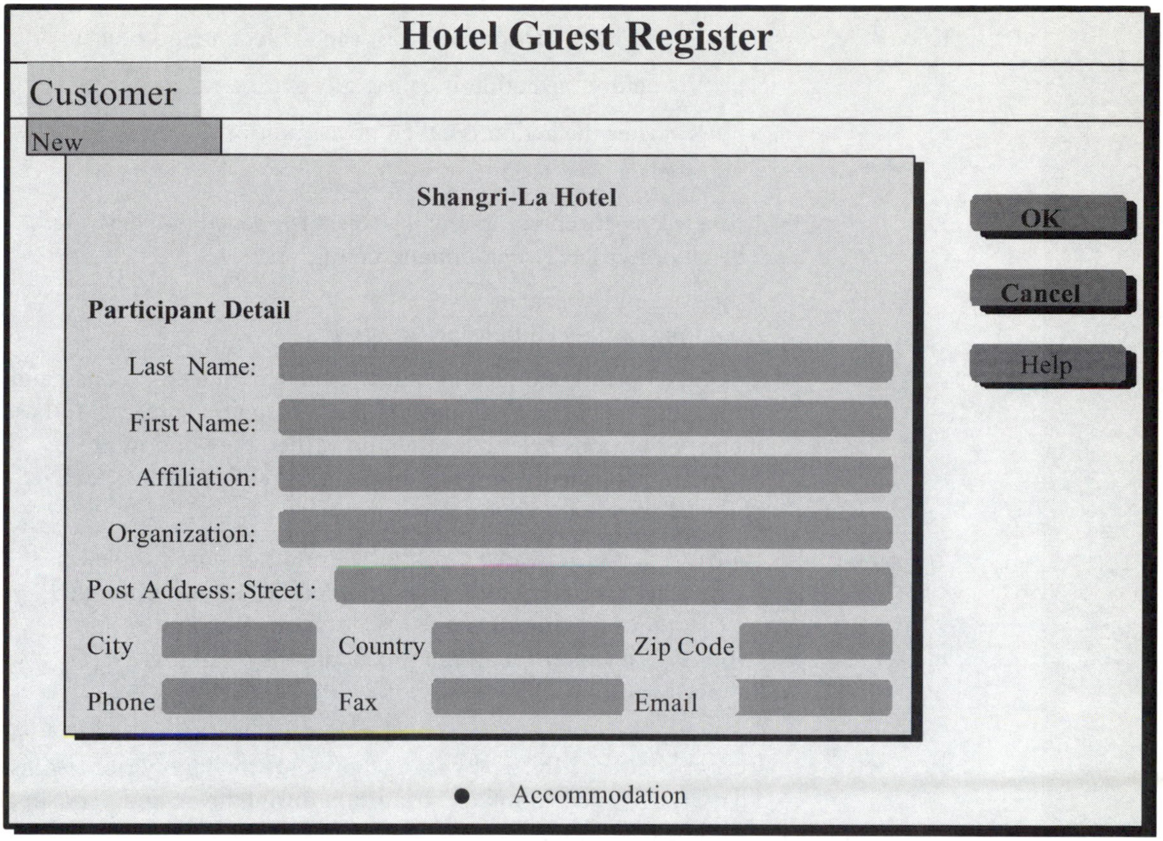

Figure 14.10   Concrete UI objects for customer

14.8 *LOGICAL DESIGN OF THE USER INTERFACE II – FLOW OF INTERACTION*

The important point to understand is that at a given point in the UI associated with the web site, there are only certain actions available to a user. Thus, any action a user is allowed to take must be associated with a set of preconditions. Furthermore, once a user takes an action, certain postconditions must hold. When one chains the pre- and postconditions for other user actions, one gets a description of the flow of navigation or flow of interaction.

When we model UI, we not only model it at each window level but also at each UI command level. Each bubble in the net represents a UI command object, and each solid bar is the action or event that is taken by the user.

1. ◯   Represents state (or condition) of each UI command object.

The ◯ before the action is called precondition.

The ◯ after the action is called postcondition.

2. ╤   Represents a user action.

3. •   It is a token. It represents the UI object is opened and activated. The UI object has two command conditions:

- opened and activated
waiting or opened but not activated

The token position indicates that the current window is open and activated. If a current UI object is just a menu or button and these menus or buttons belong to a window, then the window they belong to is opened. No more than one token is used for each UI object. Tokens can move around the Net.

4. Firing rules   (a) An action is activated if all its preconditions are fulfilled (i.e. they have a token) and all its postconditions are unfulfilled (i.e. they have no token).
(b) Firing tokens from all the preconditions to all the postconditions.

5. Weight   The weight is a number attached to the arc. It is equal to 1 throughout the FIN. The weight represents the number of tokens that are removed from a precondition during firing and deposited in a postcondition.

There are two steps involved in developing a FIN:

Step 1   **Step 2**

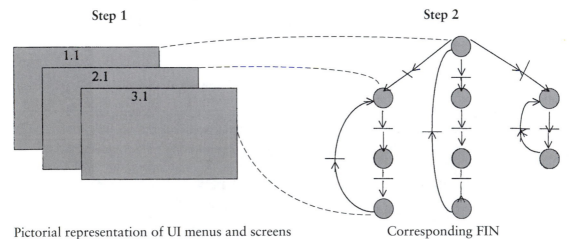

Pictorial representation of UI menus and screens   Corresponding FIN

Step 1: The pictorial representation of site architectures and web pages

Before drawing the FIN, a pictorial presentation of site architecture and web pages must be sketched according to each abstract UI object.

Step 2: Developing the FIN

1. The state (UI objects) representation

    can be used to represent a window widget (such as pop-up window, button, or menu)

    with no input action to enter this UI object, means it is in a start state, or start UI object, i.e. first window or homepage, as shown below:

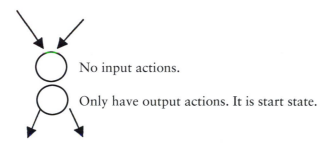

No input actions.

Only have output actions. It is start state.

2. User action representation

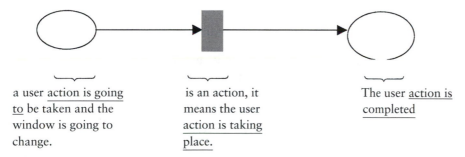

| a user <u>action is going to</u> be taken and the window is going to change. | <u>is an action, it</u> means the user <u>action is taking place.</u> | The user <u>action is completed</u> |

All preconditions satisfied must have a • black token and all postconditions must have no • token before an action can fire

3. The web site structure representation
   This consists of the site architecture found in the main pages and the required links. This is represented as a FIN.

4. Identify 3Is
   The main purpose in using FIN is to ensure that the pictorial presentation of the UI design is not:

1. illogical (flow of tasks carried out is not logical)
2. incorrect (task or screen design is incorrect)
3. incomplete (missing UI objects [windows or widgets])

When we develop a FIN, we will find some of these problems. We should, therefore, indicate where the fault is in the net. This is done by the following:

- If it is missing a screen or a window widget, we represent a dotted circle, like

- If it has an illogical flow, we represent a question mark on the net, like ?.
- If it is missing user action or system operation, we represent a dotted box, like

14.8.1 Illustrative example

This section gives the FIN for a web-based hotel guest registration system. Only a portion of the UI for this system is modelled.

Pictorial presentation of main menus

Hotel guest register homepage
Registration Booking Accommodation

The corresponding FIN for this menu is shown in Figure 14.11 and the pictorial presentation of a pop-up window is shown in Figure 14.12.

Note that each of the objects such as the AddNew page, Save button, Exit button, etc. correspond to a UI command object. Only UI command objects are used in FIN.

Chang and Dillon [1997] give further details on the use of FINs.

14.9 USABILITY TESTING AND QUALITY ASSURANCE

14.9.1 Usability testing

The field of evaluation of a UI of a web site, otherwise known as *web usability Evaluation*, [Nielsen, 1999] has become increasingly important with computer users being drawn from varied groups, from domain specialists to the average person.

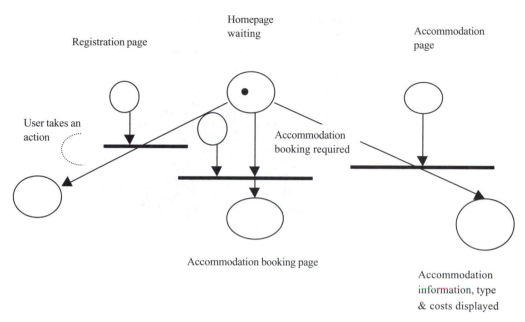

Figure 14.11   Using FIN to express the site structure

As explained in Chapter 3, the *Usability* of a computer software "is measured by how easily and how effectively it can be used by a specific set of users, given particular kinds of support, to carry out a defined set of tasks, in a defined set of environments" [Shackel, 1981].

In the literature, a variety of approaches have been adopted in order to evaluate usability of software and these can be categorized as follows: (1) empirical testing [Molich and Nielson, 1990], (2) inspection [Nielsen and Philips, 1993], (3) comparative usability measures [Dillon and Maquire, 1993], (4) formal complexity-based measures [Thimbleby, 1994], and (5) the MUSIC methodology [Bevan and Macleod, 1994].

The most useful of these from the viewpoint of web sites is empirical testing.

Empirical testing essentially involves testing the software product in a laboratory environment, which seeks to simulate as closely as possible the conditions under which the user uses it in the field. The user is asked to carry out designated tasks using the software product. The user's interaction with the system are recorded using video equipment and audio equipment, sometimes with timing markers or alternatively automatically using a software tool [Chang and Dillon, 1997]. One can also use a questionnaire. The primary focus of empirical testing is to uncover problems that the user is experiencing with the product. If the product is still in a prototype stage,

Pictorial presentation of a pop-up window

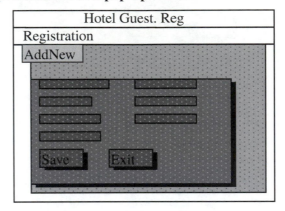

The corresponding FIN is expressed as follows:

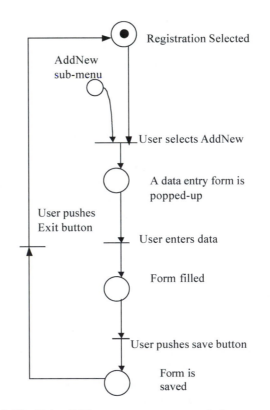

Figure 14.12 Using FIN to express a pop-up window

then the results of this testing can be utilized for refining the final version of the product. However, if the product is in the final stage of development, this approach is useful for determining whether one selects a given product. Three different testing laboratory set-ups can be utilized for empirical testing and these include (1) fixed laboratories, (2) portable laboratories, and (3) remote laboratories.

The main advantage of empirical testing is that it is able to directly monitor the performance reactions of the user to the particular interface and one does not have to rely on a usability expert trying to second-guess what a user's reaction might be. The disadvantages are that it is only useful for testing an implemented product, and therefore the ability to make changes to correct the problem immediately is greatly reduced. It can focus and identify specific problems that the user experiences with a given set of tasks but does not give an overall measure of the quality of the UI. It is also very time consuming, requiring tedious reviews of audio and video recordings if they are utilized. A new approach using automated usability testing which overcomes these weaknesses has been developed by Chang and Dillon [1997]. This helps to overcome the tedious nature of the reviews, automatically recording user actions and system messages in a database. This information in the database can then be used for display in various graphical forms and also for re-running the user actions.

There is a large body of literature on the factors which make up a usable UI. Molich and Nielsen [1990] and Bevan and Macleod [1994] have all identified factors based on different empirical studies. A study of the literature indicates that the following list of factors would give a comprehensive coverage of the notion of usability. As explained in Chapter 3, these factors include

1. System feedback
2. Consistency
3. Error prevention
4. Performance/efficiency
5. User like/dislike
6. Error recovery

The usability test layout and factors

In order to understand this we need to elaborate on the following:

1. Usability test layout and procedure
2. Test population

Practical test layout and procedure

The test layout consists of the test subject, the computer with the software being tested, and a test monitor. The test subject actually performs the given task on the software. The test monitor does not intrude on or advise the test subject how to carry out any specific action. Rather, the test monitor observes what the test subject is doing and enters a score on a checklist that is used to determine units against each of the relevant input factors discussed previously. For example, each time the test subject makes an error, one unit is recorded against the number of error items in the checklist. Note that this is a fairly minimal test setup without any expensive video cameras, audio equipment, etc. The test monitor performs the role of recording directly rather than going through an intermediate phase of video or audio recording followed by the analysis of these. The test monitor always sits behind the user and is to be unobtrusive and does not interfere with the user or prompt him in any way.

The task design during the usability test should contain a representative sample of tests that a user would actually carry out on the UI.

Basically, these tasks must be designed based on the following principles, namely, the tasks must be such that

1. they be work-related so as to simulate the manner in which the software would actually be used in the work environment;
2. they cover most of the significant functions of the package so that all significant and frequently used features of the interface are tested; and
3. the time of the test session clearly reflects work periods and is not too short so as to be artificial or too long so as to cause tiredness and fatigue to set in.

The population of test subjects considered should be sufficiently representative of the final user population in the case of the software. It is important that the testing be done by some actual users who will be utilizing the software on the internet. As the e-commerce site may have users all around the world, this could pose logistic difficulties in obtaining enough of each type of subject.

The essential criteria for the client-side GUI in e-commerce applications include the look and feel, input and output, interface operation, flow of interaction, and site maps. These should be based on the original functional requirements and the end user's perspective. In addition to testing the client-side screens, it is also necessary to usability test the server-side screens used for interaction with the e-commerce application, and backend systems or to respond to client inquiries by the e-commerce site staff.

14.9.2 Functional and system testing

Quality assurance of the e-commerce application must include the following types of tests:

1. Data validation and error handling testing
2. Database and end-to-end testing of different functions
3. Legacy interface testing
4. Exception handling testing
5. Response time and download time testing
6. Stress load testing
7. Security testing

Testing here means data input operation, data validation, system output, system feedback, and system response for both the client-side and server-side interfaces, so as to confirm that the system works correctly and efficiently. The very first stage is testing of each method or operation that the customer/user does. This is not testing the programming logic or efficiency of coding. The testing team should have flow of logic diagrams and the testing forms. This latter testing should be the responsibility of each programmer and should be done before the integration of the code and also before the database acceptance testing.

Data validation and error handling testing must ensure that

1. if the data is correctly input and submitted, the data is passed on to the right methods for processing. Feedback should also be provided to the user indicating that the data has been submitted for processing.
2. if incorrect data in range, type, or format is entered, the data is not accepted and an informative error message is generated.

Often, testers do not spend enough time on the second point, whereas this can pose real problems for a remote client who is unfamiliar with the system.

The so-called black box testing approach is normally adopted for point 2 in terms of allowed inputs and checked against expected outputs. The primary objective for test case design is to derive a set of tests that have the highest likelihood of uncovering defects in the application processes, database transactions, and data operations between users and the system.

Input/output tests are designed to be done on individual methods and objects involved in using and passing of these inputs. Correctness of expected outcome assures that the code required for input data integrity checking and provision of appropriate error and help messages are incorporated.

It is very important to enter some real data and make queries on the database to make sure that the transactions are completed. Then the server logs are examined to ensure that what was carried out on the client side actually happens on the server side.

Systematic end-to-end testing helps determine if the functions required of the system have been property implemented. In addition to this, one should do a function checklist test to ensure that *all* the functions have been implemented.

Frequently, the e-commerce system might be required to interact with a legacy system or databases. Here it is important to ensure that the interface between the e-commerce system and legacy system has been properly implemented. This requires detailed testing of different conditions under which data is interchanged between the two systems.

Exception handling testing is an important issue. When the user uses the browser to buy goods or deliver the goods on-line, there is a possibility that the user will be disconnected from the internet. This could lead to problems if there are some transactions running between the user and web system and the external system. It is very important that the web interface can handle power failure, electricity cut off, the computer being turned off, sudden disconnection, user, or external errors. There can be problems for on-line virtual markets and actions that involve money transactions. One would not want to be in the situation of the customers not knowing what happened with their money or order.

Response time or downloading time is an important issue to take into account when creating web sites. If web documents need to be downloaded with long down-loading times, users can get irritated and leave the web site. Testing the download-ing time of web documents under different speeds of connection such 28.8 Kbps/56.6 Kbps modems, T1, etc. is important. Also, testing the load time for different functions is important.

Most e-commerce systems require the handling of a large number of users at the same time. Furthermore, a large amount of data may be required by each user. Each user may also be involved in a long period of continuous use. It is important to estimate the likely number of users and carry out stress testing to determine if the system can adequately handle the required load. Loading tools are available to simulate the required conditions to allow stress testing.

For web systems involving e-commerce, security is very important. If a web system is not secure and does not convey the impression of security, customers or business partners will not use the system.

Thus, a web tester also needs to check to see if any directories will allow users or hackers to break into private sections to get hold of information on the web site.

Many web sites are now using Secure Socket Layer (SSL) for secure transac-tions. Although SSL can secure data transactions or transmissions, it does not protect the site from unauthorized entry to sensitive parts of the site's databases, and other methods such as access control have to be used in conjunction with it. Also, users may have browsers that do not support SSL and one needs to check if there is an alternate way of handling these browsers.

If a web site requires customers or users to log in to their account before they perform tasks on the web site, hackers could try to use invalid username/passwords to break into the account.

Testing of security involves

1. identification of sensitive information
2. user access level to sensitive information both for customer and e-commerce maintenance
3. method of restriction of access to sensitive information
4. administration of sensitive information

Scripting languages need to be tested because they are a constant source of security holes, and one could gain unauthorized entry to important information or resources through these. The actual details are different for each language and some even allow access to the root directory.

14.9.3 Web feature testing

Testing the features of a web site involves both the client and server sides. There are several things that need to be tested including (1) hyperlinks testing, (2) validation of HTML code, (3) script testing, (4) compatibility, (5) resolution, and (6) server-side testing [Nielsen, 1999].

There are several software tools that can be utilized for web feature testing including [O'Brien, 2000]

1. Site owner
2. Web site garage
3. Net mechanic

Also, these provide facilities for hyperlink tests, browser compatibility testing, and HTML syntax validation.

Web owners want as many users as possible to visit their site, each of which may use different platforms and different browsers. It is important, therefore, that the web site should try to be browser independent. Compatibility testing is necessary to

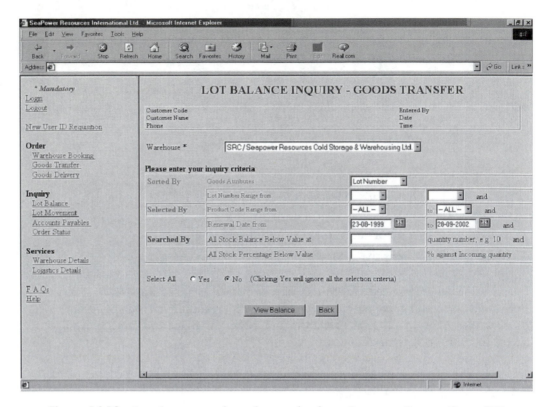

Figure 14.13 Sample screen of goods transfer from Seapower System iPowerB2B.com (using IE)

ensure that a site performs as intended across multiple operating systems and browser configurations. The web tester when performing browser compatibility testing should check if it works for the most important web browsers such as Netscape, Internet Explorer, Lynx and on different operating systems such as Mac OS, Windows, etc.

Note the same screen as it is viewed using two different browsers in Figures 14.13 and 14.14.

Errors can occur at places where the page does not follow the rules for proper HTML coding. These problems may cause a page to display incorrectly under different browsers. Several tools can be used to check this.

Compatibility problems can occur at places where you use an HTML tag or attributes that are not part of the HTML 4.0 standard and may not be supported by all browsers.

Web developers may design their web documents according to their own computer's resolution, and this could cause problems when one views these on computers with different resolutions. Hence, it is important to test whether web documents are acceptable under different screen resolutions.

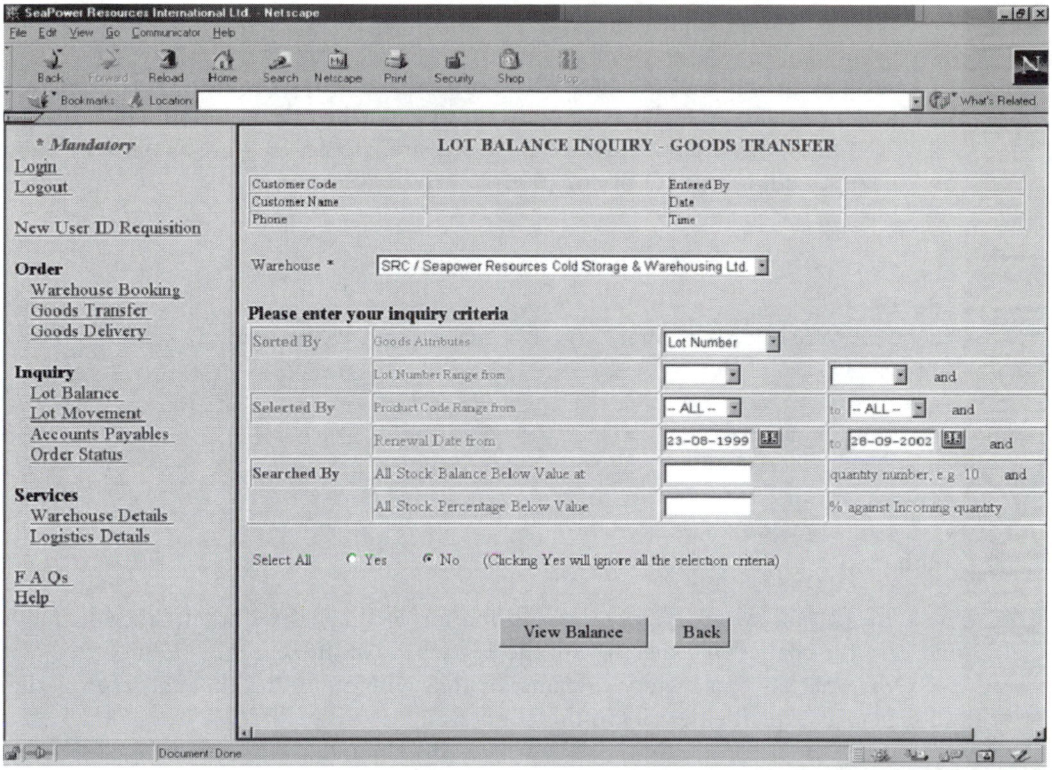

Figure 14.14 Sample screen of goods transfer from Seapower System iPowerB2B.com (using Netscape)

The web tester should always test to see whether or not the web documents are sized appropriately for printing, otherwise users may experience difficulty when printing them.

14.10 *WEB PRESENCE AND VISIBILITY*

It is not enough just to create a web site. You have to let the world know you are there. There are several techniques for doing this. The first of these is to ensure that you register with the main search engines such as Lycos, Altavista, etc. These browsers have their own indexes which they employ during keyword searches. Most of them use webcrawlers to find out and index new sites, but it pays to register with them. In addition, the webcrawlers or spiders note changes in the web site and may update indexes [Denucci, 2000; O'Brien, 2000].

Mobile agents or others often look at directory listings such as Yahoo! to identify a web site. Here, the way your web site is categorized and indexed results from a human editor for the directory service, reviewing the description of your web site.

In order to maximize your relevance score when a search engine is doing a particular search related to your site, it is important to make the title tag contain information related to the most important content of your site. Do not just use a company name or a jazzy sounding title [O'Brien, 2000].

Thus, a tag such as

```
<html>
<head>
<title> seapower: controlled temperature, warehousing, transport,
 logistics </title>
</head>
 is better than
<html>
<head>
<title> seapower </title>
</head>
```

If the title on each page contains information on the main content, this will greatly increase the chance of a match with the key words in the search.

Other mechanisms include exchanging links with other sites that address a similar audience, as explained earlier in this chapter.

14.11 *SUMMARY*

In this chapter we looked at internet and web-based advertising. We compared traditional advertising with internet-based advertising. Next, we examined different internet-based advertising techniques and strategies. Lastly, we considered business models and also measurement and pricing mechanisms.

In the second half of the chapter, we discussed web publishing. This included an examination of the issues of usability testing and quality assurance, design methodologies, authoring tools, and creation of web presence.

REFERENCES

Bevan, N. and Macleod, M., "Usability measurement in context," *Behaviour and Information Technology* (1994), 132–145.

Chang, E., "Object oriented user interface design and usability evaluation," Ph.D. Thesis, LaTrobe University, 1996.

Chang, E. and Dillon, T., "Use of perspectives for design of user interfaces," in *Int'l Conference on Object Role Models'93*, Magnetic Island, Australia, 1993.

Chang, E. and Dillon, T., "Automatic usability testing," in *Proceedings IFIP Interact 97*, 1997.

Chang, E. and Dillon, T., "The navigational aspects of the logical design of user interfaces," in *1st IEEE Int. Symp. on Object-oriented Real Time Distributed Computing ISORC'98*, Kyoto, 1998, 425–430.

Dinucci, D., Giudice, M., and Stiles L., *Elements of Web Design*, Peachpit Press, California, 2000.

Dillon, A. and Maquire, M., "Usability measurement – Its practical value to the computer industry," in *Proceedings of ACM/IFIP Human Factors in Computer System INTERCHI'93*, vol. 4, 1993, 145–148.

Dillon, T. and Tan P. L., *Object Oriented Conceptual Modelling*, Prentice-Hall, NJ, 1993.

Hanson, W. *Principles of Internet Marketing*, Thompson Learning, Southwestern College Publishing, US, 2000.

Molich, R. and Nielsen, J., "Heuristic evaluation of user interfaces," in *Proceedings of ACM Human Factors in Computing Systems CHI'90 4*, 1990, 249–256.

Nielsen, J. and Philips, V., "Estimating the relative usability of two interfaces: Heuristic, formal, and empirical methods compared," in *Proceedings of ACM/IFIP Human Factors in Computing Systems INTERCHI'93*, vol. 4, 1993, 214–221.

Nielsen, J., *Designing Web Usability*, New Riders Publishing, Indiana, USA, 1999.

O'Brien, T. E., *Commerce Handbook*, Tri-Obi Productions Pty. Ltd., Melbourne, Australia, 2000.

Schneider, G. P. and Perry, J. T., *Electronic Commerce*, Course Technology, 2000.

Shackel, B., "The concept of usability," in *Proc. IBM Software and Information Usability Symposium*, Poughkeepsie, NY, Sept. 1981.

Stering, G., Dillon, T., and Chang, E., *Proceeding of 8th IFIP Data Semantics Working*, 1999.

Thimbleby, H., "Formulating usability," *SIGCHI Bulletin* **April** (1994), 59–64.

Turban, E., Lee, J., King, D., Chung, H. M., and Lee, J. K., *Electronic Commerce – A Managerial Perspective*, Prentice Hall, Upper Saddle River, NJ, 2000.

De Troyer, O., "Designing well-structured web sites: Lessons to be learned from database schema methodology," in *Proceeding of the ER-Conference 98*, Springer-Verlag, Berlin, 1998. Lecture Notes in Computer Science.

Wielderhold, G., "Value added mediation in large scale information systems," in *Proceeding of IFIP DS-6 Conference*, Atlanta, Chapman & Hall, New York, 1995.

RECOMMENDED READING

Hanson, W. *Principles of Internet Marketing*, Thompson Learning, Southwestern College Publishing, US, 2000.

Komenar, M., *Electronic Marketing*, Wiley, New York, 1996.

Nielsen J., *Designing Web Usability*, New Riders Publishing, Indiana, USA, 1999.

Schneider, G. P. and Perry, J. T., *Electronic Commerce*, Course Technology, 2000.

Turban, E., Lee, J., King, D., and Chung, H. M., *Electronic Commerce – A Managerial Perspective*, Prentice Hall, Upper Saddle River, NJ, 2000.

Zeff, R. L. and Aronson, B., *Advertising on the Internet*, Wiley, New York, 1999.

15

Step-by-Step Exercises for Building the VBS

15.1   Introduction

15.2   Exercise 1 – VBS Homepage Design (Weeks 1 and 2)

15.3   Exercise 2 – Form Validation Using Javascript (Weeks 3 and 4)

15.4   Exercise 3 – Search Engines (Weeks 5–7)

15.5   Exercise 3A – Quick Search

15.6   Exercise 3B – Category Search

15.7   Exercise 3C – Advanced Search

15.8   Exercise 4 – Access Control (Weeks 8 and 9)

15.9   Exercise 4A – CartLogin

15.10 Exercise 4B – Create a New Customer Account

15.11 Exercise 4C – Change Password

15.12 Exercise 4D – CartLogout

15.13 Exercise 5 – Virtual Shopping (CartServices) (Weeks 10 and 11)

15.14 Exercise 6 – E-Payment (Week 12)

15.1   *INTRODUCTION*

In previous chapters, we used the VBS to explain the basic technologies for building an e-commerce system as well as the principles of e-commerce. In this chapter, we provide some step-by-step exercises for building the VBS using Java Servlet as the main programming tool. These exercises will give you hands-on programming experiences in building a B2C e-commerce system from scratch. The programming techniques applied in the exercises can in fact be adapted in many other e-commerce systems.

Altogether there are six exercises. Each exercise is devoted to building part of the system. After completing all the exercises, you will build the complete VBS, which incorporates most of the B2C e-commerce system functions including access control, shopping cart, and search engine.

It takes about 12 weeks to complete all the exercises. If this book is used for teaching a computing course in e-commerce, the exercises should fit neatly into a 12-week laboratory project for the students. It is recommended that students should form teams of three to four people to build the VBS. The exercises also provide a good reference for e-commerce programmers/developers and Information Technology managers.

In each exercise, we provide you with the objective, the program instruction, and some program hints. The objective defines the program requirements. In some cases, a flow chart is included to explain the main logic of the program. The program instruction guides you in writing the program, and the program hints help you to complete it. Of course, there are many different ways to write the programs. For your reference, the sample answers can be downloaded from the web site of this book. The program listings are labeled as Fig. Ax.y where x and y are the exercise number and program number, respectively. In other words, this chapter is designed to work in conjunction with the Web site of this book. By integrating all the programs, you can build the VBS. It is strongly encouraged that you try to write the programs yourself first. By doing so, you will learn a lot more. (For instructors who adopt this book, the "laboratory exercise version" is available for developing your own laboratory exercises.)

15.1.1   Typical e-shopping scenario

Let us first look at a typical shopping scenario for a VBS customer. To purchase some books, the customer will usually go through the following steps:

1. access the Web site of the VBS;
2. login to the VBS;
3. search for the required books;
4. select the required books and put them into a virtual shopping cart;
5. view/change the content of the shopping cart if required; and
6. check out and settle the payment.

Note that step 2 can also be deferred until check out is required. The aforementioned assumes that the customer has already registered with the VBS (i.e., he has an account in the VBS system already) and so he can login to the system at any time. The VBS should also provide a function for new customers to create an account in the VBS system.

15.1.2   VBS – system overview

Figure 15.1 gives a general overview of the major modules of the VBS system. It consists of four main systems as follows:

1. *Search engine system* – Provides different types of book search functions including quick search, category search, and advanced search.
2. *Access control system* – Provides various user login functions including creation of new user account and validation of login information.
3. *Shopping cart system* – Provides virtual shopping cart functions by using the Java Servlet session tracking technique.
4. *Checkout system* – Provides the checkout functions after shopping (it is referred to as e-payment).

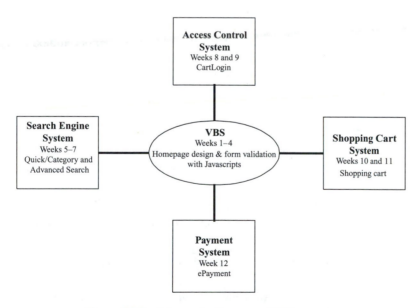

Figure 15.1   Schematic diagram of VBS system

The VBS project consists of six interrelated exercises (12 weeks) as follows:

- Exercise 1 (Weeks 1 and 2): VBS homepage design
- Exercise 2 (Weeks 3 and 4): Form validation with Javascripts
- Exercise 3 (Weeks 5–7): Search engines
- Exercise 4 (Weeks 8 and 9): Access control (CartLogin)
- Exercise 5 (Weeks 10 and 11): Shopping cart system
- Exercise 6 (Week 12): Checkout (e-Payment)

15.2   EXERCISE 1 – VBS HOMEPAGE DESIGN (WEEKS 1 AND 2)

15.2.1   Objectives

In the first two weeks, the major objective is to build the homepage of the VBS by using the nested framed page technique. Furthermore, we will also create a dynamic banner by using both the Servlet technique and the JavaScript technique. The dynamic banner can be rented out for generating advertising revenue for the VBS!

15.2.2   Program instructions

1. Build the VBS homepage by using three nested frames: banner, index, and content, as shown in Figure 15.2. The sample answer is given in Figure A1.1. Create the following HTML files for building the VBS homepage:
   - `Welcome.html`: The main welcome page/content page
   - `Top.html`: The banner page
   - `Menu.html`: The index page

   You are encouraged to design the homepage with as many web publishing techniques as possible. Of course, you can use the web publishing tools. Be innovative!

2. Using the Servlet technique, create a dynamic banner by displaying the four images as shown in Figure 15.3 in a cyclic manner. The sample answer is given in Figure A1.2.

3. Repeat step 2 by using JavaScript. The sample answer is given in Figures A1.3a–A1.3c.

4. Compare the pros and cons of using the two approaches (i.e. steps 2 and 3). Which one would you choose for your VBS system? Why?

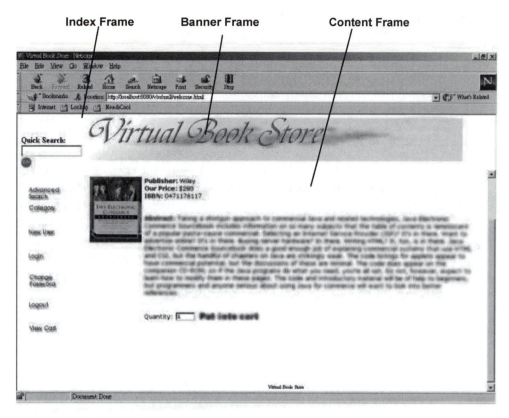

Figure 15.2   VBS homepage using nested frame page technique

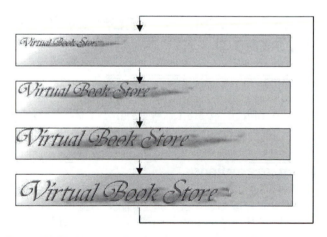

Figure 15.3   Dynamic banner based on four different images

15.2.3   Program hints

1. Nested frame pages can be created by using the `"frameset"` and `"frame"` tags. Details can be found in Chapter 3.
2. For the Servlet approach, the "dynamic" effect can be achieved by setting the response object `"resp"` of the HTML document as

   ```
   resp.setHeader("Refresh", "2");
   ```

   By doing so, it will ask the web browser to `"refresh"` the current web page once every 2 s. You should think about what to include in the web page each time and how to do it.
3. For the JavaScript approach, we cannot include the Javascript in the banner page. Why? We need to include the Javascript in a static page, otherwise it will be overwritten every time a new page is loaded. The index page is the best choice. Therefore, it is recommended that the Javascript that is used to invoke the animation in the banner page should be written in the index page.

   Let us give an overview of what should be done. In the `"welcome.html"` file, a function should be included to start the animation when the web page is loaded. In the `"menu.html"` file, an array should be used to keep track of which image is to be loaded next time. When the time comes, the image should be written in the banner page accordingly. To implement this using Javascript, please visit `http://developer.netscape.com/docs/examples/javascript/ formval/overview.html` and other Javascript references on the internet.

15.3   *EXERCISE 2 – FORM VALIDATION USING JAVASCRIPT (WEEKS 3 AND 4)*

15.3.1   Objectives

In Weeks 3 and 4, the objectives are to create an HTML form for creating a new account and to write the corresponding Javascripts for validating the input data.

15.3.2   Program instructions

1. Create an HTML form for creating a new user account. A sample is shown in Figure 15.4. The HTML form contains the following fields:
   - `Customer ID` (Text input: length 30)
   - `Password` (Password input: length 10)

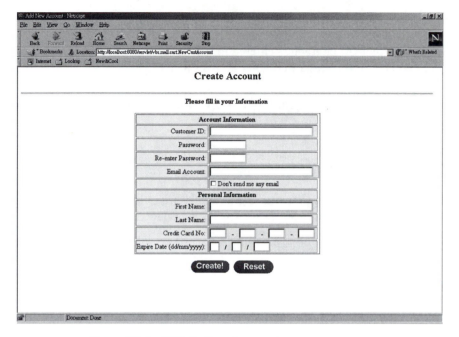

Figure 15.4   HTML form for creating a new account

- Re-enter Password (Password input: length 10)
- E-mail Account (Text input: length 30)
- A checkbox for "Don't send me any e-mail"
- First name (Text input: length 30)
- Last name (Text input: length 30)
- Credit card no.: It consists of four segments with four characters per segment
- Expiry date: There are three segments corresponding to date, month, and year
- Two buttons: "Create" for creating the account and "Reset" for resetting all fields

2. Write the Javascripts to perform the following validations*:

- to "trim" all text inputs;
- to check for the existence of "@" and "." characters in the e-mail field;
- to check whether the expiry date of the credit card is before or after current day. Return false if it is before (or equal to) current date;

---

* *Bonus*: All the form validation Javascript functions being used in the VBS system are "embedded" into the HTML file "JavaScriptCode.html" (Figure A2.4), which is invoked by the Java class "JavaScriptCode" (Figure A2.3). For clarity purpose, all the "global" constants being used in VBS system are collected into the file "MALL_CONST.java" (Figure A2.2).

- to ensure that numbers rather than characters are entered into the number fields (e.g. credit card number); and
- to ensure that the characters entered in the "Password" field are the same as that entered in the "Re-enter Password" field.

The sample HTML document for "Create New Customer Account" form validation using Javascripts is given in Figure A2.1.

15.3.3   Program hints

1. Details on HTML form elements (e.g., text input, password input, checkbox and buttons etc.) as well as an overview of JavaScript can be found in Chapter 3.
2. Please visit http://developer.netscape.com/docs/examples/ javascript/formval/overview.html to learn more about JavaScript and how it can be used to perform form validation.

15.4   *EXERCISE 3 – SEARCH ENGINES (WEEKS 5–7)*

15.4.1   VBS – System flow

In the previous two exercises, we created the "front-door" of the VBS. Using this as a start, we will build the functional modules for the VBS, which include search engines, user login, shopping cart, and checkout.

A general overview of the VBS system is shown in Figure 15.5.

As shown in Figure 15.5, the major modules are invoked by clicking the corresponding buttons in the menu page of the index frame. They include:

- Quick search button – for performing the quick search
- Advanced search button – for performing the advanced search
- Category search button – for performing the category search
- Login button – for customer login
- View cart button – for viewing the shopping cart
- Logout button – for logging out the system
- Change password button – for changing the password
- New account button – for creating a new account

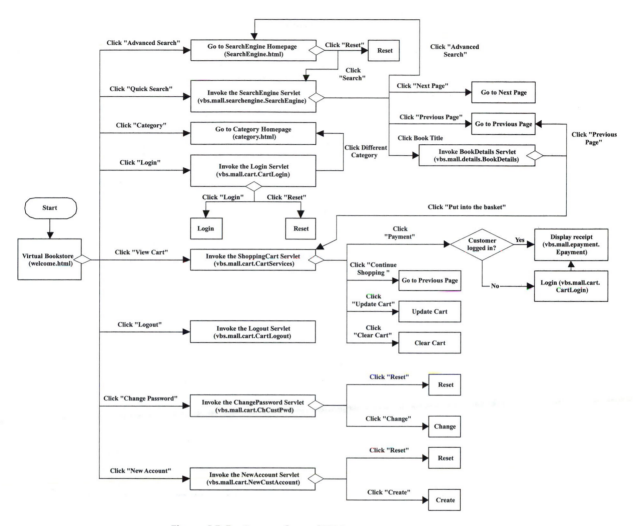

Figure 15.5   System flow of VBS

Figure 15.5 also shows the major program flow and the corresponding servlets/ HTML file being invoked in each case.

The VBS has a simple Microsoft Access database called mall.mdb. It contains the following tables:

- Bookstore – for storing the book information in the VBS
- Transaction – for storing the order information
- Customer – for storing registered customers' information.

The table fields are shown as follows:

	Fields	Descriptions
Bookstore table (bookstore)	ISBN	ISBN code
	Name	Title of the book
	Author	Author name
	Publisher	Publisher name
	Year	Year of publication
	Price	Price of book
	Category	Category of the book
	Desc	Description of the book
	Quantity	Available quantity of the book
Transaction table (transaction)	Customer	The name of the customer
	Isbn	The ISBN code of the book
	DeliveryQty	The quantity of the book delivered to the customer
	SubscribeQty	The quantity of the book ordered by the customer
Customer table (customer)	CustID	Customer ID
	Password	Password of the customer
	Email	E-mail of the customer
	GetNews	Indicate whether the customer is willing to receive latest news
	Bonus	Bonus points of the customer
	Gender	Gender of the customer
	Fname	First name of the customer
	Lname	Last name of the customer
	CreditNo1	The credit card number of the customer
	Expiry date	Expiry date of the credit card
	Address	The address of the customer

15.4.2 Objectives

In this exercise, the major objective is to build a search system that is composed of different search options:

- Quick search – based on simple keyword(s)
- Category search – based on a predefined book category
- Advance search – based on a combination of different book attributes including book name, author's name, price, etc.

15.4.3   Search engine: Program flow

Irrespective of the search techniques, the main program flow is the same as shown in Figure 15.6, which is given by the Java program `"DbQuery.java"` (Figure A3.2).

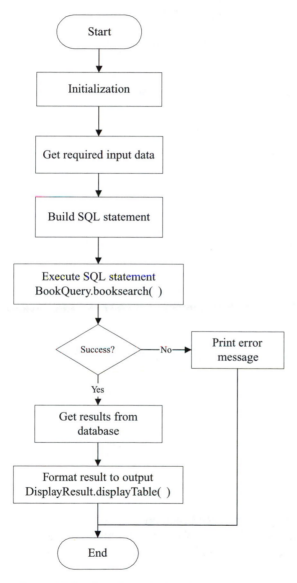

Figure 15.6   Generic logic flow for search engine

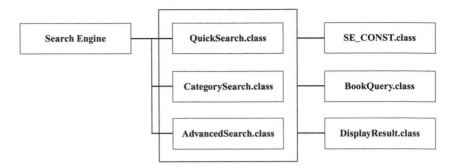

Figure 15.7   Program structure of the search engine package

For each search method, the main steps are as follows:

1. retrieve the search criteria entered by the user
2. build the SQL statement
3. collect the search results
4. format the search results in HTML format and display them

Steps 3 and 4 will be performed by two methods, namely `BookQuery.booksearch` and `DisplayResult.displayTable`, respectively.

As shown in Figure 15.7, the "search engine" package has three search programs, namely, `QuickSearch.java`, `CategorySearch.java`, and `AdvancedSearch.java` for performing quick search, category search, and advanced search, respectively.

In addition, `BookQuery.java` and `DisplayResult.java` contain the common servlet methods that can be shared by the three different search programs. `SE_CONST.java` (Figure A3.1) contains the common constant values (i.e. `String` values) that are used in the search engine programs.

15.5   *EXERCISE 3A – QUICK SEARCH*

15.5.1   Program instructions

1. Write the Quick Search Servlet (namely `QuickSearch.java`) to perform the simple keyword search. In this case, a user enters the key word in the text-box for the keyword search (see Figure 15.2). The search is then triggered by clicking the `"GO"` button.
2. The program will search for books in the database that have the specified keyword(s) in the following fields:

- book name
- author's name
- publisher
- price of the book
- year of publication
- ISBN code

3. Write two programs `BookQuery.java` and `DisplayResult.java` to perform the SQL query and format the query results, respectively. Note that these two programs can be shared by the other two search programs in the following exercises. Basically, by giving the search criteria (SQL command), the `booksearch()` method can perform the search and generate the `resultSet` object. The three different search programs can make use of `BookQuery.java` to perform the search by providing the respective search criteria. Once the resultSet object is generated, it can be passed to the `DisplayResult.class` to display the search results. The sample answers for `BookQuery.java`, `DisplayResult.java,` and QuickSearch.java are given in Figures A3.3, A3.4, and A3.5, respectively.

15.5.2 Program hints

1. Figure 15.8 shows the proposed program structure of the VBS up to the current stage. The root directory contains the `"image"` folder, the HTML files for the VBS, the `"search engine"` folder, and the `MALL_CONST.class`. By now you should have developed the HTML files. Let us explain the other components as follows.

   For ease of programming and management, a `MALL_CONST.class` can be written to define the String values that will be used throughout the VBS package. A sample can be found in Figure A2.2. The `"image"` folder contains the image files (e.g. book images, common icons, etc.) for the VBS. Similarly, `SE_CONST.class` defines the String values that will be used for the search engine package only (i.e., the three search programs only).

2. Suppose that the keyword entered by the user is `"Java."` The corresponding SQL statement for the quick search looks like this:

   ```
   Select name, author, publisher, price, ISBN, year from bookstore
   where name like "%Java%" or author like "%Java%" or publisher
   like "%Java%" ....
   ```

   Now the problem is that we need to turn the SQL `statement` into a `String` object and express it in terms of the String constants as defined in `SE_CONST.java`. Suppose that the entered keyword is stored in the variable `"keyword."` The search criteria (`bookQuery`) for the Quick search program in terms of the

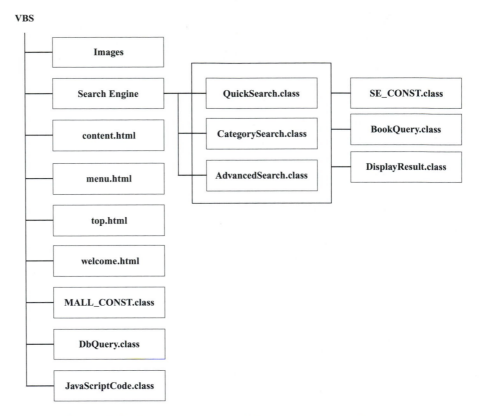

Figure 15.8 Program structure of VBS project (intermediate state)

constant values as defined in SE_CONST.java looks like the following:

```
bookQuery = "select" +SE_CONST.DB_BOOKNAME+ ","
  +SE_CONST.DB_AUTHOR+"," +SE_CONST.DB_PUBLISHER+ ","
  +SE_CONST.DB_PRICE+ "," +SE_CONST.DB_ISBN+ ","
  +SE_CONST.DB_YEAR+ "from" +SE_CONST.BOOKSTORE+ "where"
  +SE_CONST.DB_ISBN+ "like '%'";
```

```
if (!keyword.equals(""))
bookQuery +="and ("+SE_CONST.DB_AUTHOR+ "like '%" +keyword+ "%'
  or" +SE_CONST.DB_BOOKNAME+ "like '%" +keyword+ "%' or"
  +SE_CONST.DB_PUBLISHER+ "like '%" +keyword+ "%' or"
  +SE_CONST.DB_ISBN+ "like '%" +keyword+ "%' or"
  +SE_CONST.DB_CATEGORY+ "like '%" +keyword+ "%')";
```

The query contains two parts. The first part specifies the "bookQuery" string (the SQL string), which collects all the related book attributes for the query criteria. The second part appends the "keyword" string to the bookQuery to complete the whole SQL statement. In doing so, the `"like"` statement is used to perform the pattern matching.

3. Having defined the search criteria in terms of SQL, we can perform the search by `BookQuery.java`. There is a `booksearch()` method in `BookQuery.java`, which basically performs the following: (1) creates the JDBC connection, (2) executes the SQL statement, and (3) calls the `displayTable()` method of the `DisplayResult.class` to display the search result in HTML format.

4. Note that the `DisplayResult.class` needs to implement the multiple page function as described in Chapter 5.

15.6 EXERCISE 3B – CATEGORY SEARCH

15.6.1 Objective

Category search provides an HTML page (namely `category.html`) as shown in Figure 15.9 so that a user can search for the books under different categories. The category of each book is indicated by the `"category"` field in the book database (i.e. `mall.mdb`).

15.6.2 Program instructions

1. Create the category.html page similar to the one in Figure 15.9. The sample answer is given in Figure A3.6.

2. Write the Servlet CategorySearch.java to perform the category search. Basically, when the hyperlink of a particular category is clicked, the books of that category will be displayed. `CategorySearch.java` should make use of `BookQuery.java` and `DisplayResult.java` to perform the SQL query and to display the search results, respectively. The sample answer for `CategorySearch.java` is given in Figure A3.7.

15.6.3 Program hints

1. The category.html file is a simple HTML document that contains a table of hyperlinks for a user to invoke the CategorySearch program with different category parameters. A typical link is shown here:

```
<a href="servlet/vbs.mall.searchengine.CategorySearch?category=
%28e-commerce%29">Electronic Commerce</a><br>
```

In this case, a Servlet called `"CategorySearch"` with the input parameter `"category = e-commerce"` will be invoked when a user clicks this hyperlink.

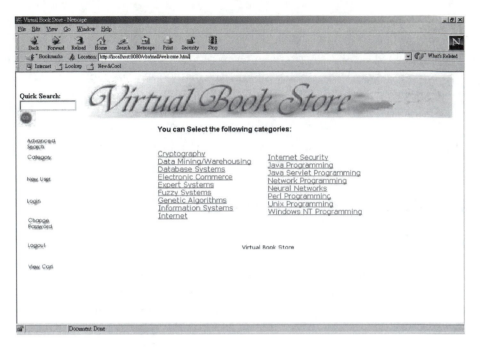

Figure 15.9 Category search screen

2. The major difference between Category search and Quick search is the SQL statement. In this case we search only for books with the specified word(s) in the category field. In terms of the constants as defined in SECONST.java, the SQL statement is

```
bookQuery = "select" +SE_CONST.DB_BOOKNAME+ ","
    +SE_CONST.DB_AUTHOR+ "," +SE_CONST.DB_PUBLISHER+ ","
    +SE_CONST.DB_PRICE+ "," +SE_CONST.DB_ISBN+ ","
    +SE_CONST.DB_YEAR+ "from" +SE_CONST.BOOKSTORE+"where"
    +SE_CONST.DB_ISBN+ "like '%' and" +SE_CONST.DB_CATEGORY+
    "like '%"+ category+ "%' order by" +SE_CONST.DB_ISBN+ " "
    +SE_CONST.ASC;
```

15.7 EXERCISE 3C – ADVANCED SEARCH

15.7.1 Objective

Compared with the previous search options, Advanced search provides the greatest flexibility because a user can perform the search based on a combination of the

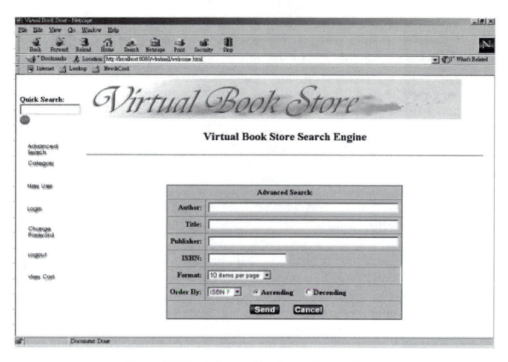

Figure 15.10 Advanced book search entry form

book attributes. The input form for the Advanced search is shown in Figure 15.10. Basically, the books that match with any of the specified keywords in the form will be displayed.

15.7.2 Program instructions

1. Construct the Advanced Book Search input form (namely Searchengine. html) with the following attributes:
   - Author name: text field (size 50)
   - Book title: text field (size 50)
   - Publisher: text field (size 50)
   - ISBN number: text field (size 20)
   - Display format: select box with three options of (1) 10 items per page, (2) 30 items per page, or (3) 50 items per page
   - Ordering: select box with three options of ordering by (1) price; (2) ISBN, or (3) year of publication

- A radio box for indicating whether the books should be displayed in ascending or descending order in accordance with the ordering criteria
- A checkbox for indicating whether the cover page image should be shown.

The form should have two buttons: `"Reset"` button for resetting the fields and `"Search"` button for triggering the search. The sample answer is given in Figure A3.8.

2. Write the corresponding Servlet program (namely `AdvanceSearch.java`). Again `AdvanceSearch.java` should make use of `BookQuery.java` and `DisplayResult.java` to perform the SQL query and to display the search results, respectively. The sample answer is given in Figure A3.9.

15.7.3 Program hints

1. The SearchEngine.html is a simple HTML form, which makes use of various HTML form elements (e.g., text boxes, radio buttons, checkboxes, list boxes, etc.). (Please refer to Chapter 3 for details.)

2. Note that in building the SQL statement, we need to take into account that some of the fields in the input form may be empty. The most straightforward way is to build the SQL query as follows by using the `"if-then"` statement during the parsing procedure.

```
bookQuery = "select" +SE_CONST.DB_BOOKNAME+ ","
  +SE_CONST.DB_AUTHOR+ "," +SE_CONST.DB_PUBLISHER+ ","
  +SE_CONST.DB_PRICE+ "," +SE_CONST.DB_ISBN+ ","
  +SE_CONST.DB_YEAR+ "from" +SE_CONST.BOOKSTORE+ "where"
  +SE_CONST.DB_ISBN+ "like '%'";

if (!author.equals(""))
bookQuery += "and" +SE_CONST.DB_AUTHOR+ "like '%" + author
  +"%'";
if (!name.equals(""))
bookQuery += "and" +SE_CONST.DB_BOOKNAME+ "like '%" + name
  +"%'";
...
```

Bonus: Book details

In order to speed up the search process and to display as many books as possible on a single page, the `DisplayResult` class will display only a concise list of books, as shown in Figure 15.11.

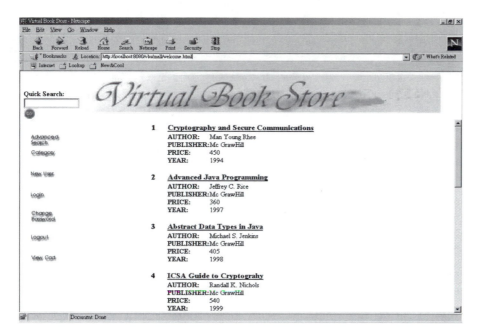

Figure 15.11   Sample book query result screen

Only when a user clicks the reference link for a particular book, the detail book summary will be displayed. (see Figure 15.12).

In fact, the `BookDetail` program is another type of search program which will use an "exact" match for matching a particular book. The program listing of this program is given in Figure A3.10 as a bonus.

15.8   EXERCISE 4 – ACCESS CONTROL (WEEKS 8 AND 9)

15.8.1   Objective

As an extension to the Servlet session tracking technique that we have learned about in Chapter 6, the main objective of this exercise is to construct a comprehensive customer's shopping cart login and account maintenance system for the VBS.

The main functions of the system include the following modules:

- shopping cart customer login module – `CartLogin.java`
- create new customer account module – `NewCustAccount.java`
- change customer account password module – `ChCustPwd.java`
- shopping cart customer logout module – `CartLogout.java`

Figure 15.12 Detail book summary

15.8.2 Program structure

Figure 15.13 shows the program structure up to the current stage. The grey boxes indicate the modules completed in the previous exercises. In this exercise, we will complete the modules of the CartLogin package.

As shown in Figure 15.13, the CartLogin system consists of four major program modules, which will be invoked accordingly when a user clicks on the respective buttons in the menu page. These modules are

- CartLogin.class – for logging into the system
- NewCustAccount.class – for creating a new customer account
- ChCustPwd.class – for changing the customer password
- CartLogout.class – for logging out of the system

In addition, there are two Servlet classes USER_CONST.class and Shopping-Cart.class. For ease of management, the former defines the constant values being used for developing the CartLogin package. The latter is a session object for customer login control. In fact, one of the unique features for the VBS system is that we make use of the ShoppingCart object (Figure A4.2) for both customer login and

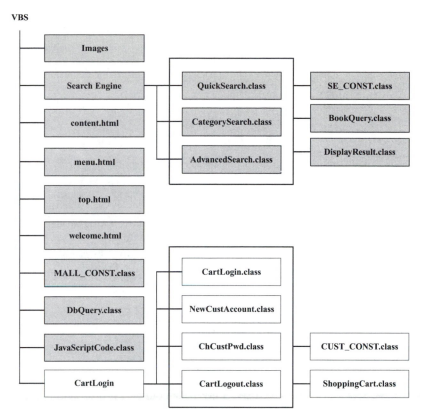

Figure 15.13 Program structure of VBS (intermediate state)

virtual shopping purpose. In other words, whenever a customer visits VBS, he will either be automatically assigned with a new shopping cart or "retrieve" the previous engaged shopping cart if his session object (ShoppingCart object) still exists. Moreover, he can log in to the VBS system (and the customer ID will be "logged" into the ShoppingCart object as well), or the system will ask for customer login when he decides to check out.

15.9   EXERCISE 4A – CartLogin

15.9.1   Objective

The system flow diagram for the CartLogin module is given in Figure 15.14.

As shown in Figure 15.14, the program logic for CartLogin is similar to the one given in Chapter 6 except that the program needs to cater for more cases as indicated

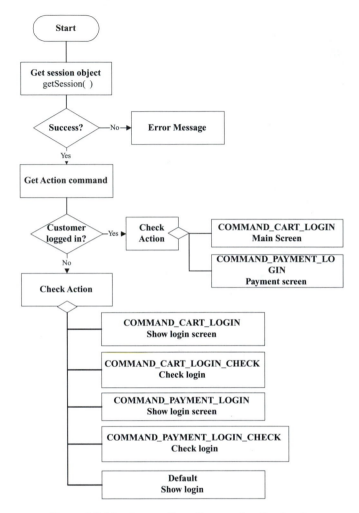

Figure 15.14   System flow diagram for CartLogin

by the "action" values passed to the server through the `HTTPServletRequest` object. The possible commands are:

- `COMMAND_CART_LOGIN` – show the customer login screen
- `COMMAND_CART_LOGIN_CHECK` – trigger the validation of the login information.
- `COMMAND_PAYMENT_LOGIN` – prompt the customer to log in when he wants to check out but he has not logged in before.
- `COMMAND_PAYMENT_LOGIN_CHECK` – trigger the validation of the login information for the case of `COMMAND_PAYMENT_LOGIN`.

Note that in general there are two login scenarios. In the first scenario, the customer requests to log in by clicking the "Login" button. In the second scenario, the system forces the customer to login because he wants to check out without logging into the system before.

The objective of the program is to cater for all the aforementioned situations.

15.9.2 Program instructions

1. For ease of management, it is recommended that the constant values to be used should be placed in a separate class file (see the sample USER_CONST in Figure A4.1).

2. Based on the program given in Chapter 6, write the CartLogin.java program to satisfy the requirements as shown in Figure 15.14. The sample answer is given in Figure A4.3.

15.9.3 Program hints

1. In fact, the CartLogin program for this exercise is very similar to the one given in Chapter 6. We just need to extend the previous program to cater for more situations.

2. Similar to the approach used in Chapter 6, the CartLogin program should consist of the following main modules:

   • doPost() – handle the different action options
   • showWelcome() – display the VBS welcome page or the "front-door"
   • showPayment() – invoke the payment module to be developed later
   • showLoginDialog() – display the login screen
   • checkLogin() – validate the login information

3. Since we need to use many field constants in the CartLogin program (and in the upcoming programs) such as for catering different "action" options, it is recommended that they be defined in a separate class file for ease of management as mentioned earlier. (Please refer to Figure A4.1.)

15.10 EXERCISE 4B – CREATE A NEW CUSTOMER ACCOUNT

15.10.1 Objective

The system flow diagram for the Create New Customer Account module is shown in Figure 15.15.

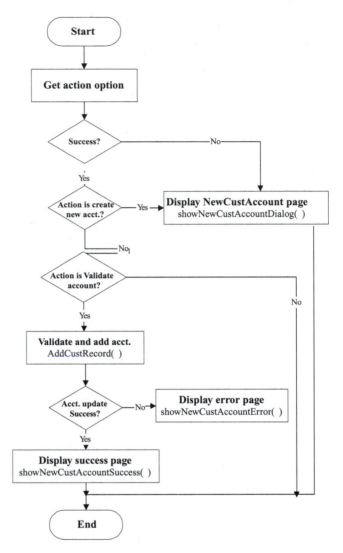

Figure 15.15 System flow for the Create New Customer Account module

The main steps are given as follows:

1. Display the new account HTML form when the customer clicks the "Create Account" button;

2. Validate the customer information after submitting the form; in particular, it is necessary to cross-check whether the user has registered already, in which case an error message should be displayed; and

3. Create the customer account by updating the database accordingly.

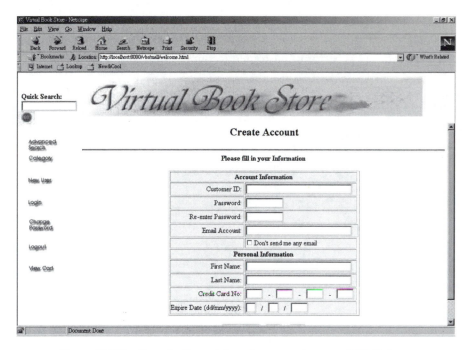

Figure 15.16 Sample Create New Customer Account HTML form

15.10.2 Program instructions

1. Design a "Create New Customer Account" form similar to the one given in Figure 15.16.
2. Write the Create New Customer Account program, namely NewCustAccount.java to satisfy the above requirements as given in Figure 15.15. Note that you need to incorporate the form created in step 1 into the NewCustAccount.java. The sample answer is given in Figure A4.4. Note that you need to perform form validation by means of JavaScript as well.

15.10.3 Program hints

You should include the following functional modules in NewCustAccount.java:

- doPost() – handles the action options
- showNewCustAccountDialog() – displays the Create New Customer Account HTML form
- showNewCustAccountSuccess() – displays the "Account Created Successfully" message

- showNewCustAccountError() – displays the Create New Account error message(s)
- addCustRecord() – performs customer account database validation

15.11   EXERCISE 4C – CHANGE PASSWORD

15.11.1   Objectives

The system flow diagram for the Change Password module is given in Figure 15.17.

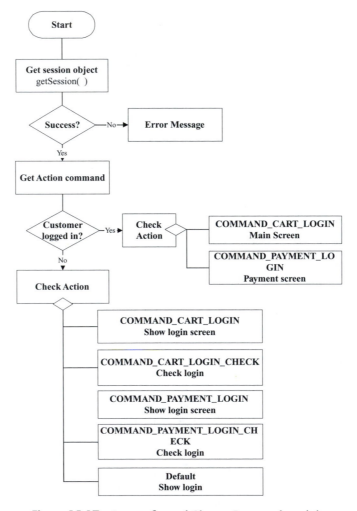

Figure 15.17   System flow of Change Password module

EXERCISE 4C – CHANGE PASSWORD

The logic is relatively straightforward. Firstly, the system checks for the "action" passed to the server. If no action is specifed, the Change Customer Password HTML form will be displayed. This HTML form will also be displayed if the action is not `"USER_CONST.COMMAND_CHANGE_PWD_CONFIRMATION"`.

When the customer submits the request for changing a password as indicated by the action of `USER_CONST.COMMAND_CHANGE_PWD_CONFIRMATION`, the password update method will be invoked (namely `CustPwdUpdate()`). After processing, the result (either success or failure) will be returned via the `showChangeCust-PwdSuccess()` and `showChangeCustPwdError()` methods, respectively.

15.11.2   Program instructions

1. Write the program Change Customer Password (`ChCustPwd.java`) to satisfy the aforementioned requirements as indicated in Figure 15.17. The change password form is as shown in Figure 15.18.

2. The program should have the following main methods:

   - `ShowChangeCustPwdError` – for showing the error messages
   - `ShowChangeCustPwdDialog` – for showing the Change Customer Password form

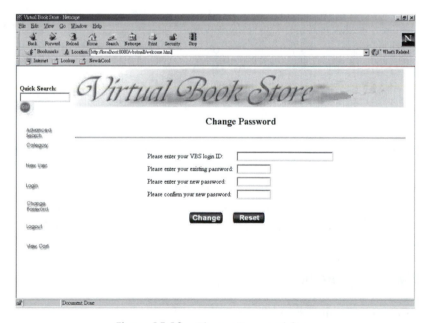

Figure 15.18   Change Password form

- `ShowChangeCustPwdSuccess` – for showing that the customer password has been changed successfully
- `CustPwdUpdate` – for updating the new customer password into the database

The sample answer is given in Figure A4.5.

15.11.3   Program hints

The program logic follows a similar approach as the Create Customer Account program.

15.12   EXERCISE 4D – CartLogout

15.12.1   Objective

The objective of the `CartLogout` module is to allow the customer to log out of the system whenever required. Technically, it eliminates the `ShoppingCart`'s session object so that a new session can be started (possibly by another customer) from the same machine.

As shown in Figure 15.19, the core program logic is very simple. Firstly, the program should check whether a session object (`ShoppingCart`) exists or not. If a session object exists, the program will clear the session object; otherwise, it will display an error message showing that the user has not logged in.

15.12.2   Program instructions

1. Write the program `CartLogout.java` for performing the log out function as indicated in Figure 15.19. The sample answer is given in Figure A4.6.
2. The program should contain the following methods, namely
   - `ShowNotLogin` – for showing that the customer has not logged in
   - `ShowLogout` – for showing that the user has logged out successfully

15.12.3   Program hint

The method for closing a session is `session.invalidate`.

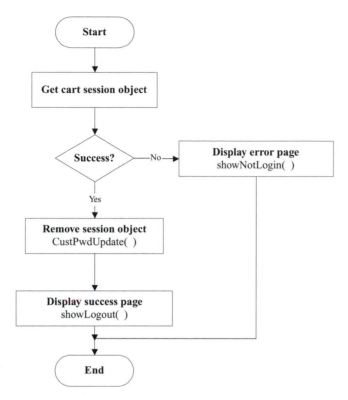

Figure 15.19 System flow for CartLogout module

15.13   *EXERCISE 5 – VIRTUAL SHOPPING (CartServices) (WEEKS 10 AND 11)*

15.13.1   Objective

In Chapter 6, we discussed how to employ the Servlet session tracking technique for supporting customer login using the ShoppingCart object.

In this exercise, we will implement another core function of the ShoppingCart object – "virtual shopping" – and demonstrate how it can be integrated into our VBS system.

15.13.2   Program structure

Figure 15.20 shows the program structure up to the current stage. The grey boxes indicate the modules completed in the previous exercises. In the following exercises,

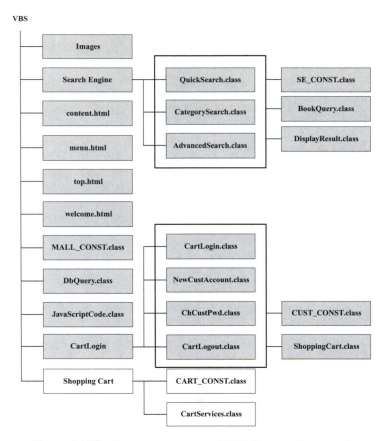

Figure 15.20   Program structure of VBS (intermediate state)

we are going to build the CartServices program within the "Shopping Cart" package (i.e. the white box).

As shown in Figure 15.20, the Shopping Cart system consists of two program modules:

- CART_CONST.class
- CartServices.class

The CART_CONST.class (see Figure A5.1) defines the constant values (e.g. action commands and field values) to be used for virtual shopping. CartServices.class provides various shopping cart services such as viewing the shopping cart content.

In the last exercise, we have introduced the shopping cart object.

The main attributes of a shopping cart to support virtual shopping are

- Customer identity (ID)
- Number of items being purchased
- Total price of the goods (books) being selected
- List of goods selected including product code, quantity of purchase, item price, and item description.

For a detailed description of the shopping cart object, please refer to Section 6.4.2 of Chapter 6.

15.13.3 CartServices: System flow

Figure 15.21 shows the flow chart of the shopping cart system for virtual shopping. The main tasks are performed by `CartService.class`.

In principle, the `CartService` program implements different virtual shopping functions, including

- `COMMAND_ADD` – add books into the shopping cart object
- `COMMAND_UPDATE` – update the information stored in the shopping cart object
- `COMMAND_CLEAR` – clear the current shopping cart object while still keeping it for later use

15.13.4 Program instruction

1. Write the `CartServices` Servlet to satisfy the requirements as indicated in the aforementioned flow chart. Work out the main logic flow of the `CartServices` program.
2. The CartServices program should have the following main modules:
   - `doPost()` – handles different types of `CartServices` commands;
   - `addItem()` – adds books (i.e. the ISBN number(s)) and order quantity into the shopping cart object (cart).
   - `updateItem()` – updates the order quantity for a particular book already in the "cart" object and removes the book from the `"cart"` object if new order quantity is zero.
   - `clearCart()` – clears all the books in the ucart object.
   - `viewCart()` – displays the current contents of the shopping cart (see Figure 15.22).

   The sample answer is given in Figure A5.2.

Figure 15.21   System flow for the CartServices

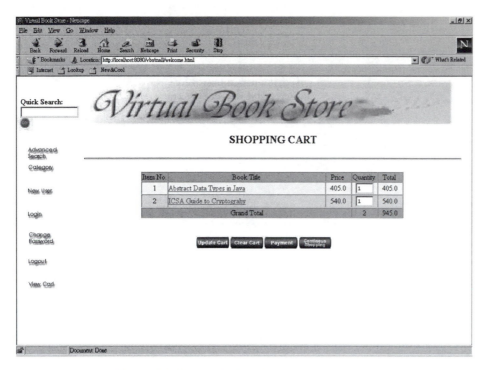

Figure 15.22 Displaying shopping cart content

15.14   *EXERCISE 6 – E-PAYMENT (WEEK 12)*

15.14.1   Objective

In the final exercise, we are going to complete the whole e-shopping procedure by performing the checkout or e-payment function. For simplicity, we assume that payment is made by simply posting the order into the transaction database. In addition, the e-payment system also performs other necessary checkout functions as follows:

• getting the customer's personal information from the database according to the user identity stored in the ulog object

• sending an e-mail to the customer for confirming the order

• displaying the books purchased

The main system logic is given in Figure 15.23.

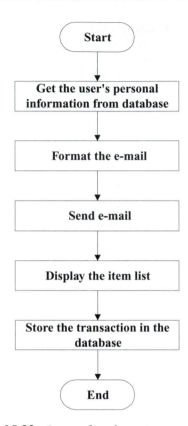

Figure 15.23   System flow for e-payment system

15.14.2   Program structure

Figure 15.24 shows that we have almost completed all the VBS program modules (all the grey boxes are the completed modules). In this exercise, we are going to complete the e-payment package, which consists of the e-payment class.

15.14.3   Program instruction

1. Create a transaction database with a table consisting of at least the following fields:

   - Customer: The name of the customer
   - ISBN: The ISBN code of the book
   - DeliveryQty: The quantity of books delivered to the customer
   - SubscribeQty: The quantity of books ordered by the customer

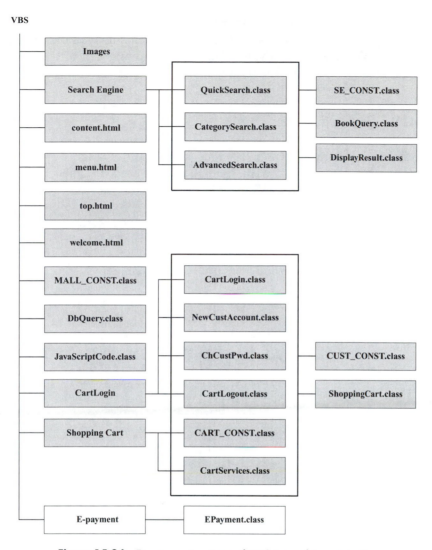

Figure 15.24 Program structure of VBS (complete version)

2. Write the e-payment Servlet program, namely "Epayment.java" to satisfy the requirements as indicated in the aforementioned flow chart.

3. The program should have the following main modules:
   - payment() – this is the entry point of the program
   - formatEmail() – it obtains the customer's personal information from the database; generates the payment notice; and calls the sendEmail() method to send an e-mail to the customer confirming the purchase

- sendEmail() – it sends the confirmation e-mail
- displayList() – it displays the order summary and invokes the updateDB method to update the transaction database accordingly ,
- updateDB() – it updates the transaction database

15.14.4   Program hints

The following program* is for sending an e-mail message "emessage" to "mailhost.vbs.com." To use the program, we need to import "sun.net. smtp.SmtpClient". The sample answer is given in Figure A6.1.

```
private void sendEmail(PrintWriter out1, String sender, String
   receiver, String subject, String emessage)
{
          PrintStream out; SmtpClient _email;
          try{
                    _email = new SmtpClient("mailhost.vbs.com");
                    _email.from(sender);
                    _email.to(receiver);
                    out = _email.startMessage();
                    out.println("From: " + sender);
                    out.println("To: " + receiver);
                    out.println("Subject: " + subject);
                    out.println(emessage);
                    out.flush();
                    out.close();
                    _email.closeServer();
          }catch(Exception e){
                    out1.println(e.toString());
          }
}
```

---

* This program is written by Gary Li; listed with his permission.

Index

Absolute URL, 70–71
Abstract Syntax One (ANS.1) notation, 222
Abstract user interface (UI) objects, 407–411
Acceptability, of payment, 286
Access control system, 429, 445–447
Acknowledgment, 35
Acquirer, 288
Action, 412–414
ACTION attribute, 79
Activated condition, 412
Active Server Page (ASP) code, 96, 100–101
ActiveX controls, 56
Address, 32
ADSL. *See* Asymmetric Digital Subscriber Line
Advanced search engine, 126–127, 151–155
Advertising, 389–426
    banners, 392–396, 430
    e-mail and, 392
    effectiveness of, 399
    pricing models and, 399–400
    quality assurance, 414–423
    usability testing, 414–419
    web presence and visibility, 423–424
Agent-based auction supporting sites, 385

Agent Transfer Protocol (ATP), 254
Agents, mobile, 251–263
Aggregation, 363
Agile wallet, 311
Aglet Software Development Kit (ASDK), 254
Aglets, 254–262
AH. *See* Authentication Header
Alert message, 90, 91
Alert protocol, 247–248
ALIGN attribute, 68, 74–75
Allow header, 44
Amazon.com, 8–9, 321, 325–328, 338
American National Standards Institution (ANSI), 367
American Online (AOL), 393
Anchor tag, 70
Andreeseen, Marc, 39
anewShop.com, 338–339
Anonymity, of payment, 286, 298
Anonymous session tracking, 176
ANS.1. *See* Abstract Syntax One
ANSI. *See* American National Standards Institution
AOL. *See* American Online
APDUs. *See* Application Protocol Data Units
API. *See* Application programming interface

Apple script, 100
Applets, 101–102
Application gateway, 238–239
Application layer, 36–38
Application programming interfaces
    (APIs), 20, 103–105
  JDBC. *See* Java Database Connectivity
  session tracking techniques, 177–195
Application Protocol Data Units (APDUs),
    308
Architecture, of web, 39–40
ARIBA, 357, 359, 364
ASC X12 standard, 367
ASCII format, 42
ASDK. *See* Aglet Software Development
    Kit
ASP. *See* Active Server Page
Association rules, 278–279
Asymmetric Digital Subscriber Line
    (ADSL), 31
Asymmetric key encryption, 207
ATP. *See* Agent Transfer Protocol
Attributes, 68, 74–75, 79–80
Auction Universe, 386
Auctions, 384–387
Audience, 402, 405–406
Authentication, 50, 175, 187, 204–205,
    216–225, 288
Authentication Header (AH), 230,
    232–233
Authorization, 44, 352
Autonomous systems, 34–35
Availability, 204

B2B. *See* Business-to-business
B2C. *See* Business-to-consumer
Babel, tower of, 274
Backend systems, 40, 96, 125, 344
Bank of America, 375
Banking, 301–303, 375–377
Banner advertising, 392–396, 430
Banner Exchange, 395
Barnes and Noble, 337
BaseT standards, 31

Basic Encoding Rules (BER), 222
Basic Rate Interface (BRI), 31
Bastion host, 240–241
Beenz, 310
BER. *See* Basic Encoding Rules
Best-effort service, 29
Bezos, Jeff, 8
BGCOLOR attribute, 74–75
BGP. *See* Border Gateway Protocol
BizTalk (MS), 359, 369
Black box testing approach, 419
Blind signature, 289–299
Block cipher, 214
Bonus points system, 310
Bookstore, virtual. *See* Virtual bookstore
BORDER attribute, 74
Border Gateway Protocol (BGP), 35
Border properties, 84
Borland JBuilder, 109
BPR. *See* Business Process Reengineering
Brand name products, 335
BRI. *See* Basic Rate Interface
Bridge, 97
Brokers, 338–341
Browsers, 60, 87, 176, 423
Burn rate, 7
Business models, 352–367
    B2B. *See* Business-to-business
    B2C. *See* Business-to-consumer
    electronic commerce and, 6, 17–21, 243
    emergent models, 342–344
    internet advertising. *See* Advertising
    internet publishing. *See* Publishing
    See also specific types, processes
Business Object, 404
Business-oriented (B2B) e-commerce, 315,
    349–372
Business platforms, 273
Business process, defined, 343
Business Process Reengineering (BPR),
    343
Business-to-business (B2B) systems, 3,
    126, 159, 315, 349–372
    auctions and, 386–387

features of, 351–352
model, 8
Trading Process Network, 10
XML and, 368–370
See also specific companies, processes
Business-to-consumer (B2C) systems, 3
Amazon.com, 8–9
applications, 126
e-commerce, 8–9, 161
model, 6–8
Priceline, 10–11
web site, 176
See also specific companies, processes
Button, 413
Buyer-oriented systems, 15, 353–357

C code, 100
C++ code, 100, 271
C2C. *See* Consumer-to-consumer systems
CA. *See* Certification authority
Cable TV, 398
Cache control, 50
Caesar cipher, 207
Calvin Klein, 400
Capital costs, 321
Capture codes, 297
Cardholder, 288
Carrier Sense Multiple Access with
    Collision Avoidance (CSMA/CA),
    31
Carrier Sense Multiple Access with
    Collision Detection (CSMA/CD),
    30–31
CartLogin, 447–449
CartServices, 455–459
Cascading style sheets (CSS), 82–86, 271
Cash-and-transfer, 301–303
Catalogs, 15, 341, 357
CBC. *See* Cipher block chaining
CDF. *See* Channel Definition Format
CDMA. *See* Code Division Multiple
    Access
CDNow, 329
CDPD. *See* Cellular Digital Packet Data

Cellular Digital Packet Data (CDPD), 32,
    267
Central processing unit (CPU), 307
CERN. *See* European Particle Physics
    Laboratory
Certificate chain, 222–223
Certificate revocation list (CRL), 225
Certification authority (CA), 220–225,
    289
CGI. *See* Common gateway interface
Challenge and response protocol,
    224–225
Change cipher protocol, 247–248
Channel Definition Format (CDF), 273
Chat rooms, 396, 400
Checkbox, 80–81
CHECKED attribute, 80
Checkout system, 429
Checksum, 226
Chemdex.com, 360
Cipher block chaining (CBC), 214, 233
Circuit level gateway, 239–240
Cisco systems, 335, 357
CLASS attribute, 86
Click-through rate, 400
Clickshare, 310
Client-server programming, 95
Client-side image map. *See* Image map
Client-side programming, 55–94
CNET store, 318
COBRA, 177
Codd, E.F., 127
Code Division Multiple Access (CDMA),
    32, 267
Code model, 342
Coin signing, 298
Collaborative filtering, 331
Collaborative supply chain management,
    365–367
Commerceone.com, 363
Common Gateway Interface (CGI), 96,
    98–100
Compartmentalized organization, 17
Compatibility, 96

Competitive pricing, 320
Compilation, of servlets, 109–110
Compiled languages, 100
Complexity-based measuring, 415
Components-based models, 342
Compression methods, 42, 51, 71, 247
Conceptual model, 342, 407
Concordia, 254
Concrete user interface objects, 62, 413
Condition, 412
Confidentiality, 204–205, 247, 288
Consistency, 58, 417
Consortiums, 364
Consumer-oriented e-commerce,
  315–348
Consumer-to-consumer (C2C) systems,
  9–10, 384–387
Container tags, 64
Content creation, 63
Content integrity, 51
Content, of web sites, 281
Content-type header, 44
Convenience, 320
Cookies, 48–49
  servlet fundamentals and, 110–115
  session tracking techniques and,
    175–176
Core server-side programming tool, 105
CORRA programming techniques, 103
Cost-effectiveness, 96
Covisint.com, 364
CPM model, 399
CPU. *See* Central processing unit
Credit card payments, 287–298, 301
CRL. *See* Certificate revocation list
Cross-selling, 391
Cryptography. *See* Encryption
CSMA/CA. *See* Carrier Sense Multiple
  Access with Collision Avoidance
CSMA/CD. *See* Carrier Sense Multiple
  Access with Collision Detection
CSS. *See* Cascading Style Sheets
Customer account creation, 449–452
Customer service, 321, 357

Customization, 13, 15, 16, 320, 344
Cybershopping, 13

Data Encryption Standard (DES),
  207–208
  temporary, 213
Data mining, 277–281
Data networks, 5
Data validation, 57
Database connectivity, 125–158, 160
Database systems, 96–97, 126–127, 359
DCM. *See* Demand Chain Management
Decision trees, 279–280
Dedicated file (DF), 308
DELETE statement, 106, 129, 133, 142
Dell, 320, 335, 357
Demand Chain Management (DCM), 13,
  351
Demand-driven model, 13
Demilitarized zone (DMZ), 242
Department stores, 317
Deposit-and-clear, 301
DER. *See* Distinguished Encoding Rules
DES. *See* Data Encryption Standard
DF. *See* Dedicated file
Dial-up modem, 30
Diffie-Hellman protocol, 209–210, 231,
  246
Digital catalogue, 15
Digital certificates, 220, 223, 224
  authentication and, 220–221
  chain, 222–223
  hierarchy of, 223
  revocation of, 225
  SET protocol and, 289
  X.509 framework, 221–222, 225
Digital envelope, 292–293
Digital goods, vs physical goods, 15
DIGITAL phenomenon, 3–4
Digital signature, 297
Digital signature standard (DSS), 210,
  217–219
Direct fund transfer, 303
Direct mailing, 318

Direct-selling, 15, 335–336
Directory services, 424
Disintermediation, 381
Disney, 384
Distance vector routing protocol, 34
Distinguished Encoding Rules (DER), 222
Distribution portals, 365
Divisibility, of payment, 286
DMZ. *See* Demilitarized zone
DNS. *See* Domain Name System
Document mark up, 273
Document object, 88
Document Object Model (DOM), 272, 276
Document Style and Semantics Language (DSSSL), 271
Document Type Definition (DTD), 268–269
DOM. *See* Document Object Model
Domain Name System (DNS), 36–37
Domino Go web Server, 104
Door-to-door sales, 318
Dot-decimal format, 32
Dotcoms, 7
Downloading time, 57, 419–420
DS. *See* Dual signature
DSS. *See* Digital Signature Standard
DSSSL. *See* Document Style and Semantics Language
DTD. *See* Document Type Definition
Dual home bastion host, 240
Dual signature (DS) method, 289–292
Dutch auction, 384
Dynamic pricing, 15
Dynamic Web Enterprises, 368
Dynamic web pages, 46–48, 98

Earnings per share (EPS), 7
eBay, 9–10, 386
E-business. *See* E-commerce
E-cash, 298–301
Ecashtechnologies.com, 298
ECB. *See* Electronic Code Book
ECC. *See* Elliptic Curve Cryptography

E-checks, 301–303
E-commerce
  advanced technologies, 21, 251–282
  advertising. *See* Advertising
  automation and, 5
  business models and, 6, 17–21, 243
  changes brought by, 13–14
  defined, 2–3
  development of, 14–18
  different perspectives on, 4–6
  electronic business model and, 17–18
  funding for, 16
  implementation of, 14–18
  key drivers of, 5
  myths about, 14–18
  physical commerce and, 2–3
  process-oriented approach, 344–345
  publishing and. *See* Publishing scenario
  retailing and, 11–13, 317–319
  security, 20
  servicing scenario. *See* Servicing scenario
  supply chain management scenario. *See* Supply chain management scenario
  three-layer model, 4
  traditional business model and, 17–18
  types of, 6–8
  typical architecture of, 19
  web page building and, 16
  web programmers and, 16–17
  See also specific applications, companies, processes
EDI. *See* Electronic Data Interchange
EDIFACT system, 367
Education, 378–379
EF. *See* Elementary file
Efficiency, 59, 96
Egghead.com, 17
Ehitax.com, 364
Electronic Code Book (ECB), 214
Electronic commerce. *See* E-commerce
Electronic data interchange, 2
Electronic Data Interchange (EDI), 351, 367

Electronic information, 5
Electronic payment. *See* Payment methods
Element Handler, 272
Elementary file (EF), 308
ElGamal algorithm, 213, 219
E-mail, 392
E-malls, 334–335
Embedded style sheets, 84–85
Emergent business model, 342–344
Empirical testing, 415, 417
Employment, 381
Encapsulating security payload (ESP)
    service, 230, 233–234
Encryption, 2, 21, 203–228
    DES, 207–208, 213
    Diffie-Hellman protocol, 209–210, 231,
        246
    dual signature, 291
    Elliptic Curve Cryptography (ECC),
        213–214
    hybrid, 213
    IDEA code, 208
    key distribution problem, 209
    private key encryption, 207–209
    process of, 205
    RSA methods, 210–213, 217–220, 291,
        298
    substitution, 207
    transposition, 207
    two types of, 207
End-to-end testing, 419
English auction, 9, 384
Enterprise Resource Planning (ERP)
    systems, 351, 370
Entertainment, 384
Entity header, 44
EPROM. *See* Erasable programmable
    read-only memory
EPS. *See* Earnings per share
Erasable programmable read-only
    memory (EPROM), 308
ERP. *See* Enterprise Resource Planning
E-R relationship, 127
Error handling testing, 419
Error prevention, 59, 417

Error recovery, 59–60
E-services, 373–388
    categories of, 374–375
ESP. *See* Encapsulating security
    payload
ESPN, 399
Ethernet connections, 30–31, 57
Eurobanner, 394–396
European Particle Physics Laboratory
    (CERN), 38–39
Event handlers, 88
E-wallet, 311
Exception handling, 419
Exit button, 414
Expires header, 44, 50
eXtensible Markup Language (XML),
    252, 267–277
    applications of, 273–275
    architecture for, 275–277
    displaying documents, 271
    Document Type Definition, 269
    HTML and, 267–268
    processing of, 271–273
    programming interfaces, 271–273
    recommended web sites for, 282
    style sheets, 271
    syntax of, 267–271
eXtensible Style Language (XSL), 271
Extent driven model, 255–256
External style sheets, 83–84

Feedback, 58, 417
File input field, 81
File transfer protocol (FTP), 36, 40
FIN. *See* Flow of Interaction Net
Financial advice, 384
Financial Services Technology Consortium
    (FSTC), 301
Firewalls, 236–242
Firing rules, 412
Flow of interaction, 61, 411
Flow of Interaction Net (FIN), 404, 407
Flowers, selling of, 328
FOBchemicals.com, 363
Fonts, 68, 84

Ford Co., 335
Form, 79–82
  Javascript and, 89–92
  object, 88
  posting, 177
  validation, 86, 89–92, 432–434
Forums, 341
4C payment methods, 286–287
Fragmentation, 247
Frames, 75–79
Franchise stores, 317
From header, 44
Front end, 96
FSTC. *See* Financial Services Technology
  Consortium
FTP. *See* File transfer protocol
Funding, 16
Fuzzy audience, 402

General Electric, 357
Generalized e-stores, 317–318
GenericServlet, 105
GEOShops, 318
GET command, 41, 47, 51, 106
GIF. *See* Graphics Interchange Format
Gift products, 328
Gigabit Ethernet standard, 31
Global certification system, 224
Global economy, 3, 5
Global reach, 321, 391
Global System for Mobile
  Communication (GSM), 267
Goodman-Kruskall Tau, 279
Graph, directed, 279
Graphical User Interface (GUI), 96, 109
Graphics Interchange Format (GIF), 42,
  71
Group-oriented pricing, 15
GSM. *See* Global System for Mobile
  Communication
GUI. *See* Graphical User Interface

Handshaking procedures, 244–247, 309
HEAD request method, 51
Headers, types of, 43–44

HFF. *See* Hidden Form Fields
Hidden Form Fields (HFFs), 81–82, 155,
  161, 177
  session tracking techniques and,
    162–170
Hierarchical organization, 15
Hierarchical trust system, 223–224
Hit rate, 399
HMAC algorithm, 216, 233
Hop-by-hop basis, 51
Horizontal rule, 64, 68
Hotel Registration system, 407–410,
  414
Hotjobs, 281
HTML. *See* Hypertext markup language
HTTP. *See* Hypertext transfer protocol
HTTPS. *See* Secure hypertext transfer
  protocol
Human resources, 370
Hybrid encryption, 213
Hyperlinks, 41, 71, 177, 275, 276, 421
Hypertext markup language (HTML), 20
  basic structure of, 64–66
  links, 69
  overview of, 63–64
  syntax of, 268
  tags, 252
  XML and, 267–268
Hypertext transfer protocol (HTTP), 19,
  27, 36, 40
  authentication scheme, 175
  entity header, 44
  overview of, 41–42
  request methods, 42–44, 51
  server response, 44–46
  servlet model, 105–106
  session tracking and, 175
  stateless protocol, 48, 98
  status codes, 45
  user identification, 175
  version 1.0, 41, 44–46
  version 1.1, 41, 49–51

I/O. *See* Input/output interface
IBM DB2, 368

IBM LMX converter, 369
IBM VisualAge, 109
IDEA. *See* International Data Encryption
    Algorithm
IETF. *See* Internet Engineering Task Force
If-modified-since header, 44
IKE. *See* Internet Key Exchange
Image map, 72–73
Images, 71–72
Inductive learning, 278
Information Age, 5
Information selling, 383–384
Informix, 134, 359
Inline style, 85–86
Input/output interface (I/O), 308
Input/output tests, 419–420
INSERT statement, 129, 130–131, 142
Inspection, 415
Integrated organization, 17
Integrated Services Digital Network
    (ISDN), 31
Integration, 367–371
Integrity, 204–205, 247, 288
Interactive entertainment, 384
Interactive servlet programs, 110–115
Interactivity, 61, 400, 411
Intercompany activities, 353, 367–368
Interface widgets, 62
International Data Encryption Algorithm
    (IDEA), 208
International Telecommunication Union
    (ITU) X.509 standard, 221
Internet, 2, 27–54
    access methods, 31
    application layer, 36–38
    layered model, 29
    link layer, 29–32
    network architecture, 28–29
    network layer, 32–35
    next generation, 38
    overview of, 28–38
    routers, 28
    security, 20
    standards, 32

transport layer, 35–36
    See also specific sites, systems
Internet advertising. *See* Advertising
Internet Engineering Task Force (IETF),
    32, 244
Internet Key Exchange (IKE), 231
Internet Protocol (IP), 32, 229
    classes of, 33
    DNS, 37
    IPv4, 38, 232
    IPv6, 38
Internet Protocol Security (IPSec), 38
    application of, 235–236
    gateway, 233
    header, 232
    protocol, 230, 230–231
    security association, 231
Internet security, 229–250
Internet Security Association and Key
    Managment Protocol (ISAKMP), 231
Internet Service Provider (ISP), 28
Internetsecure, 310
Intracompany activities, 353, 370–371
Intradomain routing, 34
Inventory, 370
Investing, 377–378
Investment information, 383
IP. *See* Internet Protocol
IPowerB2B.com, 361
IPSec. *See* IP Security Protocol
ISAKMP. *See* Internet Security Association
    and Key Managment Protocol
ISDN. *See* Integrated Services Digital
    Network
ISDN BRI. *See* Basic Rate Interface
Islands of trust, 224
ISP. *See* Internet Service Provider
Issuer, 288
ITU. *See* International Telecommunication
    Union

JADE. *See* Java-based Agent Development
    Environment
Java Applets, 56

Java-based Agent Development Environment (JADE), 262
Java Beans, 134
Java Cryptography Architecture (JCA), 103, 177
Java Database Connectivity (JDBC)
  advanced search engine, 126, 151–155
  API, 126, 136–137, 177
  cryptography, 103, 107
  diagram of, 135
  drivers, 134–136
  infrastructure, 134–135
  ODBC bridge, 97, 135, 137–138
  perspectives, 134–137
  programming, 103–106, 137–144
  servlets and, 126, 151–155
Java Remote Method Invocation (RMI), 103, 177, 254
Java Security API, 177
Java Servlet Developments Kit (JSDK), 104
Java servlets, 20, 96, 98, 101–104, 160, 429
  session tracking and, 98, 429
Java Virtual Machine (JVM), 103
Java Web Server, 104
JavaScript, 56, 86–92, 432–434
JC Penny, 318
JCA. *See* Java Cryptography Architecture
JDBC. *See* Java Database Connectivity
JIT. *See* Just-in-Time
Jobs, on internet, 381
Joint Photographic Experts Group (JPEG), 42, 71
JPEG. *See* Joint Photographic Experts Group
JPNET, 368
JSDK. *See* Java Servlet Developments Kit
Just-in-Time (JIT) systems, 13, 350
JVM. *See* Java Virtual Machine

Key distribution problem, 209
Keyed MD5, 233
Keyword searches, 60, 423
Knowledge-based systems, 342

Language interface, 100
LANs. *See* Local area networks
Last-modified header, 44
Lastminute.com, 318, 325, 331–333
Law, 21
Layered architecture, 29, 134, 275
Layout, of page, 62
Legacy interferance tests, 419–420
Linking, 69–71, 271, 344
  anchor tag pair, 69
  HTML document, 69
  hyperlinks, 41, 71, 177, 275, 421
  link layer, 29–32
  routing protocol, 34
Lists, formatting, 68–69
Live Software, 104
Load-balancing, 202
Local area networks (LANs), 30
Location object, 88
Lockbox, 303
Login, 159, 185, 187, 429
Logistics, 370
Lossless compression, 71

MAC. *See* Message authentication code
MAGICS. *See* Mobile-Agent-based Internet Commerce System
MAGNET system, 253
Maintenance, repair and operating (MRO) goods, 353
Malls, 317
Many-to-many marketing, 391
Marketing, 15, 16, 390–392
Marketplace, vs marketspace, 15
Mass customization, 321, 344
Mass marketing, 15, 390
Master file (MF), 308
Matchmaking services, 379–383
Mathematical Markup Language (MATHML), 273
MATHML. *See* Mathematical Markup Language
MD. *See* Message digest algorithms
MEB. *See* Mobile Electronic Business

Mediator, web-based, 403
Memory cards, 306
Menu, 413
Merchant, 288
Message authentication code (MAC), 216–217, 233
Message digest (MD) algorithms, 214–216
Messaging, 273
Metacontent definition, 273
METHOD attribute, 79, 100
MF. *See* Master file
Micropayment system, 303–306
Micropaymet Working Group, 310
Middleware technology, 136
Millicent system, 303–305, 310
MIME. *See* Multipurpose Internet Mail Extensions
Mining, of data, 277–281
Missing user action, 414
Mobile-Agent-based Internet Commerce System (MAGICS), 262–263
Mobile agents, 252–263
Mobile Electronic Business (MEB), 251, 263
Mod operator, 210–212
Modems, 30
Mondex system, 309–311
Mortgage information, 384
Mosaic browser, 39
Movies, 384
MRO. *See* Maintenance, repair, and operating
Multicast services, 38
Multifunctional marketing, 15
Multimedia, 56, 391
Multiplexing, 35
Multipurpose Internet Mail Extensions (MIME), 42
MUSIC methodology, 415
Mutual funds, 383
MySAP.com, 359
mySimon.com, 340

Name spaces, 275
Navigator, Netscape, 87
Net mechanic, 421
Net value, 351
Netscape Communications Corporation, 39
Netscape Enterprise Server, 104
Network architecture, 28–29, 287–298
Network layer, 32–35
Network Load Balancing (NLB), 202
Networked organization, 15
Newspapers, 383
Next generation, internet, 38
Nielson/Netratings, 393
NLB. *See* Network Load Balancing
Nodes, of domain names, 37
Nomad system, 253

Oakley key managment protocol, 231
Object-oriented conceptual model (OOCM), 404
Object-oriented (OO) scripting language, 86
Object-oriented programming (OOP) technique, 101
ODBC driver, 97, 135–138
Odyssey, 254
OI. *See* Order information
On-line catalog, 341
One-to-many marketing, 390
One-to-one marketing, 15, 391
OO. *See* Object-oriented scripting language
OOCM. *See* Object-oriented conceptual model
OOP. *See* Object-oriented programming
Open universities, 379
Opened condition, 412
Operating Resource Management (ORM), 353, 357
OPTIONS command, 106
Oracle database system, 134, 359–360, 368

Order information (OI), 289
Organization, 15, 17
Organization object model, 404
ORM. *See* Operating Resource
    Management
Overhead cost, of payment, 286

P3P. *See* Platform for Privacy References
    Syntax Specification
Packet filtering router, 237–238, 338
Page layout properties, 84
Paint Shop Pro, 71
Paragraph formatting, 67–68
Parsers, 276
PART system (Boeing), 360
PASS model, 346
Password methods, 80, 175, 219,
    452–454
Payment systems, 285–314
    4C methods, 286–287
    anonymous, 298
    authorization, 295–297
    capture, 297–298
    characteristics of, 286
    gateway, 289, 295
    instructions, 289
    overhead cost, 286
Payword protocol, 305–306, 310
Peopleware, 16
Perceptual design, 62–63
Performance, 59
Perl script, 100, 103, 271
Permission marketing, 396, 398
Persistent connections, 50
Persistent cookies, 202
Personalization, 12, 341, 391, 396
Perspectives, 407
Petri nets, 407
Petsmart.com, 337
PICS. *See* Platform for Internet Context
    Selection
Pipelining, 50
Plaintext, 205

Platform for Internet Context Selection
    (PICS), 274
Platform for Privacy References Syntax
    Specification (P3P), 274
Plugins, 56, 369
PO. *See* Purchase order
Pop-up window, 413, 416
Port numbers, 35
Portals, 396
POST commands, 43, 47, 105–106
Practical Extraction and Report
    Language. *See* Perl
Priceline.com, 10–11, 337, 339–340
Pricing models, 323, 399–400
Prime numbers, 209, 211, 212
Private key encryption, 207–209
Private key-exchange key, 291
Private signature key, 294
Procter & Gamble, 400
Procurement, 16, 353, 356, 365
Product catalog, 357
Product configuration, 357
Product, customized, 13, 15–16, 320, 344
Product searching, 251
Production planning, 16, 370
Profit margins, 322
Program Resolver, 38
Programming, 16–17, 55–94
Proton system, 309, 311
Proxy authentication, 50
Proxy server, 41, 238–239
Public key encryption, 207, 210–214, 220
Public key-exchange key, 291
Publishing, 12, 310, 389–426
    goals and criteria, 400–401
    quality assurance, 414–423
    usability testing, 414–419
    web presence and visibility, 423–424
Purchase order (PO), 368
Purchase protocols, 293–295
Purchase requisition, 355
Purchasing circles, 331, 396
PUT command, 106

Quality assurance, 414–423

Radio button, 81
RAM. *See* Random-access memory
Random-access memory (RAM), 308
Range request, 50
RDBMS systems, 134
RDF. *See* Resource Description
    Framework
Read-only memory (ROM), 308
Record protocol, 247
Referer header, 44
Relational database systems, 126–134
Relative URL, 70
Replay attack, 219, 234–235, 294
Request for Comments
    RFC 768, 35
    RFC 950, 32
    RFC 1034, 36
    RFC 1035, 36
    RFC 1700, 35
    RFC 1825-1829, 230
    RFC 1925, 42, 43
    RFC 1928, 239
    RFC 2104, 216
    RFC 2109, 48
    RFC 2401, 230, 232
    RFC 2406, 234
    RFC 2408, 231
    RFC 2409, 231
Request headers
    HTTP/1.0, 44
Request methods, 43–44, 51, 114
Request signature, 305
Requests for Quotations (RFQs),
    10, 354, 364
Resolver program, 38
Resource Description Framework (RDF),
    274
Resources Reservation protocol (RSVP),
    38
Response methods, 45–46, 116
Response time, 419, 420
Resume-writing, 384

Retailing, 11–12, 317–319
    basic features of, 331
    benefits of, 319–321
    brokers, 338–341
    direct selling, 335–336
    e-malls, 334–335
    features of, 341
    future of, 341
    generalized e-stores, 333–334
    key success factors for, 322–324
    models of, 324–341
    specialization by function, 331–333
    supplementary distribution channel,
        336–338
Reverse aggregation, 363
Reverse auction, 384
RFC. *See* Request for Comments
RFQs. *See* Requests for Quotations
Rich Text Format (RTF), 271
RIP. *See* Routing Information Protocol
RMI. *See* Java Remote Method Invocation
Robot program, 42
ROM. *See* Read-only memory
Round-robin, 202
Routing, 32–35, 38
Routing Information Protocol (RIP), 34,
    38
ROWSPAN attribute, 75
RSA encryption, 210–213, 217–220, 291,
    298
RSVP. *See* Resources Reservation Protocol
RTF. *See* Rich Text Format

SA Database (SAD), 232
SAD. *See* SA Database
Sample API for XML (SAX), 272–273
SAP R/3 system, 371
Save button, 414
SAX. *See* Sample API for XML
Scalability, 220, 223
Scaleable Vector Graphics (SVG), 274
Schemas, 275
SCM. *See* Supply-Chain Management
Screened firewall system, 242

Scrip, 303–304

Scripted languages, 86, 100, 421

Search engines, 152–155, 323, 341, 423, 429, 438–445

SearchEngine.java, 152–155

Secret keys, 291

Secure Electronic Transaction (SET), 285–298
  authentication system of, 289
  CA and, 289
  credit card payments, 287–298
  four phases of, 293
  RSA keys and, 291

Secure Hash Algorithm (SHA), 216

Secure hypertext transfer protocol (HTTPS), 40

Secure socket layer (SSL), 213, 230, 242–248, 420
  alert protocol, 247–248
  change cipher protocol, 247–248
  handshake protocol, 244–247
  record protocol, 247

Security, 96, 421
  associations, 231–232
  authentication, 204–205
  confidentiality, 204–205
  e-commerce and, 20, 204
  encryption and. *See* Encryption
  integrity, 204–205
  internet and, 20
  IPSec and, 231
  network layer, 229
  of payment, 286
  testing, 419
  transport layer, 229

Security First Network Bank (SFNB), 375

Security Policy Database (SPD), 232

Select menu, 82

SELECT statement, 129–130

Selection menu, 169

Selectors, 232

Sell-side e-commerce, 357–360

Semantics, 268

"Send and Pray" service, 29

Server logs, 420

Server-side applications (SSA), 96, 106, 160
  CGI and, 96, 98–100
  client-server programming, 95–96
  database connectivity, 125–158
  servlet fundamentals, 95–124
  session tracking and, 159–202
  testing, 421
  See also Servlets

Servicing, 12

Servlet APIs
  overview of, 103–105

Servlet book query
  advanced, 144–151
  JDBC example for, 137–144

Servlet-enabled web servers, 104

ServletRequest, 105

Servlets, 107–109
  APIs, 20, 103–105, 126, 151–155
  applets and, 102
  application of, 102
  basics, 104
  common methods for, 179–180
  compilation of, 109–110
  execution of, 109–110
  interactivity, 110–115
  Java and, 101–103
  methods used to create, 106
  request methods, 103, 114
  response methods, 116
  server-side programming, 95–124
  session-tracking. *See* Session tracking
  SimpleCart, 185

Session key, 213

Session tracking, 20, 106, 159–177
  advantages and disadvantages, 176
  API and, 177–195
  authentication, 185
  comparison of methods, 176–177
  cookies and, 175–176
  example, 180–185
  hidden form field and, 162–170

Session tracking (*cont.*)
   HTTP user identification and, 175
   server-side programming and, 159–202
   servlets, common methods for, 179–180
   shopping cart example, 185–195
   shopping in VBS, 160–161
   types of, 98
   URL rewriting and, 162–170
SET. *See* Secure Electronic Transaction
SFNB. *See* Security First Network Bank
SGML. *See* Standard Generalized Markup
   Language
SHA. *See* Secure Hash Algorithm
Shopping, 126, 161
Shopping cart, 185, 341, 429
   basic functions of, 195–196
   contents of, 195
   implementation issues, 161
   object, 161
   servlet session tracking API, 185–195
   session tracking, 185–195
   VBS example, 195–201, 447–449
Signature, blind, 289–299
SimpleCart program, 187–189
Site hosting, 63
Site owner, 421
SIZE attribute, 68
Sliding window mechanism, 35, 234, 235
Smart cards, 306–309
SMIL. *See* Synchronized Multimedia
   Integration Language
SOCKS protocol, 239
Software engineering, 341–342
Software structure model, 342
SPD. *See* Security Policy Database
Specialized stores, 317–318
Spiders, 423
SQL. *See* Structural Query Language
SSA. *See* Server-side applications
SSL. *See* Secure socket layer
Staffing, 351
Standard Generalized Markup Language
   (SGML), 64
Standards, BaseT, 31

Start tag, 273
State tracking. *See* Session tracking
Static web page, 99
Status codes, 45
Stickiness, 341
Stock evaluation, 383
Stocktrading, 377–378
Store layout, 322–323
Stream cipher, 214
Stress load testing, 419
Structural Query Language (SQL), 97,
   125
   MS server, 368
   relational database and, 128–134
   statement types, 129, 142
STYLE attribute, 85
Style sheets, 82–86, 271
Submit button, 81
Subnetting, 32–33
Substitution, encryption and, 207
Sun Microsystems Inc., 101
Sun web Server, 104
Supplementary distribution channel,
   336–338
Supply-Chain Management (SCM), 13,
   351, 365–367
Supply-driven model, 13
SVG. *See* Scaleable Vector Graphics
Sybase, 134
Symmetric key encryption, 207–209
Synchronized Multimedia Integration
   Language (SMIL), 274
Syntax, 268
System feedback, 58
System operation, 414
System testing, 419–421

Tabican system, 253
Tables, 73–75
Tags
   attributes and, 89
   formatting and, 68
Tahiti server, 254–255
Targeted marketing, 321, 344

Taxation, 21, 352
TCL code, 100
TCP. *See* Transmission Control Protocol
Telemarketing, 318, 390
TELNET, 36, 41, 338
Testing, system, 418–421
Text formatting, 66–69
Textarea, 82
Textbox, 80
Thematic web sites, 396, 398
Three-i requirements, 307
Three-tier model, 4, 5, 19, 96–98
Timing markers, 415
Token position, 412
ToysRus.com, 337
TPN. *See* Trading Procss Network
TRACE command, 106
Trading Procss Network (TPN), 10
Traditional model, 17–18, 321–322
Transferability, of payment, 286
Transmission Control Protocol (TCP),
   29, 35–36
Transport layer, 35–36
Transport mode, 234
Transposition, encryption and, 207
Travel services, 379–381
Tree structure, 37, 279
Trust system, hierarchical, 223–224
Tunnelling, 233, 236, 338

UDP. *See* User Datagram Protocol
UI. *See* User interface
Uniform resource locator (URL), 40–41
   absolute, 70–71
   hyperlinks, 41
   rewriting, 162–165
   routing, 202
   session tracking and, 162–170
Unique visitors, 399
Universal Resource Identifier (URI), 276
Unix shell scripting, 100
Unwired Planet, 263
UPDATE statement, 129, 132, 142
URI. *See* Universal Resource Identifier

URL. *See* Uniform resource locator
Usability
   advertising and, 414–419
   automated tests, 417
   factors in, 57–59, 415, 417
   publishing and, 414–419
   user interface and, 414–419
User-agent header, 44
User Datagram Protocol (UDP), 35
User interface (UI), 57
   abstract user interface object, 407–411
   flow of interactions, 411–414
   functional and system testing, 419–421
   quality assurance, 414–423
   usability testing, 414–419
   web design and publishing, 407–414
   widgets, 62
User login program, 185
User preregistration, 176
Username, 175, 219

VALIGN attribute, 75
Value-added networks (VANs), 2, 321,
   367
Value America, 333–334
Value chain concept, 6
VANs. *See* Value-added networks
VBS. *See* Virtual bookstore
Vending machines, 318
Verification path/certificate chain,
   222–223
Virtual bookstore (VBS), 105–109
   access control, 445–447
   advanced search, 126, 151–152,
      442–445
   book ordering, 127
   CartLogin, 447–449
   CartServices, 455–459
   category search, 441–442
   core server-side programming tool, 105
   customer account creation, 449–452
   exercises for building, 427–462
   form validation, 432–434
   homepage design, 430–432

Virtual bookstore (*cont.*)
 Javascript and, 432–434
 JDBC and, 105, 137–144, 151–155
 mobile agents, 256–261
 ordering system, 102, 127–128
 password changes, 452–454
 payments in, 310–311, 459–462
 relational database and, 127–128
 search engines, 126, 144–152, 434–445
 servlets and, 105–107, 137
 session tracking, 163
 shopping cart, 163, 195–201, 447–449
 shopping in, 126, 160–161, 428–429,
  455–459
 simple, 163
 system overview, 429–430
 virtual shopping, 455–459
 See also specific functions, software
Virtual marketplace, 126, 352, 360–365
Virtual Private Network (VPN), 235–236,
 311
Virtual reality, 341
Visa Cash, 309, 311
Visibility, 322–323
Visits, defined, 399
Visual Basic, 100
Volumes, of trade, 351–353
Voyager, 254
VPN. *See* Virtual Private Network

W3C Micropayment Working Group,
 311
WAE. *See* Wireless Application
 Environment
Waiting condition, 412
Wall Street Journal, 399
Wallet software, 300
Walmart, 318, 334
WAP. *See* Wireless Application Protocol
Warehousing facilities, 350
WDP. *See* Wireless Datagram Protocol
Web. *See* World Wide Web
Web pages. *See* Web site design
Web Server Farm, 202

Web site design, 421
 audience-centered design, 61
 categories of systems, 402–403
 CGI programming, 99
 client-side programming, 61
 client-side programming and, 61–62
 content creation and, 63
 dynamic, 46–48
 electronic commerce and, 16
 generation of, 46–48
 information requirements, 61
 logical design of, 61–62
 methodologies for, 401–407
 overview of, 403–407
 perceptual design and, 62–63
 site hosting and, 63
 web page design and, 61–62
Webcrawlers, 423
Weights, 412
Well-formed constraints, 270
Widgets, 62, 413
WIDTH attribute, 68, 74–75
Window widget, 413
Wireless Application Environment (WAE),
 265–266
Wireless Application Protocol (WAP),
 251–252, 263–267
Wireless Datagram Protocol (WDP), 266,
 267
Wireless links, 31
Wireless local area network, 31
Wireless Markup Language (WML),
 264
Wireless session protocol (WSP), 263,
 266
Wireless Telephony Applications (WTA),
 264
Wireless Transaction Protocol (WTP),
 266
Wireless Transport Layer Security
 (WTLS), 266
WML. *See* Wireless Markup Language
World Wide Web, 2, 27–54. *See also*
 Internet; Web

World Wide Web (WWW)
  advertising. *See* Advertising
  architecture, 39–40
  brief history of, 38–39
  data mining and, 277–281
  programming, 15–17, 55–94
  publishing. *See* Publishing
  usability, 414
  user interface. *See* User interface
  See also specific applications, sites, functions
WSP. *See* Wireless session protocol
WTA. *See* Wireless Telephony Applications
WTLS. *See* Wireless Transport Layer Security

WTP. *See* Wireless Transaction Protocol
W.W.Grainger, 361
WWW. *See* World Wide Web

X.500 naming system, 222
X.509 standard (ITU), 221, 225, 289
Xlink, 268, 271
XML. *See* eXtensible Markup Language
XOR function, 217
Xpointer, 271
XSL. *See* eXtensible Style Language

Yahoo!Store, 318, 335

Zenus Web Server, 104